Phonology

This practical and accessibly written textbook provides a thoughtfully ordered introduction to a wide range of phonological phenomena. It contains many exercises combining classic data sets with newly compiled problems. These help the student learn to discover sound patterns nested in complex linguistic data, beginning with concrete introductory examples and stepping through a series of progressively more complex phonological phenomena. It covers alternation, vowel harmony, phonemic analysis, natural classes and distinctive features, abstractness and opacity, syllable structure, tone, stress, prosodic morphology, feature geometry, and Optimality Theory. Essential reading for students of linguistics around the world.

- Begins with familiar and concrete patterns to aid student understanding.
- All data are translated into IPA, allowing students to observe trends across languages.
- Ideas are organized thematically by phenomena, allowing students to gain a wider understanding of what phonology encompasses.

ROBERT KENNEDY has taught phonology, phonetics, linguistic analysis, and dialects of English for over fifteen years. As a specialist in reduplicative phonology and morphology, accent portrayal, nickname formation, and the linguistics of team sports, he has published in *Phonology*, *American Speech*, and *Linguistic Inquiry*. He is also a widely sought media presence, cited in the *Boston Globe*, *New York Times*, *Baltimore Sun*, *Chicago Tribune*, *USA Today*, and on BBC *Sportshour*. A two-time *Jeopardy!* champion and prolific internet humorist (through his page, *lolPhonology*), he is always interested in new ways to make linguistics engaging and accessible to a broad audience.

Phonology:
A Coursebook

ROBERT KENNEDY
University of California, Santa Barbara

CAMBRIDGE
UNIVERSITY PRESS

CAMBRIDGE
UNIVERSITY PRESS

University Printing House, Cambridge CB2 8BS, United Kingdom

Cambridge University Press is part of the University of Cambridge.

It furthers the University's mission by disseminating knowledge in the pursuit of education, learning and research at the highest international levels of excellence.

www.cambridge.org
Information on this title: www.cambridge.org/9781107624948

First published 2017

Printed in the United Kingdom by TJ International Ltd. Padstow Cornwall

A catalogue record for this publication is available from the British Library

Library of Congress Cataloguing in Publication data
Names: Kennedy, Robert, 1974-
Title: Phonology : a coursebook / Robert Kennedy.
Description: Cambridge : Cambridge University Press, 2016. |
Includes bibliographical references and index.
Identifiers: LCCN 2015040100| ISBN 9781107046887 (Hardback) |
ISBN 9781107624948 (Paperback)
Subjects: LCSH: Grammar, Comparative and general–Phonology–Textbooks.
Classification: LCC P217 .K37 2016 | DDC 414–dc23 LC record available at
http://lccn.loc.gov/2015040100

ISBN 978-1-107-04688-7 Hardback
ISBN 978-1-107-62494-8 Paperback

CONTENTS

PREFACE

This textbook is an introduction to the basic methodology of phonological analysis, covering segmental alternations, phonemic analysis, features and natural classes, and suprasegmental concepts such as syllables, stress, and tone. It also includes multiple perspectives on phonological representation, including distinctive feature theory, serial rule ordering, feature geometry, and optimality theory.

The aim of this book is to make a number of abstract concepts concrete: the reader first encounters phonemes and underlying representations in readily observable patterns of alternation, and the concept then expands to include scenarios of allophony, and later to elements beyond the segment. The exposition is data-driven, which illustrates how the many tools of phonological analysis are motivated in real language phenomena, and is organized topically by types of phonological processes. It combines data from the canon of traditional phonological problem sets with other data sets which help underscore many of the same pedagogical points, and with refreshing new typological spread.

Beginning and intermediate students may both benefit from this textbook – beginners are taken on a thoughtfully ordered journey through a range of examples of phonological patterns, while intermediate students have the opportunity to learn new links among the data and theories they have encountered in their study of phonology.

This book can be used as the primary source for an introductory undergraduate or graduate course on phonology, and can also supplement other materials at the instructor's choosing. It is written so that each chapter leads students through example analyses, with problems divided into smaller, manageable chunks, interspersed with clarifying exposition. In addition, since each chapter is largely self-contained, instructors who prefer to order phonemic analysis (Chapter 5) or feature theory (Chapter 6) ahead of alternation (Chapters 2–4) may readily do so.

ACKNOWLEDGMENTS

I could not have completed this textbook or crafted it as I have without the help, guidance, support, and influence (direct and otherwise) of a host of different people: friends, peers, colleagues, and mentors, both during its development as well as in the many years leading up to it. To my colleagues at UCSB, Mary Bucholtz, Carol Genetti, Matt Gordon, Pat Clancy, Marianne Mithun, Jack Dubois, Sandy Thompson, Bernard Comrie; to friends, associates, and mentors around the world, Diana Archangeli, Mike Hammond, Dick Demers, Adam Ussishkin, Colleen Fitzgerald, Megan Crowhurst, Norma Mendoza-Denton, Cathy Hicks Kennard, Sonia Bird, Rachel Hayes, Jason Haugen, Tania Zamuner, Eric Bakovic, Sharon Rose, Rachel Walker, Kie Zuraw, Bruce Hayes, Ellen Kaisse, Colin Ewing, Marc Van Oostendorp, Joe Pater, John McCarthy, Alan Prince, Beth Hume, Ken Rehg, Stuart Davis, Lisa Davidson, Jon Jensen, and Henrietta Hung, along with no doubt many others, each of you has in passing or at length helped me hone the ways of talking about phonology accessibly to lots of different audiences. Likewise, my students in Phonology, Phonetics, and Linguistic Analysis have unwittingly but graciously shaped my understanding of what works best in the linguistics classroom. I also thank Helen Barton, Valerie Appleby, and the excellent team at Cambridge for their efforts in this project. Most of all, a very big thanks to Robin, I am eternally grateful to you for your patience, support, and understanding throughout this endeavor. And to Skyler: thanks for the wonderful natural class data!

CHAPTER 1 INTRODUCTION

Phonology is the study of the organization of sounds in human languages. It is a subfield of linguistics concerned with understanding how languages use certain sounds and combine them to build meaningful units – essentially, words. At its core, phonology begins with the observation that each language uses its own fixed set of sounds, an inventory of consonants and vowels, and that these sounds may combine into sequences in patterned ways. We call these sounds **phonemes**: contrastive sounds of language, they are not themselves meaningful, but serve as symbols which are combinable into longer sequences, to which meaning and function are in turn associated.

phoneme: a contrastive sound or category of sounds within a language.

Our methods for detecting phonemes are indirect, and involve examining the structure and form of simple and complex words. We begin with the basic task of **segmentation**, in which we observe words of a language and detect smaller components within them. In so doing, we also identify recurrent parts, component units that are found in many different words.

segmentation: the task of dividing up words into smaller components.

For example, consider the word *love*, and in particular, focus on the way the word sounds when spoken aloud. Using two different approaches to segmentation, we can identify three smaller components within the word. First, just thinking about how the sounds of the word are created, it begins with a vocal gesture with the tongue tip touching the roof of the mouth, but with air escaping around its sides. It then moves to a more open configuration, with the jaw more open, and the sound more resonant. Last, the mouth closes again, this time with the lower teeth against the upper lip, just enough to create a small amount of turbulent hissing. While there are also transitional gestures as we move from one configuration to the next, there nevertheless are three distinct phases we can identify over the course of the word, in terms of the configuration of the mouth, and in terms of the sounds that accompany each distinct physical configuration.

Alternatively, we can think of this word in comparison to other words in the same language. For example, the word *love* begins with the same component that occurs at the beginning of words such as *laugh*, *like*, and *learn*. Its next component is similar to the most resonant component of words such as *tub*, *bus*, and *dove*. Its last component is identical to the first component of *very* and the last component of *give*. The smaller components we find are called **segments**.

Exercise 1.1 Consider the following list of English words, and perform segmentation on each of them.

stoop, stop, shop, shoot, spots, those, this, spit, soothe, soup, post, pose, toss

    a. How many segments do you find in each word?
    b. How many types of segments do you find overall?

The number of segments for each word is listed as follows. Below that is a list of the types of segments, along with the words in which each segment occurs.

stoop	4
stop	4
shop	3
shoot	3
spots	5
those	3
this	3
spit	4
soothe	3
soup	3
post	4
pose	3
toss	3

s	*stoop, stop, spots, spit, soothe, soup, post, toss*
t	*stoop, stop, shoot, spots, spit, toss*
oo	*stoop, shoot, soothe, soup*
p	*stoop, stop, shop, spots, spit, soup, post, pose*
o	*stop, shop, spots, toss*
sh	*shop, shoot*
th	*those, this, soothe*
long-o	*those, post, pose*
z	*those, pose*
short-i	*this, spit*

As our data are linguistic, they are usually auditory in nature, but can be recorded visually using techniques of phonetic transcription. To return to the example of *love*, we'd transcribe the first segment as [l], the second as [ʌ], and the third as [v]. The transcription task itself enacts segmentation, as it relies on the use of specific standardized symbols, where each symbol invariantly represents some type of segment. Our spelling system (like all alphabets) is a transcription system, but for historical reasons it is not suited to the task of transcribing words to the level of detail that the analyses in this textbook require. For that reason, we rely on the IPA alphabet for all transcriptions. This textbook assumes you have knowledge of the symbols of IPA, but you may find it helpful to keep a copy of the standard IPA chart nearby should you need to refer to it.

It is important to remember that segments and transcription symbols are not the same as letters. The spelling systems of languages like English sometimes use pairs of letters to represent single sounds, or allow a given letter to represent different sounds in different words, or indeed allow the same sound to be represented with different symbols in different words.

Exercise 1.2   Transcribe the words from Exercise 1.1 into IPA notation. If you are familiar with details such as diacritics that indicate aspiration and release, you can leave them out for now. Vowels may differ by accent.

stoop	[stup]
stop	[stɒp/stɑp]
shop	[ʃɒp/ʃɑp]
shoot	[ʃut]
spots	[spɒts/spɑts]
those	[ðoʊz]
this	[ðɪs]
spit	[spɪt]
soothe	[suð]
soup	[sup]
post	[poʊst]
pose	[poʊz]
toss	[tɒs/tɑs]

We can use symbolic transcription systems because each of the segments we identify occurs in a large number of words. For example, the sound represented by [l] is a segment found in many English words; the same is true of the sounds representd by [ʌ] and by [v]. The more words we observe and perform segmentation on, the more segments we detect; with sufficient observation, we would arrive at the complete set of segments for a given language. This full set comprises the surface **inventory** of the language.

inventory: the set of sounds within a language.

As we will see, we can use the surface inventory to make inferences about what sounds are contrastive in a language, and about the nature of mental representations of words. For example, you know that *love* and *dove* are different words, in part because they begin with different segments. The fact that they differ only by their initial segments suggests that the contrast between [l] and [d] is relevant in English. In turn, we infer that the two segments represent or "belong to" different phonemic categories.

Phonology is a distinct enterprise from the study of phonetics, which is concerned with the physical properties of sounds in human language – for example, articulatory dimensions such as tongue position and vocal cord vibration, and acoustic dimensions such as loudness and resonance. The division between these fields is blurry, however, since phonemes can be described by their phonetic properties. Indeed, phonological and phonetic generalizations often interact with each other.

When we study the phonetic properties of languages, we learn that segments can be described in terms of how they are articulated in the vocal tract. Such description includes details of place and manner of articulation, nasality, and the state of the larynx. In turn, we learn that some combinations are absent from some languages. For example, English has fricatives such as [f, v, θ, ð, s, z ʃ, ʒ], and velar consonants such as [k, g, ŋ], but no velar fricatives such as [x] or [ɣ]. This does not mean such a combination is impossible; instead, it is a fact about the inventory of English segments. Different languages have different inventories of sounds. Nevertheless, in both phonology and phonetics, we often observe enough languages to infer that some sounds are more common than others. Many languages have [t] and [m], while fewer have [θ] or [ʁ].

Your phonology is part of the knowledge you have of your language. You know which sounds are a part of a language and which are not, and you know which sounds may occur together within a word and which may not. In technical terms, you have knowledge of the phonemes that comprise the phonological inventory of your language, and you also have knowledge about which phonemes can go where in words of your language, its **phonotactics**.

phonotactics: the restrictions a language places on which sounds may occur next to each other.

There is thus much more to the study of phonology than the study of the phonemic inventory of languages. The study of phonotactics shows us that languages place restrictions on the positioning and sequencing of phonemes. For example, the Japanese consonant inventory includes the consonant [t], and the vowel [i], and in general, any consonant may precede any vowel. However, the sequence of [t] followed by [i] does not occur; there are no words in which the string [...ti...] can be found. Of course, this is a fact only about Japanese phonology; some other languages may share this property, while others clearly allow the sequence [ti].

This point becomes more complex when we realize that in Japanese, as in many languages, a word may consist of more than one meaningful part. We refer to such meaningful parts as **morphemes**.

morpheme: a linguistic unit which pairs sound with meaning, and which is not composed of smaller morphemes.

The absence of [...ti...] is a basic observation about Japanese words, but also applies more specifically to Japanese morphemes. One might wonder whether this gap is a simple accident or a principled gap. In fact, if we examine words that combine more than one morpheme, we also encounter evidence which suggests that [...ti...] is actively avoided in the sound system. If you consider a **root** morpheme that ends in the consonant /t/, such as /kat/ 'win,' but try to add a **suffix** morpheme that begins with the vowel /i/, such as /-inai/ 'NEGATIVE,' you are creating a word in which the sequence [...ti...] may potentially occur.

root: a morpheme to which affixes may be attached.

affix: a morpheme attached to a root, such as a prefix or suffix.

If the combination of / kat + inai / remains intact as [...ti...], then we may conclude that the absence of [ti] among individual morphemes is indeed an accident. However, if anything changes about this sequence of sounds, we have evidence that it is truly avoided, and indeed the surface form in this case is [katʃinai]: the root's final /t/ has changed to a [ʧ].

This is an example of **alternation**, a scenario in which a morpheme has more than one surface realization, where one or more of its segments changes predictably. In this case, the root /kat/ appears as [kat-] in some contexts and [katʃ-] in others. We may say both that /t/ alternates between [t] and [ʧ], and that the morpheme /kat-/ alternates between [kat-] and [katʃ-].

alternation: a scenario in which a morpheme has more than one surface realization, depending on the linguistic context.

Within the Japanese word [katʃinai], we may still observe the form [katʃ-] as the root and [-inai] as the suffix, but since not every word built from /kat/ has [katʃ-] as its root, we refer to both [katʃ] and [kat] as *alternants* of the root. Further, while we may say that the root alternates, a more thorough examination of Japanese verbs would tell us that this is not simply a fact about morphemes such /kat-/, but about any root ending in /t/. Thus, there is a phonological alternation between [t] and [ʧ], in which they are surface realizations of the same element, but [ʧ] is the alternant that arises in a specific circumstance – preceding the vowel [i] – while [t] is the alternant that arises in other circumstances. A third alternant, [ʦ], arises just if the following vowel is [u]. Again, these are generalizations about the sound system of Japanese, not just facts associated with some individual words.

Another important concept is that although there is more than one alternant of the root, in phonological analysis we often want to identify a single, abstract mental representation for any root or morpheme. This representation is often called the **underlying form**. In Japanese, for a number of reasons that will become clear as you learn more about phonology, the underlying form of 'win' is /kat-/.

underlying form or underlying representation (UR): an abstract mental representation of a linguistic unit.

Underlying representations are usually represented in text within angle brackets, as in /kat-/. Surface alternants, instead, are represented in square brackets, as in [kat-] and [kaʧ-].

A similar term for the concept of underlying form is **lexical form**, in reference to the **lexicon** – a list of morphemes which we presume a speaker of a language knows. The lexicon of any language is a list of all its morphemes, including roots and affixes, and includes information about their form as well as their meaning and function. The lexicon is analogous to an actual dictionary, in that it is a list of forms, both their sounds and functions, but is an abstract mental construct. Every speaker of every language has a lexicon comprising the morphemes of their language. In essence, the term *lexical form* implies that the underlying representation is what is stored within the lexicon of the language.

lexicon: an abstract mental list of morphemes, consisting of their form (sounds) and their functions and/or meanings.

Phonological restrictions of the kind exemplified by the absence of [ti] in Japanese are observable just by inspecting the form of individual morphemes. Nevertheless, they are often easiest to see in scenarios of alternation, wherever prefixes or suffixes attach to roots. In some cases, certain phonological generalizations are *only* observable in the context of alternation. For this reason, we will begin our study of phonology by framing it within morphology – the study of word structure.

1.1 Organization of this textbook

This textbook therefore follows a particular path through phonology. In Chapter 2, we will begin our investigation by studying alternation in more detail: we will see many examples of phonemes taking on different forms in different phonological contexts. Chapter 3 explores alternation with zero-forms – situations where segments are deleted or inserted. We will move on in Chapter 4 to patterns of long-distance effects, where non-adjacent segments influence each other. One major example is the phenomenon of vowel harmony, a specific type of alternation seen in diverse languages around the world. We'll then focus more closely on the notion of phoneme and phonemic distribution in Chapter 5. This will prepare us to visit the notion of classes of sounds in Chapter 6, and hidden processes in Chapter 7.

We then move on to explore some other challenging types of phonological phenomena that go beyond the analysis of segments, such as syllable structure in Chapter 8, tone in Chapter 9, stress and meter in Chapter 10, and prosodic morphology in Chapter 11. Chapter 12 provides a discussion of advanced theories of phonological representation that are intended to address many of the empirical challenges along the way.

Key terms

phoneme
segment
segmentation
inventory
phonotactics
morpheme
root
affix
alternation
underlying form / underlying representation (UR)
lexicon

CHAPTER 2 ALTERNATION

Learning objectives

- Identify morphemes that have multiple alternants
- Learn the basics of morphological analysis, to identify components of complex words
- Describe the contexts in which various alternants appear
- Identify the best fit for a default alternant or underlying form
- Compose rules to derive other alternants from underlying forms

Introduction

In this chapter, we will explore how sounds may change their form because of the nature of adjacent sounds. We can see this quite clearly when morphology operates to place morphemes together – in such scenarios, sometimes a segment at the edge of a morpheme adapts to the segment at the corresponding edge of another morpheme, which provides us with concrete evidence of a default or "underlying" sound changing into something else. When the sounds of particular morphemes change like this, we infer that they **alternate** – they take one form in one context and a different form in some other context. We will begin examining the phenomenon of alternation here, and will pursue it further in the subsequent two chapters.

2.1 English plurals

For a first look at alternation, we may turn to a few basic examples from English. First, think of how nouns are made plural in English – aside from a short list of exceptions, we add a suffix spelled -s to a noun to make it plural. Under certain circumstances, we instead spell the suffix -es. Nevertheless, the phonological form of this suffix actually has three alternants; we can divide the set of all regular-pluralizing nouns into three groups, depending on which form of the suffix they take.

Exercise 2.1 For each group of words, describe the form of the English plural suffix. Remember to think in terms of sounds, not spelling. The orthographic and phonemic representations of each word in its singular form are provided; where UK and US pronunciations differ, both are shown.

a. *Phonemic representation*	*Gloss*	b. *Phonemic representation*	*Gloss*	c. *Phonemic representation*	*Gloss*
dɒg/dɑg	dog	ɹeɪk	rake	dʒʌdʒ	judge
wɒl/wɑl	wall	lɪp	lip	weɪdʒ	wage
kæn	can	stɹɹəp	stirrup	tʃɜtʃ/tʃɚtʃ	church
ɹɪm	rim	mast/mæst	mast	kaʊtʃ	couch
sɪmbəl	symbol	pɒt/pɑt	pot	pas/pæs	pass
stoʊv	stove	tɛmpəst	tempest	meɪz	maze
ɒlɪv/ɑlɪv	olive	task/tæsk	task	tɒs/tɑs	toss
bɒtəm/bɑɾəm	bottom	weɪf	waif	sɔːs/sɔɹs	source
fɪg	fig	klɪf	cliff		
deɪ	day	asp/æsp	asp		
bɔɪ	boy	hæft	haft		
kiː	key	tɹɪk	trick		
stjuː/stuː	stew				
hænd	hand				
fæŋ	fang				
stænd	stand				
kɹɪb	crib				
aʊə/aʊɹ	hour				
fɜː/fɚ	fur				
bɛː/bɛɹ	bear				

The form of the suffix for the roots in (a) is [z]; for the roots in (b) it is [s], while for the roots in (c) it is [əz].

Each noun has exactly one plural form, and everyone who speaks the language agrees on the nature of the plural form. One of way of trying to explain this knowledge is to presume that we all have acquired a lexicon which lists a pair of forms for each noun – one member of each pair is the singular, and the other is the plural. For example, we remember that the singular of *cat* is [kæt] and that *cats* [kæts] is its plural.

However, there are two facts that are unexplained by this approach: first, membership in one of the three groups above is not random, and second, people pluralize new words in consistent ways. To discover the non-randomness of the three groups, we look for something that the words in each group have in common with each other, to the exclusion of the other groups.

9

Exercise 2.2   For each column in Exercise 2.1, find a general statement that describes the final segments of each form.

The words in (c) all end in one of a small set of consonants: [s, z, ʧ, ʤ]. The words in (a) all end in a vowel or in a voiced consonant (other than [z] or [ʤ]). The words in (b) end in a voiceless consonant other than [s] or [ʧ].

The three columns actually differ not just by their choice of the form of the suffix, but also by the nature of their final segments. In fact, we can conclude from this sample of nouns that if you know the final segment of the root, you can predict the form of its plural. This means that we do not need to presume that speakers store each noun's plural form in full in their lexicon. Instead, we only store the singular form, and the plural is predictable from this.

The second unexplained fact is related to this: we agree on how to pluralize new nouns. If I told you about a new object called a *wug*, you would in all likelihood pluralize this word using [-z], because it ends in a voiced consonant like the words in (a). You could only do this by following the generalizations that already exist for noun-formation. If instead there were no principle for choosing the form of the plural affix, then at least some people would choose [-s] and others would choose [-əz], *for the same noun.*

Let us focus on the plural suffix itself: we have observed that it has more than one form, and the choice among these forms is predictable from the phonological context, based on the nature of the preceding segment. This is an example of **alternation**, a scenario in which some segment within a morpheme changes form as a function of other nearby segments.

alternation: a phonological pattern in which an underlying form has different surface forms based on its phonological context.

When we analyze patterns of alternation, we presume that a morpheme has a single underlying form, but has multiple surface forms. Alternation of a given segment is observable in situations of morphological affixation, because a particular morpheme may take one form in the absence of some other affix, but a different form in the presence of that affix.

Note that our use of *alternation* as a term also gives as forms like *alternant* and *alternate*. The **alternants** are the various forms observed in different contexts in a pattern of alternation; they may be said to **alternate**. Handling these terms is important for talking about phonological concepts, but the terminology can be tricky. Remember that this terminology is based upon the notion of *alternatives* (different options or choices) and not on *alterations* (i.e., changing one form into another). Of course this can be confusing at first because, as we have noted here, we often consider every morpheme to have a basic or default form which changes its form in some contexts. Alternation is a scenario in which a morpheme has more than one form. Each possible form – even one that matches the basic one – is an alternant.

There is more to say about the English plural alternation. First, while we have identified three alternants of the plural suffix, we can associate this with a single lexical form for the suffix itself. Since the alternants are similar to each other in form (all of them have or include an alveolar fricative), we can identify one form for the plural suffix, which undergoes minor tweaks in its makeup in some of the subgroups. In addition, we can hypothesize that one of these alternants is representative of the **underlying form** (see Chapter 1) of the suffix, unchanged at the surface, while the others are refinements that are produced in particular circumstances.

In this textbook we use the terms *phoneme* and *underlying representation* somewhat interchangeably, to refer to the abstract lexical form of a given morpheme, but the two concepts are not exactly equivalent. The phoneme is better understood as a category of sound, detectable via phonemic analysis of the type we'll see in Chapter 6, and the full set of phonemes comprises the phonemic inventory. In contrast, the components that comprise lexical representation are instantiations of the language's phonemic inventory. Affixes and roots both have lexical representations that include information about their component segments.

Traditionally, the default form of the English plural is considered to be [-z], despite what our spelling system suggests. The other two alternants occur in very specific circumstances. The [-əz] form occurs whenever the noun ends in one of [s, z, ʧ, ʤ]. By contrast, the [-z] alternant occurs basically anywhere else, or more technically, **elsewhere.**

Rather than conclude that these alternants are wholesale replacements of the basic form of the plural, we can say that each is arrived at by a relatively minor change in the phonological representation of the suffix. The [-əz] form is arrived at by inserting a vowel between a word-final **sibilant** and the [-z] of the basic suffix. The [-s] form is derived simply by changing the voicing of the consonant to match the voicelessness of the preceding consonant. Thus, *generally* the suffix is [-z], but the other alternants appear under a set of specific, simply described circumstances.

sibilant: a fricative or affricate consonant produced using the front of the tongue.

Here we have simplified the explanation of the various forms of the plural suffix. We have shortened the list of what needs to be remembered or stored in the lexicon. We have also uncovered the principles behind the choice among the three alternants, and we have made the process rely on a small set of simple statements. Thus, we have not required too much explanatory power:

we have not invoked a system which could produce drastically different alternants.

This pattern also foreshadows a few phenomena that we will see recur across languages of the world – **assimilation**, **epenthesis**, and **natural classes**.

assimilation: a process in which a segment becomes more like an adjacent segment.

epenthesis: a process in which a segment is inserted between two other segments.

natural class: a group of sounds within a language that share some feature and which trigger or undergo similar processes.

Exercise 2.3 Describe how assimilation and epenthesis are observed in the English plural alternation.

Try also to look for natural classes in the pattern.

The English plural illustrates assimilation in that the voiceless alternant appears only after voiceless sounds. It illustrates epenthesis in the vowel that appears between root-final sibilants and the sibilant consonant of the suffix.

It illustrates natural classes in that sibilant consonants behave similarly – motivating epenthesis – and voiceless consonants also behave similarly, motivating assimilation.

2.2 The English past tense

The pattern we see in the plural of nouns is reflected also in the third-person singular present tense of verbs, as shown by words such as *walks*, *runs*, *sways*, and *passes*. It is also seen in possessives, as in *Pat's*, *Tim's*, *Jay's*, and *Russ's*. In both of these additional cases, the same alternation among [s, z, əz] is evident. A slightly different pattern can be seen in past tense formation, where the alternation is instead among [d, t, əd]. If you look at the following data, you can uncover a different set of conditions under which each alternant occurs.

Exercise 2.4 Consider the following English verbs and their past tenses. Transcriptions of stems are provided, and where UK and US pronunciations differ, both are given. Describe the environments in which each alternant of the English past tense suffix occurs. Which alternant is the default form of the suffix?

a. Phonemic representation	Gloss	b. Phonemic representation	Gloss	c. Phonemic representation	Gloss
wɒk/wɑk	walk	læg	lag	hiːd	heed
tɒk/tɑk	talk	pɛg	peg	weɪd	wade

fʌs	fuss	weɪv	wave	fʌnd	fund
tɪp	tip	dʒɔɪn	join	teɪst	taste
sæp	sap	wɛl	well	weɪt	wait
nɒk/nɑk	knock	dʒʌdʒ	judge		
laf/læf	laugh	fjuːz	fuse		
		pætʃ	patch		

Like plural nouns, past tense verbs yield a voicing assimilation in the suffix where the root ends in a voiceless consonant, as the forms in (a) show. Vowels are inserted under different conditions, however: not after sibilants, but only after alveolar stops, as in (c). This should not be a surprise since the suffix also consists of an alveolar stop; given the intuition that vowels are inserted to separate segments that are too alike, it makes sense that insertion occurs in plural nouns to separate root-final sibilants from the sibilant of the suffix /-z/, but in past-tense verbs to separate root-final alveolar stops from the alveolar stop of the suffix /-d/.

2.3 Morphology

Now that we have explored alternation at a preliminary level, we should take some time to note that languages use morphology in different ways, and that what might arise as an affix in one language may arise as a separate word in another language, or not at all.

Indeed, a lot of what we will see throughout this book will be data from languages you are not familiar with. Thus, unlike examples from English, in which you are likely to be familiar with the component morphemes of complex words (for example, you know that the boundary between root and suffix in *cats* is between the *t* and *s*, and not between the *a* and *t*), you often need to discover morpheme boundaries yourself when examining new language data, a process we call **morphological analysis**.

morphological analysis: the activity of examining a set of morphologically complex words from some language, and identifying their component morphemes.

2.4 Swahili verbs

Swahili provides a good example of morphological analysis. The following data (from Fromkin, Rodman, and Hyams 2014) consist of complex words – complex because they consist of more than one morpheme. Each word is a verb with several affixes. Even though we don't necessarily know any

Swahili, the data are glossed well enough that we know the difference in function and meaning across each form.

(1)	atanipenda	'he will like me'
(2)	atakupenda	'he will like you'
(3)	atampenda	'he will like him'
(4)	atatupenda	'he will like us'
(5)	atawapenda	'he will like them'
(6)	nitakupenda	'I will like you'
(7)	nitampenda	'I will like him'
(8)	utanipenda	'you will like me'
(9)	utampenda	'you will like him'
(10)	atanipiga	'he will beat me'
(11)	atakupiga	'he will beat you'
(12)	atampiga	'he will beat him'
(13)	ananipiga	'he is beating me'
(14)	anakupiga	'he is beating you'
(15)	anampiga	'he is beating him'
(16)	amenipiga	'he has beaten me'
(17)	amekupiga	'he has beaten you'
(18)	amempiga	'he has beaten him'

In morphological analysis, we attempt to identify and isolate each individual morpheme. We do this by comparing a small number of words at a time. Any pair of words may share some element of form (the segments they comprise) as well as meaning. Conversely, where two words diverge in form, we infer that this change is reflected in the change of their meaning. Consider the pair of words (1) and (2), repeated below:

(1)	atanipenda	'he will like me'
(2)	atakupenda	'he will like you'

These forms differ in the highlighted segments: where [atanipenda] has **ni**, [atakupenda] has **ku**. Likewise, where [atanipenda] is glossed as 'he will like *me*,' [atakupenda] is glossed as 'he will like *you*.' We thus infer that the element [ni-] carries the function indicated by *me*, and the element [ku-] carries the function indicated by *you*.

Thus far we have not done enough to figure out what function or functions are represented by the initial sequence [ata-], or by the final sequence [-penda]. But we can apply the same approach to pairs of words that differ in different elements; for example, let's now consider (2) and (6), where both words have [ku-].

(2)   atakupenda   'he will like you'
(6)   nitakupenda   'I will like you'

These forms instead differ in the initial component: where [atakupenda] has [a-], [nitakupenda] has [ni-], and we infer that [a-] corresponds to 'he' while [ni-] corresponds to 'I.'

We can use this method to isolate all the component morphemes in these data.

Before moving on, let us acknowledge a few technicalities. First, while the glosses we have used suggest that morphemes like [a-] or [ni-] correspond to English pronouns, the Swahili morphemes are more appropriately referred to as inflectional affixes that indicate agreement and tense. Thus [a-] does not truly mean 'he'; instead, it is the prefix that appears at the start of the verb when its subject is third person singular. Likewise [ku-] does not mean 'you'; it is the prefix that appears only before the root when the object is second person singular. Second, the form [ni-] is used for both subject and object agreement, but that does not make these the same form. When absolutely initial, [ni-] is a subject agreement prefix; when it immediately precedes the root, it is an object agreement prefix.

Third, all affixes which precede the root are prefixes, despite the fact that they themselves may also be preceded by some other morpheme. For example, [ku-] in (2) [atakupenda] is a prefix, even though it is not word-initial. You may be familiar with the term *infix*, an affix which occurs within some other morpheme. The affix [ku-] is *not* an infix, however, because it is not placed within some other morpheme. It is simple a prefix preceded by additional prefixes. It is common practice to include a hyphen in the representation of the affix to indicate that it is a prefix.

Exercise 2.5   Identify each morpheme in the data in (1)–(18) above.

a-	'he'
ni-	'I'
u-	'you'
ta-	'will'
na-	'is V-ing'
me-	'has V-ed'
ni-	'me'
ku-	'you'
m-	'him'
tu-	'us'

wa-   'them'
-penda   'like'
-piga   'beat'

One thing to note about the Swahili data is that each morpheme has a constant, unchanging form. The first-person subject agreement morpheme is always [ni-], and the second-person object agreement morpheme is always [ku-]. Thus, there is no alternation in form for any of these morphemes, which makes morphological analysis of these data rather straightforward.

Often we instead see data in which some morphemes do have different forms, analogous to the three-way alternation in English plural noun formation or past-tense verb formation, but in languages whose word structure may be unfamiliar, as it is in Swahili. Let us now turn to Luganda, which illustrates just such a scenario.

2.5 Luganda

Examine the following data from Luganda (Halle and Clements 1983), paying attention to morphological analysis:

(1)   ẽnato   'a canoe'
(2)   ẽnapo   'a house'
(3)   ẽmpipi   'a kidney'
(4)   ẽŋkoosa   'a feather'
(5)   ẽmmããmmo 'a peg'
(6)   ẽŋŋõõmme 'a horn'
(7)   ẽnnĩmiro 'a garden'
(8)   ẽnugẽni   'a stranger'
(9)   akaato   'little canoe'
(10)   akaapo   'little house'
(11)   akapipi   'little kidney'
(12)   akakoosa   'little feather'
(13)   akabããmmo 'little peg'
(14)   akagõõmme 'little horn'
(15)   akadĩmiro 'little garden'
(16)   akatabi   'little branch'

If we compared just (2) [ẽnapo] and (3) [ẽmpipi], we might conclude that [ẽ-] corresponds to the English 'a,' leaving [-napo] as 'house' and [-mpipi] as 'kidney.' But if we compare [ẽnapo] and (10) [akaapo], we instead could infer that [ẽn-] means 'a,' leaving [apo] as 'house' and then [aka-] as 'little.' Something must therefore be alternating: either [ẽ-] is a prefix and the root alternates between [apo] and [napo], or the root is [apo] and the prefix alternates between [ẽn] and [ẽm]. We are faced with an analytical choice, as schematized below:

Alternating roots	*Alternating prefix*
ẽ + napo	ẽn + apo
ẽ + mpipi	ẽm + pipi
aka + apo	aka + apo
aka + pipi	aka + pipi

The better analysis turns out to be the one that attributes alternation to the prefix, because the alternative analysis is much more unwieldy. We arrive at this conclusion by considering both analyses in more detail: if we follow the alternating-root hypothesis, that the prefix is invariantly [ẽ], we'd need to add a statement to the effect that [napo] is a preferred alternant for the root following a vowel prefix. But the diminutive prefix [aka-] also ends in a vowel, and [apo] is the root form instead of [napo]; that is, if there is some pressure to choose [napo] following [ẽ-], yielding [ẽnapo], then it remains unexplained why the same pressure does not yield *[akanapo].

We could save this approach by saying that [napo] is preferred just when the preceding vowel is [e], not [a], but this added level of specificity nevertheless suggests that the nasal consonant is somehow "called for" by the indefinite prefix [ẽ]. Moreover, when we turn to roots like [pipi], this analysis forces us to presume this root alternates between [pipi] and [mpipi]. The story we had been using to explain the appearance of [napo] in [enapo] – that the root uses a consonant-initial alternant after the prefix [ẽ] – no longer explains what happens with [empipi], where the root would already begin with a consonant, so an additional nasal consonant does not seem as motivated. Thus, the conditions under which a nasal consonant is inserted seem to be pretty disparate and haphazard.

Now we can return to the simpler analysis, which holds that [apo] is invariantly the root for 'house,' that [pipi] is invariantly the root for 'kidney,' and that the form of the prefix alternates between [ẽn] and [ẽm]. Note also that a third alternant appears in forms such as (4) [ẽŋkoosa].

Exercise 2.6 Describe the environments in which each of the alternants of the indefinite prefix appears.

These alternants are fairly easy to describe in terms of their distribution; [ẽŋ], with a velar nasal, appears where the root begins with a velar stop; [ẽm] appears where the root has a bilabial stop, and [ẽn] appears otherwise. The fact that the nasal consonant assumes the place of articulation of the root's initial consonant makes this an example of **place assimilation**.

The next analytical challenge is to make sense of the forms in (5)–(7) and (13)–(15), in which an additional element of alternation appears.

place assimilation: a process in which a segment adopts place features of an adjacent segment.

Exercise 2.7   a.   What are the alternants of the Luganda roots in (5)–(7) and (13)–(15)?
          b.   Which is the default form of each alternating Luganda root?

mããmmo, bããmmo	'peg'
ŋõõmme, gõõmme	'horn'
nĩmiro, dĩmiro	'garden'
ugẽni	'stranger'
tabi	'branch'

The choice of default is not always easy, and needs to take numerous types of observations into account. In the discussion of the English plural noun formation, we assumed that [-z] is the default form because it occurs in the widest set of environments. The same argument could be made for the basic prefix [ẽn-] in Luganda: it appears before alveolars, and before vowels.

However, in choosing among /bããmmo/ and /mããmmo/ for the default root for 'peg,' we have only two forms, so we cannot determine from these data which root has a wider distribution. Here we would need to turn to typological information – knowledge gathered from the study of a multitude of languages. We will investigate phonological typology in greater detail in later chapters, but we can introduce how it would help us here. In essence, we are choosing between two analyses. In one, we assume /bããmmo/ to be the default, which requires a proposal that [b] becomes [m] after another nasal consonant; thus, /ẽn + bããmmo/ → [ẽmmããmmo]. In the other analysis, we assume [mããmmo] to be the default, but this forces an additional proposal that [m] turns into [b] between vowels, to account for the appearance of [b] in [akabããmmo].

Nasalization after /n/	*Denasalization between vowels*
ẽn + bããmmo → ẽmmããmmo	ẽn + mããmmo → ẽmmããmmo
ẽn + gõõmme → ẽŋŋõõmme	ẽn + ŋõõmme → ẽŋŋõõmme
ẽn + dĩmiro → ẽnnĩmiro	ẽn + nĩmiro → ẽnnĩmiro
aka + bããmmo → akabããmmo	aka + mããmmo → akabããmmo
aka + gõõmme → akagõõmme	aka + ŋõõmme → akagõõmme
aka + dĩmiro → akadĩmiro	aka + nĩmiro → akadĩmiro

Typological evidence tells us that languages do not tend to turn [m] into [b], or more generally tend not to take away the nasal component of a nasal stop – certainly not between vowels. This disfavors the analysis that /mããmmo/ is an underlying form. Conversely, languages *do* tend to add a nasal component to an oral stop if it is adjacent to some other nasal sound. This favors the analysis that /bã̃mmo/ is an underlying form. Together, both cross-linguistic generalizations lead us to choose the latter approach. It does not mean the other approach is completely impossible, but if we were to stick with it, we would want much more compelling reasons to do so.

The steps needed to derive alternants are often expressed as rules, which operate on input forms and change something about them. Rules are needed to help sort out when one alternant occurs instead of another. In Luganda, we need to propose that speakers follow a rule which changes the place of articulation of nasal consonants to match the place of articulation of an immediately following consonant. This operates on /ẽn/ in /ẽn + pipi/ to produce [ẽmpipi].

2.6 Example rules

(a)   n → m / ___ [bilabial]
(b)   n → ŋ / ___ [velar]

In Chapter 6, we will explore how to make such rules more precise, but some explanation is still warranted here. First, each rule has a **target**, the segment which it applies to, and a restructuring, which is what the rule does to the target. For example, in (a), the target is /n/, and it is restructured to [m]. The restructuring relationship is indicated with an arrow. Crucially, the target of the rule is a segment, not the full morpheme; the rules only refer to the segment /n/, not to the morpheme /en/.

target: the segment or unit to which a phonological rule applies.

Second, each rule refers to an **environment**, which specifies the conditions under which it applies, separated from the restructuring component with a single slash. In (a), the conditions indicate that the change happens to /n/ if it precedes a bilabial segment. This is expressed by notating a blank underlined space to represent the position of the target, and specifying [bilabial] to the right of the blank space. In other words, the rule essentially says "the consonant /n/ becomes [m] if it occurs in a position where the following sound is bilabial."

environment: the context in which a target is found.

In Luganda, even though we have three alternants for the indefinite prefix, we only need two rules: one changes the prefix to [em] before bilabials, and another changes it to [eŋ] before velars. In all other circumstances, the prefix remains unchanged, and therefore surfaces as [en]. In later chapters, we will see how to combine these into a single rule.

If the target were sensitive to a preceding sound instead of what follows, the conditions would indicate this by specifying the context before the blank space. This would be the case for English plurals, as shown below:

2.7 Rules for English plural

/z/ → [əz] / [sibilant] ___

/z/ → [s] / [voiceless] ___

It is a general tenet that a simple phonological account subjects all forms in a language to the same set of rules – thus, it is important to compose the rules in such a way that they operate only on targets that match a certain description. Without a specification of a condition or context, a rule such as (2.6(a)) would change *every* [n] in Luganda into [m]. But by including the conditions, we may subject forms such as /ẽn + apo/ to it, and since its /n/ does not precede /b/ or /p/, the rule will not affect it. In other words, the rule that changes the place of articulation for nasals applies to the consonant of /ẽn-/, but only if the consonant is followed by another consonant. If the following segment is a vowel, as in [ẽnapo], then the rule does not apply.

Multiple rules may apply within one language. In Luganda, a separate rule needs to be proposed to handle the nasalization of root-initial consonants. It must be separate because it applies in different forms, and it targets different segments.

Exercise 2.8 Propose a second rule to account for the nasalization of root-initial consonants in Luganda.

As with the place assimilation in the prefix, we could propose a separate rule for each type of consonant that alternates:

b → m / m ___

d → n / n ___

g → ŋ / ŋ ___

However, we can note that [b, d, g] are similar consonants; they are all voiced stops. Since they share some articulatory properties and undergo a parallel phonological process, we can think of them as a natural class, and formulate a single rule that applies to all three. We assume in such rules that unless otherwise stated, the consonant named as the target maintains all of its other features. In this case, the target has its own place of articulation, which stays the same following the change created by the rule.

[voiced stops] → [nasal] / [nasal] ___

We will return to the notion of rules that apply to groups of sounds in Chapter 6.

For each of the rules we have written for Luganda, we have assumed a particular underlying representation. The rules are then written to reflect these assumptions. In the case of alternating roots, our choice of default form relied on typological evidence: oral stops becoming nasal near nasal sounds is more typical than nasal stops becoming oral between vowels. For the prefix, the choice depended on the more general distribution of the [en-] alternant. In our next test case, we will further explore what is meant by a general distribution of an alternant.

2.8 Indonesian

Examine the following data from Indonesian (Halle and Clements 1983), which illustrate a simple and a prefixed form for each of numerous roots. We may assume in this case that the simple form is equivalent to the root. We may proceed with morphological analysis of these data as we did with Luganda, making note of morphemes with multiple forms.

Simple form	Prefixed form	Gloss	Simple form	Prefixed form	Gloss
lempar	məlempar	'throw'	isi	məɲisi	'fill up'
rasa	mərasa	'feel'	undaŋ	məŋundaŋ	'invite'
masak	məmasak	'cook'	gambar	məŋgambar	'draw a picture'
nikah	mənikah	'marry'	dəŋar	məndəŋar	'hear'
ɲatso	məɲatso	'chat'	bantu	məmbantu	'help'
ambil	məɲambil	'take'			

Exercise 2.9 a. Identify each alternant of the Indonesian prefix.

b. Identify the conditions under which each alternant appears.

The prefix has several alternants: [mə-] if the root begins with [l, r, m, n, ŋ]; [məŋ-] if the root begins with a vowel or [g], [mən-] if the root begins with [d], and [məm-] if the alternant begins with [b].

Now our task is to decide which of these several forms of the prefix most closely corresponds to its default representation; in other words, we will identify the underlying representation of the prefix.

First, we may exclude [məm-] and [mən-] from consideration, as they occur in quite specific environments; in fact, each ends in a consonant which matches the place of articulation of the root's initial consonant. As such, they seem to have a very predictable distribution. Thus, we are left with [mə-] and [məŋ-] as possible underlying representations.

In favor of choosing [mə-] is the fact that it occurs before a seemingly wide range of consonants. In contrast, [məŋ-] seems parallel to [məm-] and [mən-] in that it assimilates to the place of the following consonant, at least in [məŋgabar], and also occurs in the relatively specific environment of vowels.

However, the context for [məŋ-], which includes both [g] and all vowels of the language, is difficult to characterize as some kind of specific, easily identifiable or unifiable group, mainly because [g] is unlike the rest of the segments which follow [ŋ]. In contrast, the context for [mə-], which includes just liquids and nasals, does have a common set of properties: they are voiced consonants, and indeed we can refer to them as resonants or **sonorants**. In fact, in Chapter 5 we will use data such as these to motivate the notion of "sonorant" as a **natural class** of sounds in languages.

sonorant: a class of segments including vowels, liquids, nasals, and glides.

natural class: a class of segments which share some common phonological feature (see §6.1 for a fuller definition).

Because they are all sonorant, we can actually characterize the group of sounds before which [mə-] occurs as a very specific set. Likewise, [məŋ-] now remains as the alternant with the most general distribution, confirmed by the fact that it occurs before a widely disparate set of sounds: vowels, as well as the consonant [g]. We cannot summarize this group of sounds as succinctly as we can for liquids and nasals. As a result, we conclude that [məŋ-] has the widest, least specific distribution, and therefore this is the alternant which corresponds most closely to the underlying representation.

We can restate the difference in the distribution of [məŋ-] and [mə-] with reference to terms of logical connectives. When we describe the set of sounds which [məŋ-] precedes, we rely on a disjunction, OR. That is, when describing the environments in which this alternant appears, we mean it can occur before vowels OR velar stops, and we cannot describe this set of sounds without using this disjunctive connector OR. In contrast, we do not need to use any descriptive statement using OR to characterize the environments in which [mə-] occurs: it is simply the set of sonorant consonants.

Exercise 2.10 Construct rules that produce the various alternants of /meŋ-/.

ŋ → Ø / __ [sonorant consonants]
ŋ → m / __ [bilabial]
ŋ → n / __ [alveolar]

These three rules account for the distribution of the alternants of the Indonesian prefix. Note again that the rules refer only to /ŋ/ as their target, and not to /məŋ/.

2.9 Malay

A similar pattern is observable in Malay, but with some notable differences. As with Indonesian above, examine the following Malay data (Sidharta 1976). The data exemplify a prefix that carries a number of varying functions, so for the purposes of this discussion we only need identify it as the prefix, and the forms in the table below show unprefixed nouns next to their prefixed counterparts. We may again assume that the simple form is equivalent to the root.

Base nouns	Prefixed	Gloss
tulis	penulis	'writer'
toloŋ	penoloŋ	'assistant'
tipu	penipu	'cheater'
suruh	peɲuruh	'messenger'
siram	peɲiram-an	'a watering'
sapu	peɲapu	'broom'
pukul	pemukul	'hammer'
potoŋ	pemotoŋ	'slaughterer'
pindah	pemindah-an	'a shift'
minta	peminta-an	'a request'
mamah	pemamah	'cud chewer'
lepas	pelepas	'starter'
lawat	pelawat	'visitor'
kurang	peɲurang-an	'a decrease'
kira	peɲira-an	'counting'
kenal	peŋenal-an	'introduction'
judi	peɲdʒudi	'gambler'

jimat	peɲdʒimat	'thrifty one'
gentar	peŋgentar	'coward'
geli	peŋeli	'ticklish one'
dapat	pendapat-an	'acquisition'
tʃeramah	pentʃeramah	'lecturer'
tʃari	pentʃari-an	'livelihood'
bunuh	pembunuh	'killer'
buka	pembuka	'opener'
batʃa	pembatʃa	'reader'
atur	peŋatur	'arranger'
ambil	peŋambil-an	'collection'

Exercise 2.11 Conduct a morphological analysis of these data, making note of morphemes with multiple forms.

In Malay, the prefix may appear as [pen-], [pem-], [peɲ-], [pe-], or [peŋ-]. The choice appears to be sensitive to the root's initial consonant: [pen-] occurs when the root begins with an alveolar stop; [pem-] occurs if the root begins with a bilabial consonant; [peɲ-] occurs if the root begins with [s] or with a palatal consonant; and [pe-] occurs if the root begins with a lateral or nasal. [peŋ-] occurs otherwise – where the root has an initial vowel or velar stop. The distribution of [peŋ-] suggests that, like the Indonesian prefix, this one matches the underlying representation.

However, you may have noticed that some of the roots also alternate in Malay. Thus, even though the prefix appears as the alternate [pen-] in [penulis], the root has an initial [t] when unprefixed, as in [tulis]. That is, the consonant of the prefix assimilates to a segment that is not present at the surface.

Exercise 2.12 Which other roots alternate in Malay?

tulis, toloŋtipu, pukul, potoŋ, pindah, kurang, kira, kenal
suruh, siram, sapu
judi, jimat

Any root that begins with a voiceless stop or fricative in its unsuffixed form has this kind of alternation. In such cases, the root's initial consonant is retained when there is no prefix, as in [tulis, sikam, pukul], but when the prefix appears, the initial consonant is lost, as in [menulis, meɲikam, memukul].

Another alternation is seen in roots with voiced palatals: [judi] and [jimat] both have an initial palatal glide when unprefixed, but a voiced affricate when prefixed, as in [peɲdʒudi] and [peɲdʒimat].

We can infer that three different things happen in Malay: a process of assimilation occurs, in which the prefix's final consonant adopts the place of articulation of the root's initial consonant. A process of deletion occurs, in which the root-initial consonant is deleted after a nasal consonant, as long as it is voiceless and not an affricate. Third, roots with initial /j/ have their own particular alternation.

Exercise 2.13 Construct rules that account for the alternation in the form of the prefix.

In the list below, there are three separate assimilation rules; in Chapter 6, we will return to these rules to combine them into a single process. A fourth rule is included to account for the deletion of the prefix /ŋ/ before roots with initial sonorants.

ŋ → ɲ / __ {s dʒ tʃ j}
ŋ → n / __ [alveolar]
ŋ → m / __ [labial]
ŋ → Ø / __ [sonorant]

Exercise 2.14 Construct rules that account for the alternations seen in some roots.

One rule is needed to delete voiceless segments after the nasal consonant, and another is needed to treat the alternation in roots with initial [j].

[voiceless, non-affricate consonant] → Ø / [nasal consonant] __
/j/ → [dʒ] / ɲ __

If you imagine a scenario in which underlying forms are fed through a series of phonological rules, the rule that accomplishes the assimilation process must occur first, before the deletion rule. Otherwise, if deletion occurred first, the root-initial consonant would be gone, and there would be no record of its place of articulation for the prefix consonant to assimilate to.

2.10 Karo

By now it should be clear that alternation can happen in both affixes and roots. In the Indonesian and Malay examples, we saw root alternation, where the unprefixed roots were equivalent to the underlying form. In the data set from Karo (Gabas 1999), we see that this is not necessarily a fact we can assume.

(1)	ˈpəgat	'burn'	oˈpəgat	'burned me'	eˈpəgat	'burned you'
(2)	penaˈoj	'dance'	owenaˈoj	'I danced'	ebenaˈoj	'you danced'
(3)	taˈti	'bring'	oɾaˈti	'brought me'	eɾaˈti	'brought you'

(4) 'toj   'see'   o'toj   'saw me'   e'toj   'saw you'
(5) kuruʔ'cu 'saliva'   oguruʔ'cu 'my saliva'   eguruʔ'cu 'your saliva'
(6) 'kun   'stomach'   o'kun   'my stomach'   e'kun   'your stomach'

Exercise 2.15 Identify the alternating roots in Karo.

The form for 'dance' varies across contexts between [pena'oj], [-wena'oj], and [-bena'oj]. Likewise, 'bring' appears as [ta'ti] or [-ɾa'ti], and 'saliva' appears as [kuruʔ'cu] or [-guruʔ'cu].

In each of these roots, we see a voiceless consonant when there is no prefix, and voiced consonant otherwise. Other roots have voiceless consonants in every equivalent context.

Exercise 2.16 Determine the underlying forms of the alternating roots in Karo.

The best candidate for the underlying forms is the root as it appears in the second person column, as in /ɾa'ti/, /bena'oj/, and /guruʔ'cu/.

If we focus on 'bring,' we need to choose either /ta'ti/ or /ɾa'i/ as the underlying representation. If we presume that /ta'ti/ is the underlying form, based on the fact that it is how the unprefixed root appears, we need to create a rule that voices /t/ between vowels. On the one hand, the same rule could apply to each of the other alternating roots, but on the other, we cannot prevent it from also applying to the non-alternating roots, wrongly generating forms such as *[o'ɾoj].

The alternative is to choose the alternants with initial voiced consonants as the underlying forms, and rely on a rule of initial devoicing to account for the alternants that appear when there is no prefix.

2.11 Other kinds of assimilation

Many of the patterns of alternation we have seen involve some process of assimilation, where a segment at the edge of a morpheme undergoes some change in its form in order to become more like an adjacent segment from another morpheme. So far, we have seen assimilation patterns in which a consonant adopts the place, nasality, or voicing of an adjacent consonant. We are about to expand our knowledge of assimilation, looking at patterns which instead involve interactions between consonants and vowels.

2.12 Catalan

Now examine the following data from Catalan (Mascaró 1976, Bermúdez-Otero 2001). In this case the complex forms are not actually roots and affixes;

instead we have words which are preceded by articles. Even so, we may apply the methods of morphological analysis to isolate and identify component morphemes. Regardless, we see in these data that some of the morphemes have alternations in their form.

[um buto]   'a button'
[əl βuto]   'the button'
[uŋ gos]   'a dog'
[əl ɣos]   'the dog'

Exercise 2.17 Identify the alternating forms of each Catalan root. Under what conditions does each alternant appear?

Each root begins with a voiced stop consonant when preceded by the indefinite article, as in [um buto] and [uŋ gos], but when preceded by the definite article, the root's initial consonant is instead a voiced fricative made at the same place of articulation.

Which is the underlying form of the root? A larger set of data would provide distributional evidence that it is the form with an initial stop – it occurs if preceded by a pause, and when preceded by most consonants. The fricative variant occurs just when preceded by a vowel and liquids. In addition, though we have not yet discussed typological considerations, this is an example of **spirantization** – the change of a stop to a fricative between vowels or sonorants – which is much more common than the change of a fricative to a stop at the beginning of a word. It is also an example of an **intervocalic effect**, in which a specific allophone appears only between vowels or sonorants.

spirantization: a process in which stop consonants become fricatives.

intervocalic effect: any process in which a consonant undergoes a phonological change by virtue of occurring between two vowels.

The implications of these data are several. First, we see that alternation may occur within roots rather than simply in affixes, as we also saw in Luganda, Malay, and Karo. Second, we see that alternation can occur not just in processes of affixation, but also at the juncture of separate words. Third, and more to the point here, we see that a consonant may be affected by adjacent vowels. In Catalan, consonants that occur between vowels are in a sense weakened. The change of stop to fricative is one of numerous types of phonological changes that occur in intervocalic contexts. We may see voiceless consonants becoming voiced, stops becoming fricatives, fricatives becoming sonorants, or consonants becoming glides.

We will return to Catalan spirantization in depth in Chapter 6.

2.13 English flapping

Many English varieties illustrate a similar phenomenon in which the consonants /t/ and /d/ both alternate with another sound, [ɾ], called either a *flap* or a *tap*. Such alternation is observable when one of these consonants occurs at the end of a root which is then suffixed. Some other English varieties use [ʔ] instead of [ɾ] in these same contexts.

weɪt	'wait'	weɪɾəd	'waited'	weɪɾɪŋ	'waiting'
hiːt	'heat'	hiːɾəd	'heated'	hiːɾɪŋ	'heating'
pæt	'pat'	pæɾəd	'patted'	pæɾɪŋ	'patting'
saɪt	'cite'	saɪɾəd	'cited'	saɪɾɪŋ	'citing'

Exercise 2.18   Identify the alternants of each root, and propose an underlying representation.

- [weɪt] alternates with [weɪɾ-]
- [hiːt] alternates with [hiːɾ-]
- [pæt] alternates with [pæɾ-]
- [saɪt] alternates with [saɪɾ-]

Although there is actually insufficient evidence to make a definitive choice in the above data, the forms which end in [-t] are more suitable choices for the underlying representation.

Would we want to assume these roots end in /t/ or /ɾ/? If we considered only the above data, either choice would be plausible at first (as long as we abstract away from the clue given to us from our own spelling system). We could propose a word-final /t/ which becomes [ɾ] just when followed by a vowel, or we could propose a word-final /ɾ/ which becomes [t] just when word-final.

Nevertheless, if we widen our scope of inquiry to determine when exactly [t] appears, the contexts are of a wider range: when in final position of an utterance (or before a pause), when followed by a consonant-initial word (as in *wait for*), or when followed by a consonant-initial suffix (as in *waits*). This suggests a more general set of cases in which [t] occurs, whereas [ɾ] has a more specific distribution, requiring a vowel to follow. This leads us to conclude that such roots end with /t/.

2.14 More English flapping

Further support for this conclusion comes from roots in which [ɾ] alternates with [d] instead. In this set of data, the facts are similar: [ɾ] occurs before a vowel; [d] occurs otherwise.

weɪd	'wade'	weɪɾəd	'waded'	weɪɾɪŋ	'wading'
hiːd	'heed'	hiːɾəd	'heeded'	hiːɾɪŋ	'heeding'
pæd	'pad'	pæɾəd	'padded'	pæɾɪŋ	'padding'
saɪd	'side'	saɪɾəd	'sided'	saɪɾɪŋ	'siding'

For us to posit root-final flaps which lose their flaphood in word-final contexts, we no longer have a sensible account: some words would end in /ɾ/ but change it to [t], while others would end in /ɾ/ but change it to [d]. This choice is not predictable; thus, we place the /t/ vs. /d/ distinction as a property of the root-final consonant, and allow either to become [ɾ] before a vowel.

As a result, we have identified another phonological process in which a particular sound (in this case, a stop consonant) weakens in an intervocalic context. Though the flap is quite similar to [d], it is also less occlusive and consonantal in its articulation; indeed, the same articulation is used in other languages as /r/.

The facts about flapping in English are more complex than presented here. Flaps may occur within morphemes, as long as they precede an unstressed vowel, but the following sound may also be a syllabic resonant (as long as it is not /n/). Thus, *data* [deɪɾə], *city* [sɪɾi], *ditto* [dɪɾo], *bottle* [bɑɾl], and *bottom* [bɑɾm] all have flaps, but *button* [bʌʔn] does not, despite the consonant occurring after a stressed vowel and before an unstressed syllable. Likewise, *detergent* [dətʰɚdʒnt], *rotisserie* [ɹotʰɪsɚi], *retort* [rətʰoɹt], and *petunia* [pətʰunja] all maintain voiceless (indeed, aspirated) [tʰ] by virtue of the stressed vowel that follows. At the ends of roots, flapping may occur even if the following vowel is stressed, as phrases such as *get on, get it, get Albert* all illustrate.

Even despite these complicated nuances in the distribution of flaps in English, these data illustrate a phenomenon of **neutralization**: two different phonemes share a common alternant.

neutralization: two different phonemes share a common alternant (see §7.4 for a fuller definition).

2.15 German neutralization

Neutralization is not uncommon, and among consonants is often found at the ends of words. Consider the following data from German, particularly the form of the unsuffixed and suffixed roots. Note that the root vowels also show some changes, but we will ignore these in this problem.

| [taːgə] | 'days' | [taːk] | 'day' |
| [følkəʁ] | 'peoples' | [fɔlk] | 'people' |

[ʁɛːdəʁ]	'wheels'	[ʁaːt]	'wheel'
[laɪdən]	'to suffer'	[laɪt]	'sorry'
[ʁaːtən]	'to advise'	[ʁaːt]	'advice'
[bʁaːvəʁ]	'obedient'	[bʁaf]	'good'
[høfə]	'courtyards'	[hɔf]	'courtyard'
[ʁeguŋ]	'movement'	[ʁɛksam]	'active'
[zaːgən]	'to say'	[zaːktə]	'said'
[ʁaːdɛln]	'to pedal'	[ʁaːtfaʁən]	'to cycle'
[bʁaːvəʁ]	'obedient'	[bʁaːfhaɪt]	'good behavior'
[ʃtɔʏbən]	'to dust'	[ʃtɔʏpçən]	'dust particle'
[bøzə]	'wicked'	[boshaft]	'malicious'

Exercise 2.19   Which roots alternate? What generalizations can you make about the alternating and non-alternating roots?

While there are numerous suffixes illustrated in these data, the roots can still be extracted, and many of them show an alternation where there is a final voiceless consonant in one alternant but a final voiced consonant in the other.

The following pairs of alternants illustrate the alternating roots: [taːg- ~ taːk], [ʁɛːd- ~ ʁaːt] [laɪd- ~ laɪt], [bʁaːv- ~ bʁaf-], [ʁeg- ~ ʁɛk], [ʁaːd- ~ ʁaːt], [zaːg- ~ zaːk], [ʃtaʊb- ~ ʃtɔʏp-], [bøːz- ~ bøːs].

Among such roots, the alternants with final voiced consonants are always followed by vowel-initial suffixes, while the alternants with final voiceless consonants either have no suffix or are followed by consonant-initial suffixes.

More generally we see that some roots consistently have voiceless consonants, while others alternate between voiceless and voiced; moreover, the voiced consonant always appears before a vowel-initial suffix. In addition, there are no roots which invariantly end in voiced consonants.

Were we to focus solely on alternating forms such as [taːk] ~ [taːgə] and [laɪt] ~ [laɪdən], we might conclude that this is another example of intervocalic voicing – a segment which is voiceless when word-final, alternating with a voiced form between vowels. Given that the voiceless form occurs in an unsuffixed root, we might further conclude that this is the basic form – but non-alternating forms such as [ʁaːt] ~ [ʁaːtən] and [høf] ~ [høfə] present some difficulty. These too should be seen as having voiceless consonants, but in their suffixed forms, the consonant remains voiceless. Thus, if all these roots underlyingly contain voiceless consonants, we will struggle for an account of why only some undergo intervocalic voicing.

The alternative is to consider roots such as [taːk] to contain underlyingly voiced consonants, which in the absence of any suffix become voiceless at the end of the word: thus /taːg/ arises as [taːk]. But if a vowel-initial suffix is attached to these roots, as in [taːg + ə], the consonant then becomes intervocalic and maintains its voicing, as in [taːgə].

Thus we characterize German as have a devoicing pattern: voiced consonants are made voiceless in certain circumstances. Since they then have a voiceless alternant that is identical at the surface to other voiceless consonants, this is another example of neutralization.

Exercise 2.20   Construct a rule that predicts the devoicing pattern in German.

[voiced consonants] → [voiceless] / ___]$_{\text{WD}}$
[voiced consonants] → [voiceless] / ___ [consonant]

2.16 Palatalization

The vowel-driven effects we saw in Catalan and English are examples of consonants weakening in some sense; these patterns can also be seen as types of assimilation. For example, a stop becoming a fricative makes the consonant a little more open in its constriction, thus moving slightly towards a vocalic segmental configuration. Similarly, intervocalic voicing of consonants illustrates an assimilation of the consonant to the voicing of the surrounding vowels.

There are also examples of consonants assimilating their place features to nearby vowels; most notable of these is palatalization, in which an alveolar or velar consonant changes to a palatal consonant adjacent to a front vowel. We may now return to some Japanese data we first encountered in Chapter 1.

2.17 Japanese

Examine the following forms in Japanese (Halle and Clements 1983). Note that every verb root has a final /-u/ which only appears when there is no other suffix. For this analysis, you can assume that this vowel is not actually part of the root. With this in mind, you should be able to find a pattern of alternation that arises only in some roots.

Present	Negative	Volitional	
ʃinu	ʃinanai	ʃinitai	'die'
jomu	jomanai	jomitai	'read'
jobu	jobanai	jobitai	'call'
katsu	katanai	katʃitai	'win'

kasu	kasanai	kaʃitai	'lend'
waku	wakanai	wakitai	'boil'
ʦugu	ʦuganai	ʦugitai	'pour'
karu	karanai	karitai	'shear'

Exercise 2.21　First, determine the form of the negative and volitional suffixes. Then, identify any alternation you see in the form of the verb root.

The negative suffix is /-anai/ and the volitional suffix is /-itai/. Both forms are invariant, and can be extracted from the data with basic morphological analysis.

　　The roots are more complicated, as two of them alternate. In particular, 'win' alternates between [kaʦ-], [kat-], and [katʃ-], and 'lend' alternates between [kas-] and [kaʃ-]. All other roots have no alternation.

Exercise 2.22　Describe the conditions that seem to apply to the alternating roots.

Both roots alternate between alveolar and post-alveolar places of articulation. They end in alveolar consonants before the [-anai] suffix, and post-alveolar consonants before the [-itai] consonant. The root meaning 'win' has a third alternant that appears only before the final [-u] of the present form; the alternant here is still alveolar but is realized as an affricate in [kaʦu].

　　The other roots are consistent in that they have the same final consonant in both inflected forms; for example [ʃin-anai] and [ʃin-itai] both have a root-final [n]. Other roots of this type include [jom-], [job-], [wak-], [ʦug-], and [kar-].

　　For the alternating roots, the final consonant changes in response to the following vowel: the root has an alveolar consonant before the initial low vowel of the negative suffix [-anai], but a post-alveolar consonant before the high front vowel of the volitional suffix [-inai]. Moreover, this alternation is only found among coronal obstruents: the liquid /ɾ/ and the nasal /n/ do not alternate.

Exercise 2.23　Construct a rule that predicts the palatalization pattern in Japanese.

[alveolars] → [post-alveolar] / ___ i

As with other analyses, our next step would be to determine which form is underlying, but there is not quite sufficient evidence in these data to make this choice. However, several other facts about Japanese phonology converge upon us choosing the alveolar form. First, the alveolar form is found before any vowel except [i], with the additional point that [ʦ] is another alternant appearing only before [u]. Thus while /s/ has two alternants, with [ʃ] appearing in the specific circumstance of [i], /t/ has three alternants, with [ts] and [tʃ] both appearing in specific circumstances. Both phonemes have a general distribution for their remaining alternant. Thus, the palatal alternant appears in a restricted environment.

Some additional aspects of Japanese phonology deserve comment. First, some of the non-alternating roots do undergo alternation before other suffixes not shown here. Second, the distributional facts about Japanese /s/ and /t/ are not simply facts of alternation; they are generally true of these phonemes, such that even within roots, [ʃ] but not [s] may precede [i], and likewise [tʃ] but not [t] may precede [i]. This aspect of the data can then be approached from a phonemic analysis perspective, using the tools we learn in Chapter 5.

2.18 Dakota

Another example of palatalization emerging in the context of morphophonemic alternation can be seen in Dakota (Shaw 1978). Take some time to peruse the data below.

(1)	kʰá	'to mean'
(2)	nitʃʰá	'she means thee'
(3)	kʔú	'to give'
(4)	nitʃʔú	'she gives it to thee'
(5)	kilówaⁿ	'to sing for another one'
(6)	nitʃílowaⁿ	'she sings for thee'
(7)	makʰute	'he shoots at me'
(8)	wakʰute	'I shoot at him'
(9)	nitʃʰute	'he shoots at you'

Exercise 2.24 Determine the forms of the roots and prefixes in the Dakota data below.

Bare roots: kʰá, kʔú, kilówaⁿ
Prefixed forms: nitʃʰá, nitʃʔú, nitʃílowaⁿ, makʰute, wakʰute, nitʃʰute

Before addressing the alternation in these data, some morphological analysis is necessary, especially since these data illustrate a particular morphological phenomenon we have not yet seen in this text.

In short, the form of the verb in Dakota changes as a function of both the subject and object. Comparing just the first two forms [kʰá] and [nitʃʰá], we note the presence of [ni-] in one form but not the other. Using only this pair of words, we cannot determine whether this form relates to the third-person subject agreement, second-person object agreement, or both, but a look at the remainder of the forms suggests in fact that the prefix indicates both subject agreement and object agreement all at once. Here is a brief summary of the morphological conditions under which each prefix appears.

- [ni-] appears where the subject is third person and the object is second person, as in [nitʃʰá, nitʃílowaⁿ, nitʃ'ú, nitʃʰute]
- [ma-] appears where the subject is third person and the object is first person, as in [makʰute]
- [wa-] appears where the subject is first person and the object is third person, as in [wakʰute]

The remaining forms appear to lack prefixes, and they are glossed without any agreement information.

There are two ways to make sense of the functions of the prefixes. First, it is possible that all third-person agreement is null in the language, so [ni-] indicates solely second-person object agreement; [ma-] indicates solely first-person object agreement, and [wa-] indicates only first-person subject agreement. Alternatively, each prefix is a **fusional morpheme** that simultaneously indicates both object and subject agreement. We would need more data illustrating more combinations of subject and object agreement to sort out this question.

fusional morpheme: a morpheme that carries more than one function at once, for example tense and subject agreement, or subject and object agreement.

Regardless of the particular morphological analysis, we still may conclude that some forms in the Dakota data have no prefixes, while others do have prefixes.

Exercise 2.25   Describe the alternation in Dakota roots. Which roots alternate, and under what conditions do their alternants appear?

It should be clear that each of the roots alternates, in that its initial consonant differs as a function of its environment. In brief, each root has an initial velar stop (whether aspirated, glottalized, or plain), but when occurring with the [ni-] prefix, the root-initial consonant appears as a post-alveolar affricate instead.

Moreover, the prefixes *ma-* and *wa-* produce no such change; both have low vowels, while the prefix *ni-* has a high vowel. We may thus conclude that the consonants [k] and [tʃ] are in an alternation relationship, whereby the post-alveolar alternant [tʃ] appears just in the specific context of a preceding vowel [i]. Thus, like Japanese, a pattern of palatalization is evident in which some non-palatal consonant acquires a palatal place of articulation in the context of the high front vowel [i].

Exercise 2.26 Construct a rule that predicts the palatalization pattern in Dakota.

[velars] → [post-alveolar] / i ___

Summary

In this chapter, we have seen a variety of types of alternations, which are phonological patterns in which a segment in some morpheme reacts to the presence of adjacent or proximate segments by changing its form. In alternation patterns, the adjacency of sounds is brought about by morphological processes that place morphemes together in the creation of complex words. Alternation often entails some process of assimilation between adjacent segments, where one segment adapts to another by assuming similar place or manner features.

We have seen that consonants may affect each other, as well as vowel-to-consonant effects, whereby consonants assimilate to vowels along dimensions such as voicing, aperture, and place of articulation. Many of these assimilatory processes seem quite clearly to result in structures that are somehow easier or simpler to produce or pronounce. Nevertheless, it is important not to view phonology simply as a mechanism to reduce articulatory effort; many of the types of sequences that are resolved via phonological assimilation in some languages are nonetheless physiologically possible.

Moreover, if phonology in language were simply a set of effort-reducing processes, then without any counteractive principles, it could run amok and reduce every structure to the easiest, most effortless form. Yet we do not see this – languages maintain large sets of phonemes and tolerate some relatively effortful sequences. Indeed, phonology is better characterized as a continuous balance between allowing phonemes to assume adaptive, assimilatory alternants, and maintain contrasts between them, to the extent of sacrificing ease of articulation concerns. We return to this point in detail in Chapter 12.

We will revisit assimilatory effects in Chapter 5, where instead of alternation, the evidence will come from morpheme-internal phonemic analysis. In the following chapters, we will examine some additional types of alternation. In Chapter 3, we will survey various deletion patterns, which can be construed as "alternations with zero," where a phoneme is simply not realized in a particular morphophonemic context. In Chapter 4, we will explore alternations that involve something other than adjacent segments, such as vowel harmony, a special type of assimilation that occurs among nearby (but non-adjacent) vowels.

Key terms

segment
sound
phoneme
alternation
underlying representation
alternant
rule
target
epenthesis
natural class
sonorant
sibilant
neutralization
assimilation
spirantization
palatalization

References and further reading

Bermúdez-Otero, Ricardo. 2001. Voicing and continuancy in Catalan: a nonvacuous Duke-of-York gambit and a Richness-of-the-Base paradox. Ms., University of Manchester. Available online at www.bermudez-otero.com/Catalan.pdf

Fromkin, Victoria, Robert Rodman, and Nina Hyams. 2014. *An Introduction to Language, 10th edition*. Boston: Wadsworth.

Gabas, Nilson, Jr. 1999. A grammar of Karo, Tupı (Brazil). Doctoral dissertation, University of Californa, Santa Barbara.

Halle, Morris, and George N. Clements. 1983. *Problem Book in Phonology*. Cambridge, MA: MIT Press.

Mascaró, Joan. 1976. Catalan phonology and the phonological cycle. Doctoral dissertation, Massachusetts Institute of Technology.

Sidharta (Sie Ing Djiang). 1976. *The Consonantal and Vowel Systems of Malay and Huayu: A Contrastive Analysis*. Singapore: Chinese Language Centre, Nanyang University.

Tsukida, Naomi. 2004. Seediq. In K. Alexander Adelaar and Nikolaus Himmelmann (eds.), *The Austronesian Languages of Asia and Madagascar.* Abingdon, Oxon, and New York: Routledge, 291–325.

Review exercises

Karo

Examine the following data from Karo (Gabas 1999):

'cu	'big'	'cuɾem	'big'
'pɨj	'lazy'	'pɨjɾem	'lazy'
'tãw	'far'	'tãwɾem	'far'
'kĩn	'hard'	'kĩnnem	'hard'
'wɨn	'curved'	'wɨnnem	'curved'
'kap	'fat'	'kaptem	'fat'
'pãt	'beautiful'	'pãttem	'beautiful'
'wãk	'sick'	'wãktem	'sick'

The forms in the right column all contain a variant of the same suffix. Identify all such variants and describe the conditions under which each variant occurs.

Sediq (Formosan)

Examine the following data from Sediq (Tsukida 2004):

Unsuffixed	Imperative	Gloss
kajak	kijapi	'cut (meat)'
atak	tapi	'cut (with scissors)'
tsehak	tsehepi	'lick'
tsupecik	tsupucipi	'suck'
ruberuk	ruburubi	'broil'
eluk	lebi	'close'
tugejak	tugujaki	'belch'
gemuk	gumuki	'cover'
talaŋ	tulami	'run'
kututiŋ	kututiŋi	'fall'
kubahaŋ	kubahaŋi	'hear'
geleiŋ	guliiŋi	'hide'
dakin	dukili	'grow'

betun	buteli	'kick'
sukuxun	sukuxeli	'thresh'
ʦukun	ʦukuli	'push'
tekan	tukani	'pound (rice)'
requn	ruqeni	'swallow'

These data illustrate alternation in Sediq roots.

a. Identify the imperative suffix and note any alternations you detect in consonants. Do not be concerned with any changes you see in vowels (and there are many).

b. Propose underlying representations of the roots and rules that predict the appearance of their alternants.

CHAPTER 3 ALTERNATION WITH ZERO

> ## Learning objectives
>
> - Identify alternations involving the presence or absence of segments
> - Describe the contexts in which each alternant appears
> - Determine whether an alternation with zero is insertion or deletion
> - Compose rules to derive other alternants from underlying forms

Introduction

In the previous chapter we saw many examples of phonological processes in which phonemes adapt to their environment. We characterized this generally as the phenomenon of assimilation, under which a sound adopts some or all characteristics of nearby sounds. Palatalization, spirantization, intervocalic voicing, and word-final devoicing are all manifestations of phonemes adapting to their environments.

Through such analysis we have seen that phonemes alternate – they take on different forms in different phonological contexts. Alternation is a phenomenon in which the phonological form of a morpheme changes based on context, observable where different morphological structure yields different phonological environments. You should recall that this is true of phonemes within root morphemes as well as within affixes.

In this chapter we expand our understanding of alternation to include scenarios in which segments may be present in one alternant but missing in another.

3.1 Persian

Consider the Persian data below (from Windfuhr 1979), which include singular and plural nouns. Morphological analysis of the first ten forms yields a fairly consistent result: the plural morpheme appears to be [-an]. For example, compare the singular forms [zæn] 'woman' and [hæsud] 'envious' with their plural forms, [zænan] and [hæsudan].

	Singular	*Plural*	*Gloss*
(1)	zæn	zænan	'woman'
(2)	læb	læban	'lip'
(3)	hæsud	hæsudan	'envious'
(4)	bæradær	bæradæran	'brother'
(5)	bozorg	bozorgan	'big'
(6)	mæleke	mælekean	'queen'
(7)	valede	valedean	'mother'
(8)	kæbire	kæbirean	'great'
(9)	ahu	ahuan	'gazelle'
(10)	hamele	hamelean	'pregnant'
(11)	bætʃtʃe	bætʃtʃegan	'child'
(12)	setare	setaregan	'star'
(13)	bænde	bændegan	'slave'
(14)	azade	azadegan	'freedom'

However, the plural of forms (11)–(14) follows a different generalization: each has the sequence [-gan] in the plural rather than [-an], as in [setaregan] 'stars.' Thus, some plurals have an extra [g], while others don't.

Now we are faced with a dilemma, because it is not immediately clear where the [g] comes from – that is, which morpheme does it belong to, and what are the circumstances that determine its presence or absence?

Note that the issue here is basically that: the presence or absence of [g], which can be rephrased as [g] alternating with zero.

There are several analytical choices here, one of which will ultimately fit the data the best. Either the [g] is part of the root (and disappears in some contexts), part of the suffix (and disappears in some contexts), or it is not really part of either, and it just appears in some contexts. Our analysis is a matter of choosing among these three competing hypotheses.

3.1.1 Hypothesis: g-insertion

Let us deal with the third option, **g-insertion**, first. According to this approach, the [g] which appears in some plurals is not a member of either morpheme. Likewise, the roots are always invariant, and the plural suffix is invariantly [-an]. For example, the root for 'star' would be /setare/, and when /-an/ is added, the [g] is inserted between the two:

/ setare + an /	UR
	insert [g] between vowels
[setaregan]	output

The approach needs an account of why [g] is inserted. We may note that each root in which [g] appears in the plural ends in /e/, so perhaps there is a rule which inserts [g] between /e/ and /a/. Indeed, an appeal to such a rule is a necessary consequence of this approach. However, there are other roots which end in /-e/ which do not undergo this process; for example, the plural of /kæbire/ is [kæbirean], with no inserted [g]. Consequently, the g-insertion hypothesis appears to be untenable.

3.1.2 Hypothesis: [gan] and [an] are allomorphs

Another option is to presume that the /g/ is part of the plural morpheme – and thus that [gan] and [an] are two allomorphs of the plural suffix. In this approach, we need some way to account for why each allomorph appears – perhaps [gan] appears in one set of circumstances, while [an] appears in the converse set of circumstances. This therefore calls for a rule that deletes [g], and to do so we would need to find a specific environment in which this occurs.

setare + gan	læb + gan	kæbire + gan	UR
NA			g-deletion
setaregan	læban	kæbirean	output

As with the g-insertion approach, this option runs into some difficulty. On the one hand, [gan] always occurs after root-final [e], but on the other, there are some roots with final [e] that do not receive the [gan] allomorph, as in [kæbirean] 'great-PL.' In other words, whatever rule deletes /g/ from /gan/ must do so after consonants, as well as after some (but not all) instances of /e/. Thus, a simple rule to produce [gan] in a particular circumstance does not seem to be available.

3.1.3 Hypothesis: Alternating /g/ is part of the root

The last option is to construe the alternating [g] as a member of the roots. Likewise, the plural suffix in this approach is invariantly [an]. The implication here is that some of the roots alternate: any root which has a final [g] in its plural also has a final underlying /g/, which is deleted from its unsuffixed form. To account for this pattern, we may note that each such root also has /e/ before its final /g/. Thus, the rule expresses this generalization, using the symbol Ø to represent the result of deletion.

g → Ø / e _]$_{WD}$

setareg	setareg + an	bozorg	kæbire	kæbire + an	UR
setare					g-deletion
setare	setaregan	bozorg	kæbire	kæbirean	output

41

The analysis thus works as follows: word-final /g/ is deleted if preceded by /e/; if the preceding sound is something else, as in [bozorg], the /g/ stays. In the presence of a plural suffix, root-final /g/ is never word-final, and so it remains, as in [setaregan]. Plurals forms built from roots without final /g/ obviously have no [g] in their plural either, as in [kæbirean].

Ultimately this analysis is one of deletion, a patttern in which an underlying segment alternates with zero. The zero alternant appears in a specific circumstance (i.e., the environment e__]), while the [g] alternant appears more generally elsewhere. Moreover, here is a case where the alternation clearly arises in the root itself, and not in the affix.

Since the undeleted [g] alternant has the more general distribution, our construal of the pattern as one of deletion comports with the notion that *general* forms are more telling of underlying representations than are *specific* forms. Alternatively, we can note that the zero alternant's distribution is entirely *predictable*, so it is more sensible to encode the presence of [g] in lexical entries rather than the absence of it.

3.2 Fijian

Now consider the following data from Fijian (Crowley 1992b). The left-hand forms are simple verbs, while those on the right are derived passive forms.

(1)	'see'	rai	raiða
(2)	'take'	tau	taura
(3)	'carry'	kau	kauta
(4)	'make'	ðaka	ðakava
(5)	'give'	soli	solia
(6)	'dry'	siŋa	siŋana
(7)	'push'	bili	biliŋa
(8)	'repay'	sau	sauma
(9)	'shave'	toro	toroja
(10)	'go away'	jawa	jawaka

At first glance the pattern may seem less obvious here than our final conclusion for Persian. In short, the Fijian passive is clearly produced by adding a suffix, but the additional segmental material differs quite specifically for each root: [-ða] for 'see,' [-ra] for 'take,' [-ta] for 'carry,' and so on. The question is this, what governs the choice of different consonant for each suffix?

Exercise 3.1 Describe two plausible approaches to these data, differing by where you would place the boundary between the root and the suffixes.

In one approach, the underlying root is identical to the unsuffixed form. Alternatively, some of the roots have final consonants which are present in the suffixed forms but are lost from the unsuffixed forms.

Let us first test the hypothesis that the underlying roots are identical to the unsuffixed forms. For example, /rai/ would mean 'see,' and is [rai] in its simple form; likewise, its suffix is [-ða], and its passive is [raiða].

Exercise 3.2 Assume that the underlying roots are identical to the unsuffixed forms as you answer the following questions.
a. Describe the various forms of the passive suffix.
b. Is it possible to predict the form of the passive suffix, based on the form of the unsuffixed root?

If the underlying roots are the same as the unsuffixed forms, then we are left with ten allomorphs of the passive suffix: [-ða, -ra, -ta, -va, -a, -na, -ŋa, -ma, -ja, -ka]

In these data we have a different form of the suffix for each root, so we cannot possibly identify any generalizations governing their distribution.

Since the following sound is always [a], we can only turn to the preceding segments – the root-final vowels – to make this prediction. But these immediately preceding segments are not helpful: roots which seem to end in /u/ take either of three consonants, as in [kauta], [taura], and [sauma], while roots that seem to end in [a] take any of three other consonants, as in [ðakava], [siŋana], and [jawaka]. The choice of these consonants seems to be just about impossible to predict with any accuracy.

Let us then test the alternative hypothesis that the underlying roots include final consonants which are lost from the unsuffixed forms. For example, /raið/ would mean 'see,' and is [rai] in its simple form, but the final consonant remains in the passive form [raiða].

Exercise 3.3 Assume that the underlying forms in Fijian have final consonants, and answer the following questions with this in mind.
a. What are the underlying forms of the suffix and root in this account?
b. Compose a single rule that will account for the alternation you observe here.

The suffix is invariantly [-a] in this approach. The underlying representations of the roots are as follows: /raið, taur, kaut, ðakav, soli, siŋan, biliŋ, saum, toroj, jawak/.

All the alternation can be handled with a single rule:

[consonant] → Ø / ___]$_{WD}$

The alternative root-allomorphy hypothesis encodes that the choice of consonant to appear in the passives is essentially *not* predictable – and as such, it is a property of the lexical entry of each root. Indeed, the lexicon is exactly where unpredictable (learned) information must reside – and moreover, this is equivalent to concluding that the underlying representation of 'see' is actually /raið/.

The final-consonant deletion rule is not so different from that of Persian, except that it affects consonants more generally, rather than just one member of the inventory. In addition, this approach quite cleanly handles the behavior of 'give': as /soli/, it has no final consonant underlyingly, so it is [soli] when unsuffixed, and because of its root-final vowel, it shows no alternation between simple and passive form, where it appears as [solia].

3.3 Paamese

Another example of an alternation between a segment and zero is found in Paamese (Crowley 1992a: 129). Consider the following data, which include morphologically simple nouns, along with two additional inflected forms.

(1)	aim	'house'	aimok	'this house'	aimos	'only the house'
(2)	ahat	'stone'	ahatuk	'this stone'	ahatus	'only the stone'
(3)	ahin	'woman'	ahinek	'this woman'	ahines	'only the woman'
(4)	atin	'cabbage'	atinuk	'this cabbage'	atinus	'only the cabbage'
(5)	atas	'sea'	atasik	'this sea'	atasis	'only the sea'
(6)	metas	'spear'	metasok	'this spear'	metasos	'only the spear'
(7)	ahis	'banana'	ahisik	'this banana'	ahisis	'only the banana'
(8)	ahis	'rifle'	ahisuk	'this rifle'	ahisus	'only the rifle'

Exercise 3.4 Describe two plausible approaches to these data, differing by where you would place the boundary between the root and the suffixes.

In one approach, the underlying root is identical to the unsuffixed form. Alternatively, the roots have final vowels which are present in the suffixed forms but are lost from the unsuffixed forms.

Exercise 3.5 Assume the first analysis, that the root is identical to the unsuffixed form.
a. Describe the various forms of the definite suffix and of the exclusionary suffix.
b. Is it possible to predict the form of either suffix, based on the form of the unsuffixed root?

In this approach, the definite suffix has four alternating forms: [-ok], [-uk], [-ek], and [-ik], and the exclusionary also has four forms: [-os], [-us], [-es], and [-is]. There does not appear to be anything about the root that helps determine which of these forms appears.

Exercise 3.6 Now assume the second analysis, that the roots have final vowels which are lost in the unsuffixed forms.
a.   What are the forms of each underlying suffix and root in this account?
b.   Compose a single rule that will account for the alternation you observe here.

In this approach, the definite suffix is invariantly [-k], and the exclusionary is invariantly [-s].

The roots have final vowels, as in [aimo-, ahatu-, ahine-, atinu-, atasi-, metaso-, ahisi-, ahisu-].

All the alternation can be handled with a single rule:

$$[\text{vowel}] \rightarrow \emptyset\ /\ \underline{\qquad}\ ]_{\text{WD}}$$

In the Paamese data, there are vowels which alternate with zero: they are absent from the ends of unsuffixed roots, as in [ahat] and [ahin], but appear ahead of suffix consonants, as in [ahatok] and [ahinuk]. Since the nature of these vowels is unpredictable, we consider them to be part of the root. We must also propose a rule of final-vowel deletion that deletes vowels just in word-final position; the consonant suffixes "protect" root-final vowels by rendering them outside the scope of the deletion rule.

The patterns we have seen so far involve segments (consonants in some cases, vowels in others) being lost at word margins, but being retained at morphological junctures. However, the converse scenario is also observable: segments being lost at junctures but retained at word margins. Diola Fogny provides a useful example, as the data below show.

3.4 Diola Fogny

Examine the following data from Diola Fogny (Sapir 1965; John Alderete p.c.), where the underlying forms and morphology of a number of complex words are provided for you. Note that many of the morphemes have underlying final consonants; these consonants remain unchanged in word-final position. However, we may note a few things that happen when a morpheme-final consonant is followed by another consonant within a complex word.

	Underlying form	Surface form	Gloss
(1)	ni-maŋ-maŋ	nimammaŋ	'I want'
(2)	ni-ŋan-ŋan	niŋaŋŋan	'I cried'
(3)	na-ʤum-to	naʤunto	'he stopped'
(4)	ni-gam-gam	nigaŋgam	'I judge'
(5)	pan-ʤi-maɲʤ	panʤimaɲʤ	'you-pl will know'
(6)	na-tiŋ-tiŋ	natintiŋ	'he cut through'
(7)	ku-boɲ-boɲ	kubomboɲ	'they sent'
(8)	uʤuk-ʤa	uʤuʤa	'if you see'
(9)	let-ku-ʤaw	lekuʤaw	'they won't go'
(10)	kob-kob-en	kokoben	'yearn for'
(11)	a-ʤaw-bu-ŋar	aʤabuŋar	'voyager'
(12)	na-laɲ-laɲ	nalalaɲ	'he returned'
(13)	na-joken-joken	najokejoken	'he tires'
(14)	na-waɲ-am-waɲ	nawaɲawaɲ	'he plowed for me'
(15)	e-rent-rent	ererent	'it is light'
(16)	na-maɲʤ-maɲʤ	namamaɲʤ	'he knows'

Exercise 3.7 Describe what happens wherever morphemes with final consonants are followed by consonant-initial morphemes.

Two different patterns can be seen here: either the morpheme-final consonant assimilates to the place of the following consonant (1)–(7), or it is completely deleted (8)–(16).

Exercise 3.8 Describe the circumstances that determine whether place assimilation or deletion is to occur.

Place assimilation happens in a special circumstance, namely where an underlying nasal consonant is followed by an obstruent or by another nasal consonant, as in (3) /na-ʤu**m**-to/ → [naʤu**n**to]. The morpheme-final consonant is instead deleted if it is not nasal, as in (8) /uʤu**k**-ʤa/ → [uʤuʤa], or if it is a nasal followed by liquid or glide, as in (12) /na-la**ɲ**-laɲ/ → [nalalaɲ].

Diola Fogny thus provides an example of a different kind of zero-alternation: one in which an underlying segment is deleted, specifically within a word rather than at an edge.

3.5 English cluster reduction

A similar pattern can be seen among English roots which end with two consonant sequences, the second of which is a stop. In the casual speech of some speakers, the second consonant is deleted if the root receives a consonant-initial suffix. The following data illustrate this; where UK and US pronunciations differ, both are given.

(1)	æpt	apt	æpli	aptly
(2)	dɛft	deft	dɛfli	deftly
(3)	tækt	tact	tæklǝs	tactless
(4)	ǝdʒɛkt	eject	ǝdʒɛks	ejects
(5)	ask/æsk	ask	ast/æst	asked
(6)	rɪft	rift	rɪfs	rifts
(7)	lɪft	lift	lɪfs	lifts
(8)	kloʊð	clothe	kloʊz	clothes

Since this is a casual-speech phenomenon, it is subject to some variation: some speakers may delete the second consonant even in unsuffixed circumstances, and variably at that. Others may never delete at all. But the crucial pattern is between the two extremes – some speakers are more likely to delete in the suffixed circumstance than in the unsuffixed circumstance.

Let us now turn to a more complex alternation pattern involving vowels which appear in some morphological contexts but not others. While the morphological structure definitely plays a role, it is not a matter of segments alternating with zero at morpheme boundaries.

3.6 Tonkawa

Examine the following data from Tonkawa (Hoijer 1949), an indigenous language once spoken in Alabama. We will see all the relevant forms first, and then focus on individual subsets.

(1)	a.	picnoʔ	'he cuts it'
	b.	wepcenoʔ	'he cuts them'
	c.	kepcenoʔ	'he cuts me'
	d.	picnanoʔ	'he is cutting it'
	e.	wepcenanoʔ	'he is cutting them'
	f.	kepcenanoʔ	'he is cutting me'
	g.	picen	'castrated one, steer'

(2)	a.	notxoʔ	'he hoes it'
	b.	wentoxoʔ	'he hoes them'
	c.	kentoxoʔ	'he hoes me'
	d.	notxonoʔ	'he is hoeing it'

    e.   wentoxonoʔ   'he is hoeing them'

    f.   kentoxonoʔ   'he is hoeing me'

    g.   notox   'hoe'

(3) a.   netloʔ   'he licks it'

    b.   wentaloʔ   'he licks them'

    c.   kentaloʔ   'he licks me'

    d.   netlenoʔ   'he is licking it'

    e.   wentalenoʔ   'he is licking them'

    f.   kentalenoʔ   'he is licking me'

(4) a.   naxcoʔ   'he makes it a fire'

    b.   wenxacoʔ   'he makes them a fire'

    c.   kenxacoʔ   'he makes me a fire'

    d.   naxcenoʔ   'he is making it a fire'

    e.   wenxacenoʔ   'he is making them a fire'

    f.   kenxacenoʔ   'he is making me a fire'

Let us first examine all the affixed forms built from the verb root meaning 'cut' from (1a–f), repeated here:

a.   picnoʔ

b.   wepcenoʔ   'he cuts them'

c.   kepcenoʔ   'he cuts me'

d.   picnanoʔ   'he is cutting it'

e.   wepcenanoʔ   'he is cutting them'

f.   kepcenanoʔ   'he is cutting me'

Exercise 3.9 Using the basic steps of morphological analysis, identify any prefixes you see in the forms in (1). If you are unsure of the position of any boundaries, you should refer to the full data set in (1)–(4).

By comparing (1b) [wepcenoʔ] and (1c) [kepcenoʔ], we may infer that something about the former indicates third-person plural object agreement, while something in the latter indicates first-person singular object agreement. This is supported by a similar comparison (1e) [wepcenanoʔ] and (1f) [kepcenanoʔ].

b.   wepcenoʔ   'he cuts them'

c.   kepcenoʔ   'he cuts me'

e.   wepcenanoʔ   'he is cutting them'

f.   kepcenanoʔ   'he is cutting me'

In short, the paired forms differ in their initial segments, suggesting that they include different prefixes to indicate different object agreement. However, the boundary between the object agreement prefix and the rest of the form cannot be definitively determined from these forms: we could analyze the third-person plural object form as [w-], [we-], or [wep-], among other choices. It thus helps to turn to some forms which lack object agreement. The noun [picen] and the form [picno?] provide this comparison: we may infer that the root begins with [p], and thus that the object prefixes are [we-] and [ke-]. Moreover, we see the same elements [we-] and [ke-] occuring with other roots, as forms involving other roots in (2)–(4) show, for example (2b) [wentoxo?]. These facts suggest that the prefixes contain more than just [w-] and [k-], and do not contain as much as [wep-] and [kep-].

Exercise 3.10   Using the basic steps of morphological analysis, identify any suffixes you see in the forms in (1). If you are unsure of the position of any boundaries, you should refer to the full data set in (1)–(4).

A comparison of (1b) [wepceno?] 'he cuts them' and (1e) [wepcenano?] 'he is cutting them' suggests that the latter includes a morpheme indicating a progressive aspect. This analysis is supported by the analogous comparison of (1c) [kepceno?] and (1f) [kepcenano?]. We could infer, tentatively, that [-an] is the progressive marker, but we will explore this more below.

(1b)   wepceno?   'he cuts them'
(1e)   wepcenano?   'he is cutting them'
(1c)   kepceno?   'he cuts me'
(1f)   kepcenano?   'he is cutting me'

Moreover, (1g) [picen] has a meaning related to the concept of cutting, but is not glossed as a verb with a third singular subject; it also lacks the [-o?] sequence. Let us therefore analyze [-o?] as a third-person singular subject agreement suffix.

In (1e) [wepcenano?], we tentatively analyzed the progressive aspect to be represented by [-an] and third-person subject agreement to be represented by [-o?]. These claims warrant further discussion, since we could alternatively assign boundaries in different places, as in [we-pce-na-no?]. However, if we compare with other roots, we can refine our morphological analysis. Consider first (2b) [wentoxo?] 'he hoes them', alongside [wepceno?] 'he cuts them.'

(1b)   wepceno?   'he cuts them'
(2b)   wentoxo?   'he hoes them'

49

This comparison makes it clear that the third-person singular subject suffix can only be [oʔ], leaving the analysis as [we-pcen-oʔ] for 'he cuts them.' We then infer in turn that [an] is the progressive form in [wepcen-an-oʔ].

However, let us again compare across roots, this time with progressives: (1e) [wepcenanoʔ] 'he is cutting them' and (2e) [wentoxonoʔ] 'he is hoeing them' lead to a different analysis: that [-an] is not clearly the progressive. Instead, [-n] is a more plausible conclusion for the progressive suffix, leading us to analyze these as [we-pcena-n-oʔ] and [we-ntoxo-n-oʔ]. This claim is further supported by reference to (3e) [we-ntale-n-oʔ] 'he is licking them': the vowel that precedes the progressive [-n] changes for different roots, suggesting that it is part of the root.

(1e)   wepcenanoʔ   we-pcena-n-oʔ   'he is cutting them'
(2e)   wentoxonoʔ   we-ntoxo-n-oʔ   'he is hoeing them'
(3e)   wentaleno?   we-ntale-n-oʔ   'he is licking them'

Exercise 3.11   Assuming that [ke-] and [we-] are prefixes, [-n] and [-oʔ] are suffixes, what are the alternants of the root meaning 'cut'?

Based on our tentative analysis, there are five allomorphs of 'cut': [picn-] as in [picn-oʔ]; [pcen] as in [we-pcen-oʔ], [picna] as in [picna-n-oʔ], [pcena] as in [we-pcena-n-oʔ], and [picen], which is how it appears with no affixes. We repeat the data from (1) with our presumed morpheme boundaries below:

a.   picn-oʔ   'he cuts it'
b.   we-pcen-oʔ   'he cuts them'
c.   ke-pcen-oʔ   'he cuts me'
d.   picna-n-oʔ   'he is cutting it'
e.   we-pcena-n-oʔ   'he is cutting them'
f.   ke-pcena-n-oʔ   'he is cutting me'
g.   picen   'castrated one, steer'

Exercise 3.12   Produce a similar revised morphological analysis for the remaining three verbs.

(2)   a.   notx-oʔ   'he hoes it'
       b.   we-ntox-oʔ   'he hoes them'
       c.   ke-ntox-oʔ   'he hoes me'
       d.   notxo-n-oʔ   'he is hoeing it'
       e.   we-ntoxo-n-oʔ   'he is hoeing them'
       f.   ke-ntoxo-n-oʔ   'he is hoeing me'
       g.   notox   'hoe'

(3) a.   netloʔ   'he licks it'
     b.   wentaloʔ   'he licks them'
     c.   kentaloʔ   'he licks me'
     d.   netlenoʔ   'he is licking it'
     e.   we-ntale-n-oʔ   'he is licking them'
     f.   ke-ntale-n-oʔ   'he is licking me'

(4) a.   naxc-oʔ   'he makes it a fire'
     b.   we-nxac-oʔ   'he makes them a fire'
     c.   ke-nxac-oʔ   'he makes me a fire'
     d.   naxce-n-oʔ   'he is making it a fire'
     e.   we-nxace-n-oʔ   'he is making them a fire'
     f.   ke-nxace-n-oʔ   'he is making me a fire'

At this point, we have a more finalized picture of the morphological analysis. The affixes do not alternate, but each verb root has upwards of four alternants. The next step would be to figure out the underlying form of the verb roots. Given the allomorphs [picn], [pcen], [picna], [pcena], and [picen] for 'cut,' there seems to be a lot of alternation to deal with, though some additional facts may be observed. First, if there is ever a vowel between the first two consonants, it is always [i]; if there is ever a vowel between the second and third consonants, it is always [e], and if there is ever a root-final vowel, it is always [a]. We may briefly entertain that these vowels are inserted, but such an approach is untenable, since the other verb roots contain different vowels in alternation with zero.

Thus, let us consider that each of these vowels is present underlyingly, and that the root is /picena/. How, then, do we determine the circumstances for each allomorph? The deletion of /i/ from /picena/ at first glance may seem elusive, since its immediate environment of [p__c] is constant. Something beyond the immediately adjacent segments must be responsible for triggering deletion. Moreover, when we look to the other roots, the vowels of each are deleted under similar circumstances: as a function of their position, irrespective of the precise consonants that are adjacent. We will rely on these observations after perusing the alternants of the other roots.

Exercise 3.13 Arrange the data to compare alternants of roots, with a different root on each line, and four forms for each root: third singular subject and object; third subject and third plural object; third singular subject and object progressive; third subject and third plural object in progressive.

a.	picn-oʔ	we-pcen-oʔ	picna-n-oʔ	we-pcena-n-oʔ
b.	notx-oʔ	we-ntox-oʔ	notxo-n-oʔ	we-ntoxo-n-oʔ
c.	netl-oʔ	we-ntal-oʔ	netle-n-oʔ	we-ntale-n-oʔ
d.	naxc-oʔ	we-nxac-oʔ	naxce-n-oʔ	we-nxace-n-oʔ

Some parallels are notable across verb roots: each has an alternant CVCC, CCVC, CVCCV, and CCVCV, and these alternants appear in identical contexts. In addition, the other roots show the same kinds of facts about their vowels as we saw for the forms of 'cut.' For example, wherever the [n] and [t] of 'lick' are separated by a vowel, it is [e], as in [netloʔ] and [netlenoʔ]; wherever the [t] and [l] are separated by a vowel, it is [a], as in [wentaloʔ] and [wentalenoʔ]. Whenever there is a progressive suffix, the preceding vowel is [e], as in [netlenoʔ] and [wentalenoʔ].

This provides additional support that /picena/ is the underlying form for 'cut,' and /netale/ is the root for 'lick.' The other roots are /notoxo/ and /naxace/. Now we can attempt to model the circumstances under which vowels are deleted in surface forms.

Exercise 3.14 Since the four roots have each of their vowels deleted under parallel circumstances, you may answer the following questions with regard to /picena/.

a. What do the forms in which /i/ of /picena/ is deleted have in common?
b. What do the forms in which /e/ is deleted have in common?
c. What do the forms in which /a/ is deleted have in common?

a. The /i/ in /picena/ is deleted when there is an object agreement prefix. Alternatively, the vowel is deleted if it is the second underlying vowel.
b. The /e/ in /picena/ is deleted when there is no object agreement prefix, but there is at least one suffix. Alternatively, it is deleted if it is the second underlying vowel.
c. The /a/ is deleted from /picena/ when followed by [-oʔ] or if there is no suffix at all.

We can describe the deletion pattern strictly in terms of morphological context, but also strictly in terms of phonological context. Indeed, the first two patterns are in fact very parallel: the first vowel is retained, but the second one is deleted. It thus makes sense to adhere to a phonological explanation; additional evidence comes from the fact that the deletion of the root's first vowel happens whether the prefix is [we-] or [ke-].

The failure of /e/ to be deleted in the absence of any affix is also phonological: deleting it would yield [picn], with a word-final cluster, but the data suggest such sequences are impossible. When we create rules to handle these data, it will be necessary to be specific enough to account for this.

Vowels are thus deleted in three basic circumstances: after the second consonant, before a vowel, and word-finally.

Exercise 3.15   Construct rules that properly delete vowels in Tonkawa.

Vowel → Ø / C V C __ C V
Vowel → Ø / __ V
Vowel → Ø / __]$_{WD}$

We should note here that the predictability of an allophone or allomorph's occurrence converges with its more general or "elsewhere" distribution. In this case, we conclude that the vowels are present underlyingly and deleted (rather than absent underlyingly, and inserted), because the nature of the vowel is not predictable. Likewise, if we consider the zero-form of any vowel to be an alternant, it has a specific distribution: after the second consonant or before other vowels. In other words, any given vowel is present underlyingly, and is deleted under specific circumstances, but retained elsewhere.

3.7   Insertion

Every pattern we have seen in this chapter so far has involved a scenario of a segment alternating with zero, and in each case we have settled on an analysis in which the segment is present underlyingly, deleted in some circumstances, but kept in the converse set of circumstances. Many situations of segment/zero alternation, however, do not call for the segment to be present underlyingly.

3.8   Kahabu Kahabu

Consider the following data from Kahabu Kahabu (Li 1997). Turn your attention first to the prefix which occurs in the present: it has three forms, [m], [ma], and [mu].

	Present	*Imperative*	
(1)	ma-xatukun	xatukul-i	'climb'
	m-daxan	daxal-i	'dig'
	mu-xuʔun	xuʔul-i	'pull'
(2)	m-kən	kan-i	'eat'
	ma-hatan	pa-hatan-i	'laugh'

Exercise 3.16 Describe the conditions under which each form of the present prefix occurs. Make sure that the conditions you describe do not overlap. For example, be specific enough so that the conditions you describe for [ma] are fully distinct from those you describe for [m] and [mu].

The [ma] form appears before fricatives followed by [a]; the [mu] form appears before fricatives followed by [u]. The [m] alternant appears before stop consonants.

3.9 Alternation in Kahabu Kahabu

We may simplify these conditions as follows: the CV forms occur before roots which begin with fricatives; otherwise the prefix is [m]. In addition, the vowel in the prefix, if it has one, is the same quality as the first vowel of the root. Thus, it is predictable whether the prefix has a vowel, and if a vowel occurs, its quality is also predictable.

In such a scenario, we do not need to posit an underlying vowel for the prefix; instead, it can be inserted by rule, and a second rule can be used to set its quality. When we write rules of insertion, we again rely on the notation of [Ø], but now instead of being the result of a rule, it is the target.

Exercise 3.17 Compose a rule that inserts a vowel in the appropriate circumstances, and a second rule that determines the appropriate quality of vowel.

Ø → [a] / m __ [fricative]
[a] → [u] / m __ [fricative] u

In fact, several approaches are possible; we could plausibly insert [u] and change it to [a] just in case the inserted vowel is in the environment [m __ [fricative] a]. Alternatively, we could create two separate insertion rules, one inserting [a] and the other [u], but this would fail to capture the generalization that vowels generally are inserted under a single set of circumstances.

For the sake of completeness, aside from the vowel-zero alternation of our focus, note that some roots have a final alternation of [l] ~ [n], while others do not. This suggests a pattern of neutralization; those that alternate have underlying final /l/ which stays as such when suffixed, as in [daxal-i], but which is changed to [n] in word-final contexts, as in [daxan].

3.10 Turkish

Another insertion pattern can be seen in Turkish, in forms which include a derivative suffix /msI/; we notate this with the symbol /I/ since this vowel differs across roots. In the data below (Lees 1961, Lewis 1967), we may consider the unsuffixed roots to be representative of the underlying forms; two of them end in the vowel /a/, while the other two end in consonants. The addition of the suffix /msI/ is seamless in the vowel-final roots; the suffix vowel appears as [ɨ], as in [karamsɨ]. However, with the consonant final roots, the suffix creates the potential for a three-consonant sequence, and to avoid this, a vowel is inserted between the root and suffix, as in /rapor + msI/ → [rapor**u**-msu].

kara	'black'	karamsɨ	'blackish'
maɟara	'cave'	maɟaramsɨ	'cavernous'
rapor	'report'	raporumsu	'report-like'
duvar	'wall'	duvarɨmsɨ	'wall-like'

Exercise 3.18 Construct a rule that inserts a vowel in the appropriate circumstances in Turkish. Do not be concerned with the quality of the vowel; you may have it insert [ɨ].

$$\emptyset \rightarrow ɨ \ / \ C \ \_\_ \ CC$$

As we have already noted, the inserted vowel and the vowel of the suffix itself both vary in Turkish. The vowels' quality in these cases is an example of *vowel harmony*, a phenomenon we explore in more detail in Chapter 4. At this point, we are concerned mainly with the fact that a vowel is inserted at all.

We may also ask whether an alternative analysis is possible, in which the alternating vowel is present in the underlying form of the affix, and deleted after root-final [a]. For example, this would entail /kara + ImsI/ → [karamsɨ]. In the given data, we cannot rule this possibility out, but there is still reason to side with the insertion account. Recall that at the surface, we observe a vowel-zero alternation, and the vowel consistently appears as a high vowel (with its backness and roundness predictable from context). In other words, the vowel's quality and its position are both predictable. When a segment/zero alternation can be analyzed such that the form of the segment is predictable like this, it is readily analyzable as a pattern of insertion.

3.11 Serbo-Croatian

For an example of a pattern in which a segment/zero alternation is indubitably a function of insertion, let us turn to the gender agreement suffixes of Serbo-Croatian adjectives. The data below (Kenstowicz 1994) show a series of adjectives and the form they take when accompanying masculine, feminine, neuter, or plural nouns. This discussion will proceed with some preliminary morphological analysis.

	Masc	*Fem*	*Neut*	*Pl*	*Gloss*
(1)	mlád	mladá	mladó	mladí	'young'
(2)	púst	pustá	pustó	pustí	'empty'
(3)	zelén	zelená	zelenó	zelení	'green'
(4)	ʧést	ʧestá	ʧestó	ʧestí	'frequent'
(5)	bogat	bogata	bogato	bogati	'rich'
(6)	suntʃan	suntʃana	suntʃano	suntʃani	'sunny'
(7)	rapav	rapava	rapavo	rapavi	'rough'
(8)	ledan	ledna	ledno	ledni	'frozen'
(9)	dóbar	dobrá	dobró	dobrí	'good'
(10)	jásan	jasná	jasnó	jasní	'clear'
(11)	sítan	sitná	sitnó	sitní	'tiny'
(12)	óʃtar	oʃtrá	oʃtró	oʃtrí	'sharp'
(13)	mókar	mokrá	mokró	mokrí	'wet'

Exercise 3.19 Conduct a morphological analysis just of the first seven forms (1)–(7). What are the forms of the various suffixes? What is the form of each unsuffixed root? For this analysis, pay no attention to the position of the acute accent.

The suffixes have invariant forms in this subset of data: the feminine is always [-a]; the neuter is always [-o], and the plural is always [-i]. The roots comprise whatever is leftover if you remove any of these suffixes; for example; [mlada] means 'young-FEM'; [-a] is the feminine suffix, while [mlad-] is the root.

The masculine forms thus appear to be unsuffixed: there is no additional form in the masculine adjectives, so we infer that an adjective root when appearing by itself is functioning as masculine.

Exercise 3.20 Now extend your analysis to the forms in (8)–(13). What are the forms of the various suffixes? What is the form of each unsuffixed root?

The suffixes continue to be consistent across these forms: the feminine is always [-a]; the neuter is always [-o], and the plural is always [-i].

Now, however, the roots alternate: there are internal vowels in the masculine forms which alternate with zero in the suffixed forms; for example there is an [a] in (8) [ledan] which is missing from [ledna] and [ledno]. In such a scenario of segment/zero alternation, we are confronted with a choice between an insertion account and a deletion account.

Exercise 3.21 Propose two competing analyses of these alternating roots. What are the underlying forms in each analysis? What additional rules would be needed in each analysis to handle the alternation seen in (8)–(13)?

The two analyses differ as to whether the alternating vowel is present underlyingly or not.

In a deletion account, the vowel is present underlyingly, as in /ledan/, and it remains in the unsuffixed masculine form as [ledan], but is deleted in the presence of a suffix; hence, /ledan + o / → [ledno].

The deletion rule would be as follows:

/a/ → Ø / C ___ CV]$_{WD}$

In an insertion account, the vowel is not present underlyingly; instead, it is inserted specifically when there is *no* suffix, and the suffixed adjectives undergo no insertion. Hence, these forms end in sequences of consonants underlyingly; for example /ledn/ becomes [ledan] in the masculine, and the neuter form is realized as /ledn + o/ → [ledno].

The insertion rule would be as follows:

/Ø / → [a] / C ___ C]$_{WD}$

Looking only at the forms in (8)–(13), there is no way to choose one analysis over the other, but the forms in (1)–(7) provide a clue as to which analysis is appropriate.

Exercise 3.22 Use the data in (1)–(7) to choose between the insertion and deletion accounts for Serbo-Croatian. Your argument should take the following form: if either analysis employs a phonological rule which predicts unattested surface forms in any data point, you must revise or reject the analysis. If an analysis is consistent with all forms in (1)–(7), it remains as a viable option to account for the data.

The deletion account entails a rule which deletes a root-internal vowel. In (8)–(13), the deletion rule works appropriately, deleting putative /a/ from /ledan + o/ to yield [ledno]. But the same rule would force deletion to occur in forms such as (3) or (5). That is, the same analysis has us postulate /bogat/, and the deletion rule would apply to /bogat + o/, incorrectly yielding *[bogto].

Conversely, the insertion account posits no underlying /a/ as a second vowel in any of the alternating roots in (8)–(13). The non-alternating form [bogat] comes from underlying /bogat/ (whose second vowel *is* present underlyingly) while the alternating form [ledan] comes from /ledn/.

That there is an insertion pattern is therefore unequivocal, given the difference between [bogato] and [ledno] – their different behavior is a function of their different underlying representations. We also have corroborative evidence in that the alternating vowel is always of a predictable quality: in roots that have such an alternating vowel, it is always [a] when it appears. Thus, we can say that the alternating vowel is predictable both in its position and its quality.

Summary

In this chapter we have investigated scenarios where a segment is in an alternating relationship with zero – in other words, it appears in some contexts, and under different, complementary conditions it is absent. Some of these patterns have been analyzed as *deletion*, where an underlying segment persists at the surface, but only in some contexts. Conversely, other patterns are more clearly *insertion*, where a non-underlying segment appears in some contexts at the surface.

At first glance, such alternations may seem fundamentally different from those in the previous chapter, which all involve some type of assimilation, where underlying segments remain in each of their surface contexts, but adapt to them in some way. However, segment/zero alternations can instead be seen as a special subtype of assimilation: rather than a phoneme undergoing some assimilatory change in its articulation, the context achieves a sort of assimilatory adaptation simply by dropping a segment (in the case of deletion) or by interceding a segment (in the case of insertion). That is, deletion and insertion patterns both seem to resolve certain potential sequences which for some reason are deemed to be avoided.

As we saw in Chapter 2, we ought not to interpret the manifestation of insertion or deletion patterns as evidence that phonology is merely a set of effort-reducing principles. Again, many of the types of sequences that are avoided with epenthesis or deletion are physiologically possible, and a phonologically impossible sequence in one language may still be attested in many others.

In the next chapter, we will see some more types of alternation, each of which is much less plausibly characterized simply as an ease of articulation effect, and which instead can be construed as driven by the desire to maintain contrast or perceptibility.

Key terms

epenthesis
insertion
deletion
cluster reduction
competing analyses
hypothesis testing

References and further reading

Crowley, Terry. 1992a. *A Dictionary of Paamese*. Canberra: Pacific Linguistics.
Crowley, Terry. 1992b. *An Introduction to Historical Linguistics*, 2nd edition.
    Auckland: Oxford University Press.
Halle, Morris, and George N. Clements. 1983. *Problem Book in Phonology*.
    Cambridge, MA: MIT Press.
Hoijer, Harry. 1949. *An Analytical Dictionary of the Tonkawa Language*. Berkeley,
    CA: University of California Press.
Kisseberth, Charles. 1970. Vowel elision in Tonkawa and derivational constraints.
    In J. L. Sadock and A. L. Vanek (eds.), *Studies Presented to Robert B. Lees by his
    Students*. Champaign, IL: Linguistic Research, 109–137.
Kuroda, S-Y. 1967. *Yawelmani Phonology*. Research Monograph no. 43.
    Cambridge, MA: MIT Press.
Lees, Robert. 1961. *The Phonology of Modern Standard Turkish*. Uralic and Altaic
    Series 6. Indiana University Publications.
Lewis, Geoffrey. 1967. *Turkish Grammar*. Oxford University Press.
Li, Paul Jen-kuei. 1997. Course on Formosan languages. Linguistics Society of
    America Summer Institute. Cornell University, Ithaca, NY.
Newman, Stanley S. 1946. The Yawelmani dialect of Yokuts. In C. Osgood and H.
    Hoijer (eds.), *Linguistic Structures of Native America*. New York: The Viking
    Fund, 222–248.
Sapir, J. David. 1965. *A Grammar of Diola-Fogny*. West African Language
    Monographs 3. Ibadan: Cambridge University Press.
Windfuhr, G. L. 1979. *Persian Grammar*. The Hague: Mouton.

Review exercises

Diegueño

Examine the following data from Diegueño (Halle and Clements 1983):

ʔaːkat	'I cut a long object'
maːkat	'you cut a long object'

aːkat	'he cuts a long object'
ʔətʃuːkat	'I bite off'
mətʃuːkat	'you bite off'
tʃuːkat	'he bites off'
mətuːkat	'you cut into chunks'
tuːkat	'he cuts into chunks'
ʔaːmar	'I cover a long object'
maːmaḷʲ	'you sweep'
mətʃuːxʷar	'you chew'
tʃuːkʷar	'he makes a speech'
ʔətuːmar	'I cover a chunky object'
ʔətalʲ	'my mother'
mətalʲ	'your mother'
ʔətalʲtʃ	'our mother'
mətalʲtʃ	'your (plural) mother'

a. Perform a morphological analysis of these forms.

b. Identify any forms that include a segment/zero alternation. Are these better analyzed as an insertion pattern or a deletion pattern?

Yokuts

The following data from Yokuts (Newman 1946, Kuroda 1967) illustrate an interaction between numerous alternations: some vowel alternate by length and other do not; other vowels alternate between [i] and [u], and still others alternate with zero. For this exercise, you should focus only on those vowels that alternate with zero. In addition, the vowels that alternate with zero are sometimes [i] and other times [u].

		Aorist	Passive	Aorist future	Gloss
(1)	a.	xatit	xathin	xatnit	'eat'
	b.	gopit	gophin	gopnit	'take care of infant'
	c.	gijit	gijhin	gijnit	'touch'
	d.	mutut	muthun	mutnut	'swear'
(2)	a.	saːpit	saphin	sapnit	'burn'
	b.	goːbit	gobhin	gobnit	'take in'
	c.	meːkit	mekhin	meknit	'swallow'
	d.	ʔoːtut	ʔothun	ʔotnut	'steal'
(3)	a.	panat	panaːhin	panaːnit	'arrive'
	b.	hojot	hojoːhin	hojoːnit	'name'

	c.	ʔilet	ʔileːhin	ʔileːnit	'fan'
	d.	cujot	cujoːhun	cujoːnut	'urinate'
(4)	a.	paxaːtit	paxathin	paxatnit	'mourn'
	b.	ʔopoːtit	ʔopothin	ʔopotnit	'arise from bed'
	c.	hibeːjit	hibejhin	hibejnit	'bring water'
	d.	sudoːkut	sudokhun	sudoknut	'remove'

a. Perform a morphological analysis of these forms.

b. Identify any forms that include a segment/zero alternation. Are these better analyzed as an insertion pattern or a deletion pattern?

CHAPTER 4 OTHER KINDS OF ALTERNATION

Learning objectives

- Identify non-adjacent triggers of segment alternation
- Become familiar with triggers, targets, and directionality in vowel harmony
- Describe the contexts in which each alternant appears
- Identify the best fit for a default alternant or underlying form
- Compose rules to derive other alternants from underlying forms
- Identify non-assimilatory cases of segment alternation

Introduction

So far much of the phonological alternation we've witnessed has involved *adjacent* sounds, where one segment has an effect on the form of some other segment immediately next to it, either before or afterwards. Consonant assimilation, intervocalic effects, and palatalization are examples of such *local* phenomena. Some phonological patterns, however, do not clearly involve segments adapting to adjacent segments. In addition, the morphophonology of many languages allows non-adjacent segments to have an effect on each other.

The most common type of such effects is called vowel harmony, in which a vowel adopts some or all features of some nearby (but usually non-adjacent) vowel.

vowel harmony: a process in which vowels become similar or identical to nearby vowels.

4.1 Mongolian

Let us first explore some suffix alternations in Mongolian (Svantesson *et al.* 2005). Look over the data below, paying attention to the vowels in each suffix.

Direct past	*Causative*	*Gloss*
it-ʤe	it-uʤ	'eat'
ʃiit-ʤe	ʃiit-uʤ	'decide'
uc-ʤe	uc-uʤ	'see'
tuuʤ-ʤe	tuuʤ-uʤ	'jump'
tuir-ʤe	tuir-uʤ	'be stunned'
zeeʤ-ʤe	zeeʤ-uʤ	'decorate'
og-ʤo	og-uʤ	'give'
cʰoor-ʤo	cʰoor-uʤ	'decrease'
xʊnj-ʤa	xʊnj-ʊʤ	'pleat'
ʊʊrʃ-ʤa	ʊʊrʃ-ʊʤ	'evaporate'
ʊiʤ-ʤa	ʊiʤ-ʊʤ	'cry'
jaw-ʤa	jaw-ʊʤ	'go'
saatʰ-ʤa	saatʰ-ʊʤ	'be delayed'
sairx-ʤa	sairx-ʊʤ	'brag'
ɔr-ʤɔ	ɔr-ʊʤ	'enter'
cʰɔɔr-ʤɔ	cʰɔɔr-ʊʤ	'be pierced'
cʰoiʤ-ʤɔ	cʰoiʤ-ʊʤ	'dart out'

Exercise 4.1 Identify the alternants of each suffix.

The direct past suffix has four alternants: [ʤe], [ʤo], [ʤa], and [ʤɔ]. The causative has two alternants: [uʤ] and [ʊʤ].

Exercise 4.2 Describe the distribution of the causative. Pay attention to the vowels of the roots.

The [uʤ] alternant follows roots with the vowels [i, u, e, o, ui]. The [ʊʤ] alternant follows roots with the simple vowels [a, ʊ, ɔ], and with the diphthongs [ʊi], [ai], and [oi].

Since the vowel of the suffix changes as a function of the vowel of the root, we can call this an example of vowel harmony. In addition, we can infer that the vowels [i, u, e, o] share some feature, while [a, ʊ, ɔ] have some other feature, and it is this difference between the groups that determines the choice of the suffix. Sometimes we characterize the first group as consisting of **tense** vowels, while the second group is **lax** – this is a typical way of describing these vowels as they occur in English. Furthermore, since the diphthongs [ʊi], [ai], and [oi] pattern together with [a, ɔ, ʊ], we can tentatively presume that they share the same feature.

In many harmonic languages, vowels such as [i, u, e, o] are called Advanced Tongue Root (ATR) – it is not the same phonetic property as what distinguishes tense vowels in English, but ATR vowels acoustically resemble English tense vowels, while non-ATR vowels acoustically resemble English lax vowels.

The symbols we use to transcribe ATR vowels are often identical to those we use to record "tense" vowels of English, while non-ATR vowels use the same symbols as "lax" vowels of English. However, ATR should not be equated with tenseness. ATR is a phonological feature with a clear phonetic correlate: the difference between ATR and non-ATR is produced with different configurations of the root of the tongue, in the pharynx. In contrast, tenseness and laxness in English vowels are more phonological than phonetic, as there is no consistent phonetic gesture that determines whether a vowel is tense or lax. Instead, to differentiate them, we turn to distributional facts, such as the restriction that only tense vowels may occur in final open syllables. It just so happens that the acoustic forms are quite similar, so that non-ATR vowels sound similar to lax vowels, while ATR vowels sound similar to tense vowels.

Following this description, then, the [uʒ] alternant itself has an ATR vowel, and it occurs when the root also has an ATR vowel. Likewise, the [ʊʒ] alternant has a non-ATR vowel and co-occurs with roots that also have non-ATR vowels. Again, for this analysis we continue with the notion that the diphthongs [ʊi], [ai], and [oi] are also phonologically non-ATR. Overall, the vowel of the suffix *matches* the vowel of the root in the ATR dimension.

Exercise 4.3 Construct a rule that will make the suffix vowel [ATR] in the appropriate circumstances. You will need to determine an appropriate underlying form to do this.

As long as the vowel of the causative is underlyingly [ʊ], a rule changing it to [u] after ATR vowels will derive the appropriate distribution of the alternants of the direct past suffix.

ʊ → u / [ATR vowel] C ___

It should be noted that the output of the rule, [u], is itself [ATR], and as a result it matches the preceding vowel for this feature. Such likeness of vowel features is indicative of vowel harmony.

Furthermore, when we introduce binary features in Chapter 6, we will see that vowels could be specified with a negative value for some features – so the non-ATR vowels could be [-ATR] here. It would then be just as plausible to assume /u/ is the underlying vowel, and that the rule changes it to [-ATR] only after other [-ATR] vowels.

Exercise 4.4 Describe the distribution of the direct past. Again, pay attention to the vowels of the roots.

[ʒe] occurs after roots with [i], [e], and [u].
[ʒo] occurs after roots with [o].
[ʒa] occurs after roots with [a] and [ʊ].
[ʒɔ] occurs after roots with [ɔ].

Like the direct past, the causative in Mongolian is harmonic, as its vowel changes according to the vowel of the root. Obviously it is more complicated, however, as it has four alternants that differ in more than just ATR. Even so, we will be able to make some principled generalizations about the conditions for each alternant.

Exercise 4.5   Come up with a way to distinguish each set of conditioning vowels, using terms referring to vowel height, backness, roundness, and ATR.

[i], [e], and [u] are either front, high, or both.
[o] is the only back non-high ATR round vowel.
[a] and [ʊ] are back, unround, and non-ATR.
[ɔ] is the only back non-high non-ATR round vowel.

Three of the alternants appear only after particular types of back vowels, while [ʤe] occurs in the remaining circumstances. We may then infer that [ʤe] has a more general distribution, and is suitable as a choice for the underlying form of the suffix. As a result, we can compose rules which derive the other alternants under specific circumstances.

Exercise 4.6   Construct rules that derive the suffix vowels for the Mongolian causative.

e → o / [back, ATR, round, non-high] C ____
e → ɔ / [back, non-ATR, round, non-high] C ____
e → a / [back, non-ATR] C ____

The first rule derives [ʤo] if the root vowel is [o], and the second rule derives [ʤɔ] if the root vowel is [ɔ]. The third rule derives [ʤa] in the remainder of back-vowel circumstances, basically where the root contains [ʊ] or [a].

Some additional comment is warranted here, as we have required three rules for this suffix, whereas the direct past needed only one. We should then consider whether some refinement could simplify this analysis. In fact, the causative suffix always matches the root vowel for ATR, which suggests the same rule from Exercise 4.3 above could be at work here – it just needs to be generalized to make all non-ATR vowels into ATR vowels, rather than just changing [ʊ] to [u]. Consequently, with a more general rule, the rules for [ʤo] and [ʤɔ] can be combined, since now they do not need to make any reference to ATR.

The combined version of these first two rules is below:

e → ɔ [back, round, non-high] C ____

We can then rely on the rule from Exercise 4.3 to ensure that the suffix has [o] instead of [ɔ] after roots with [o].

The third rule needs to remain specified as is, applying only to non-ATR vowels, to prevent [ʤa] being the alternant where the root contains [u]. Since none of the vowels [i, e, u] fits the structural descriptions of any of the rules presented here, the suffix stays as [ʤe] for roots with each of them.

Despite the range of rules needed here, they converge upon harmonic behavior, as each assigns some feature to the suffix vowel that is also present in the root.

4.2 Turkish

Like Mongolian, Turkish has a harmonic pattern in which the vowels of its suffixes alternate. Take a moment to peruse the following data (adapted from Lewis 1967, Hony and Iz 1957, Jensen 1995), which require a step of morphological analysis, but paying particular attention to the form of the suffixes.

(1)	geldi	'he came'
(2)	geldim	'I came'
(3)	gelmedi	'he didn't come'
(4)	gelmedim	'I didn't come'
(5)	satti	'he sold it'
(6)	sattim	'I sold it'
(7)	satmadi	'he didn't sell it'
(8)	tuttu	'he held it'
(9)	tuttum	'I held it'
(10)	itʃti	'he drank'
(11)	itʃtim	'I drank'
(12)	itʃmedi	'he didn't drink'
(13)	gørdy	'he saw'
(14)	gørdym	'I saw'
(15)	gørmedi	'he didn't see'
(16)	gørmedim	'I didn't see'

Exercise 4.7 a. Perform a morphological analysis of the Turkish data.
 b. What are the forms of each root?
 c. What are the alternants of each suffix?

 a. These forms contain roots followed by one or more suffixes. The negative suffix is closest to the root, followed by the past-tense suffix, followed by subject agreement. There are two different agreement suffixes in the data: first person singular and third person singular.

b. The roots in these data include [gel] 'come,' [sat] 'sell,' [tut] 'hold,' [itʃ] 'drink,' and [gør] 'see.'

c. Each of the four suffixes has multiple alternants:
   - The past-tense suffix has two alternants: [-d] as in [gel-d-i], and [-t] as in [itʃ-t-i].
   - There is a negative suffix with two alternants, [-me] and [-ma].
   - The suffix indicating third-person agreement has four alternants: [-i], as in [geld-i], [-ɨ], as in [satt-ɨ], [-u], as in [tutt-u], and [-y], as in [gørd-y].
   - The suffix indicating first-person agreement has four analogous alternants: [-im], as in [geld-im], [-ɨm], as in [satt-ɨm], [-um], as in [tutt-um], and [-ym], as in [gørd-ym].

The form of the roots is extractable by comparing negatives and non-negatives. For example, [geldi] 'he came' and [gelmedi] both contain the sequence [gel-], and their difference in form suggests that [-me] is the negative suffix here. The difference between [sattɨ] and [satmadɨ] is parallel, pointing towards [sat-] as the root; the same conclusion can be drawn for [itʃ-] from [itʃti] and [itʃmedi] and [gør-] from [gørdy] and [gørmedi]. Only the root in [tuttu] and [tuttum] is unclear, but it can be determined as [tut] once we establish that the last [t] indicates past tense.

Exercise 4.8   a. Describe the distribution of the allomorphs of the past-tense suffix.
b. Describe the distribution of the allomorphs of the negative suffix.
c. Describe the distribution of the allomorphs of the agreement suffixes.

a. For the past-tense suffix, [-t] appears when following a voiceless consonant, and [-d] appears otherwise.

b. For the negative suffix, [-me] occurs with the roots [gel], [itʃ] and [gør], while [-ma] occurs with the roots [sat] and [tut].

c. A more complex pattern is evident in the agreement suffixes. The third-person agreement suffix has four alternants: [-ɨ], as in [sat-t-ɨ] and [sat-ma-d-ɨ], [-u], as in [tut-t-u], [-y], as in [gørd-y], and [-i], as in [gel-d-i] and [itʃ-t-i]. This last form also appears after the negative suffix alternant [-me], as in [gør-me-d-i].

The alternation in the past-tense suffix is a simple example of voicing assimilation: the suffix consonant becomes voiceless only after voiceless consonants. This is similar to what we saw in English noun plurals and verb past-tense suffixes in §§2.1–17.

However, the other suffixes alternate in a way that is sensitive to non-adjacent segments: their vowel quality changes depending on the preceding vowel, despite the consonants that separate them. Moreover, the alternation is assimilatory: the suffix vowels adopt the backness of the preceding vowel. This phenomenon is indicative of vowel harmony.

The negative suffix alternates just by backness: it is [a] when the preceding vowel is a back vowel, any of [a, o, u, ɨ]; it is [e] when the preceding vowel is a front vowel, any of [i, y, ø, e]. As such, the backness of the negative suffix *matches* the backness of the preceding vowel.

The third-person agreement suffix matches both the backness and roundness of the preceding vowel: it is front and unround after front unround roots, as in [geld-i] and [itʃt-i]; it is front and round after front round roots, as in [gørd-y]; it is back and round after back unround roots, as in [tutt-u], and it is back and unround after back unround roots, as in [satt-ɨ].

The suffix indicating first-person agreement alternates in an analogous manner: [-im] after front unround vowels, as in [geld-im]; [-ym] after front round vowels, as in [gørd-ym]; [um] after back round vowels, as in [tutt-um], and [-ɨm] after back unround vowels, as in [satt-ɨm].

Two aspects are worthy of additional comment: first, the agreement suffixes additionally harmonize in their roundness, while the negative suffix does not. Second, the co-occurrence of the negative and agreement suffixes offers some additional insight into the nature of vowel harmony, as we can explore below.

Exercise 4.9 Re-examine the Turkish forms from (13)–(16).

(13) gørdy   'he saw'
(14) gørdym   'I saw'
(15) gørmedi   'he didn't see'
(16) gørmedim   'I didn't see'

How do the agreement suffixes respond to the negative suffix?

The agreement suffixes have round front vowels when they directly follow the root [gør]. However, when a negative suffix occurs between the root and the agreement suffix, the agreement suffix is front but unround.

These last two forms show that the vowel of any given suffix is sensitive to the immediately preceding vowel, and not necessarily to the root vowel. In particular, when an agreement suffix follows the negative, it agrees in roundness with the negative suffix, regardless of whether the root has a round vowel. For example, in [gør-me-d-i], the final vowel is [i] and crucially not [y]; if this suffix cared about the roundness of the root vowel, we would expect [gørmedy]. Instead, the third-person suffix vowel looks only to the immediately preceding vowel – the [e] of the negative – and no further. Consequently the agreement suffix is unround, like the immediately preceding morpheme's vowel, and not round, despite the roundness of the root's vowel.

Turkish suffix vowels thus harmonize along two dimensions: they adopt the backness and, in some cases, the roundness of the preceding vowel. But they maintain their own height. Moreover, harmony proceeds iteratively from the root to each successive vowel.

Exercise 4.10 Propose underlying forms for each harmonizing suffix. Create rules that determine the appropriate variants.

For each suffix, since there is no definitive evidence that suggests any of its alternants has a wider distribution, any of them is a plausible choice, as long as the accompanying rules are adequate to account for the distribution of alternants.

For the negative suffix, we could choose /ma/ as the underlying form. The accompanying rule would change [back] vowels to [front] vowels only after [front] vowels.

[back vowel] → [front] / [back vowel] C _____

Conversely, if we chose /me/ as the underlying form, the accompanying rule would change [front] vowels to [back] vowels after back vowels.

The same ambiguity of choice is evident in the agreement suffixes: whatever the roundness of the underlying vowel, the rule must assign the opposite roundness in specific contexts. However, we ought to choose the same backness as we do for the negative suffix, so that we may use the same back-harmonizing rule.

Thus we could choose /ɨ/ as the underlying form for third person and /ɨm/ for first person. We need no additional backness-harmonizing rule, but we do need a rule that adds roundness only after round vowels.

[high, unround vowel] → [round] / [round vowel] C _____

The fact that all suffix vowels harmonize for backness, but only high vowels harmonize for roundness, is captured by the different phrasing for the two rules: the backness-harmony rule applies to all vowels, while the roundness-harmony rule only applies to high vowels. The restriction of roundness harmony to high vowels is an example of **height-dependent roundness harmony**.

In later chapters we will revisit the notation system for differentiating vowels: rather than call them [back] and [front], [unround] and [round], we will characterize them with binary features, for example [±back], [±round], and [±high]. With such a representational system, we can rewrite the rules so that they simply change feature values for their targets; for example, the roundness rule would change a vowel from [-round] to [+round], only after [+round] vowels.

The Turkish system presents an interesting symmetry, in that every possible combination of three binary dimensions (height, backness, and roundness) is observed among its eight vowels. Furthermore, suffix vowels maintain their height but otherwise alternate in a balanced manner: every possible combination of roundness and backness is observed in both agreement suffixes. However, often a vowel harmony system presents some asymmetrical or unbalanced aspects, and Turkish itself also provides several basic examples of this. Foremost, recall that the negative suffix only alternates in backness, and not in roundness. Consider also the forms in the next section, which illustrate another suffix we have not yet seen.

4.3 More Turkish

(17)	gelijor	'he is coming'
(18)	gelijorum	'I am coming'
(19)	gelijordu	'he was coming'
(20)	satijorum	'I am selling it'
(21)	tutujor	'he is holding it'
(22)	tutujordu	'he was holding it'
(23)	gøryjorum	'I am seeing'

Exercise 4.11 Identify the additional suffix and its alternants.

Here we see a suffix indicating a progressive interpretation with four alternants: [-ijor], [-ɨjor], [-ujor], and [-yjor].

Note that the first vowel of this suffix alternates as any other high vowel of a suffix would: it adopts the frontness and roundness of the preceding vowel. The second vowel in this suffix, however, is invariantly [o], and never alternates. This intractability makes it an **opaque** vowel; its resistance to the harmonic pattern is referred to as *opacity*. Moreover, consider the vowels in the morphemes which occur afterwards: they harmonize with [o], adopting its backness and roundness, regardless of whatever precedes the opaque vowel, as in the final [u] in [gelijordu] and [gøryjorum] show. Thus, the opaque vowel of /Ijor/ stops the harmonic pattern and establishes its own.

opaque segments: segments which do not participate in a harmonic pattern.

There are several ways in which we could attempt to encode the opacity of the second vowel in this suffix. Clearly, it does not behave as other suffix vowels do, so its underlying form must reflect this. One approach would be to stipulate it as an exception, immune to the rules of harmony, such that it remains as [o] even after the rules we devised in Exercise 4.10. Subsequent vowels would then harmonize with it.

An alternative, more abstract approach is to consider the possibility that suffix vowels general have *no* specification for [±round] or [±back]; in such an approach, phonologists often resort to capital symbols to represent underlying forms that lack one or more features. For example, we would represent the third-person suffix as /I/ underlyingly and the negative suffix as /A/.

The rules in Exercise 4.10 would have to be reformulated to make any unspecified vowels [+back] after [+back] vowels and [−back] after [−back] vowels (and likewise for the roundness specification). The exceptionality of /Ijor/ is in the full specification of its second vowel: since it is underlyingly /o/, the revised harmony rules cannot apply to it. In this alternative approach, the opaque vowel differs from other suffix vowels in its underlying form rather than in its immunity to certain rules.

4.4 Hungarian

Some additional issues of vowel harmony can be observed in Hungarian, which like Turkish has vowel harmony occurring within its suffixing morphology. Examine the following data from Hungarian (Kornai 1987), paying attention to the vowels of the suffixes.

Stem	Dative	Ablative	As X	Gloss
had	hadnak	hadtoːl	hadul	'army'
haːz	haːznak	haːztoːl	haːzul	'house'
juk	juknak	juktoːl	jukul	'hole'
kuːt	kuːtnak	kuːttoːl	kuːtul	'well'
hold	holdnak	holdtoːl	holdul	'moose'
loː	loːnak	loːtoːl	loːul	'horse'
in	innak	intoːl	inul	'tendon'
hid	hidnak	hidtoːl	hidul	'bridge'
heːj	heːjnak	heːjtoːl	heːjul	'crust'
bab	babnak	babtoːl	babul	'bean'
baːb	baːbnak	baːbtoːl	baːbul	'puppet'
rum	rumnak	rumtoːl	rumul	'id.'
huːr	huːrnak	huːrtoːl	huːrul	'chord'
bot	botnak	bottoːl	botul	'stick'
droːt	droːtnak	droːttoːl	droːtul	'wire'
ʒir	ʒirnak	ʒirtoːl	ʒirul	'fat'
ceːl	ceːlnak	ceːltoːl	ceːlul	'goal'

hit	hitnek	hittøːl	hityl	'belief'
viːz	viːznek	viːztøːl	viːzyl	'water'
fej	fejnek	fejtøːl	fejyl	'head'
eːrv	eːrvnek	eːrvtøːl	eːrvyl	'argument'
hølɟ	hølɟnek	hølɟtøːl	hølɟyl	'lady'
tøːɟ	tøːɟnek	tøːɟtøːl	tøːɟyl	'udder'
sylt	syltnek	sylttøːl	syltyl	'roast'
tyːz	tyːznek	tyːztøːl	tyːzyl	'fire'
tøk	tøknek	tøktøːl	tøkyl	'pumpkin'
føːr	føːrnek	føːrtøːl	føːryl	'skin'
fyst	fystnek	fysttøːl	fystyl	'smoke'
byːn	byːnnek	byːntøːl	byːnyl	'sin'

Exercise 4.12   What are the alternants of each suffix?
Under what conditions does each alternant appear?

Each suffix has a back and a front alternant: [nak] alternates with [nek]; [toːl] alternates with [tøːl], and [ul] alternates with [yl].

Roots with back vowels always take suffixes with back vowels, as in [hadnak], [juknak], and [holdnak]. Roots with some types of front vowels always take front suffixes, as in [tøknek] and [syltnek].

However, the situation for roots with /i/ or /e/ is more complicated. Some such roots take front suffixes, as in [hitnek] and [eːrvnek], while others take back suffixes, as in [hidnak] and [ceːlnak].

We can say that the choice of alternant is at least partially predictable: most vowels have a consistent choice, while only /i/ or /e/ are problematic. No other type of vowel behaves like this in Hungarian. Nevertheless, each root is consistent within its own paradigm: each /i/ root either always uses front alternants, as in [hitnek], [hittøːl], and [hityl], or always uses back alternants, as in [hidnak], [hidtoːl], and [hidul].

We may divide both phonemes /i/ and /e/ into two groups: those that show front-vowel harmony, as in [hitnek], and those that show back-vowel harmony, as in [hidnak].

We could then infer that there is something about the back-vowel-choosing roots that is underlyingly distinct from the front-vowel-choosing roots. In short, perhaps [hidnak] and [ceːlnak] underlyingly contain back vowels, which accounts for their choice of back-vowel suffixes.

The exceptional back-harmony vowels of words like [hid] are not opaque; instead, they act as if they are back vowels despite not appearing as such at the surface. This is inferred simply from the fact that, like other roots with obviously back vowels, they take suffixes with back vowels. This is an **abstract** analysis: it relies on the possibility that despite being identical in form at the surface, the /i/ of [hid] and the /i/ of [hit] are different vowels at an abstract level of underlying representation. An abstract approach also entails the existence of a rule that turns abstract segments into their surface forms; we will explore such analyses in more detail in Chapter 7.

Exercise 4.13 Determine underlying forms for the alternating suffixes, and write a rule that accounts for their alternation. You may ignore the abstract roots such as [hid] and [ceːl].

We can assume that all suffix vowels are underlyingly front, in which case, our vowel harmony rule changes them to back vowels only after roots with back vowels.

[vowel] → [back] / [back vowel] C ___

This rule assumes that /y/ is changed to [u], [ø] is changed to [o], and [e] is changed to [a].

If we instead assume that the suffix vowels are underlyingly back, the rule instead needs to be formulated to change them to front vowels only after front vowels.

The facts of Hungarian vowel harmony are more complex than presented here, where the data are limited to suffixes which alternate only by backness. Some suffixes also have alternations in roundness, yielding three-way alternations in some cases and four-way alternations in others. The complication here is that again similar-looking vowels trigger different behavior.

An analysis of these suffixes is possible but beyond the scope of this chapter; even so, it should be noted there is a basic parallel between the solution we proposed for [hit] vs. [hid] and a solution here. In particular, wherever seemingly identical vowels have different harmonic behavior, we infer they are somehow abstractly different from each other in their underlying representation.

A second complication in Hungarian relates to the same surface vowels [i] and [e], which in multisyllabic words can exhibit the phenomenon of transparency. For example, in words such as [radir-nak], the first vowel is back and the second is front – but the suffix vowel harmonizes with the first vowel. Transparency is converse to harmonic opacity: in transparency, the harmonic feature seems to jump across the transparent vowel, while opaque vowels block its transmission from one vowel to the next.

Turkish and Hungarian together illustrate systems of harmony in which features of roots spread from earlier to later, and from root to affix. This is not to imply that the opposite directions are impossible, and in fact other languages illustrate some different directions of harmonic effects. The analyses in §§4.5–4.7 pursue this in more detail.

4.5 Pulaar

Consider the following data from Pulaar (Paradis 1986); the table below includes nouns in their singular and diminutive plural forms.

cɔf-ɔn	'chick, dim. pl.'	sof-ru	'chick, sing.'
cɛr-kɔn	'rifle butt, dim. pl.'	ser-du	'rifle butt, sing.'
ᵐbɛɛl-ɔn	'shadow, dim. pl.'	ᵐbeel-u	'shadow, sing.'
pɛɛc-ɔn	'slot, dim. pl.'	peec-i	'slot, sing.'
ᵐbɛɛl-ɔn	'puddle, dim. pl.'	beel-i	'puddle, sing.'
ⁿdɔg-ɔ-w-ɔn	'runner, dim. pl.'	dog-oo-ru	'runner, sing.'

First, we may note that the diminutive plural suffix has several different forms: [-ɔn] in most cases, but [-kɔn] in [cɛr-kɔn]. Nevertheless, for this exercise, let us not be concerned with any differences in consonants: what is important is that this suffix consistently has the vowel [ɔ] within it. Likewise, the other suffixes all indicate plurality, and again some variance among them is evident: notably, some include one of several consonants such as in [-du] or [-ru], while others consist merely of the vowel [-u] or [-i]. Beyond these details, the singular suffix always contains at least a high vowel, either [u] or [i].

Exercise 4.14 Do the roots or suffixes alternate in Pulaar?
Identify the alternants of each morpheme that alternates.

The roots clearly alternate, as every root has a non-ATR vowel in the diminutive plural but an ATR vowel in the singular form. The suffixes have various forms but do not alternate along the ATR dimension. Although we have acknowledged several forms of the diminutive plural, it differs only in the presence or absence of a consonant. Likewise, while we have seen multiple forms of the singular suffix, it always has a high ATR vowel.

If we abstract away from the consonants which appear only in some of the suffixes, we may note that the quality of the suffix's vowel is consistent within each column: it is always [ɔ] in the diminutive plural, and it is always a high ATR vowel in the singular. The same is true of the root vowels within each column: in the diminutive plural column, the root always contains either [ɛ] or [ɔ], while in the singular column, the root always has either [e] or [o].

Exercise 4.15 Under what conditions does each root allomorph appear?

Every root has a corresponding alternant in each column; for example, [cɔf-] in the diminutive group corresponds to [sof-] in the other. The alternation in the root vowel is a function of the suffix vowel: wherever the suffix includes [ɔ], the root contains either [ɛ] or [ɔ]; wherever the suffix contains [i] or [u], the root contains [e] or [o].

Note that the changes in vowels also precipitate changes in the initial consonants: for example, some roots have initial [s] before ATR vowels but [c] before non-ATR vowels.

Because this pattern involves vowels affecting nearby vowels, we may consider this another example of vowel harmony. Like Mongolian, we see the vowels [e, o, u, i] behaving in one way, to the exclusion of [ɛ] and [ɔ], suggesting that [e, o, u, i] share some other feature that [ɛ] and [ɔ] lack. Studies of the phonology of African languages commonly rely on the feature of Advanced Tongue Root to model the process of vowel harmony. In Pulaar, the suffix vowels [u, i] are ATR, and affect the vowels of preceding root morphemes, causing them to have an ATR configuration as well. Conversely, the vowel [ɔ] in the diminutive suffix is not ATR, and so neither is the vowel in the root that precedes it.

Exercise 4.16 Construct a rule that will make the root vowel [ATR] in the appropriate circumstances. You will need to determine an appropriate underlying form to do this.

As long as the root vowel is underlyingly non-ATR, a rule changing it to ATR before ATR vowels will derive the appropriate alternant of each root.

[vowel] → [ATR] / ___ C [ATR vowel]

Some other aspects of Pulaar ATR harmony are worthy of further comment. Consider the additional data below, paying attention to the activity of the low vowel [a].

4.6 More Pulaar

faji	'fat'
lammi	'dirty'
bɔɔt-aa-ri	'dinner'
pɔɔf-aa-li	'breath'
nɔdd-aa-li	'call'
ŋgɔr-aa-gu	'courage'

Exercise 4.17 Does [a] participate in ATR harmony in Pulaar?
a. Does it alternate?
b. Does it cause alternation?

There is no evidence of [a] alternating in Pulaar. In the data in above, the vowel [a] is always followed by an ATR vowel. However, forms like [bɔɔt-aa-ri] suggest that [a] blocks ATR harmony and causes preceding vowels to be non-ATR.

Without considering forms with a non-ATR suffix (such as the diminutive [-ɔn]), we cannot conclude whether [a] is part of a pattern of alternation. We could only do so if we could observe the same roots co-occurring with suffixes that contain lax non-ATR vowels such as [ɔ]. In such a circumstance, a root that maintained [a] could be concluded to be non-alternating; conversely, any change in the root's vowel would suggest that low vowels also harmonize.

Nevertheless, we still can conclude that, in some sense, the low vowel [a] does not participate in tongue root harmony in Pulaar. This follows from the fact that root vowels remain non-ATR if they are separated from an ATR suffix by an intervening morpheme containing [a]. For example, in the form [pɔɔf-aa-li], the final suffix includes the ATR vowel [i]; if the directly precedent [a] were affected by this, it too would be ATR via harmony, and likewise we would expect an ATR vowel in the root as well. Because this does not happen – instead a non-ATR vowel remains in the root – we conclude that the vowel [a] is opaque in Pulaar ATR harmony.

The patterns of vowel harmony we have seen have illustrated numerous variations on how the phenomenon may manifest itself in languages of the world. Some languages harmonize along dimensions of backness or roundness; others harmonize by tongue-root features. Harmony may proceed from earlier to later in a word or vice versa, and it may proceed from root to affix or vice versa. Further, some vowels may resist a harmonic alternation, either by opaquely preventing surrounding vowels from harmonizing or by transparently allowing them to do so.

One of the key aspects of harmonic vowel systems is that each vowel falls into one of several groups. We can characterize this as follows: every vowel is a member either of (a) the set of vowels that has a positive value for the harmonic feature, (b) the set of vowels that has a negative value for the harmonic feature, or (c) the set of vowels that do not participate in harmony.

Alternation in harmony is evidenced when a given phoneme has a surface alternant from each of the harmonic sets.

Of course, the relationship between the surface vowels and the underlying vowels can be complicated, as we have already seen for Hungarian. The data there suggest that there is one type of [i] which is underlyingly /i/, because it precipitates front-vowel suffix alternants. Yet there is another surface [i] which is underlyingly /ɨ/, because it precipitates back-vowel suffixes.

4.7 Maasai

A comparable scenario arises in Maasai. Consider the first subset of Maasai data below (from Tucker and Mpaayei 1955), which consists of forms marked for subject agreement in first-person, second-person, and third-person singular present tense.

	1st sing.	*2nd sing.*	*3rd sing.*	*Gloss*
(1)	a-rɪk	ɪ-rɪk	ɛ-rɪk	'cause nausea'
(2)	a-ɪlɛp	ɪ-ɪlɛp	ɛ-ɪlɛp	'ascend'
(3)	a-bɔl	ɪ-bɔl	ɛ-bɔl	'hold its mouth'
(4)	a-bʊl	ɪ-bʊl	ɛ-bʊl	'prosper'
(5)	a-raɲ	ɪ-raɲ	ɛ-raɲ	'sing'
(6)	a-rik	i-rik	e-rik	'lead it'
(7)	a-lep	i-lep	e-lep	'milk it'
(8)	a-bol	i-bol	e-bol	'open it'
(9)	a-bul	i-bul	e-bul	'pierce it'

Exercise 4.18 Identify those morphemes that alternate and those that don't. For the alternating morphemes, under what conditions does each alternant appear?

The verb roots themselves do not alternate; they have the same vowels in each column. Likewise, the first singular prefix is invariantly [a-], so it also does not alternate.

The second- and third-person prefixes alternate between ATR and non-ATR vowels. The vowel of the second-person prefix alternates between [ɪ] and [i]; it is [ɪ] before the roots in (1)–(5), but [i] before the roots in (6)–(9). The vowel of the third-person prefix alternates between [ɛ] and [e] under the same conditions: it is [ɛ] before the roots in (1)–(5), and [e] before the roots in (6)–(9).

Note that the ATR prefix vowels [i] and [e] always occur before roots with ATR vowels, [i, u, e, o], while the non-ATR prefix vowels always appear before roots with non-ATR vowels [ɪ, ʊ, ɔ, ɛ]. Thus, the prefixes clearly harmonize with the root vowels by their ATR features. The fact that roots with [a] also receive [ɪ] and [ɛ] as their agreement suffixes (as in [ɪ-raɲ] and [ɛ-raɲ]) suggests that [a], while non-alternating, is itself non-ATR.

Exercise 4.19 Construct a rule that will make the prefix vowels [ATR] in the appropriate circumstances. You will need to determine appropriate underlying forms to do this.

As long as the prefix vowel is underlyingly non-ATR, a rule changing it to ATR before ATR vowels will derive the appropriate alternant of each root.

[non-low vowel] → [ATR] / ___ C [ATR vowel]

This one rule will alter both /ɪ/ and /ɛ/, rendering them [i] and [e] respectively, before roots with ATR vowels. If we were to assume the underlying forms of the prefixes were already ATR, we would need to rewrite this rule to make them non-ATR only before non-ATR vowels.

Let us turn to another subset of Maasai data, indicating the formation of a progressive aspect. As before, we see the first-person subject agreement prefix [a] and the second-person prefix, which alternates harmonically between [i] and [ɪ]. Now, however, different material follows the root. There is a suffix that alternates between [ɪta] or [ito], and in the second-person plural there is additional reduplication, rendering the suffix as [ɪta-ta] or [ito-to]. We may presume that the suffix marks progressive aspect, while reduplication marks plural subject agreement.

	1st sing.	2nd pl.	Gloss
(1)	a-rɪk-ɪta	ɪ-rɪk-ɪta-ta	'causing nausea'
(2)	a-ɪlɛp-ɪta	ɪlɛp-ɪta-ta	'ascending'
(3)	a-bɔl-ɪta	ɪ-bɔl-ɪta-ta	'holding its mouth'
(4)	a-bʊl-ɪta	ɪ-bʊl-ɪta-ta	'prospering'
(5)	a-raɲ-ɪta	ɪ-raɲ-ɪta-ta	'singing'
(6)	a-rik-ito	i-rik-ito-to	'leading it'
(7)	a-lep-ito	i-lep-ito-to	'milking it'
(8)	a-bol-ito	i-bol-ito-to	'opening it'
(9)	a-bul-ito	i-bul-ito-to	'piercing it'
(10)	a-iruk-ito	iruk-ito-to	'believing him'

Exercise 4.20 Describe the alternation in the progressive suffix.

The progressive suffix has two forms, [ɪta] and [ito]. The first form appears after non-ATR roots and itself contains two non-ATR vowels, [ɪ] and [a]. The second form appears after ATR roots and contains two ATR vowels, [i] and [o].

Like the second-person subject prefix, the first vowel of the suffix alternates between [ɪ] and [i], harmonizing with the ATR feature of the root. However, the final vowel of the suffix is curious, because it alternates between [a] after non-ATR vowels and [o] after ATR vowels. Thus, unlike the first-person subject prefix, which is invariantly [a], in the suffix, the vowel [a] has an ATR counterpart.

We may draw the conclusion that suffixing harmony works slightly differently from prefixing harmony in Maasai, since the vowel /a/ alternates in one circumstance but not the other. If this is the case, then the suffixing harmony rule should be formulated to reflect this difference.

Exercise 4.21 Compose a different harmony rule that accounts for all alternation in the Maasai suffixes.

[vowel] → [non-low ATR] / [ATR] C ___

This rule differs from the prefixing rule in Exercise 4.19 in two ways. First, it targets all vowels, not just non-low vowels, so it also targets /a/. Second, it produces an output that is itself a non-low vowel; thus, it leaves most target vowels unchanged in terms of their height, as all Maasai vowels except /a/ are non-low to begin with. As a consequence, when the rule applies to /ɪ/, the ATR output is [i], which is non-low, but when it applies to /a/, the ATR output is the non-low vowel [o].

Maasai illustrates several additional interesting aspects to vowel harmony. Like Mongolian and Pulaar, it is an ATR harmony system, but here we have evidence of harmony proceeding in both directions away from the root, such that vowels in the prefixes and suffixes both harmonize with the vowels of the root. Moreover, the specific details of the harmonic process differ in the rightward and leftward harmony rules. Furthermore, Maasai has an apparently opaque vowel in its prefix system, but when we include suffixes in the analysis, we see instead that a single surface vowel, [o], serves as the ATR counterpart to two distinct non-ATR vowels, [ɔ] and [a].

Patterns of vowel harmony are notable for several reasons: first, they involve segments responding to features of other segments, but non-locally – what matters for the alternating vowels in such cases is not the features of adjacent consonants, but of vowels farther afield within the same word. Second, they are still quite clearly patterns of assimilation, in that the alternating vowel ends up adopting one or more features of the conditioning vowel. In some cases, these features are backness or roundness, and in others the features are instead characterized with the ATR dimension. We have also seen numerous patterns in which the height of the target and/or the height of the conditioning vowel is also relevant.

The remainder of this chapter will focus on patterns that are not vowel-harmonic, but are still either non-local or non-assimilatory. Let us first examine the following data from Balinese.

4.8 Balinese

Take some time to peruse the following data (Edmundo Luna p.c), which include bare nouns alongside related forms that have a suffix indicating definiteness. The suffix can be analyzed as having two alternants, [e] and [ne], and several of the nouns also exhibit some alternation in their final consonants. Aside from these few details, the real focus of this exercise will be the quality of the vowels.

(1)	kədɪs	'bird'	kədise	'the bird'
(2)	sabʊʔ	'belt'	sabuke	'the belt'
(3)	bale	'hall'	balene	'the hall'

(4)	bwajɤ	'crocodile'	bwajane	'the crocodile'
(5)	təgal	'garden'	təgale	'the garden'
(6)	kambɪŋ	'goat'	kambiɲe	'the goat'
(7)	odalan	'temple festival'	odalane	'the temple festival'
(8)	məsolah	'dance'	məsolahe	'the dance'
(9)	əndəʔ	'Balinese ikat'	əndəke	'the Balinese ikat'
(10)	dʒauʔ	'type of demon'	dʒauke	'the type of demon'
(11)	pradɤ	'gold leaf'	pradane	'the gold leaf'
(12)	antʃur	'type of adhesive'	antʃure	'the type of adhesive'
(13)	dolɔg	'type of rice warehouse'	dologe	'the type of rice warehouse'
(14)	təbu	'sugarcane'	təbune	'the sugarcane'
(15)	tali	'rope, tie'	taline	'the rope, tie'
(16)	gɔŋ	'gong'	goɲe	'the gong'
(17)	gambəlan	'gamelan ensemble'	gambəlane	'the gamelan ensemble'
(18)	laŋɪt	'sky'	laɲite	'the sky'
(19)	borɛh	'skin lotion'	borehe	'the skin lotion'
(20)	idʊp	'life'	idupe	'the life'

Exercise 4.22 Identify the conditions in which [ne] appears as the definite suffix.

The alternant [ne] appears with roots which end in vowels when unsuffixed, for example [bale] is suffixed as [balene] and [tali] is suffixed as [taline]. Roots with final consonants in their unsuffixed form have [e] as their suffix, for example [təgal] is suffixed as [təgale].

Exercise 4.23 Identify any other roots which alternate in their final consonants.

There are three roots that end in [ʔ] in their unsuffixed form but [k] in their suffixed form; for example the unsuffixed [əndəʔ] is [əndəke] when suffixed.

These roots are probably best analyzed as having a final underlying /k/ which is rendered [ʔ] when there is no suffix. The opposite scenario is plausible, but we while we do see [k] elsewhere in the data, we do not see any other examples of [ʔ]. This suggests simply that [ʔ] is a predictable allophone of /k/. Nevertheless, the specifics of the analysis are inconsequential, as the presence of the [ʔ] in the unsuffixed forms ensures that the preceding vowel is not word-final. This leads us to the main point of the analysis.

Exercise 4.24 Describe the alternation in root vowels, by following these steps:
a. Identify all the vowels that alternate, and list the alternants together.
b. Determine the conditions under which each alternant appears.
c. Identify any vowels that do not alternate – that are identical in their suffixed and unsuffixed forms, regardless of the conditions you determine above.

a. The pairs of alternants are as follows:

[ɪ, i], as in [kədɪs, kədise] and [kambɪŋ, kambiɲe]
[ʊ, u], as in [sabʊʔ, sabuke] and [antʃʊr, antʃure]
[ɔ, o], as in [dolɔg, dologe] and [gɔŋ, goɲe]
[ɛ, e], as in [borɛh, borehe]
[ɤ, a], as in [bwajɤ, bwajane] and [pradɤ, pradane]

b. For the lax/tense pairs, the lax or non-ATR alternant appears before word-final consonants, while the tense or ATR alternant appears before a sequence of a consonant followed by another vowel.

For the pair [ɤ, a], the vowel [ɤ] appears word-finally, while the vowel [a] appears in non-word-final positions.

c. There are other forms which contain [a] whether suffixed or not; for example, [təgal, təgale] and [odalan, odalane]; the vowel remains unchanged in [odalan] even before the word-final consonant.

Several other roots have no alternation but also have no word-final consonant; for example [balene, təbune, taline] are [bale, təbu, tali] when unsuffixed, but this is not inconsistent with the generalizations in (b) above, since in this case there is no word-final consonant which would provide the conditions for the vowels to be lax.

In nearly every pair of alternating vowels, there is a lax or non-ATR alternant, either [ɪ], [ʊ], [ɔ], or [ɛ] and a tense or ATR alternant, either [i], [u], [o], or [e]. The non-ATR alternants appear before word-final consonants, and the ATR alternants appear elsewhere.

The only pair of alternating vowels that does not fit this pattern is [ɤ, a], which are not distinct by ATR, and which are subject to a different set of conditions: [ɤ] occurs word-finally, and [a] occurs elsewhere.

Exercise 4.25 Determine the underlying representation for the alternants [ɤ, a], and construct a rule that accounts for their alternation.

The underlying vowel for this pair is best seen as [a], since [ɤ] only occurs in the specific context of word-final position, and [a] occurs in all other contexts. The rule that accounts for this is as follows:

[a] → [ɤ] / __]₍ᴡᴅ₎

Exercise 4.26 Determine the underlying representation of the ATR/non-ATR vowels, and construct a rule that accounts for the alternation that affects all of them.

The underlying vowels are [ATR], because such vowels have a wider distribution. The non-ATR vowels only appear in the specific context directly before word-final consonants. The rule that accounts for this alternation is as follows:

[ATR vowel] → [non-ATR] / ___ C]$_{WD}$

This rule must include the word boundary to ensure that the pattern does not apply before all consonants throughout the word. Note also that since this rule explicitly references word-final consonants, it will not overapply and change the final vowel in unsuffixed roots with final vowels such as [bale] or [təbu].

In this data set, we have ended up with an analysis in which the underlying forms necessarily are the [ATR] vowels, which become non-ATR in a specific context. In the other languages of this chapter that use an ATR distinction (e.g., Mongolian, Pulaar, Maasai), we could afford to be equivocal. The choice of the ATR or non-ATR alternant was inconsequential for those analyses (aside from the consequences on the specifics of the accompanying rules). In those cases, we went with underlying non-ATR vowels, and the rules added the ATR specification to them.

In Balinese, however, the rule must remove the ATR specification, because the distributional evidence forces us to posit ATR vowels underlyingly. It might seem strange to construct a rule that does this, but we will see in Chapter 6 that a binary approach to feature specification will make these analyses more sensible: some rules may change [+ATR] vowels to [−ATR], while others may do the opposite. With this approach, features aren't removed; instead, their positive or negative values are respecified.

4.9 Woleaian

We conclude this chapter with a different data set which, like the examples from Balinese, is not assimilatory in any sense, but like the harmony patterns, it illustrates another type of non-local phenomenon. In Woleaian, some vowels exhibit a dissimilatory alternation. Examine the following data (from Sohn 1975, Sohn and Tawerilmang 1976), which juxtapose plain verbs with causatives. The causatives all contain a prefix which is either [xa-] or [xe-].

Some other aspects of the data require comment. In many cases, there is some additional segmental material in the causative which essentially acts as a transitive-marking suffix. These additional final segments are not predictable and can be ignored for this exercise. In addition, in some other cases not shown here, there is alternation in the root-initial consonant such that it too differs between the plain verbs and the causatives.

4.10 Forms with [xa-]

(1)	ppʷeʃ	'to be hot'	xappʷeʃ	'to roast, burn, heat'
(2)	ʃexau	'to be greedy'	xaʃexauw	'make him greedy'
(3)	ʃʉw	'to leave'	xaʃʉwa	'make it move away'
(4)	kit	'tiny, little'	xakiti	'make them small'
(5)	kʉŋ	'ringing'	xakʉŋʉ	'ring it, make it clang'
(6)	luʃ	'coconut syrup'	xaluʃo	'make it syrup like'
(7)	nes	'to curl'	xanesʉ	'bend it'
(8)	nʉr	'shade'	xanʉr	'hat'
(9)	pej	'to bend over'	xapeja	'slant it'
(10)	pø	'to be empty'	xapøw	'empty it'
(11)	ɸʷoŋ	'night'	xaɸʷoŋ	'to say goodbye to'
(12)	rep	'to be near'	xarepa	'approach it'
(13)	rous	'to be painful'	xarousa	'hurt him'
(14)	six	'to be mad'	xasixe	'make him angry'
(15)	sʉ	'to stand'	xasʉw	'build it'
(16)	tʃetʃ	'to tremble'	xatʃetʃ	'to shake, wave, swing'
(17)	tix	'slant'	xatixe	'tilt it'
(18)	tuɸʷ	'go down'	xatuɸʷ	'make a deep hole in the ground'
(19)	xʉ	'burning'	xaxʉw	'set a fire to it'

4.11 Forms with [xe-]

(1)	ppʷar	'to be curved'	xeppʷaro	'bend it'
(2)	ʃɒʃɒ	'load'	xeʃɒʃɒ	'load it'
(3)	faniij	'watch it'	xefaniij	'take care of him'
(4)	ffas	'to laugh'	xeffas	'to make a joke'
(5)	kail	'strong'	xekaila	'strengthen it'
(6)	kaɸʷ	'dull'	xekaɸʷu	'cause it to become dull'
(7)	lɒ	'waves'	xelɒw	'make it wavy'
(8)	mak	'to break away'	xemak	'to distribute'
(9)	matʃ	'to fall'	xematʃo	'chop it down'
(10)	mʷal	'to hide'	xemʷalo	'hide it'
(11)	naŋ	'to lift oneself up'	xenaŋ	'to lift'
(12)	pak	'to be impatient'	xepak	'to hurry'
(13)	rax	'to be counted'	xerax	'read it'
(14)	tal	'rope, line'	xetal	'to walk in line'
(15)	tɒlap	'to be wasted'	xetɒlepa	'waste it'
(16)	taɸʷ	'taboo'	xetaɸʷu	'forbid it'

(17)	tɒtɒ	'to catch, support'	xetɒtɒ	'assistant'
(18)	t͡ʃau	'to be unwilling'	xet͡ʃauw	'make him reluctant'
(19)	wal	'to be covered'	xewalʉ	'cover it up'
(20)	was	'hurt'	xewasʉ	'hurt him'
(21)	xaʃ	'to decay'	xexaʃi	'cause it to decay'
(22)	xaɸʷ	'infected'	xexaɸʷu	'cause it to be infected'

Exercise 4.27 Describe the conditions under which the alternants [xa-] and [xe-] appear.

The form [xe-] appears if the root's first vowel is [a] or [ɒ]. The form [xa-] appears before roots with any other kind of vowel.

Exercise 4.28 Choose the underlying form for the prefix.
Compose a rule that accounts for the alternation in the form of the causative.

Since the distribution of [xe-] is limited to a specific context, we can posit [xa-] as the underlying form of the prefix. We can compose the rule as follows:

[a] → [e] / ___ C [low vowel]

The actual rule ends up being quite simple once we put aside the additional complications in the causative stems. The process resembles vowel harmony in that the target vowel responds to some other vowel despite intervening consonants, but in Woleaian the process is dissimilatory – the target ends up being less like the vowel in its conditioning environment.

We can still make sense of the layers of unpredictability if we draw an analogy with Fijian (§3.12) and Paamese (§3.23). In Fijian, it seemed at the surface that the passive suffix contained any of a long list of unpredictable consonants, but the analysis ultimately settled on associating these consonants with the underlying forms of the roots. In the absence of the passive suffix [-a], the root-final consonants were deleted, but when the passive suffix is there, the final consonant is "protected" from deletion.

A similar analysis is available here – one could posit the [-o] of [xemat͡ʃo], the [-w] of [xapøw], the [-i] of [xakiti], and the [ʉ] of [xewalʉ] to be unpredictable allomorphs of a transitive suffix. Alternatively, we could treat them as parallel to the various consonants of Fijian, which entails associating them with the root. Accordingly, they are missing from the bare root, but present in the derived form, presumably because they are protected from deletion. The difference is that in Fijian, an explicit final segment protects the root-final consonant from deletion, but in Woleaian, any extra segment filling this role is itself deleted. This is schematized below, where "C" stands in for a mysterious segmental affix that is deleted during the derivation.

4.12 Sample derivations

[kit] vs. [xakiti]

	/ kiti / 'small'	/ xa + kiti + C / 'make it small'
Final deletion	kit	xa kiti
a → e	NA	NA
	kit	xakiti

[matʃ] vs. [xematʃo]

	/ matʃo / 'fall'	/ xa + matʃo + C / 'chop it down'
Final deletion	matʃ	xa matʃo
a → e	NA	xe matʃo
	matʃ	xematʃo

4.13 Problem roots in Woleaian

There are additional roots in Woleaian that have an unexpected alternation in their vowels. Examine the following subset of data:

(1)	faŋ	'to let'	xafeŋa	'let it go'
(2)	far	'to fit'	xafera	'fit it'
(3)	law	'to be scared'	xalew	'scare it'
(4)	pak	'impatient'	xapeka	'make him hurry'
(5)	pal	'dried'	xapela	'dry it'
(6)	tap	'be ready'	xattepa	'touch it'
(7)	fetal	'to move'	xefatela	'make him go'
(8)	ɸʷerax	'brave man'	xeɸʷarexa	'make him brave'
(9)	texaʃ	'to rise'	xetaxeʃa	'throw it'

Exercise 4.29 Describe the alternation that occurs in these roots.
What are the consequences of this alternation for the form of the causative prefix?

The roots in (1)–(6) have [a] in their bare form, such as [faŋ] and [law], but rather than derive [xefaŋ] and [xelaw], their root vowels change to [e], and the causative prefix thus stays as [xa], yielding [xafeŋa] and [xalew]. Conversely, the roots in (7)–(9) have [e] as their first vowel, but this vowel switches to [a] in the causative, and the prefix accordingly is [xe].

Since these exceptional roots also alternate between [a] and [e], and since [a] can convincingly be posited as the underlying vowel for the alternating causative prefix, we can argue that these roots also have underlying [a]. Furthermore, we have already noted that many causatives undergo an additional unpredictable change in their form beyond the addition of the prefix, also receiving an extra final vowel or consonant.

Exercise 4.30 Account for the behavior of these roots. Why do (1)–(6) change their root vowels, unlike the low-vowel roots in §4.11? Why do (7)–(9) also change their root vowels?

Simply put, all the roots in (1)–(9) above have multiple instances underlying /a/, including a final vowel that is maintained in the causative but lost from the bare root, analogously to the root-final segments discussed in §4.12.

The final [a] of the causatives impacts the preceding vowels of the words. In (1)–(6), the final vowel is lost from the bare root; for example, /paka/ surfaces as [pak]. However, the final [a] is maintained in the causative / xa + paka /. This forces the root's first /a/ to raise to [e], and as a consequence, the prefix maintains the low vowel, as in [xapeka].

The bare forms in (7)–(9) also lose their final vowel, but since they still have two vowels remaining, the first is raised to [e] to dissimilate from the second. For example, /taxaʃa/ surfaces as [texaʃ]. When the final vowel of /xa + taxaʃa/ is maintained in the causative, only the middle vowel is raised, leaving the first vowel as [a]. The causative is then [xe-], as in [xetaxeʃa].

The fact that the presence or absence of the final vowel here has an impact on preceding vowels suggests that the [a]-raising rule "knows about" the output of the deletion process. That is, the deletion of the final segment happens first, and the a-raising rule applies second. Thus, where a final /a/ remains, the directly precedent vowel is raised, but if the final /a/ is deleted, the directly precedent vowel stays low. We can illustrate this with some more sample derivations.

4.14 Sample derivations

[pak] vs. [xapeka]

	/ paka / 'impatient'	/ xa + paka + C / 'make him hurry'
Final deletion	pak	xa paka
a → e	NA	xapeka
	pak	xapeka

Finally, the form [xalew] is problematic, because its root vowel should raise only if the final /a/ remains, but in this case, the vowel that triggers the raising pattern is missing. We would have to propose an additional rule that deletes /-a/ only after /w/, and order this rule critically after the [a]-raising rule.

The Woleaian data have motivated several extra layers of analysis: mysterious segments that protect root-final vowels, and others that precipitate raising before themselves disappearing. These inject a degree of abstractness into the phonological analysis of Woleaian. We have already seen an example of abstractness in Hungarian, where we concluded that some vowels are underlyingly back and unround, despite never appearing as such at the surface. In addition, the analysis invokes the notion of the critical ordering of different phonological rules with respect to each other. We will explore several examples of both abstractness and rule ordering in Chapter 7.

Summary

In this chapter, we have explored numerous phonological phenomena that are not readily characterized as assimilation of segments for the sake of articulatory ease. Much of this is seen through the lens of vowel harmony, which we have explored from a number of angles. We have seen that harmony may proceed either left-to-right or right-to-left, and may also proceed from root to affix or vice versa. Moreover, harmonic systems make use of a range of vowel features – in some languages, roundness and backness seem to spread among vowels, while in others, the operative feature is instead Advanced Tongue Root.

While harmony is like other segmental processes in that it entails segments reacting to the form of nearby segments, it differs in the non-local relationship between targets and triggers. Furthermore, we again must not assume that vowel harmony is merely a process that reduces the effort needed in producing words; that is, one might easily assume that the fewer kinds of vowels in a word, the easier it is to pronounce. We should avoid such causational hypothesizing, for several reasons. First, it should be noted that the consonants which occur between harmonizing vowels remain stable, and in some sense interrupt the vowel gesture. That is, we cannot infer that a harmonizing language allows the tongue to stay "more still" by keeping vowels similar or identical – because the articulation of the consonant precludes the tongue from standing still. Second, sometimes the vowels held constant are inherently more challenging, in that they are rare in languages of the world, often for acoustically grounded reasons. This actually suggests an alternative perspective about harmony, that it repeats particular vowel features not just to reduce articulatory effort, but also to ensure they are perceivable – reducing the amount of effort needed in perceiving words.

Key terms

vowel harmony
transparency
opacity
abstractness

Advanced Tongue Root (ATR)
height-dependent harmony
roundness harmony
dissimilation
sample derivation

References and further reading

Applegate, Richard B. 1972. Ineseño Chumash grammar. Doctoral dissertation, University of California, Berkeley.

Archangeli, Diana, and Douglas Pulleyblank. 1994. *Grounded Phonology*. Cambridge, MA: MIT Press.

Archangeli, Diana, and Douglas Pulleyblank. 2007. Harmony. In Paul de Lacy (ed.), *The Cambridge Handbook of Phonology*. Cambridge University Press, 353–377.

Clements, G. N. 1976a. The autosegmental treatment of vowel harmony. In W. U. Dressler and O. Pfeiffer (eds.), *Phonologica* 19. Innsbrucker Beiträge zur Sprachwissenschaft, 111–119.

Clements, G. N. 1976b. *Vowel Harmony in Nonlinear Generative Phonology: An Autosegmental Model*. Bloomington: Indiana University Linguistics Club.

Clements, G. N. 1985. Akan vowel harmony: a nonlinear analysis. In Didier L. Goyvaerts (ed.), *African Linguistics: Essays in Memory of M. W. K. Semikenke*. Studies in the Sciences of Language Series 6. Amsterdam: Benjamins.

Clements, G. N., and E. Sezer. 1982. Vowel and consonant disharmony in Turkish. In Harry van der Hulst and Norval Smith (eds.). *The Structure of Phonological Representations: Part II*. Dordrecht: Foris, 213–356.

Cohn, Abigail C. 1992. The consequences of dissimilation in Sundanese. *Phonology* 9: 199–220.

Cole, Jennifer. 1991. *Planar Phonology and Morphology*. New York: Garland.

Hony, H. C., and Fahir İz. 1957. *A Turkish–English Dictionary*. Oxford: Clarendon Press.

Hulst, Harry van der. 1985. Vowel harmony in Hungarian: a comparison of segmental and autosegmental analyses. In Harry van der Hulst and Norval Smith (eds.), *Advances in Nonlinear Phonology*. Dordrecht: Foris, 267–303.

Hyman, Larry M. 1995. Nasal consonant harmony at a distance: the case of Yaka. *Studies in African Linguistics* 24: 5–30.

Jensen, John T. 1990. *Morphology: Word Structure in Generative Grammar*. Amsterdam: Benjamins.

Johnson, D. C. 1980. Regular disharmony in Kirghiz. In R. Vago (ed.), *Issues in Vowel Harmony*. Amsterdam: Benjamins, 201–236.

Kornai, András. 1987. Hungarian vowel harmony. In Megan Crowhurst (ed.), *Proceedings of the 6th West Coast Conference on Formal Linguistics*. Stanford Linguistics Association, 147–161.

Krämer, Martin. 2003. *Vowel Harmony and Correspondence Theory*. Berlin: Mouton de Gruyter.

Lewis, Geoffrey. 1967. *Turkish Grammar*. Oxford University Press.

McDonough, Joyce. 2003. *The Navajo Sound System*. Dordrecht: Kluwer.

Oberly, Stacy. 2003. An optimality-theoretic analysis of Navajo sibilant harmony. *Coyote Papers: University of Arizona Working Papers in Linguistics.*

Paradis, Carole. 1986. Phonologie et morphologie lexicales: les classes nominales en peul (fula). Doctoral dissertation, University of Montreal.

Poser, William J. 1982. Phonological representation and action-at-a-distance. In Harry van der Hulst and Norval Smith (eds.), *The Structure of Phonological Representations*. Dordrecht: Foris, 121–158.

Savà, Graziano. 2005. *A Grammar of Ts'amakko*. Cushitic Language Studies 22. Cologne: Rüdiger Köppe.

Schachter, Paul, and Victoria A. Fromkin. 1968. A phonology of Akan: Akuapem, Asante, Fante. UCLA Working Papers in Phonetics 9. Los Angeles: Phonetics Laboratory, University of California.

Sohn, Ho-Minh. 1975. *Woleaian Reference Grammar*. Honolulu: University Press of Hawaii.

Sohn, Ho-Minh, and Anthony F. Tawerilmang. 1976. *Woleaian–English Dictionary*. Honolulu: University Press of Hawaii.

Svantesson, Jan-Olof, Anna Tsendina, Anastasia Karlsson, and Vivan Franzén. 2005. *The Phonology of Mongolian*. Oxford University Press.

Tucker, Archibald N., and J. Tompo Ole Mpaayei (1955) *A Maasai Grammar with Vocabulary*. London: Longmans, Green & Co.

Walker, Rachel, and Sharon Rose. 2011. Harmony. In John Goldsmith, Jason Riggle, and Alan C. L. Yu (eds.), *The Handbook of Phonological Theory*. Hoboken, NJ: Wiley-Blackwell.

Review exercises

Ts'amakko (Cushitic)

Examine the following data from Ts'amakko (Savà 2005):

ɓaɗ	'to hide'	ɓaɗ-as	'to make hide'
ɠabb	'to take'	ɠabb-as	'to make take'
bas	'to do'	bas-as	'to make sb. do'
zaq'	'to slaughter'	zaq'-as	'to make sb. slaughter'
tʃ'ur	'to throw'	tʃ'ur-aʃ	'to make sb. throw'
ʃukuj	'to be scared'	ʃukuj-aʃ	'to scare'

a. Describe the alternants of the causative suffix in Ts'amakko.

b. Under what conditions does each alternant appear?

Yaka

Examine the following data from Yaka (Hyman 1995):

sól-ele 'deforest'
jád-idi 'spread'
kúːnd-idi 'bury'
kém-ene 'moan'
nútúk-ini 'bow'
méːŋg-ene 'hate'

a. Assume the above forms in Yaka all have a variant of the same suffix. In what ways does this suffix alternate?
b. Construct a rule that accounts for the vowels of the suffix.
c. Construct a rule or rules that account for the consonants of the suffix.

Sundanese

Examine the following data from Sundanese (Cohn 1992):

kusut   'messy'
rahɨt   'wounded'
k-ar-usut   'messy' pl.
r-ar-ahɨt   'wounded' pl.
l-al-əga   'wide' pl.

Describe the position and alternation in the Sundanese plural morpheme.

Latinate English

Examine the following list of latinate vocabulary, making note of the forms of the suffix. Describe the conditions under which each suffix alternant appears.

circular
velar
ideal
vestigeal
annual
vital

alveolar

virginal

solar

polar

angular

areal

regal

ordinal

tabular

scalar

Now consider the two additional forms: *pl*ạ*nar* and *global*.

- How do these complicate your generalization?
- Is there any way to express the generalization precisely enough to make these unexceptional?

Ineseño Chumash and Navajo

Examine the following data from Ineseño Chumash (Poser 1982, Applegate 1972) and Navajo (McDonough 2003, Oberly 2003), two languages that are not related but which nevetheless have a similar phonological process. The underlying morphological structure is provided for you, because the morphology of both languages is often highly opaque. Nevertheless, you should be able to detect a basic alternation that affects various prefixes in each language.

Ineseño Chumash

UR	Surface	Gloss
/s-ixut/	[sixut]	'it burns'
/s-ilakʃ/	[ʃilakʃ]	'it is soft'
/p-iʃ-al-nan'/	[piʃanan']	'don't you two go'
/s-iʃ-tiʃi-yep-us/	[sistisiyepus]	'they two show him'

Navajo

UR	Gloss		Surface	Gloss
jiʃ-ø-tʃʼid	øimp/1st-classifier-'scratch'		jiʃ tʃʼid	'to scratch it'
jiʃ-ø-dʒíːs	øimp/1st-classifier-'pull, tow'		jis dʒíːs	'to drag it'
jiʃ-tʃa	1st-'cry'		ji-ʃ-tʃa	'I cry'

jáʃ-ł-tiʔ	preverb/1st-classifier-'speak'	já-ʃ-tiʔ	'I speak'
ʃ-iz-ø-tał	1st.obj-sperf/3rd-classifier-'act with the feet'	siz tał	'it gave me a kick'
ʃ-ooh-ł-ził	1st.obj-sperf/2nd-classifer-'grab'	soo sił	'you two are grabbing me'
ʃ-dʒ-ł-ɣoʒ/	1st.obj-3rd.subj-classifier-'tickle'	ʃidʒiłhoʒ	's/he is tickling me'
sis-l-jool	sperf.1s-classifier-'lay huddled, cowering'	ʃiʃ-dʒool	'I lie huddled'

Describe the segmental alternation that these data exemplify.

Akan

Examine the following complex forms from Akan (Schachter and Fromkin 1968, Archangeli and Pulleyblank 1994), which all have one of two prefixes, and most of which also have a suffix. Even without a morpheme-by-morpheme gloss, you should be able to conduct a morphophonological analysis of these data.

e-bu-o	'nest'
o-kusi-e	'rat'
e-sĩnĩ	'piece'
o-fiti-i	'he/she pierced it'
o-be-tu-i	'he/she came and dug it'
o-susu-i	'he/she measured it'
e-tene	'it (news) spreads'
ɛ-bʊ-ɔ	'stone'
ɔ-kɔdɪ-ɛ	'eagle'
ɛ-pʊnʊ	'door'
ɔ-tʃɪrɛ-ɪ	'he/she showed it'
ɔ-bɛ-tʊ-ɪ	'he/she came and threw it'
ɔ-fʊrʊ-ɪ	'he/she went up'

a. How many prefix forms appear in these data? Can you group any of these together as likely allomorphs of a common morpheme? Under what conditions does each allomorph appear?
b. How many suffix forms appear in these data? Can you group any of these together as likely allomorphs of a common morpheme?
c. Create rules that account for the prefix and suffix alternations.

Now examine the next subset of data. What do you infer about the vowel [a]?

kasa	'to speak'
ɔ-kasa-ɪ	'he/she spoke'
ɔ-rɪ-kasa	'he/she is speaking'
bɛ-da	'come sleep'
ɔ-fata	'he/she deserves'
ɔ-ba-a	'he/she came'
ɔ-bɛ-ba	'he/she will come'
mɛ-ba	'I will come'

Kirghiz

Examine the following data from Kirgiz (Johnson 1980):

Definite past	Past participle	Verbal noun	Stem
bildi	bilgen	bilyː	'know'
berdi	bergen	beryː	'give'
kyldy	kylgøn	kylyː	'laugh'
kørdy	kørgøn	køryː	'see'
kɪldɨ	kɪlgan	kɪluː	'do, perform'
aldɨ	algan	alguː	'take'
tutu	tutkan	tuttuː	'hold'
boldu	bolgon	boluː	'be, become'

a. Conduct a morphological analysis of these data. What are the forms of the definite past, past participle, and verbal noun suffixes?

b. Propose underlying representations for the definite past and verbal noun suffixes. You should be able to create a single rule that handles all alternation for both forms.

c. Check if your rule also handles the past participle suffix. You should be able to craft it so it handles at least seven of the eight forms. Which form is problematic for your analysis? Can you create a second rule to deal with it?

CHAPTER 5 PHONEMIC ANALYSIS

Learning objectives

- Learn the basics of phonemic analysis
- Understand contrastive and predictable distributions
- Identify scenarios of complementary distribution
- Identify the best fit for a default allophone or underlying form
- Compose rules to derive other allophones from underlying forms

Introduction

In previous chapters we have seen evidence for the phoneme arising in situations of morphological complexity: a segment within a given morpheme changes its form based on its context. We then conclude that a single underlying phoneme has multiple possible output forms.

A relationship between a phoneme and its surface forms can also be seen independently of morphological complexity, just within single morphemes themselves. We can detect such relationships using the technique of **phonemic analysis**, a method in which we examine the contexts in which particular segments occur. The goal of phonemic analysis is to identify the set of contrastive sounds that exist within the lexicon of underlying forms in a language. In so doing, we typically reduce a relatively larger set of surface sounds to a relatively smaller set of underlying sounds.

5.1 The concept of the phoneme

At its core, phonemic analysis involves comparing the distributions of two or more segments in a language and determining whether they are contrastive. We can detect that two sounds are contrastive if they suffice to differentiate two words. Consider the words *mail* and *nail*: in phonetic transcription, we would notate them as [meɪl] and [neɪl]. As such, we see that they share some segments, but differ in their initial consonant: the difference between [m] and

94

[n] is relevant in the language. As a result we infer that [m] and [n] are contrastive in English, and that they represent different phonemes: in other words, they come from different underlying forms.

phonemic analysis: a method of phonological analysis that explores the contextual distribution of segments within a language.

phoneme: a category of sound that is contrastive within a language.

When we discuss phonemes, we represent them in angle brackets, as we would when referring to underlying forms. Thus, /n/ and /m/ are different phonemes.

From the approach of phonemic analysis, the concept of phoneme is defined a little differently from what we have seen so far. When we examine alternation, we characterize the phoneme just as the underlying form for a given segment – but in this domain of phonology, the notion of contrast emerges as an important component of the definition of the phoneme. Thus, the definition here should not be taken as a contradiction of our previous usage; instead, it is an enriched view. Moreover, as we will see, the notion of phoneme within alternation and within phonemic analysis converges upon the concept of an abstract category that may have more than one surface form.

5.2 Minimal pairs

The pair of words *mail* and *nail* exemplify an important analytic tool, one we call the **minimal pair**. A minimal pair is a pair of words that differ at the surface just by a single phoneme, and serves as a convenient shortcut to identify phonemes within languages.

minimal pair: a pair of words differing by a single phoneme.

Minimal pairs may differ in segments in any position, but their remaining segments must be in equivalent positions. For example, words may be minimal pairs if their medial segments differ, as in *seat* [sit] and *set* [sɛt] or nibble [nɪbəl] and nickel [nɪkəl], and if their final segments differ, as in *bat* [bæt] and *bad* [bæd]. On the other hand, *dab* [dæb] and bed [bɛd] are not minimal pairs: while they both contain [b] and [d], and differ only in their vowels, their remaining segments are not in equivalent positions.

Minimal pairs show that the sounds which distinguish them are different phonemes. Thus, the minimal pair *sit* and *set* shows /ɪ/ and /ɛ/ to be different phonemes.

While it should be no surprise that different languages have different minimal pairs, the tool of the minimal pair also helps illustrate differences in the phonemic inventories of languages. In Thai, for example, we can find a minimal triplet (like minimal pair, but with three words all differing by one segment) like that below:

Thai:

[bàa]   'shoulder'
[pàa]   'forest'
[pʰàa]   'to split'

These three words indicate that /b/, /p/, and /pʰ/ (aspirated [p]) are different phonemes. The fact that /p/ and /pʰ/ are different phonemes in Thai but not in English represents a major phonological difference between the languages. While English has words with [pʰ], it has no minimal pairs that are distinct only in having [pʰ] or [p].

Exercise 5.1   Consider the following data from Nepali (Genetti 1994). Are [t], [tʰ], [d] different phonemes? Look for minimal pairs to support your answer.

(1)   badal   'cloud'
(2)   swad   'flavor'
(3)   tal   'pool; lake'
(4)   dam   'money'
(5)   rat   'night'
(6)   tʰal   'plate'
(7)   tarikʰ   'date'
(8)   tʰam   'pillar'
(9)   dal   'lentil'

These three sounds are all different phonemes. The minimal pair [tal] and [dal] shows that /t/ and /d/ are different phonemes; the minimal pair [tʰal] and [tal] shows that /tʰ/ and /t/ are different phonemes.

Exercise 5.2   Now consider these data from Finnish (Carol Genetti p.c.). Are [t] and [d] different phonemes? Look for minimal pairs to support your answer.

(1)   kadot   'failures'
(2)   kate   'cover'
(3)   katot   'roofs'
(4)   kade   'envious'
(5)   kuːsi   'six'
(6)   liːsa   'Lisa'

(7)   madon   'of a worm'
(8)   maton   'of a rug'
(9)   ratas   'wheel'
(10)   radan   'of a track'

Several minimal pairs exist that show [t] and [d] to be different phonemes: for example, [kadot] vs. [katot] and [kate] vs. [kade].

Note that there are other pairs of Finnish words that are not quite minimal pairs, but which are consistent with the notion of /t/ and /d/ being contrastive. In particular, consider [ratas] and [radan]: they are not minimal pairs as they differ in their medial and final consonants, but they still give some support to the idea that /t/ and /d/ are contrastive. Notably, [t] occurs in the environment of [a __ a], as does [d]. These words thus exemplify **near-minimal pairs**: words in which two sounds are in contrastive environments, considering just their immediate phonological context, and irrespective of phonemic differences in farther positions.

Near-minimal pairs can be quite useful in phonemic analysis, because often a contrast exists in a language despite their being no actual minimal pairs to make it obvious. Indeed, the existence of a minimal pair provides definitive support for a phonemic contrast, but the lack of a minimal pair does not immediately force us to conclude that two sounds are not contrastive.

near-minimal pairs: forms that illustrate a phonemic contrast by virtue of containing different segments in equivalent immediate contexts.

5.3 Karo minimal and near-minimal pairs

In the following data from Karo (Gabas 1999), we can observe minimal and near-minimal pairs. Pay particular attention to the obstruents; there are four places of articulation (labial, alveolar, palatal, and velar), and such consonants may be voiceless stops, voiced stops, or fricatives.

(1)   abiˈpːɛ   'his lip'
(2)   cadn   'to pluck'
(3)   ʔit   'small'
(4)   tik   'mosquito'
(5)   aciˈbɛ   'root'
(6)   iˈcɨi   'water'
(7)   ˈjaβa   'rodent species'
(8)   aɣaˈja   'cocoa'
(9)   cãn   'cat'

(10) e'çɛt   'your name'
(11) cadn   'fire'
(12) 'karo   'macaw'
(13) i'tːɨ   'deer'
(14) caʔ'kĩn   'monkey species'
(15) e'cːɛt   'your name'
(16) nəp   'wasp (one species)'
(17) pɛ'wit   'honey, sweet'
(18) ko'kːõ   'hawk'
(19) a'ja   'cocoa'
(20) ná'cək   'hole'
(21) pa'gɔdn   'friend'
(22) maʔ'pɛ   'gourd'
(23) naʔ'tɔ   'tapir'
(24) mo'pːik   'guan (one species)'
(25) oguruʔ'cu   'my saliva'
(26) para'mit   'spider'
(27) tadn   'to beat'
(28) pa'kːɔ   'fish (one species)'
(29) 'jaba   'rodent (one species)'
(30) çadn   'fire'

Exercise 5.3 a. Find minimal pairs that exemplify contrast between [t] and [c].
           b. Find a near minimal pair that exemplifies contrast between [ɣ] and [β].
           c. Find a near minimal pair that exemplifies contrast between [k] and [c].
           d. Find a near minimal pair that exemplifies contrast between [kː] and [g].

           a. The forms [tadn, cadn] and [i'tːɨ, i'cːɨ] are minimal pairs that illustrate contrast between [t] and [c].
           b. The forms [jaba] and [jaβa] are not a minimal pair as they mean the same thing.
           c. The forms ['karo] and [cadn] are a near minimal pair in which [k] and [c] are in parallel immediate contexts; word-initial and followed by [a].
           d. [pa'kːɔ] and [pa'gɔdn] illustrate a near minimal pair that suggests a contrast between [kː] and [g], since both consonants occur in the immediate environment [a__ɔ].

The Karo data provide some additional implications: in particular, we can use it to focus on contrasts between groups of sounds. Certainly place of articulation is contrastive among obstruents; we can determine that [b, d, g] are contrastive with each other, as are [p, t, c, k] and [β, ɣ]. Nevertheless, it is more challenging for us to find contrasts between types of manner. We lack evidence that fricatives and stops are contrastive, because there are no pairs contrasted by [b] and [β], or by [c] and [ç].

We can use this circumstantially to wonder about contrast between [g] and [ɣ]. In this last case, even a near-minimal pair is difficult to find; the closest we get to establishing contrast is with [aɣaˈja] on the one hand against [paˈgɔdn] and [oguruʔˈcu] on the other.

Thus, while the tighter near-minimal pairs show place contrasts because of the exact likeness of the immediate environments (for example, [a__a] or ₍wᴅ₎[__a]), we can make a more general proposal that stops and fricatives can both occur word-initially and between vowels.

Even so, the same cannot be said of the distribution of voiced and voiceless stops in Karo. If we return to the full data set, we see that there are no minimal pairs that are distinguished by voiced versus voiceless stops (except where the voiceless stop is *also long*). In fact, we cannot even find a near-minimal that suggests a contrast between voiced stops and short voiceless stops. Voiced stops only seem to occur between vowels, or after a vowel and before a nasal, while short voiceless stops occur at word edges, or adjacent to a glottal stop.

We infer from this that the two sounds do not ever occur in the equivalent environment, which accounts for the absence of minimal and near-minimal pairs. This scenario is commonly known as **complementary distribution**. If two sounds are in complementary distribution, we conclude they are **allophones** of a common phoneme, and likewise that their surface forms differ as a function of their different environments.

Indeed, while phonemic analysis at times uncovers evidence of contrast, in other instances we instead uncover evidence of allophonic distribution. The remainder of this chapter will focus on identifying and describing scenarios of allophony.

complementary distribution: a scenario in which two sounds never occur in equivalent phonological contexts.

allophones: sounds whose distribution is complementary.

5.4 Allophonic and complementary distribution

Allophonic distribution and complementary distribution refer to the same set of affairs but focus on different aspects of the phenomenon: allophony refers to the sharing of a common phonemic category by two allophones, while complementarity refers more directly to their different contexts.

Moreover, when two sounds are clearly allophonic, we can say their forms are predictable, derived by rule from a common underlying phoneme. For example, in Karo we would choose either voiced or voiceless consonants to be underlying, and then formulate a rule to derive the complementary sound in a specific context.

Exercise 5.4   Choose an underlying form for the voiced/voiceless pairs in Karo, and compose a rule to derive the converse allophone.

The voiceless variants are more appropriate choices as underlying phonemes. To derive the voiced allophones, one would use the following rule:

[stop] → [voiced] / [voiced] ___ [voiced]

As with our analyses of alternants in the previous chapters, our choice of underlying form is closely linked to specificity and predictability. In Karo, the short voiceless stops have a wider, more general distribution: they occur word-initially, word-finally, and next to other voiceless sounds, while the voiced stops occur specifically just in the context of being surrounded by other voiced sounds. The rule thus predictably derives the voiced allophone in this specific context.

Complementary distribution is central to the understanding of allophony in phonemic analysis, so it does not hurt to repeat some crucial concepts here, to ensure that we associate contrast with phonemic status and predictability with allophonic status.

Two sounds are separate phonemes if they occur in equivalent environments. As such, they are contrastive, and they have an overlapping distribution.

Two sounds are allophones of a common phoneme (and are thus not contrastive) if they never occur in equivalent environments. As such they are predictable variants, and they occur in complementary distribution.

The crucial point to remember is that two sounds are contrastive (i.e., different phonemes) even though they occur in overlapping (i.e., the same) environments. Likewise, two sounds are allophones (i.e., from the same phoneme) if they occur in non-overlapping (i.e., different) environments.

5.5 English voiceless stops

Allophony is quite widely observed in the phonology of the world's languages, and English provides another helpful example. Consider voiceless stops in English; at a narrow level of phonetic description, we can actually detect two kinds of English voiceless stops: aspirated stops [pʰ tʰ kʰ] which occur word-initially or at the beginnings of stressed syllables, and unaspirated stops, which occur in any other context. The following data illustrate this distribution; where UK and US pronunciations differ, both are given.

- Aspirated – [pʰ tʰ kʰ]: word-initially OR beginning of stressed syllable

pʰɪn	'pin'
pʰas/pʰæs	'pass'
pʰəθɛtək/pʰəθɛɾək	'pathetic'
əpʰɑːt/əpʰɑɹt	'apart'
səpʰoʊz	'suppose'
ɪmpʰɛː/ɪmpʰɛɹ	'impair'
tʰɒs/tʰɑs	'toss'
tʰoʊn	'tone'
tʰəɹɪfɪk	'terrific'
ətʰoʊn	'atone'
ɹətʰeɪn	'retain'
meɪntʰeɪn	'maintain'
kʰeɪt	'Kate'
kʰɪs	'kiss'
kʰənɛtɪk/kʰənɛɾɪk	'kinetic'
ɹəkʰɔːd/ɹəkʰɔɹd	'record'
əkʰɒst/əkʰɑst	'accost'
kʰəŋkʰɒkt/kʰəŋkʰɑkt	'concoct'

- Unaspirated – [p t k]: elsewhere (after consonants, word-finally, at beginning of unstressed syllables)

spɪn	'spin'
kɹɪspi	'crispy'
sʌpəl	'supple'
nɪp	'nip'
stoʊn	'stone'
deɪtə	'data' (only in non-flapping dialects)
noʊt	'note'
tʰeɪk	'take'
nɪkəl	'nickel'
skeɪt	'skate'

Exercise 5.5 Is the difference between aspirated and unaspirated stops in English contrastive or allophonic?

For each place of articulation, the aspirated and unaspirated forms are in complementary distribution: aspirated forms occur in one set of contexts, while unaspirated forms occur only in the converse set of contexts. We may then conclude that [p] and [pʰ] are allophones of a common phoneme, as are [t] and [tʰ], and as are [k] and [kʰ].

Exercise 5.6 For each pair of allophones, is the underlying phoneme aspirated or unaspirated? Construct a rule that derives the complementary allophone from the underlying phoneme.

In each pair, the unaspirated form has a more general distribution. The aspirated allophone occurs in a very specific set of circumstances: in initial position of a word or stressed syllable. As a result, the following two rules easily predict the occurrence of the aspirated allophones.

[voiceless stop] → [aspirated] / ᴡᴅ[___
[voiceless stop] → [aspirated] / ꜱᴛʀᴇꜱꜱᴇᴅ-ꜱʏʟʟ[___

In fact, we will see in later chapters that these two rules can be collapsed into a single rule that derives aspiration at the beginning of a metrical foot, which unites word-initial positions with the beginnings of stressed syllables.

It is helpful to remember that phenomena like the allophony of aspiration in English are language-specific facts about the language's phonology, and while there may be some phonetic motivation behind them, they are not hard truths that apply in every language. In fact, two sounds may have an allophonic distribution in one language but a contrastive distribution in another, and this is easily shown for aspiration. Recall from §5.2 that Thai has a minimal pair [paa] vs. [pʰaa]; this shows that [p] and [pʰ] are different phonemes, and they are contrastive. Meanwhile, in English, we saw that there are no minimal pairs that differ just by the presence or absence of aspiration, so here, [p] and [pʰ] are allophones, in complementary distribution.

We will now proceed through numerous examples of allophony in other languages, with same basic examples followed by increasingly more complex patterns. Let us begin with a simple inspection of forms from Dolakha Newar.

5.6 Dolakha Newar

Examine the following data from Dolakha Newar (Genetti 2009), paying attention to the distribution of [ɖ] and [r].

(1)	burgi	'I gave birth'
(2)	ɖwaku	'big'
(3)	ʧer	'head'
(4)	ɖonə	's/he stood'

(5)	ḍiɲi	'I slept'
(6)	sərə	'horse'
(7)	ḍeɳu	's/he cut it'
(8)	turi	'millet'
(9)	jor	'pairs'
(10)	nibar	'sun'
(11)	si	'louse'
(12)	hi	'blood'
(13)	kũ	'smoke'
(14)	sā	'cow'
(15)	bo	'plate'
(16)	ʧʰu	'cook'
(17)	kõsa	'bone'
(18)	ṭəṭən	'spoon'
(19)	səkʰi	'dung'
(20)	ṭap	'earrings'
(21)	kaːlat	'wife'
(22)	saːɳat	'friend'
(23)	kok	'crow'
(24)	gwaːrtak	'round'
(25)	tʰaːm	'pillar'
(26)	barkʰun	'pigeon'
(27)	ṭaen	'far'
(28)	baːrpaːŋ	'tomato'
(29)	bujiŋ	'housefly'
(30)	ḍʰor	'jackal'
(31)	ʧʰer	'head'
(32)	kaːpal	'forehead'
(33)	sel	'marrow'
(34)	ʧaːnas	'midnight'
(35)	ḍas	'bedbug'

Exercise 5.7 Identify all segments that are used in surface forms in this language. It may help to divide them up by vowels and consonants.

The consonants here are b, p, t, ṭ, ḍ, r, l, s, ʧ, j, k, g, w, k, m, n, ɳ, ŋ.
The vowels are u, i, a, e, o, ə.

We have identified eighteen consonants and six vowels – there may be others, but this is what we can determine from these limited data. If we dig deeper, some additional generalizations become apparent. While some consonants are

103

too infrequent for us to make any statements about (e.g., [ʧ]) we can see that some of them occur in a wider set of circumstances than others.

Exercise 5.8 Describe in simple terms where you may find each of the following consonants: [b p ɖ t r s n l].

Most of the consonants may occur in either initial or intervocalic position. However, [ɖ] only occurs initially, while [r] occurs in other positions, but never initially.

The set of environments in which [ɖ] occurs is distinct from the set of environments in which [r] occurs: [ɖ] occurs word-initially, and [r] occurs *everywhere except* in word-initial position. In other words, [r] occurs elsewhere. Viewed this way, these two sounds are in a non-overlapping or complementary distribution.

The systematicity of this distribution calls for rules to account for these generalizations, to limit the occurrence of segments in certain positions. Are we to assume there are rules of the type, "Do not have morphemes with initial /r/," and "Do not have morphemes with non-initial /ɖ/"? Such statements represent limitations on lexical entries, but not generalizations about surface form.

When two sounds like this have complementary distribution, we infer (as we did with English aspirated and unaspirated stops) that they are allophones of the same phoneme. In Dolakha Newar, [ɖ] and [r] are two allophones of a common underlying phoneme.

The next step in phonemic analysis is to determine the nature of the underlying phoneme that has [ɖ] and [r] as its surface forms. Here we have several choices: either underlyingly it is /ɖ/, /r/, or some other form, and the choice we make then leads us to formulate a rule to derive the surface distribution patterns. The third choice is unnecessarily complicated (though there are circumstances in which it could make sense; not here). Thus we are to choose between /ɖ/ or /r/ as the underlying phonemes.

Exercise 5.9 State in simple terms the rule you would need to propose if /r/ were the underlying phoneme.
Do the same but suppose /ɖ/ were the underlying phoneme.

If we choose /r/ as the phoneme, we need a rule that changes /r/ to [ɖ] in word-initial position; this rule leaves other instances of /r/ unchanged, yielding [r] elsewhere. If conversely we choose /ɖ/, we need a rule that changes /ɖ/ to [r] between vowels, before consonants, or at the ends of words. We could rephrase this more simply to "after vowels." This rule leaves other instances of /ɖ/ (namely initial ones) unchanged.

Either approach fits the data; nevertheless, in phonemic analysis, usually one of the choices is more appropriate than the other. Note that we only need one rule, as long as we assume there is a single phoneme, and the rule together with the choice of underlying phoneme ensures the desired distribution of the two allophones.

The ultimate consequence of this phonemic analysis is twofold. First, we have reduced the number of phonemes we need to propose for the language, as we have taken the observed surface segments [r] and [ɖ] and assigned them to the same unitary phonemic category. Second, we have also expressed in formal terms a systematic generalization regarding the distribution of these two allophones.

Note the important terminological practice that we refer to both [ɖ] and [r] at the surface as allophones. If we choose one as the phoneme (for example, /r/), it is tempting but inappropriate to think of /r/ as the phoneme and [ɖ] as the only allophone. Instead, we think of /r/ as the phoneme, and [r] and [ɖ] as the allophones.

There is a parallel here with alternation of the type we saw in the previous chapters. In alternation, a given morpheme may contain a phoneme which changes its form in certain circumstances. In allophonic distributions, a given phoneme has multiple surface forms, again dependent on the phonological circumstances, but these conditions are not produced by combining morphemes – instead, they are observed just in the sequence of phonemes within morphemes.

The following data sets provide opportunities to apply phonemic analysis in increasingly more complicated manners. Let us turn next to Persian.

5.7 Persian

Examine the following data from Persian (Carr 1993), paying attention to the distribution of [r], [ɾ], and [ɽ].

(1)	rah	'road'
(2)	bazgiːɽ	'towel'
(3)	ziɾa	'because'
(4)	ran	'paint'
(5)	farsi	'Persian'
(6)	ruz	'day'
(7)	omɽ	'life'
(8)	siɾini	'pastry'
(9)	barg	'leaf'
(10)	biɾan	'pale'

Exercise 5.10 Describe the distribution of [r], [ɾ], and [r̥].

> These three segments have a three-way complementary distribution. The voiceless [r̥] can only occur in final position; the flap [ɾ] can only be intervocalic, while the trill [r] may be initial or pre-consonantal.

Exercise 5.11 Determine which allophone has the most general distribution.

> The trill [r] has the most general distribution, as the contexts in which it occurs are more disparate than the others. We are led to conclude that it is identical to the underlying phoneme.

Exercise 5.12 Propose rules that change /r/ to [ɾ] in some circumstances and [r̥] in others.

> /r/ → [ɾ] / V ___ V
> /r/ → [r̥] / ___]_WD

> That /r/ is the best choice for the phoneme should be clear as we formulate the rules that govern the occurrence of allophones. If we were to choose either of the other two sounds as the underlying representation of the phoneme, we would not be able to construct a single rule that alters the underlying phoneme to produce [r]. We would need one rule to yield [r] in the environment _WD[___, and another to do so in the environment V ___ C. There is no way to combine these environments into a single rule.
>
> These rules change underlying /r/ into [ɾ] between vowels, into [r̥] word-finally, and leave it unchanged otherwise. As such, this rule system characterizes [r, ɾ, r̥] as the three allophones of a single phoneme /r/.

5.8 Ganda liquids

The phonemic analysis we have conducted so far pays much attention to the position of allophones within words: initial and final positions seem relevant, as do positions where an allophone occurs between a vowel and a consonant. In the following discussion of Ganda, the circumstances of allophony need to be described with a finer degree of detail. Examine the following data (from Halle and Clements 1983), paying attention to the occurrence of [l] and [r].

(1)   kola   'do'
(2)   lwana   'fight'
(3)   buulira   'tell'
(4)   lya   'eat'
(5)   luula   'sit'

(6)	omugole	'bride'
(7)	lumonde	'sweet potato'
(8)	eddwaliro	'hospital'
(9)	oluganda	'Ganda language'
(10)	olulimi	'tongue'
(11)	wulira	'hear'
(12)	beera	'help'
(13)	jjukira	'remember'
(14)	eryato	'canoe'
(15)	omuliro	'fire'
(16)	effirimbi	'whistle'
(17)	emmeeri	'ship'
(18)	eraddu	'lightning'
(19)	wawaabira	'accuse'
(20)	lagira	'command'

Exercise 5.13 List the environments in which [r] and [l] occur in Ganda.

[r] occurs intervocalically, in the following specific environments:

i__a

i__o

i__i

e__i

e__a

[l] occurs initially and intervocalically, in the following specific environments:

o__a

u__i

ᵂᴰ[__j

ᵂᴰ[__u

o__e

a__i

o__u

ᵂᴰ[__a

If we think only in general terms of intervocalic position, then it would seem that [r] and [l] are not in complementary distribution in Ganda, since they both can occur between vowels. However, the specific intervocalic contexts are not clearly overlapping.

107

Exercise 5.14 Describe any generalizations you can about the environments of [r] and [l], with attention to whether their distribution can be shown to be complementary.

Each of the intervocalic contexts for [r] has a front vowel before it: either [e] or [i]. None of the contexts for [l] has a preceding [e] or [i]; we thus conclude that they are indeed in complementary distribution: the set of contexts for [r] does not overlap with the set of contexts for [l]. Consequently, they are allophones of the same phoneme.

We may note that similar vowels may occur after either of the two types of consonants: each may be followed by [a] or [i]. From this we can infer that the following environments for [l] and [r] are overlapping; thus the identity of the subsequent vowel has no bearing on whether we see [l] or [r]. However, this does not mean that [l] and [r] are in contrastive distribution; it only means that the following sound is inconsequential to the description of their distribution.

Because the sounds that follow [l] and [r] have no bearing on their distribution, only the preceding vowel is needed to determine which of the two occurs. Thus, we can formalize the environment in which [r] occurs as [front vowels] ___, and [l] occurs elsewhere.

Exercise 5.15 Identify the underlying phoneme for [l] and [r], and compose a rule to account for its allophony.

Of the two sounds, [l] has a more general distribution, since it occurs after three different vowels, and also occurs word initially. The rule that changes /l/ to [r] is provided below:

/l/ → [r] / [front vowel] ___

If we were to formalize a system in which /r/ changes into [l], we would need several rules to establish the allophony. However, if we propose /l/ as the phoneme, a single rule is needed that changes it to [r] after front vowels.

This rule will change underlying /l/ to [r] only after front vowels, and will leave it unchanged otherwise. Thus, the rule characterizes [r] and [l] as two allophones of the phoneme /l/.

5.9 Limbu (Tibeto-Burman; Nepal)

Another allophonic pattern that pays attention to details about the types of adjacent segments is seen in Limbu. Examine the following data (from van Driem 1987, adapted from Carol Genetti p.c.), paying attention to the distribution of the vowels [ɔ] and [ʌ]:

(1)   tʌʔmaʔ   'have sewn'
(2)   sʌkma   'breath'
(3)   keːdzʌŋ   'gale, tempest'
(4)   cʌtmaʔ   'be on time'
(5)   canʌkwa   'cooked red millet'
(6)   nambʱɔr   'sunburn'
(7)   pɔʔeːʔl   'winnowing basket'
(8)   pɔŋmaʔ   'be broken up'
(9)   tʌk   'cooked rice'
(10) sʌrʌŋ   'small sour lemon'
(11) hʌŋ   'hole'
(12) mɔttoː   'opinion'
(13) mɔja   'vulture'
(14) peːdʌk   'frog'
(15) pɔkwa   'basket'
(16) jʌmaʔ   'demolish'

Exercise 5.16   List the environments in which [ɔ] and [ʌ] occur in Limbu.

[ɔ] occurs in the following specific environments:

bʱ__r
p__ʔ
p__ŋ
m__t
m__j
p__k

[ʌ] occurs in the following specific environments:

t__ʔ
s__k
z__ŋ
c__t
n__k
t__k
s__r
r__ŋ
h__ŋ

d__k

j__m

Exercise 5.17 Look for a way to make more general statements to describe the contexts in which [ɔ] and [ʌ] occur. Are they in complementary distribution?

The vowel [ɔ] always occurs following a bilabial consonant, either [p], [m], or [bʱ]. The vowel [ʌ] occurs after any other type of consonant, but never after bilabials. Thus, we conclude that the two vowels are in complementary distribution.

As with the Ganda liquids, if the sounds of our analysis are both followed by an identical type of segment, we do not immediately take this as evidence of overlapping distribution. For example, in Limbu, [ɔ] in [pɔkwa] and [ʌ] in [sʌkma] are both followed by [k], but their distribution is still not overlapping, as they are still differentiated by the preceding sound. We could only call this an overlapping distribution if the two sounds [ɔ] and [ʌ] were found to occur in an identical context, with some identical sound beforehand and some other identical sound afterwards.

Exercise 5.18 Identify the underlying phoneme for [ɔ] and [ʌ], and compose a rule to account for its allophony.

Of these two vowels, [ʌ] has a more general distribution, which makes it a suitable choice for the phoneme. Conversely, [ɔ] has a more specific distribution, which can be easily described in the conditioning environment of the rule, as we see below:

/ʌ/ → [ɔ] / [bilabial] ___

This rule changes underlying /ʌ/ to [ɔ] only after bilabial consonants; the vowel remains unchanged otherwise. As such, the rule characterizes [ʌ] and [ɔ] as two allophones of the phoneme /ʌ/.

5.10 Greenlandic

Another example of a fairly specific conditioning environment is seen in Greenlandic. Examine the following data (from Fortescue 1984), paying particular attention to the distribution of [i] and [e]:

(1)   ivnaq   'bluff'
(2)   ipeʁaq   'harpoon strap'

(3)	imɑq	'sea'
(4)	tuluvɑq	'raven'
(5)	sɑvɑ	'sheep'
(6)	nunɑ	'land'
(7)	nɑnoq	'bear'
(8)	iseʁɑq	'ankle'
(9)	igɑ	'pot'
(10)	seʁmeq	'glacier'
(11)	qɑsɑloq	'bark'
(12)	ikusik	'elbow'
(13)	qilɑluvɑq	'white whale'
(14)	qɑtigɑk	'back'
(15)	sɑkiɑk	'rib'
(16)	ugsik	'cow'
(17)	neʁdloq	'goose'
(18)	mɑʁːɑq	'clay'
(19)	oʁpik	'tree'

Exercise 5.19   Describe the distribution of [i] and [e] in Greenlandic. Begin by listing the specific environments in which each occurs, and then reduce these to more general statements. Are these sounds in complementary distribution?

The vowel [e] occurs in the following contexts:

p__ʁ
s__ʁ
m__q
n__ʁ

The vowel [i] occurs in these contexts:

wᴅ[__v
wᴅ[__p
wᴅ[__m
wᴅ[__s
wᴅ[__g
wᴅ[__k
s__k
k__ɑ
s__k
p__k

Narrowing our view to just the vowel [e], we see that it always is followed by a uvular consonant, either the stop [q] or the fricative [ʁ]. Conversely, no instance of [i] is followed by a uvular consonant; thus, regardless of the preceding sound, the two vowels are in complementary distribution.

Exercise 5.20 Identify the underlying phoneme for [i] and [e].
Compose a rule to account for the allophonic pattern between them.

Since [e] has a more specific distribution, occurring only before uvular sounds, we can deem it to have a predictable occurrence; consequently, the underlying phoneme is better characterized as identical to the other allophone [i]. A rule to account for their allophony is as follows:

/i/ → [e] / __ [uvulars]

5.11 Parallel allophonic patterns

Much of what we have seen has involved a single phoneme with two or more surface allophones.

But if we return to the data in §5.10 and focus instead on [o] and [u], we would note a parallel allophonic pattern: [o] occurs only before uvulars, while [u] occurs anywhere except before uvulars. Like [i] and [e], then, [u] and [o] are in complementary distribution. The parallel is quite extensive: the higher vowel is the one with the wider distribution in both allophonic patterns, leading us to infer a more general rule that lowers high vowels to mid vowels before uvulars.

Indeed, phonemic analysis often leads us to similar conclusions: that multiple phonemes display parallel allophonic distributions. For example, recall the English aspiration data from §5.5, in which each of three voiceless stops has a pair of unaspirated and aspirated allophones, always with the same distributional restrictions: [pʰ, tʰ, kʰ] are each restricted to the initial position of a word or stressed syllable, while [p, t, k] occur in other contexts. We will see a similar example in Kongo below.

5.12 Kongo

Examine the following data from Kongo (Halle and Clements 1983); you should focus on the distribution of alveolar and palatal stops and fricatives.

(1)   tobola   'to bore a hole'
(2)   tʃina   'to cut'

(3)	kesoka	'to be cut'
(4)	knoʃi	'lion'
(5)	zenga	'to cut'
(6)	ʒima	'to stretch'
(7)	kasu	'emaciation'
(8)	ʧiba	'banana'
(9)	nselele	'termite'
(10)	lolonʒi	'to wash'
(11)	zevo	'then'
(12)	aʒimola	'alms'
(13)	nzwetu	'our house'
(14)	kunezulu	'to heaven'
(15)	tanu	'five'

Exercise 5.21 In the data above, describe the distribution of [t, s, z] on one hand, and [ʧ, ʃ, ʒ] on the other.

The first group of sounds, which are all alveolar, occur in the following environments:

[t]	[s]	[z]
ᵂᴰ[__o	e__o	ᵂᴰ[__e
e__u	a__u	n__w
ᵂᴰ[__a	n__e	e__u

The second group of sounds, which are all palatal, occur in the following environments:

[ʧ]	[ʃ]	[ʒ]
ᵂᴰ[__i	o__i	ᵂᴰ[__i
		a__i
		n__i

Exercise 5.22 State whether there seem to be any restrictions on the distribution of any of the sounds [t, s, z, ʧ, ʃ, ʒ].

Note that we have guided this analysis towards treating [t, s, z] as a group of similar sounds, and [ʧ, ʃ, ʒ] as another group of sounds. The alveolar sounds can occur anywhere except before the vowel [i]. The palatal sounds occur only before [i]. Thus, the distribution of the two groups of sounds is complementary.

Within each group, however, we can detect some contrastive or overlapping distribution; we then conclude that [t], [s], and [z] are associated with different phonemes, and [ʧ], [ʃ], and [ʒ] are also associated with different phonemes. So it seems that we have some conflicting evidence – there are clearly numerous phonemes represented within these six segments, but there is also good reason for us to suspect at least some allophonic relationships can be uncovered.

Note that since the two groups are in complementary distribution, each sound in one group is in complementary distribution with each sound of the converse group. Thus, [t] is in complementary distribution with each of [ʧ, ʃ, ʒ]. Consequently, we could argue that [t] and one of the three palatal sounds are allophones of some phoneme, and likewise for [s] and [z].

Exercise 5.23 For each of the alveolar sounds, identify the one palatal sound that it most resembles.

The most challenging link involves [t], which we conclude is most comparable to [ʧ], since they are both voiceless non-fricatives. The voiceless fricatives [s] and [ʃ] are similar, differing only by place of articulation, as is the case for the voiced fricatives [z] and [ʒ]. We can infer that each pair of sounds represents a pair of related allophones; [t] and [ʧ] are allophones of the same phoneme, as are [s] and [ʃ], and as are [z] and [ʒ].

Exercise 5.24 • For each pair of allophones, propose an underlying phoneme, and briefly state why you make this choice.
• Formulate rules that derive the surface variants from the basic phonemes you have proposed.

In every pair of allophones, the alveolar variant is the more suitable phoneme. Each of [t], [s], and [z] has a more general distribution, while [ʧ], [ʃ], and [ʒ] have a very specific distribution, only occurring before [i]. The rules that derive the palatal alternants are provided below:

/t/ → [ʧ] / __ [i]
/s/ → [ʃ] / __ [i]
/ʃ/ → [ʒ] / __ [i]

These rules change underlying alveolar sounds into palatals only before [i]; alveolar sounds that occur in other environments do not meet the structural description of the rule, so they are left unchanged.

These three rules occur in the exact same environment, __ [i], suggesting perhaps that in some sense they are the same rule. We may consider finding a way to collapse these rules into a single process. For the time being, the rule below would accomplish this:

[alveolar] → [palatal] / ___ [i]

This rule would leave every other aspect of the target phoneme intact, so that /s/ and /z/ would stay as fricatives as they change to [ʃ] and [ʒ], and /z/ in particular would retain its voicing. We will see in Chapter 6 that there are some more precise mechanisms by which we can refer to alveolars and palatals.

Note, however, that the change from /t/ to [tʃ] involves more than just a shift in place of articulation, as the output of the process is an affricate. We would need to refine this analysis to account for this, either by claiming that palatal stops in Kongo can only be affricates, or by amending the rule to have this precise effect.

5.13 Central Alaskan Yup'ik

While in Kongo we see that several phonemes respond similarly to the same specific conditioning environment, we can also find examples of allophonic distribution where a conditioning environment is more nuanced than basic word position or adjacency next to any instantiation of a particular segment. This is what we will see in Central Alaskan Yup'ik – take some time to examine the data below (from Jacobson 1984), paying attention to the distribution of plain and aspirated voiceless stops.

(1)	pəluq^h	'ash'
(2)	arnaq^h	'woman'
(3)	aquq^h	'middle finger'
(4)	iika	'my eye'
(5)	aŋut^{h}q^h	'man'
(6)	aŋut^{h}k^h	'two men'
(7)	aŋut^{h}t^h	'three or more men'
(8)	kaːnək^{h}tʃak^h	'something that looks like frost'
(9)	pistəŋuːt^h	'they are servants'
(10)	plaːiinaq^h	'string'
(11)	arnak^h	'two women'
(12)	arnat^h	'three or more women'
(13)	tuqmik^h	'bucket, pail'
(14)	kuik^h	'river'
(15)	p^{h}ki	'concerning travel'

Exercise 5.25   There are four places of articulation for aspirated stops in Yup'ik: bilabial, alveolar, velar, and uvular. Describe their distribution in the above data, first by listing specific environments, and then by providing a general description for each.

- The stops [kʰ] and [qʰ] can occur word finally, either after vowels or other consonants. [kʰ] also occurs after a vowel and before the affricate [tʃ].
- The stop [tʰ] occurs word finally and before other stop consonants.
- The stop [pʰ] occurs before [k].
- There is one instance of [q] occurring after a vowel and before [m]; all other instances of the plain stops [p t k q] occur before vowels.

Exercise 5.26   State whether there is evidence of complementary distribution in these data.

As with the alveolar/palatal allophony in Kongo, this analysis lends itself to splitting the sounds in question into two main groups: aspirated stops and plain stops. These two groups of sounds occur in different, non-overlapping environments: plain stops are always followed by vowels or nasals, while aspirated stops precede other stops, affricates, or are word final. Thus, their distribution is complementary, and we can say that each sound in one group is an allophone, related to an allophone from the complementary group. In other words, [p] and [pʰ] are allophones of the same phoneme, as are [t] and [tʰ], [k] and [kʰ], and [q] and [qʰ].

Exercise 5.27   Determine the underlying phonemes for the plain and aspirated stops in Yup'ik.
Formulate a general rule that accounts for their allophony.

If we assume that each pair of allophones is subject to the same set of restrictions on their distribution, we infer that that plain stops have a more restricted distribution, occurring only before vowels and nasals. Aspirated stops occur elsewhere. We may then conclude that the aspirated stops are identical to the underlying phonemes, and that the plain stops can be derived by rule in a specific set of environments.

Preliminarily we may propose two rules to effect this: one that applies before vowels, and one that applies before nasal consonants.

[aspirated stop] → [plain stop] / ___ [vowel]
[aspirated stop] → [plain stop] / ___ [nasal]

Since the two rules apply the same change to the same group of target sounds, we have reason to seek a way to collapse them into a single rule. This would be possible if we could somehow express the conditioning environment in more succinct terms. One option is to rephrase it as a process that applies simply before voiced sounds; this does limit the process of deaspiration to the appropriate contexts, and makes the additional prediction that there may be other sounds before which aspirated stops lose their aspiration. For example, it suggests that the same process may occur before voiced stops or fricatives – nevertheless, the data in this section suggest there are no voiced stops or fricatives in Yup'ik anyway, so the question may be moot.

It may also be that we would still want to analyze the process as occurring only before nasals and vowels, leaving out other types of voiced segments. We will see in the next chapter that we can rely on the notion of a *natural class* to do so, using the category of **sonorants** (see Chapter 2). Vowels, liquids, and nasals are sonorant, while stops and fricatives are not. If we follow this route, we could collapse the two rules as follows:

[aspirated stops] → [plain stops] / ___ [sonorants]

This single rule applies to aspirated stops at any place of articulation, and renders them as plain stops only if the following sound is a vowel or nasal consonant. Aspirated stops in other environments are left unchanged.

Summary

In this chapter we have analyzed languages to identify their phonemic inventories, the sets of sounds they employ to provide contrast in form between words. Minimal and near-minimal pairs are convenient tools for us to discover contrastive oppositions. Conversely, we have also seen that single phonemes sometimes have multiple allophones, contextually determined variants whose form is predictable from the phonological environment.

There are some parallels to be drawn between the patterns of alternation we saw in previous chapters and the patterns of allophony we have seen here: many allophonic restrictions have analogues in alternation patterns. For example, the Kongo data in §5.12 illustrate allophony of underlying alveolars, but the rules we derived are reminiscent of the process of palatalization we have seen in Japanese (§2.17) and Dakota (§2.18). Similarly, the intervocalic voicing in Karo in §5.3 resembles an alternation seen in English (§§2.13–14), and the Persian final devoicing in §5.7 resembles an alternation seen in German (§2.15).

Moreover, we have seen in this and previous chapters that alternations and allophonic restrictions often apply analogously to multiple phonemes that share some common properties. For example, the allophony of aspiration in English applies to all voiceless plosives; palatalization in Kongo and Japanese applies to all alveolars; devoicing in German applies to all obstruents. Likewise, the conditioning environment may sometimes comprise a group of similar sounds: deaspiration in Yup'ik applies before any sonorant; Ganda rhotics must occur after non-low front vowels; Greenlandic high vowels are lowered before any uvular.

The fact that phonological rules may apply to groups of sounds, and that their environments may also invoke groups of sounds, motivates a deeper discussion of the ways in which sounds pattern together in phonology, and the ways for us to express this in our generalizations and rule notations. The next chapter tackles this question by pursuing the notion of binary features as a way of identifying groups of sounds in the phonological systems of languages.

Key terms

phonemic analysis
phoneme
allophone
allophony
contrastive distribution
complementary distribution
minimal pair
near-minimal pair
aspiration
environment
underlying form

References and further reading

Carr, Phillip. 1993. *Phonology*. London: Macmillan.

Fortescue, Michael. 1984. *West Greenlandic*. Croom Helm Descriptive Grammars. London: Croom Helm.

Fromkin, Victoria, Robert Rodman, and Nina Hyams. 2014. *An Introduction to Language*, 10th edition. Boston: Wadsworth.

Gabas, Nilson, Jr. 1999. *A grammar of Karo, Tupı (Brazil)*. Doctoral dissertation, University of California, Santa Barbara.

Genetti, Carol. 1994. Introduction (with a sketch of Nepali grammar). *Santa Barbara Papers in Linguistics*, vol 6: *Aspects of Nepali Grammar*. Santa Barbara CA: Department of Linguistics, UCSB, 1–41.

Genetti, Carol. 2009. *A Grammar of Dolakha Newar*. Berlin: De Gruyter Mouton.

Gordon, Matthew. 2014. Phonology: organization of speech sounds. In Carol
    Genetti (ed.), *How Languages Work*. Cambridge University Press, 49–70.
Halle, Morris, and George N. Clements. 1983. *Problem Book in Phonology*.
    Cambridge, MA: MIT Press.
Hayes, Bruce. 2009. *Introductory Phonology*. Cambridge, MA: Blackwell.
Jacobson, Steven A. 1984. *Yup'ik Eskimo Dictionary*. Fairbanks, Alaska: Alaska
    Native Language Center.
Odden, David. 2005. *Introducing Phonology*. Cambridge University Press.
van Driem, George. 1987. *A Grammar of Limbu*. Berlin: Mouton.

Review exercises

Estonian

Examine the following data from Estonian (Gordon 2014). Note that there
are three degrees of length indicated here: long consonants are marked as
[tː], while double-long consonants are marked as [tːː].

talːː	'lamb'
lina	'flax'
talːa	'of the sole'
kanːː	'jug'
linːa	'of the town'
pakːi	'of the package'
panʲːː	'bread'
vilːː	'wool'
pala	'piece'
vilʲː	'blister'
talʲi	'winter'
linːːa	'into the town'
laːːtʲ	'nature'
halːː	'frost'
talʲːi	'stable'
palʲːː	'ball'
saːːt	'you get'
paki	'gust'
pakːːi	'into the package'

Examine the distribution of the various lengths of [t], [k], [a], [l], [n], [lʲ],
and [nʲ].

a. Is the difference between short and long segments contrastive? Cite minimal or near-minimal pairs for as many phonemes as you can identify.

b. Is the difference between long and double-long segments contrastive? Cite minimal or near-minimal pairs for as many phonemes as you can identify.

Roviana (Austronesian, Solomon Islands)

igana	'fish'
doŋo	'look'
reɲe	'fast'
onomo	'six'
mila	'betel chewing'
eɲa	'turn'
meke	'and'
motu	'earth oven'
ene	'walk'
ŋuzu	'mouth'
munu	'morning'
lima	'five'
toloŋavulu	'thirteen'
vesuŋavulu	'eighty'
ziŋara	'red'
tama	'father'
gina	'maybe'
mari	'very'
ɲira	'strong'
ginani	'thing'
boɲi	'night'
taɲin	'hold'
noma	'big'
liketoŋa	'none'
nuquru	'enter'
ŋohoro	'coconut'
ɲeta	'three'
mamaleɲi	'voice'
siaŋavulu	'ninety'

Examine the distribution of [m], [n], [ɲ], [ŋ].

a. Describe the environments in which each nasal consonant occurs.

b. Which pairs of consonants are phonemically contrastive?

c. Are there any pairs of consonants in complementary distribution? If so, describe the environment in which each occurs.

Karo

Re-examine the data from §5.3.

a. Describe the environments for short voiceless stops, long voiceless stops, and voiced stops.

b. Are there any long voiced stops?

c. Is the difference between voiced and short voiceless stops allophonic or phonemic?

d. Is the difference between long and short voiceless stops allophonic or phonemic?

e. What are the underlying contrasts for the stop consonants of Karo? In what contexts are these contrasts available?

Akan

Take a moment to look back to the Akan review exercise from the end of Chapter 4. Now examine the following additional data from Akan, paying attention to the distribution of [a] and [ə]. In what contexts can each vowel occur? Describe in words why we can infer that they are allophones of the same phoneme, and construct a rule that accounts for their distribution.

baɲtʃɪ	'cassava'
a-kʊkɔ	'fowl'
a-pʊntʃɪrɛnɪ-ɪ	'frog'
dʒʷarɪ	'to bathe'
jarɪ	'to be ill'
wa-tʊ	'he/she has thrown it'
ma-çʷɛ	'I have looked at it'
a-mɪna	'hole'
a-bɛrɛwa	'old woman'
pɪra	'to sweep'
wʊwa	'bee'
sika	'money'

kosua	'egg'
m-moʤa	'blood'
bisa	'to ask'
o-kura	'he/she is holding'
pətiri	'to slip'
ŋʷəsĩ	'to sneeze'
kəri	'to weigh'
wə-tu	'he has dug it'
ə-furuma	'navel'
nəɲçʷi-e	'cow'
jəfunu	'belly'
kaŋkəbi	'millipede'
bə-ji-e	'witchcraft'

CHAPTER 6 NATURAL CLASSES AND DISTINCTIVE FEATURES

Learning objectives

- Identify groups of sounds that behave similarly (as natural classes)
- Understand major class and place features
- Express groups of sounds using binary distinctive features
- Compose rules that operate on features rather than segments

Introduction

In this chapter we will explore a system of classifying segments into groups, so that we can express phonological processes as generalizations that affect classes of sounds rather than individual segments. We will thus pursue the notion of using **distinctive features** to describe segments as **natural classes**. Basically, we will argue that wherever two or more segments behave similarly (i.e., they either trigger or undergo the same phonological process), we have evidence that they share some distinct specification of features.

This chapter is designed so that different features emerge from the data that are presented. The philosophy is that features are always motivated or justified by the patterns: if two segments behave similarly, then they share some kind of feature specification, and if they behave differently, there is something in their feature make-up that distinguishes them. Nevertheless, students often find it helpful to be able to resort to a reference chart if they need to find a way to formalize the differences or similarities among segments that are relevant in an analysis. For this reason, there is a reference chart at the end of the chapter that summarizes features for all symbols of the IPA. This should be used sparingly: do not include too many features in any rules that require specification; use only enough to identify a particular set of sounds as a group within some language.

6.1 Processes and groups of sounds

In many of the problem sets we have seen so far, we have observed that a particular process seems to occur in or because of more than one type of segment. For example, in §2.1, we saw that the English plural suffix is [-əz] after sibilants and [-s] after all other voiceless segments; likewise, in Kongo §5.12), we saw that all alveolar obstruents are subject to the same allophonic restrictions.

When we encounter such patterns, it is intuitive to think that the same process is affecting more than one phoneme, but the formal notation we have adopted so far does not express this. Instead, we have allowed either (a) multiple rules to exist, in a sense, side-by-side, or (b) a single rule to be able to conjure up multiple phonemes, but in a heavy-handed manner. As we explore more phonological patterns, we begin to see that these approaches are not appropriate, in that they introduce or assume mechanisms that transcend what is typical of the phonological systems of languages. In this chapter, we will encounter ways of expressing phonemes formally as groups that we call **natural classes**. We will identify and express natural classes using specific combinations of **distinctive features**.

natural class: a group of sounds within a language that trigger and/or undergo the same phonological process, providing evidence that they ought to be represented with a unique combination of features.

distinctive features: components of phonemes that help distinguish them from each other; phonemes that act similarly can be said to share one or more features.

6.2 Luganda

For example, consider again the process of place assimilation in the indefinite prefix in Luganda, from Chapter 2.

(1)	ẽnato	'a canoe'
(2)	ẽnapo	'a house'
(3)	ẽmpipi	'a kidney'
(4)	ẽŋkoosa	'a feather'
(5)	ẽmmããmmo	'a peg'
(6)	ẽŋŋõõmme	'a horn'
(7)	ẽnnĩmiro	'a garden'
(8)	ẽnugẽni	'a stranger'
(9)	akaato	'little canoe'
(10)	akaapo	'little house'
(11)	akapipi	'little kidney'
(12)	akakoosa	'little feather'
(13)	akabããmmo	'little peg'

(14)   akagōōmme   'little horn'
(15)   akadīmiro   'little garden'
(16)   akatabi   'little branch'

We had drawn the conclusion that the prefix underlyingly is /en/, and the nasal consonant adapts its place of assimilation to the consonant that begins the root. This implies then that /n/ becomes /m/ before bilabials and /ŋ/ before velars. As we restate this in more formal terms, we arrived at a pair of rules, as in (a) below.

a.   /n/ → [m] / __ [bilabial]
     /n/ → [ŋ] / __ [velar]

Indeed, these rules already assume a feature: rather than have /n/ become [m] before [b] or [p], we have expressed the process as one that occurs before **bilabials**. This entails that [b] and [p] are a natural class of sounds that have the same effect on a preceding /n/.

If you want to imagine what phonology would be like without reference to any such features, we would actually need to expand the number of rules in (a) to four. For example, without features, rule (a) would have to be split into a rule that creates [m] before [b], and another that creates [m] before [b], and likewise the rule that creates [ŋ] would need to be expressed as two separate processes.

b.   /n/ → [m] / __ [p]
     /n/ → [m] / __ [b]
     /n/ → [ŋ] / __ [k]
     /n/ → [ŋ] / __ [g]

The rule that nasalizes [b], [d], and [g] after nasal consonants would similarly need to be exploded. Clearly this creates an unwieldy, rule-heavy system. More pressing is the fact that there are generalizations missing from this system: there are four different rules that all apply to /n/, and it is a coincidence that they happen to produce a pattern of nasal assimilation. If phonological systems allowed this proliferation of rules to occur in human languages, this approach would fail to account for why other combinations of targets and triggers to do not occur. For example, a language with the following set of rules is possible according to this approach:

c.   /n/ → [m] / __ [k]
     /n/ → [m] / __ [b]
     /n/ → [ŋ] / __ [p]
     /n/ → [ŋ] / __ [g]

In prose terms, this system changes /n/ to [m] before either [k] or [b], but /n/ to [ŋ] before either [p] or [g]. Quite frankly, no known language has any phonological process which applies to its /n/ like this. If we would want our system of rule formation to reflect what is humanly learnable, then the expression of rules just as objects that apply to individual segments (as inputs, outputs, and triggers) is inappropriate.

Moreover, any attempt at collapsing the rules into some kind of disjunctive notation will not address this shortcoming. For example, we could combine (b) into something like the following:

d. /n/ → [m] / __ {p, b}

In this case, an apparently single rule applies before either [p] or [b]. But the same counterargument applies here – there is nothing preventing a rule such as the following from occurring:

e. /n/ → [m] __ {k, b}

Thus, we should dispose with such an overwrought rule approach for two reasons: first, it does not capture the generalizations of natural classes (which makes it too weak in terms of its explanatory worth); second, it suggests that odd, unlikely processes are equivalently learnable (which makes it too strong in terms of its predictiveness and typological fit).

The alternative is to adopt a system of specification and description that allows us to refer to [p] and [b] as a natural class. Our usage of the feature bilabial did exactly this: now, instead of a rule applying to /n/ before a coincidentally similar pair of consonants, the rule applies to a class of sounds: exactly those that are specified as bilabial. The same approach allows us to craft a rule to handle the velar alternant:

a. /n/ → [m] / __ [bilabial]
    /n/ → [ŋ] / __ [velar]

This approach is descriptively powerful enough to capture the fact that [p] and [b] behave similarly as triggers – they do the same thing to a preceding /n/. Meanwhile, it is not too powerful in a predictive sense, in that as long as we adhere to a sensible system of features, we are prevented from allowing (for example) a system in which [p] and [g] act as a group on the one hand, and [k] and [b] act as a group on the other.

We will see later in this chapter that we can also combine the velarizing and labializing rules into a single process of place assimilation.

In addition, we can extend this approach to the process by which root-initial voiced consonants become nasalized following the /en/ prefix. In this part of the system, [b] [d] and [g] become [m], [n], and [ŋ] respectively.

Without features, we would have to propose a separate rule for each; with features, however, we can create a single rule that applies to all sounds in the language that are both **voiced** and **stops.**

[voiced, stop] → [nasal] / [nasal] ___

The feature combination of [voiced, stop] identifies the specific natural class of voiced stops. Note crucially that this description of the target is a **conjunction**, not a disjunction: it specifies sounds that have both features, rather than applying to any sound that is either voiced or a stop.

6.3 Binary features

It is standard convention in phonology to employ **binary features**, each of which allows a positive or negative specification. Thus, rather than say that some segments are [**voiced**], we instead call them [**+voiced**]. Conversely, voiceless sounds are [**–voiced**] – they have the opposite specification for the same feature. This reduces the number of features we need in our theory; instead of having both [**voiced**] and [**voiceless**], we have one feature, [**±voiced**]. This also provides an inherent account for why sounds cannot have conflicting features like [voiced] and [voiceless] at the same time: since there is only one feature that can be specified in one way, there is never even the risk that a self-contradictory specification could be learnable.

binary feature: a phonological feature for which phonemes may be specified positively or negatively.

The number of features proposed by phonologists is quite large, spanning manners and places of articulation along with laryngeal features for consonants, and tongue and lip configuration for vowels. Such lists of features are usually assembled with cross-linguistic completeness in mind – in other words, in order to find ways of specifying the differences between all possible segments, a similarly large number of features is required. In practice, however, the number of features we need to draw upon to describe a given language's processes is smaller, as any given language uses only a small subset of the sounds that are available in human language.

In the remainder of this chapter, we will allow the patterns to dictate what features are necessary. Our basic approach will be to observe a pattern, note whether groups of segments behave similarly, and wherever they do, we will look for a way to describe exactly those sounds, to the exclusion of other segments in the same language.

6.4 English plurals

The pattern of English plural formation that we examined in Chapter 2 serves as another example of how to group sounds into classes. Recall the generalization:

/z/ becomes   [s]   after   [k, t, p, f, θ]

                [əz]   after   [z, s, ʧ, ʤ, ʃ, ʒ]

                [z]   after   [v, b, m, ð, l, r, n, ŋ]

By now it should be clear that having a separate rule for each contextual phoneme would be highly unwieldy, and would also fail to capture the generalizations that occur within the data. As to these generalizations, note that each of the first two groups can be described quite succinctly: the first comprises all the voiceless obstruents of the language (with the exception of those voiceless sounds that occur in the second group). The second group, meanwhile, consists of sounds which are fricatives or affricates occurring somewhere behind the teeth but ahead of the velum. Phoneticians refer to such sounds as **sibilants**: as fricatives or affricates, they have a fricated release and produce a relatively louder turbulent noise compared to fricatives produced at labial, interdental, or velar locations. Thus we may refer to this second group quite simply as the sibilants. The third group is quite disparate in comparison – it has voiced fricatives, stops, and sonorants, as well as vowels.

To have a more efficient account that chooses which of the plural allomorphs to use on any given noun, we can appeal to these general descriptions. As there are three allomorphs, it will make sense for us to have more than one rule of plural formation.

The first rule will apply to the most specific subset of conditioning phonemes, the sibilants.

plural → [əz] / [+sibilant] _____

The second rule will apply to another specific subset of sounds, voiceless obstruents. We may refer to these sounds just as [−voiced] sounds, as only obstruents may be [-voiced] in English.

plural → [s] / [−voiced] _____

These rules may be said to apply disjunctively: if one version applies, the other does not.

As they are stated, either rule could apply in an environment after a voiceless sibilant such as [s]. We address this by ordering the rules with respect to one another: we apply one rule, and if it has an effect, we do not apply the second rule. If the first rule does not have an effect, we apply the second rule.

Exercise 6.1   Which rule needs to apply first?

The sibilant rule applies first. With the opposite ordering, [s] would be added to words ending with voiceless sibilants.

We do not actually need a third rule: if we assume that /z/ is the underlying representation of the morpheme, then the suffix stays unchanged as [z] wherever neither rule applies. Thus, if the root-final segment is neither sibilant (in which case, the [əz] alternant does not arise) nor voiceless (in which case, the [s] alternant does not arise), then in the remaining cases, the [z] alternant arises.

6.5 Yup'ik

Sometimes classes of sounds are relatively obvious, like "voiceless consonants" or "sibilants." In other cases, a larger set of sounds seems to transcend the phonetic categories that we are familiar with. We already saw something like this with Central Alaskan Yup'ik in §5.13, where plosives have two allophones; stops are unaspirated before vowels and nasal consonants, and aspirated elsewhere. The data are repeated below:

(1)	pəluq^h	'ash'
(2)	arnaq^h	'woman'
(3)	aquq^h	'middle finger'
(4)	iika	'my eye'
(5)	aŋut^{h}q^h	'man'
(6)	aŋut^{h}k^h	'two men'
(7)	aŋut^{h}t^h	'three or more men'
(8)	kaːnək^{h}ʧak^h	'something that looks like frost'
(9)	pistəŋuːt^h	'they are servants'
(10)	plaːiinaq^h	'string'
(11)	arnak^h	'two women'
(12)	arnat^h	'three or more women'
(13)	tuqmik^h	'bucket, pail'
(14)	kuik^h	'river'
(15)	p^{h}ki	'concerning travel'

In Chapter 5 we called upon two rules two account for this allophony:

[aspirated stop] → [plain stop] / ___ [vowel]
[aspirated stop] → [plain stop] / ___ [nasal]

Since the two rules have the same effect, we should consider that in fact they operationalize the same procedure. The implication is that vowels and nasal consonants somehow form a group of sounds, simply because they have similar effects on preceding plosives. We can capture this in the rules by rewriting them as a single statement whose environment specifies all segments that are vowels or nasals. We do so not by formalizing this disjunction, but simply by specifying the features that these two subgroups of sounds have, to the exclusion of others.

In this case, we can rely on the phonological feature [±sonorant] to do this work: vowels, nasals, liquids, and glides are all [+sonorant], while fricatives, affricates, and stops are [–sonorant]. The new rule can be expressed as follows:

[aspirated stop] → [plain stop] / ___ [+sonorant]

We prefer this approach because it captures the fact that vowels and nasal consonants behave similarly. The alternative of formalizing a disjunction is not different from relying on two separate rules, and it introduces the idea of a single process applying in a very disparate set of environments (say, before vowels or before voiceless fricatives, but not before other types of sounds).

6.6 Cambodian

Now let's examine the following data from Cambodian (Halle and Clements 1983), paying particular attention to the initial consonant sequences of each word. Note that in every case, there is either (a) a basic sequence of two consonants, (b) a sequence in which the initial consonant is aspirated, or (c) a sequence in which the first two consonants are separated by an excrescent [ə].

(1)	praə	'to use'
(2)	phək	'to drink'
(3)	thaa	'to say'
(4)	chaa	'to fry'
(5)	ksac	'sand'
(6)	psaa	'market'
(7)	trəj	'fish'
(8)	craən	'much, many'
(9)	kraw	'outside'
(10)	khae	'month, moon'
(11)	spɨj	'cabbage'
(12)	skŏəl	'acquainted with'
(13)	snaa	'crossbow'
(14)	sɲiəm	'quiet'
(15)	slap	'to die'
(16)	stiŋ	'river'

(17)	smaw	'grass'
(18)	sɲaeŋ	'to fear'
(19)	srəj	'woman'
(20)	pʰtĕəh	'house'
(21)	pʰkaa	'flower'
(22)	pʰɲaə	'to send'
(23)	tʰpŏəl	'cheek'
(24)	tʰməj	'new'
(25)	tʰŋaj	'day sun'
(26)	cʰpuŋ	'to inhale'
(27)	cʰmaa	'cat'
(28)	cʰɲaaj	'distant'
(29)	kʰtĕəh	'skillet'
(30)	kʰmae	'Khmer'
(31)	kʰɲom	'I, my, me'
(32)	pʰcŏəp	'to attach'
(33)	pʰnum	'mountain'
(34)	pʰŋuut	'to bathe'
(35)	tʰkaəŋ	'illustrious'
(36)	tʰnam	'herb'
(37)	cʰkae	'dog'
(38)	cʰnaŋ	'kettle'
(39)	kʰcəj	'to borrow'
(40)	kʰnoŋ	'in, inside'
(41)	məcul	'needle'
(42)	məriəm	'finger, toe'
(43)	məhoup	'food'
(44)	ləɲiəc	'afternoon'
(45)	lʰhoŋ	'papaya'
(46)	lʰmɔɔm	'sufficient'
(47)	məteeh	'a pepper'
(48)	məʔɑɑp	'an herb'
(49)	mənŏəh	'pineapple'
(50)	məlup	'shade'
(51)	məsaw	'flour'

Exercise 6.2 For this analysis, assume that neither the aspiration or the excrescent [ə] is part of the underlying form.

    a.   Under what conditions do aspiration and schwa-insertion appear?

    b.   Provide a generalization that describes the consonants which instigate each process.

c. Provide a generalization that describes the scenario in which neither process applies.

Aspiration occurs where the initial consonant is a voiceless stop and the second consonant is either a stop or a nasal.

Insertion of [ə] occurs where the initial consonant is a nasal or lateral.

These two generalizations suggest that in some circumstances, stops and nasals behave similarly, while in others, nasals and laterals behave similarly. Where different sounds behave similarly, they ought to be identifiable in a formal sense as a natural class of sounds. To unify stops and nasals on the one hand in opposition to everything else, phonologists use the feature [±continuant]: stops and nasals are [−cont], while fricatives, liquids and glides are [+cont]. To unify nasals with liquids, to the exclusion of stops and fricatives, we can again appeal to the feature [±sonorant]: nasals and liquids are [+son], while stops and fricatives are [−son].

In formal terms, this allows our derivational formalism to refer to classes of sounds in simple, general terms. With these types of features, we can identify stops and nasals as exactly that group of sounds that is [+cons, −cont], and we can identify nasals and liquids as exactly those sounds that are [+cons, +son]. In other words, we have recast the basic terminology of *stop, fricative, nasal, lateral* and so on as combinations of primitive binary features.

Exercise 6.3 Using features like [±cont] and [±son], create rules that produce aspiration and schwa insertion in the appropriate environments in Cambodian.

[−cont, −voi] → [aspirated] / $_{WD}$[___ [−cont]
Ø → [ə] / $_{WD}$[[+son, +cons] ___ [+cons]

The first rule specifically picks out voiceless stops as the target, and aspirates them before [−cont] sounds, which can only be stops or nasal consonants.

The second rule inserts [ə] between two word-initial consonants, as long as the first is sonorant (nasal or liquid). It is important to include the specification [+cons] for the preceding consonant, to preclude vowels from fitting the structural description.

If we did not admit [−cont] as a feature, and instead adhered to terms like *stop* and *nasal*, our rules would be much more disjoint. For example, the aspiration rule would essentially say, in a formal sense, "aspirate a stop before a nasal OR stop consonant," or we would need two separate rules, and the fact that they produce the same result (aspiration) would actually be an accident in the account. Without these binary features like [−cont] (but with these disjunctive practices that serve in their stead), the formal system could just as easily group highly dissimilar sounds together, for example by aspirating only before stops or glides, but not liquids, fricatives, or nasals. The binary feature system, in contrast, does not have any mechanism to refer to stops and glides as a group to the exclusion of other consonants, nor does it need to, as such sounds typically do not behave similarly in the phonological systems of languages.

6.7 Catalan

The next data set, showing alternating forms of Catalan adjectives, allows us to explore this use of binary features further, but with the added challenge in the identification of underlying representation for some forms. As this discussion is focused more on the features and natural classes, let us move quickly through the initial morphological analysis.

First, we can assume that the Catalan feminine suffix is /-ə/, and that masculine forms in these data are unsuffixed. We will then divide the data into several groups, differentiated by their alternation pattern. The first group consists of roots that do not alternate according to the presence or absence of a suffix, for example, the pairs [baʃ, baʃə], [tot, totə], and [pɔk, pɔke]. The underlying forms are uncontroversial for this group: we can consider them equivalent to the unsuffixed forms. (Data in §§ 6.8–6.10 are from Bermúdez-Otero 2001.)

6.8 Non-alternating Catalan adjectives

	Masc sing.	*Fem sing.*	*Gloss*
(1)	əkel^j	əkel^jə	'that'
(2)	siβil	siβilə	'civil'
(3)	ʃop	ʃopə	'drenched'
(4)	əspɛs	əspɛsə	'thick'
(5)	baʃ	baʃə	'short'
(6)	tot	totə	'all'
(7)	pɔk	pɔkə	'little'
(8)	mal	malə	'bad'
(9)	əskerp	əskerpə	'shy'
(10)	sɛk	sɛkə	'dry'
(11)	gros	grosə	'large'
(12)	koʃ	koʃə	'lame'
(13)	brut	brutə	'dirty'

133

(14)	nu	nuə	'nude'
(15)	əgzaktə	əgzaktə	'exact'
(16)	suβlim	suβlimə	'sublime'
(17)	kru	kruə	'raw'

A second group has roots whose final consonants change as a function of affixation: [kəzat, kəzaðə], [orp, orβə], [frənses, frənsezə], [sek, seɣə], [rotʃ, roʒə].

6.9 Catalan adjectives with manner/voicing alternations

(1)	frənses	frənsezə	'French'
(2)	kəzat	kəzaðə	'married'
(3)	rɔtʃ	rɔʒə	'red'
(4)	orp	orβə	'blind'
(5)	sek	seɣə	'blind'
(6)	grok	groɣə	'yellow'
(7)	kandit	kandiðə	'candid'
(8)	prəsis	prəsizə	'precise'
(9)	gris	grizə	'grey'
(10)	bwit	bwiðə	'empty'
(11)	botʃ	boʒə	'crazy'
(12)	lʲark	lʲarɣə	'long'
(13)	fəʃuk	fəʃuɣə	'heavy'
(14)	puruk	puruɣə	'fearful'
(15)	frɛt	frɛðə	'cold'

The remaining forms have a segment missing in one form or the other. For example, the pairs [bo, bonə], [səɣu, səɣurə], [fɔr, fɔrtə], [bɛr, bɛrðə], [al, altə], and [dulen, dulente] all have a segment in the feminine that is missing from the masculine.

6.10 Catalan adjectives with segment/zero alternations

(1)	dropu	dropə	'lazy'
(2)	flɔɲdʒu	flɔɲdʒə	'soft'
(3)	səɣu	səɣurə	'sure'
(4)	səɣəðo	səɣəðorə	'reaper'
(5)	sa	sanə	'healthy'
(6)	bo	bonə	'good'
(7)	du	durə	'hard'

(8)	kla	klarə	'clear'
(9)	əlβi	əlβinə	'albino'
(10)	pla	planə	'level'
(11)	sərɛ	sərɛnə	'calm'
(12)	al	altə	'tall'
(13)	fɔr	fɔrtə	'strong'
(14)	sor	sorðə	'deaf'
(15)	san	santə	'saint'
(16)	prufun	prufundə	'deep'
(17)	dəsen	dəsentə	'decent'
(18)	əstuðian	əstuðiantə	'student'
(19)	kur	kurtə	'short'
(20)	bɛr	bɛrðə	'green'
(21)	kəlɛn	kəlɛntə	'hot'
(22)	fəkun	fəkundə	'fertile'
(23)	dulen	dulentə	'bad'
(24)	blaŋ	blaŋkə	'white'

Exercise 6.4 Identify the underlying forms of the Catalan roots in §6.9.

The roots in §6.9 end underlyingly in voiced consonants (as seen in their feminine forms) but have the manner features of the final consonants of their masculine forms. For example, the root for [orp ~ orβə] 'blind' is /orb/, with a final voiced stop, whose voicing is retained in the feminine [orβə] and whose stop is maintained in the masculine [orp].

The voicing alternation is still evident if the root-final consonant is always a fricative. It is voiceless in the masculine, but it is voiced in the feminine, for example [gris ~ grizə]. Since there are some words in §6.8 that have voiceless consonants in both their masculine and feminine forms, as in [gros ~ grosə], we cannot infer that root-final voiceless consonants become voiced intervocalically. Instead, analogous to the pattern seen in §2.15 for German, we should consider this a case of final devoicing, where the root-final consonant is underlyingly voiced, and becomes voiceless in the absence of a suffix. Where there is a feminine suffix, the root-final consonant retains its voicing.

The data are more complicated than this, however. Many of the root-final consonants also differ in their manner features: they are fricatives in the feminine but stops or affricates in the unsuffixed masculine. Pairs such as [sek ~ seɣe] and [rotʃ ~ roʒə] illustrate this.

Since each such sound is a fricative in the feminine, but is either an affricate or stop in the masculine, it is a simpler account if we assume that the manner of articulation in the masculine is more indicative of the underlying form. Then we can rely on a single rule that turns either affricates or stops into fricatives in intervocalic position.

The converse approach, a rule turning fricatives into stops in word-final position, would be problematic for two reasons: first, it would be difficult to account for why some fricatives alternate with affricates (e.g., /ʃ/ → [tʃ]) while others alternate with stops (e.g., /β/ → [p]). Second, it would be similarly difficult to address the fricative /z/ in [gris, grizə], which is not subject to any alternation of manner.

To summarize so far, the forms in §6.8 all have final voiceless consonants, while the forms in §6.9 all have final voiced stops or fricatives. Moreover, within the data in the second group only, there are two distinct patterns of alternation: final devoicing, which devoices root-final consonants in the masculine forms, and intervocalic lenition, which we call **spirantization**, which applies to root-final stops in the feminine forms.

This analysis introduces the additional peculiarity that underlying voiced stops, as in /orb/, never appear as such in root-final position: they are either devoiced in the masculine, as in [orp], or spirantized in the feminine, as in [orβə]. Let us now formalize these patterns using binary features.

Exercise 6.5　Using at least some of the features [±cons], [±voi], [±cont], [±son], write two rules that account for the alternations seen in root-final obstruents in the words in §6.9.

Spirantization:　[+voi, −cont, −son] → [+cont] / V ___ V
Devoicing:　　　[+voi, −son] → [−voi] / ___]ᴡᴅ

The first rule uses [−cont] to target obstruents and [+voi] to limit its effect to voiced ones. It changes any such sound to [+cont] between vowels, thus rendering them fricatives.

The second rule finds any voiced obstruent, regardless of whether it is a stop, fricative, or affricate, and makes it voiceless in word-final position.

Note that a crucial part of this analysis is the reliance on the feature [−cont], which we use to target stops and affricates as a single class of sounds subject to spirantization, and on the feature [−son], which we use to limit final devoicing to obstruents (stops and fricatives).

We have not yet dealt with the third group of Catalan forms, those which lose a consonant in the masculine column. We may identify here two subgroups: some of these roots have a single root-final consonant which remains before the feminine suffix, as in [bɔnə] and [durə], but which is lost in the masculine forms, as in [bɔ] and [du]. All of these roots end in /n/ or /r/.

The remaining roots have underlying sequences which remain as such before the feminine suffix, as in [altə] and [fɔrtə], but which are reduced to single consonants in the masculine, as in [al] and [fɔr]. To be more precise, these underlying sequences always consist of a sonorant consonant followed by an alveolar consonant.

Exercise 6.6   Identify the underlying forms of the Catalan roots in the third group.

Each of these roots shows an alternation of a final segment with zero, but since the segment differs across cases, its form is unpredictable. We thus conclude that the alternating segment in each case is present underlyingly, maintained in the feminine forms, and deleted from the masculine forms.

There are actually two distinct deletion patterns: one targets root-final sonorants, which are deleted from masculine forms, and the other targets root-final obstruents which follow sonorant consonants.

Exercise 6.7   Using at least some of the features [±cons], [±voi], [±cont], [±son], [±nas], write two rules that account for the deletion patterns seen in root-final obstruents in Catalan.

Sonorant deletion   [+cons, +son] → Ø / ___]
Obstruent deletion   [+cons, –son] → Ø / [+cons, +son] ___]

The first rule uses [+cons, +son] to target nasals and liquids as a class of sounds. It will only delete these word finally, not other sonorants (such as vowels) or other consonants (such as obstruents).

The second rule uses [–son] to limit its target to obstruents, and also relies on [+con, +son] to specify the triggering environment. Formulated like this, it will only delete obstruents after sonorant consonants, not after vowels.

Again, this analysis relies strongly on binary features to identify sonorant consonants as a natural class of sounds, to the exclusion of vowels and other consonants.

Note that a crucial part of this analysis is the reliance on the feature [+son], which we use to target nasals and liquids as a single class of sounds, and on [–son], which we use to limit post-sonorant deletion to obstruents (stops and fricatives).

There are a few loose ends in our Catalan discussion that deserve merit. First, we have evidence that the ordering of at least some of these rules is consequential. In particular, the obstruent deletion rule must apply later than the sonorant deletion rule; otherwise, forms such as /fɔrt/ in the masculine would feed through each. They would first lose their final obstruent in the obstruent-deletion step, which would leave the sonorant in word-final position (i.e., /fɔr/), making it subject to sonorant deletion, resulting in *[fo]. As this is not the intended result, the opposite ordering applies: sonorant deletion applies first; in /fɔrt/, the sonorant is not word-final so it remains in the form. The subsequent application of obstruent deletion produces the appropriate form [fɔr], and now it is too late for sonorant deletion to apply.

Second, we see in this third group that some of the forms which are subject to the obstruent–zero alternation also undergo spirantization when the obstruent remains in the root. For example, /berd/ → [ber], but /berd + ə/ → [berðə]. This tells us the spirantization rule applies to these obstruents, even though they are not intervocalic. In fact, this just happens if the preceding sonorant is a liquid; it does not happen if the sonorant is nasal, as the form [prufundə] shows: there is a [d] rather than [ð] after the nasal sonorant.

Exercise 6.8   Rephrase the spirantization rule to apply to voiced obstruents that follow /r/.

The following two rules are possible approaches.

Spirantization   [−son, +voi] → [+cont] / [+son,+cont] __ V
Spirantization   [−son, +voi] → [+cont] / [+son,−nas] __ V

The resolution here is to identify the preceding environment of spirantization as a larger class of sounds than just vowels. Since at least some sonorant consonants also allow spirantization to occur in a following consonant, the preceding environment must not be specified simply as [−cons]; instead we can call it more generally [+son]. However, we must also restrict it so as not to apply after nasals. Thus, we may appeal to additional specifications such as [−nas] or [+cont]. Either approach allows us to come up with a feature combination that treats vowels and [r] as a natural class of sounds, next to which obstruents are spirantized.

The [+cont] feature is probably the best analysis here, given other data that suggest that spirantization occurs not just after vowels and liquids, but also after fricatives.

6.11 More spirantization in Catalan

[buv ðiaɾi]	'daily puff'
[əvɣa]	'Afghan'
[ʃɛv ɣəʎart]	'dashing chef'
[ez βlaw]	'is blue'
[ez ðu]	'is hard'
[dəzɣləsa]	'to defrost'

The Catalan data (Bermúdez-Otero 2001) illustrate intervocalic effects, word-final effects, and several patterns of word-final deletion. Each of these targets is sensitive to classes of sounds that unite more than one phonetic type – sometimes stops and affricates, sometimes nasals and liquids, sometimes liquids and vowels. These classes are best captured with conjunctive combinations of binary features. Let us now turn to another data set in which an appeal to natural classes is helpful, in the prefixing pattern of Malay.

6.12 Malay

We examined Malay in §2.9 as an example of alternation, where the form of the prefix /peŋ/ changes depending on the initial segment of the root. We now return to these data to explore their implications for natural classes (data from Sidharta 1976).

Before we apply a feature analysis of the data, we should refamiliarize ourselves with a basic morphophonemic analysis, with attention to any alternation found in the roots or prefix.

	Base nouns	*Prefixed*	*Gloss*
(1)	tulis	penulis	'writer'
(2)	toloŋ	penoloŋ	'assistant'
(3)	tipu	penipu	'cheater'
(4)	suruh	peɲuruh	'messenger'
(5)	siram	peɲiram-an	'a watering'
(6)	sapu	peɲapu	'broom'
(7)	pukul	pemukul	'hammer'
(8)	potoŋ	pemotoŋ	'slaughterer'
(9)	pindah	pemindah-an	'a shift'
(10)	minta	peminta-an	'a request'
(11)	mamah	pemamah	'cud chewer'
(12)	lepas	pelepas	'starter'
(13)	lawat	pelawat	'visitor'
(14)	kurang	peŋurang-an	'a decrease'
(15)	kira	peŋira-an	'counting'
(16)	kenal	peŋenal-an	'introduction'
(17)	judi	pendʒudi	'gambler'
(18)	jimat	pendʒimat	'thrifty one'
(19)	gentar	peŋgentar	'coward'
(20)	geli	peŋgeli	'ticklish one'
(21)	dapat	pendapat-an	'acquisition'

(22) ʧeramah   penʧeramah   'lecturer'
(23) ʧari   penʧari-an   'livelihood'
(24) bunuh   pembunuh   'killer'
(25) buka   pembuka   'opener'
(26) batʃa   pembatʃa   'reader'
(27) atur   peŋatur   'arranger'
(28) ambil   peŋambil-an   'collection'

In Malay, the prefix may appear as [pen-], [pem-], [peɲ-], [pe-], or [peŋ-], depending on the root's initial segment: [pen-] occurs when the root begins with an alveolar stop; [pem-] occurs if the root begins with a bilabial consonant: [peɲ-] occurs if the root begins with [s] or with a palatal consonant, and [pe-] occurs if the root begins with a lateral or nasal. The form [peŋ-] occurs otherwise – where the root has an initial vowel or velar stop, which suggests that it matches the underlying representation.

Some of the roots also alternate in Malay. Thus, even though the prefix appears as the alternate [pen-] in [penulis], the root has an initial [t] when unprefixed, as in [tulis]. That is, the consonant of the prefix assimilates to a segment that is not present at the surface.

Where the root-initial consonant is a voiceless stop; the prefix is [pe-] and seems to trigger nasalization in the initial consonant of the root. A similar pattern is observed if the root has an initial [s].

Wherever the root begins with a nasal or liquid, the prefix is [pe-] and the root remains unchanged.

Where the root begins with a voiced obstruent, the prefix ends in a nasal consonant homorganic with the root initial consonant. A similar pattern is noted for roots with an initial [j], which appears instead as [ʤ] after the prefix nasal.

In vowel-initial roots, the prefix is [peŋ-].

Exercise 6.9   Express each of the above generalizations using a combination of binary specifications of some or all of the following features: [±cons], [±cont], [±son], [±nas], [±voi], and [place].

Your rules should presuppose a single underlying form for each morpheme.

It may be useful to conceive first of rules that affect the prefix, and then produce whatever rules are also needed for roots.

The best choice for the underlying representation of the prefix is /peŋ/, since this is the form that appears before vowels.

One rule is needed to delete the nasal consonant before sonorants:

ŋ → Ø / __ [+cons, +son]

And a second rule is necessary to derive the place assimilation pattern:

ŋ → [α place] / ___ [+cons, α place]

The notation [α place] represents place features, so /ŋ/ appears as [ɲ] if the root has an initial [s], but given the transcription we assume that [ɲ] is palatal while [s] is alveolar. We return to this issue below.

A third rule deletes root-initial voiceless consonants after the prefix's nasal consonant:

[+cons, –voi] → Ø / [+nas, +cons] ___

This third rule must apply last, in order to ensure that the nasal consonant has already adapted its place features to the root consonant. It must also specifically not apply if the root begins with an affricate.[1]

A final rule is necessary to account for the alternation of root initial [j ~ ʤ]. Given that the prefix acts as if the root has an initial obstruent, let us treat /ʤ/ as underlying, and propose a rule which changes it to [j] in word-initial position.

We still require a fuller account of what happens to root-initial /s/, which triggers assimilation to a palatal in the prefix consonant. This pattern, along with the loss of the consonant in prefixed forms, suggests that /s/ *behaves like* voiceless stops. We could adopt a natural class approach and find some combination of features that unites [s] with voiceless stops, but the problem is that doing so would also bring affricates into the class. That is, a rule targeting [+cons, –son, –voi] identifies not just [p, t, k, s] as a class, but also includes [ʧ]. This is a problem because /ʧ/ does not behave similarly – it is not deleted after the prefix nasal.

There are several resolutions to this problem: first, we may appeal to something like [±affricate] to isolate the class. This feature is not typically used, but it may work for this language, and concretely the data motivate it.

Alternatively, we could analyze /s/ abstractly as the surface form of what underlying *really is* a voiceless stop – a palatal one to be exact. If these roots begin with /c/, then the prefix nasal consonant would be [ɲ], and the /c/ is deleted afterwards. An additional rule changing all remaining /c/ to [s] would also be needed.

Regardless of the approach, the Malay data exemplify natural classes at work in a number of ways. First, either voiceless stops behave differently from other obstruents, or voiceless stops and fricatives form a natural class; second, nasals and liquids trigger similar phonological processes as well.

The patterns in these languages show that consonants often act similarly, despite not having the exact same manner features. Sometimes nasals and liquids behave similarly, motivating [+son] as a feature, and other times obstruents behave similarly, motivating [−son]. Sometimes stops and nasals behave similarly, motivating [−cont], while fricatives and liquids behave similarly, motivating [+cont].

In the following sections, we will investigate groupings of consonant place features. We have seen that some discussion of place features has been necessary, but so far we have not come across evidence of consonants of different places of articulation acting in similar ways. We turn to this phenomenon next, in a discussion of natural classes of consonant place.

6.13 The Arabic article

In this section we will explore the form of the definite article in Baghdadi Arabic. In the first data set, the article always appears as the lateral liquid [l]. This is true as long as the root begins with a vowel or any of a multitude of consonant places of articulation. Data are from Youssef 2013.

l-beet	'the house'
l-mooz	'the bananas'
l-kaːtib	'the clerk'
l-qisim	'the part'
l-xeel	'the horses'
l-ħaliːb	'the milk'
l-wakit	'the time'
l-ʔakil /l-akil	'the food'
l-paːja	'the step'
l-fadʒir	'the dawn'
l-ġutˤiṇ	'the cotton'
l-hazal	'the joking'
l-ɣada	'the lunch'
l-ʕinab	'the grapes'
l-joom	'the day'
l-ʔisim/l-isim	'the name'

The next subset of data illustrates an alternation in the form of the definite marker: instead of a lateral liquid, it appears as a complete assimilation of the root-initial consonant. This pattern emerges where the root's initial segment is a consonant with an interdental, alveolar, or palatal place of articulation.

t-timan	'the rice'
s-sahal	'the easy'
d-daris	'the lesson'

z-zibid	'the butter'
θ-θoob	'the shirt'
ðˤ-ðˤaːbutˤ	'the officer'
n-naːr	'the fire'
tʃ-tʃaːkuːtʃ	'the hammer'
tˤ-tˤooba	'the ball'
sˤ-sˤuːrˤa	'the picture'
d-daːma	'the checkers'
ʃ-ʃahar	'the month'
ð-ðahab	'the gold'
r-rukkaːb	'the passengers'
l-leela	'the night'
dʒ-dʒuntˤa	'the suitcase'

Exercise 6.10   Determine whether the form of the article is a predictable alternation.

The form of the article is predictable. In the first subset of data, there are no initial interdentals, alveolars, or palatals, and the definite marker is always [l]. In the second set of data, the initial segment is always one of these three places of articulation.

Since interdentals, alveolars, and palatals trigger the same phonological behavior in Arabic, we have evidence of them forming a natural class. We use the term *coronal* to refer to such sounds. As phonetic corroboration, they have a common articulatory property of using the front of the tongue to create a consonant constriction.

The formal expression of this phonological feature is [COR]. It is common practice in phonology not to use positive or negative specifications for coronal sounds, as the use of [−COR] would imply that this identifies a natural class of sounds. However, phonological processes which target *everything except coronals* are not typically found. Thus, we express the natural class of coronals only with the presence of the unitary (or "privative") feature [COR]; each consonant either has it or does not. As we will see, non-coronal sounds made at other places of articulation have their own unitary place features.

Obviously the feature [COR] subsumes a number of more precise places of articulation, which still require further specification in their features. In the Arabic data, we see three degrees of place within [COR]: interdental, alveolar, and palatal. There are numerous approaches to dividing these up with features, but note that we need not appeal directly to something like [+interdental], [+alveolar], and [+palatal].

In short, we may use [±anterior] to distinguish palatals from the remainder, and [±distributed] to distinguish dentals from the remainder.

Thus only the dentals are [–distributed], only the palatals are [–anterior], and the alveolars in particular are [+dist, +ant]. There is some phonetic relationship observable here; [±anterior] refers to whether the front of the tongue is relatively forward or retracted, and as the palatals are farther back in place, they alone are [–anterior]. Likewise, [±distributed] refers to whether the blade of the tongue is pressed up against the alveolar ridge or hard palate; since the interdentals instead use the tongue tip, they are [–distributed]. Note that some phonologists express this with the term [+apical]. Also, the fourth combination, [–ant, –dist], describes sounds that situate the tongue tip towards the palate, which can be used to identify retroflex consonants.

Exercise 6.11   Identify which features the definite marker adopts in Arabic coronal place assimilation.

The /l/ of the definite marker adopts the same value for the [±ant] and [±dist] features of the root's initial consonant if it is coronal. Crucially, it also adopts [±son], [±cont], and [±nas].

If a segment assumes the same feature value as a sound in its environment, we use **alpha notation** to express this. Alpha notation is a rule-writing convention in which assigning a feature with the value α allows it to assume the same value for some other feature also specified as α. In other words, if two feature elements are both [α feature], they are both [–feature] or both [+feature].

In rules of assimilation, the alpha variable needs to be expressed in a feature of the triggering environment and in a feature of the target or structural change. For example, if a sound becomes [α ant] before a [α ant] sound, it becomes [–ant] if the environment is [–ant] and [+ant] if the environment is [+ant].

[+cons, COR] → [α ant, β dist] / ___ [+cons, COR, α ant, β dist]

Exercise 6.12   Using different Greek characters for each assimilating feature, fill out the rule for the remaining features.

[+cons, COR] → [α ant, β dist, γ son, δ cont, ε nas, –lat] / ___ [+cons, COR, α ant, β dist, γ son, δ cont, ε nas, –lat]

It is important that we use a different variable for each feature; otherwise, the rule would require different features with the same variable to have the same value.

Note also that we include [–lat] because all products of assimilation are non-lateral coronals. The definite marker remains [l] before [+lat] coronals.

In summary, the definite marker in Arabic assimilates only to following coronal consonants, a pattern which we could not express uniformly without a [COR] feature.

6.14 A child phonology pattern

These next data offer additional support for the notion of a coronal place node. These forms were produced by a child learner of English between the ages of 2 and 3;6 years.

(1)	bæk	'black'
(2)	bu	'blue'
(3)	biz	'breeze'
(4)	bɪŋ	'bring'
(5)	baʊn	'brown'
(6)	bʌʃ	'brush'
(7)	daɪ	'dry'
(8)	dʌp	'dump'
(9)	dʌk	'dunk'
(10)	fɛk	'fleck'
(11)	faɪ	'fly'
(12)	fiː	'free'
(13)	ɪt hnɑt	'it's not'
(14)	jæp	'lap'
(15)	jɪk	'lick'
(16)	jɑts	'lots'
(17)	peɪt	'paint'
(18)	pæt	'plant'
(19)	peɪ	'play'
(20)	pʌm	'plum'
(21)	pun	'prune'
(22)	ɹɛd	'red'
(23)	ɹaɪd	'ride'
(24)	keɪp	'scrape'
(25)	kim	'scream'
(26)	kuː	'screw'
(27)	kʌb	'scrub'
(28)	sɪp	'ship'
(29)	sɪp	'shrimp'
(30)	keɪt	'skate'
(31)	kʌk	'skunk'

(32)	kaɪ	'sky'
(33)	kaɪlo	'Skyler'
(34)	siv	'sleeve'
(35)	sɪp	'slip'
(36)	sɪpəli	'slippery'
(37)	maɑo	'small'
(38)	maɪo	'smile'
(39)	sæp	'snap'
(40)	pɛk	'speck'
(41)	pɪʊ	'spill'
(42)	pæʃ	'splash'
(43)	pɪt	'split'
(44)	pɑt	'spot'
(45)	peɪ	'spray'
(46)	pɛdɪŋ ʧiz	'spreading cheese'
(47)	pɪko	'sprinkle'
(48)	sɑp	'stop'
(49)	seɪt	'straight'
(50)	sɑː	'straw'
(51)	siŋ	'string'
(52)	saɪp	'stripe'
(53)	tiː	'tree'
(54)	tʌk	'truck'
(55)	taɪ	'try'
(56)	tizo	'tweezer'

For this discussion, we may assume the underlying form for these words is equivalent to the adult forms; in other words, the child has lexical representations that include consonant sequences which nonetheless are reduced to single consonants in her surface forms. While this may seem like a strong assumption to make, we will see that her patterning is sensitive to differences among the adult forms.

Exercise 6.13   a.   Identify all word-initial sequences in which only the first consonant is retained in the child's productions.

      b.   Identify all word-initial sequences in which only the second consonant is retained in the child's productions.

      a.   The child keeps the first consonant if the initial adult sequence is [bɹ], [bl], [pɹ], [pl], [tɹ], [dɹ], [fɹ], [fl], [sl], [sn], [st], [ʃɹ], [kɹ], [kl], [gɹ], [gl]

      b.   The child keeps the second consonant if the adult sequence is [sm], [sp], [sk]

Exercise 6.14   Using distinctive features, provide a description of the consonant sequences in the group that loses the second consonant. Be specific enough to ensure that the description does not apply to the consonant sequences that instead lose their initial consonant.

The second consonant is lost from [+cons][+cons, COR] sequences.

6.15   Natural classes in child phonology

Every initial sequence in the group of forms that loses its second consonant contains an obstruent followed by a coronal consonant. Sometimes the second consonant of such sequences is sonorant; at other times it is an obstruent, so our description should make no reference to [±son]. Thus, we can describe these as a sequence of [+cons][+cons, COR]. The forms that lose their first consonant contain [s] followed by a non-coronal sonorant.

Exercise 6.15   Compose two rules two produce these deletion patterns. You may assume that your second rule only applies to forms that the first rule does not apply to.

[+cons, COR] → Ø / $_{\text{WD}}$[[+cons] ___
[+cons] → Ø / $_{\text{WD}}$[___ [+cons]

So far, our discussion of place features has settled on [COR] as a way of grouping alveolar, dental, and palatal sounds as a natural class. This has proved useful especially in our analysis of Arabic.

Let us think counterfactually for a moment: without the grouping effect that [COR] provides for us, we would still need a notational system that allows rules to apply to a list of different places of articulation. But if the system allows us to propose rules that apply to any consonant that is either [+alveolar], [+dental], or [+palatal] (as the data motivate), then there is nothing that precludes rules that apply to [+labiodental], [+alveolar], and [+velar]. This might not seem like a problem, but a system in which a rule targets exactly these sounds – to the exclusion of [bilabial], [interdental], and [palatal] – is typologically unusual, if not unattested.

6.16   Kongo

A return to the phonemic analysis of Kongo from §5.12 will illustrate a similar point. The data are repeated below; as before, let us focus on the distribution of alveolar and palatal sounds.

147

(1)	tobola	'to bore a hole'
(2)	tʃina	'to cut'
(3)	kesoka	'to be cut'
(4)	knoʃi	'lion'
(5)	zenga	'to cut'
(6)	ʒima	'to stretch'
(7)	kasu	'emaciation'
(8)	tʃiba	'banana'
(9)	nselele	'termite'
(10)	lolonʒi	'to wash'
(11)	zevo	'then'
(12)	aʒimola	'alms'
(13)	nzwetu	'our house'
(14)	kunezulu	'to heaven'
(15)	tanu	'five'

The alveolar sounds [t, s, z] can occur anywhere except before the vowel [i]. The palatal sounds [tʃ, ʃ, ʒ] occur only before [i]. Thus, the distribution of the two groups of sounds is complementary.

The alveolar sounds are better chosen as the underlying sounds, since they have a more general distribution. The palatals have a specific context of occurring before [i]. As a result, we may construct a rule that changes alveolars to palatals only before [i]; any alveolar that is not in such an environment will remain unchanged in its place of articulation. In Chapter 5, the rule we proposed was as follows:

[alveolar] → [palatal] / __ [i]

Exercise 6.16 Rewrite the palatalization rule using the features [COR] and [±ant]

[COR] → [–ant] / __ [i]

The approach we used above uses the [COR] feature, and treats this allophonic pattern as a matter of degree of anteriority with coronals. Without the grouping effect of [COR], we'd need to rely instead on primitive features like [+alveolar] and [+palatal]. In such an approach, the rule would change [+ALV] to [+PAL] in the context of __ [i], which does not adequately capture the fact that alveolars and palatals are adjacent to each other in articulatory space. Moreover, if place features can be changed willy-nilly like this, the same primitive system would allow odd hypothetical scenarios like [+LAB] → [+PAL] (in a language in which alveolars are also used). Such extreme place-changing rules are not observed in natural languages.

6.17 Other major places of articulation

Our discussion has only handled places of articulation that range between interdental and palatal. Of course, there are consonants that are produced ahead of the teeth and behind the palate – each of these can also be represented with major class features of place. We turn next to the dorsal sounds, represented with the feature [DOR], which covers velars and uvulars.

6.18 Cuzco Quechua

In Cuzco Quechua there is an allophonic pattern observed among velar and uvular consonants. The following data (from Odden 2005) illustrate this pattern; take some time to inspect the data, and make some generalizations about the distribution of velar and uvular stops and fricatives (i.e., [k, x, q, χ]).

(1)	qori	'gold'
(2)	q'omir	'green'
(3)	moqo	'runt'
(4)	phulju	'blanket'
(5)	tulju	'bone'
(6)	suti	'name'
(7)	tʃilwi	'baby chick'
(8)	tʃhaɴqaj	'granulate'
(9)	qetʃuŋ	'he disputes'
(10)	musoχ	'new'
(11)	jaɴqaŋ	'for free'
(12)	qhelja	'lazy'
(13)	tʃeqaŋ	'straight'
(14)	noqa	'I'
(15)	tʃeχniŋ	'he hates'
(16)	aχna	'thus'
(17)	qosa	'husband'
(18)	alqo	'dog'
(19)	karu	'far'
(20)	qaŋkuna	'you pl.'
(21)	t'eχwaj	'pluck'
(22)	wateχ	'again'
(23)	waχtaj	'hit!'
(24)	waqaj	'tears'
(25)	waxtʃa	'poor'
(26)	thakaj	'drop'

(27) ʧoχlu   'corn on the cob'
(28) niŋri   'ear'
(29) hoq'ara   'deaf'
(30) jujaŋ   'he recalls'
(31) api   'take'
(32) oɴqoj   'be sick!'
(33) ʧhitʃiŋ   'be whispers'
(34) aɴqosaj   'toast'
(35) p'isqo   'bird'
(36) ʧuŋka   'ten'
(37) ʧulju   'ice'
(38) q'eɴqo   'zigzagged'
(39) qaŋ   'you'
(40) ʧaxra   'field'
(41) soχta   'six'
(42) ljixlja   'small shawl'
(43) qara   'skin'
(44) seɴqa   'nose'
(45) atoχ   'fox'
(46) pusaχ   'eight'
(47) ʧ'aki   'dry'
(48) aŋka   'eagle'
(49) haku   'let's go'
(50) kaŋka   'roasted'
(51) waleχ   'poor'
(52) reχsisqa   'known'

Exercise 6.17 a. What is the distribution of velar fricatives? What about uvular fricatives?

b. What is the distribution of velar stops? What about uvular stops?

Both velar and uvular fricatives appear to have a restricted distribution; they never occur before vowels. The stops, on the other, are always followed by vowels. Thus, we may infer that [k] and [x] are in complementary distribution, and that [q] and [χ] are as well.

The environment that follows the fricatives seems more general: fricatives occur either word-finally or before other consonants, while stops may only occur before vowels. A tentative conclusion would therefore be to treat the fricatives as underlying, and then to propose a rule which turns them into stops in the specific pre-vocalic environment. Crucially, segments at other places of articulation in Cuzco Quechua are not subject to the same allophony. Therefore, velars and uvulars are behaving as a class of sounds here.

Exercise 6.18 Compose a rule that derives the appropriate allophones for velars and uvulars in Cuzco Quechua.

$$[\text{DOR}] \rightarrow [-\text{cont}] / \underline{\quad} [+\text{syll}]$$

This rule assumes underlying dorsal fricatives, and changes them to stops before vowels. It targets velars and uvulars, but no other places of articulation. As we did with subtypes of coronal sounds, we may note here that without [DOR], we would need separate rules (or a disjoint rule) to account for the Quechua patterns. Moreover, doing so would not adequately capture the fact that the process only affects sounds that are very similar to each other in articulatory space, and such a model of feature specification has no way to preclude phonological systems in which, for example, [+bilabial] and [+velar] are subject to allophonic differences in [±cont], while [+alveolar] and [+uvular] are not.

We will see in Chapter 8 that the environments of pre-consonant and word-final can be united into a single notion of *syllable margin*. Thus, these sounds are stops if they occur at the beginning of a syllable (word initially, or between two vowels), and are fricatives if they occur at the end of a syllable (word-finally, or before another consonant).

6.19 Hezhen

For more evidence to support the notion of a dorsal feature, let us turn to Hezhen (Zhang *et al.* 1989). In the following data, examine the distribution of consonants as a function of adjacent vowels.[2]

(1)	niŋgə	'hose'
(2)	mangəmɔ	'oak'
(3)	qɔlu	'county'
(4)	qurpan	'boat'
(5)	kiaulu	'oar'
(6)	kɑskʰe	'bird'
(7)	ʒtatʰqʰuli	'cold'
(8)	qʰumakʰə	'deer'
(9)	kʰəqu	'cuckoo'
(10)	χoni	'sheep'
(11)	χula	'read'
(12)	xəŋkʰə	'cucumber'
(13)	xəi	'forehead'
(14)	miŋan	'thousand'

(15)	xatχʊn	'salty'
(16)	sɔŋu	'cry'
(17)	soktu	'get drunk'
(18)	səbə	'marten'
(19)	sabə	'shoe'
(20)	pitʰxə	'book'
(21)	pɔzu	'clot'
(22)	pʰitɕʰikə	'match'
(23)	apʰkʰa	'universe'
(24)	χɔlqʊŋ	'rope'
(25)	fʊtɕin	'princess'
(26)	pu	'give'
(27)	tʰuksu	'cloud'
(28)	χotʊŋ	'fast'
(29)	tɕɔlo	'stone'
(30)	puda	'mean'
(31)	tʰikdə	'rain'
(32)	tarmi	'wide'
(33)	tamixin	'tobacco'
(34)	tʰioqo	'chicken'
(35)	tʰumakʰi	'tomorrow'
(36)	mɔrin	'horse'
(37)	pɔrqʰu	'color'
(38)	sura	'flea'
(39)	uɬzə	'meat'
(40)	iɬka	'flower'
(41)	lɔχʊŋ	'sword'
(42)	luqʰu	'arrow'
(43)	fa	'window'
(44)	falən	'floor'
(45)	xəzu	'say'
(46)	qʰuzʊŋkʰi	'energetic'

Exercise 6.19 a. What is the distribution of velar fricatives and stops?
b. What is the distribution of uvular fricatives and stops?
c. Do the sounds [k, x, q, χ] represent four separate phonemes, or are any of them in allophonic relationships with each other?

The uvulars occur before the vowels [o, ɔ, u, ʊ]. The velars occur elsewhere. Because of this complementary distribution, we can conclude that [k] and [q] are allophones of a common phoneme, as are [x] and [χ].

Exercise 6.20   Determine the underlying phoneme for each pair of allophones, and propose a single rule using features to account for the alternation seen in each. Use the feature [±back] to distinguish velar from uvular.

The velars are better choices as underlying phonemes, since they occur before front vowels, low vowels, and word-finally. Uvulars occur in the specific context before back, non-low vowels.[3] Since uvulars are more predictable, we can easily write a rule that accounts for their occurrence.

[DOR] → [+back] / ___ [−cons, −low, +back]

In summary, the Hezhen dorsal consonants are subject to alternation in their specific place features. We can only capture the fact that this pattern applies to velars and uvulars by uniting them with the [DOR] feature; without it, the fact that uvulars and velars are so closely associated with each other would be a mysterious accident. As such, these data are the dorsal equivalent to the coronal phenomenon we saw in Arabic: velar and uvular are finer points of place within dorsal in the same way that dental, alveolar, and palatal are for coronal.

6.20 Bilabials and labiodentals

The last portion of consonant space for us to handle comprises the labial sounds, bilabials and labiodentals, which can be united with the feature [LAB]. To see this feature in action, let us explore the process of diminutive reduplication in English.

English wordplay allows a partial-reduplication pattern which repeats a word, where the second instance has its initial consonants replaced with [p]. For example, *Georgie Peorgie*, [dʒɔɹdʒi pɔɹdʒi]. In some cases, the second word begins with [w]. Examine the data below to determine if the choice between [p] and [w] in the second element is predictable.

6.21 Expressive reduplication in English: / f, p, b / form a group

hokie pokie	polly wolly
georgie porgie	fishy wishy
rollie pollie	piggy wiggy
woolie pullie	boogie woogie
easy peasy	fuzzy wuzzy
higgledy piggledy	napper wapper

153

nancy pancy
alex palex
hodge podge
hanky panky
andy pandy

Exercise 6.21 What is true of the words which receive a [w]-initial reduplicant?

Each word that has a w-form has at least one consonant involving the lips within it, either bilabials such as [p], [b], or labiodentals such as [f]. We can express this simply as the presence of a **labial** feature, [LAB], in the root. By default, the second word begins with [p], unless it contains a [LAB] sound, in which case the second word instead begins with [w].

You may be able to think of other similar expressive forms that use [w] but which have no labial consonant in their root, such as *teeny-weeny*. We should not consider these as counterexamples to the generalization: either these are derived by a different process (in effect, blending *tiny* and *wee*), or they represent a different pattern, by which [w] may occur in a wider distribution, and not just where the root contains a labial sound. If we pursue the latter possibility, it remains relevant that some speakers have a strict alternation between [p] and [w] in this pattern, and this is the system we are analyzing. Likewise, it is also relevant that even among speakers with a looser distribution of [w] (allowing, for example, *Nancy Wancy*), the same laxity does not extend to [p]: that is, such a speaker may allow both *Nancy Wancy* and *Nancy Pancy*, but only *fuzzy wuzzy* and never **fuzzy puzzy*.

It is only with the feature [LAB] that we are able to group bilabials and labiodentals into a class together. Without [LAB], we would need several independent statements restricting the form of the reduplicative consonant to match the observed patterns, and as we saw when discussing coronal and dorsal sounds, if a language could accidentally target [bilabial] and [labiodental] sounds for a single process, it could also accidentally target [labial] and [palatal] sounds, to the exclusion of intervening places of articulation.

The use of major place features like [LAB], [COR], and [DOR] does three things for us: first, it captures the fact that some phonological processes apply to all members of a major place class, but not to members of other place classes. Second, it allows us to model fine grains of place assimilation within each major place feature, without extending such alternation to other place features. Third, it precludes scenarios in which segments alternate wildly with sounds outside their own place group.

154

6.22 Vowels

We have seen that distinctive features are useful tools for identifying classes of consonants that behave similarly in phonological patterns. The same approach can be applied to patterns of allophony and alternation in vowels.

Vowel articulation can be summarized as a combination of tongue height, tongue backness, and lip rounding. In phonetic terms, we may distinguish high vowels, mid vowels, and low vowels, but in phonology we often find patterns in which vowels of several adjacent degrees of height work similarly. This is exactly the kind of scenario that calls for a feature-based approach. In fact, a number of data sets from this and previous chapters provide evidence for the notion of natural classes of vowels.

6.23 Ganda

The allophonic distribution of [l] and [r] in Ganda from §5.8 is an example of such a system. The data are repeated below.

(1)	kola	'do'
(2)	lwana	'fight'
(3)	buulira	'tell'
(4)	lya	'eat'
(5)	luula	'sit'
(6)	omugole	'bride'
(7)	lumonde	'sweet potato'
(8)	eddwaliro	'hospital'
(9)	oluganda	'Ganda language'
(10)	olulimi	'tongue'
(11)	wulira	'hear'
(12)	beera	'help'
(13)	jjukira	'remember'
(14)	eryato	'canoe'
(15)	omuliro	'fire'
(16)	effirimbi	'whistle'
(17)	emmeeri	'ship'
(18)	eraddu	'lightning'
(19)	wawaabira	'accuse'
(20)	lagira	'command'

Exercise 6.22 a. List all vowels that appear in the data.

b. Assuming the transcription is consistent with IPA notation, arrange these vowels in a table by their height and backness.

155

a. There are five vowels here: [i, u, e, o, a].

b. Phonetically, we arrange them as follows:

	front	back
high	i	u
mid	e	o
low	a	

There are five vowels in Ganda, two each at high and mid levels of tongue height, and a single low vowel. Without any additional phonological evidence, we cannot readily determine whether the low vowel [a] is front or back.

Recall that the phoneme /l/ has [r] as an allophone, appearing only after [i] and [e]. This suggests that these vowels form a natural class.

Exercise 6.23   Describe [i] and [e] as a group, to the exclusion of the other three vowels. Use a conjunction of descriptive terms, rather than a disjunction. Express them as a natural class using binary features.

The vowels [i] and [e] comprise the class of non-low front vowels. In binary feature specification, they are [−cons, −low, −back] or [−cons, −low, +front].

The feature [−low] allows us to unite mid and high vowels as a natural class without turning to a disjunctive description. In addition, as there are only two degrees of backness here, we may freely rely on either [±back] or [±front] as a distinctive feature.

Exercise 6.24   Rewrite the Ganda liquid allophony rule using distinctive features.

[+cons, +son, +lat] → [−lat] / [−cons, −low, −back] ___

6.24 Greenlandic

For another familiar allophonic pattern to illustrate vowel height, we can return to Greenlandic from §5.10. The data are repeated below; recall that in these data, the vowels /i, u/ are lowered to [e, o] only before uvulars.

(1)   ivnɑq   'bluff'
(2)   ipeʁaq   'harpoon strap'
(3)   imɑq   'sea'
(4)   tuluvɑq   'raven'
(5)   sɑvɑ   'sheep'
(6)   nunɑ   'land'
(7)   nɑnoq   'bear'
(8)   iseʁaq   'ankle'

(9)	iga	'pot'
(10)	seʁmeq	'glacier'
(11)	qasaloq	'bark'
(12)	ikusik	'elbow'
(13)	qilaluvaq	'white whale'
(14)	qatigak	'back'
(15)	sakiak	'rib'
(16)	ugsik	'cow'
(17)	neʁdloq	'goose'
(18)	maʁːaq	'clay'
(19)	oʁpik	'tree'

Exercise 6.25   a.   List all vowels that appear in the data.

b.   Assuming the transcription is consistent with IPA notation, arrange these vowels in a table by their height and backness.

a.   There are five vowels here: [i, u, e, o, a].

b.   Phonetically, we arrange them as follows:

	front	back
high	i	u
mid	e	o
low		a

Exercise 6.26   Describe [i] and [u] as a group, to the exclusion of the other three vowels. Do the same for [e] and [o]. Use conjunctions of descriptive terms, rather than disjunctions. Express them as a natural class using binary features.

The high vowels [i, u] form the class of high vowels in Greenlandic, and are specified as [–cons, +high, –low].

The mid vowels [e, o] form the class of mid vowels in Greenlandic, and are specified as [–cons, –high, –low].

Exercise 6.27   Rewrite the Greenlandic vowel allophony rule using distinctive features.

[–cons, +high, –low] → [–high] / ___ [DOR, +back]

Using the two binary features of [±high] and [±low] allows us to express an alternation limited just to the set of [–low] vowels. By targeting [–low] vowels, we avoid bringing [a] into the alternation, and we also preclude either non-low phoneme from lowering excessively to [a]. If we instead stick with a disjunctive system that could target "[high] or [mid]" as a natural class, we would lack a formal way of expressing the fact that vowels which are close to each other in phonetic space also group together phonologically. A disjunctive approach would not prevent us from targeting, for example, "[high] or [low]" vowels to the exclusion of mid ones.

We may further note that the Hezhen data from §6.19 provide more evidence for the use of [±low] as a vowel feature, since velars are rendered dorsal only after non-low back vowels. The rule we proposed there critically relies on [–low] to ensure that velars become uvular only before non-low vowels, and not before [ɑ].

[DOR] → [+back] / ___ [–cons, –low, +back]

6.25 Dumi (Tibeto-Burman; Nepal)

In the patterns discussed above, vowel height features help delimit natural classes, but some of the phenomena involve only front or back vowels. For example, it is only back [–low] vowels that trigger dorsal allophony in Hezhen, and it is only front [–low] vowels that trigger liquid allophony in Ganda. Such languages have just two degrees of vowel backness, so either [±back] or [±front] would suffice to account for the patterns.

Let us now turn to Dumi, in which the backness dimension is more complex. Examine the following data (from van Driem 1993), paying attention to the distribution of [ts] and [tʃ].

(1)	tsampi	'fermented millet'
(2)	tsaːniʔkpa	'delicious'
(3)	tsəmpəlɨ	'ant'
(4)	tsərnɨ	'pay'
(5)	tsɨrnɨ	'be sour'
(6)	tsɨmrɨ	'spine'
(7)	tʃeʔpsaːlu	'fibula'
(8)	tʃiːl	'alert'
(9)	tʃelpɨ	'maiden home'
(10)	tʃili	'anger, wrath'
(11)	tʃuba	'heart'
(12)	tʃume	'needle'
(13)	tʃɔpmʃi	'finger'
(14)	tʃɔ	'summit, peak'

Exercise 6.28   a.   List all vowels that appear in the data.

b.   Assuming the transcription is consistent with IPA notation, arrange these vowels in a table by their height and backness.

c.   Describe the distribution of the affricates [ts] and [tʃ].

a. There are seven vowels here: [i, ɨ, u, e, ə, ɔ, a].
b. Phonetically, we arrange them as follows:

	front	central	back
high	i	ɨ	u
mid	e	ə	o
low		a	

c. The affricates [ts] and [tʃ] are in complementary distribution: [ts] occurs only before [ɨ, ə, a], while [tʃ] occurs before front or back vowels. Since [ts] occurs in a more specific set of circumstances, we can construe [tʃ] to be the underlying phoneme.

Exercise 6.29 a. Describe [ɨ, ə, a] as a group, to the exclusion of the other three vowels.
b. Express them as a natural class using binary features.
c. Write a rule that uses this natural class in its structural description.

The three vowels that follow [ts] are all central vowels. We can specify them as [–cons, –front, –back], and the rule that uses them is below:

[–cont, +sibilant, –ant] → [+ant] / ___ [–cons, –back, –front]

This rule uses natural classes to identify and change the target consonant, and also to identify the conditioning environment. This example clearly illustrates the link between our reliance on "general" distribution to choose underlying phonemes with our use of binary features to highlight natural classes. In this case, the distributional facts lead us to propose /tʃ/ as the underlying phoneme, because the converse allophone [ts] has a narrower distribution, while the distribution of [tʃ] cannot be described in any more precise terms than "elsewhere." Meanwhile, the specificity of [ts]'s environment translates neatly into a precise featural specification, and our reliance on both [±back] and [±front] allows us to isolate central vowels as a natural class without turning to an ad hoc feature like [±central].

Summary

In this chapter we have explored numerous phenomena in which multiple phonemes behave in similar ways. We have seen patterns of allophony and alternation in which two or more phonemes each show analogous allophonic behavior in similar or identical circumstances. We have also seen patterns in which one or more phonemes responds to multiple segments that share one or more phonological feature. All of this points toward the idea that within languages, different phonemes often act in similar manners, either triggering or undergoing parallel phonological processes. Such parallel behavior is described with the terminology of natural classes.

To capture these phenomena, we have turned to a precise system of featural notation that allows our rules and generalizations to encode natural classes. This system appropriately characterizes natural classes with the featural descriptions that are common to them, and precludes the risk of disparate sounds being identified as natural classes.

We now have established several basic tools of phonology: the underlying/ surface relationship, phonemic analysis, and distinctive features. With these in place we can proceed in subsequent chapters to more complicated analyses involving crucially ordered sequences of rules, obscure or abstract underlying representations, and phenomena that transcend the segmental level of representation.

Key terms

features
natural classes
distinctive features
binary features
manner features
sonorant
obstruent
continuant
liquid
place features
major place features
labial, coronal, dorsal
high
low
front
back

References and further reading

Anderson, Stephen. 1985. *Phonology in the Twentieth Century*. University of Chicago Press.
Bermúdez-Otero, Ricardo. 2001. Voicing and continuancy in Catalan: a nonvacuous Duke-of-York gambit and a Richness-of-the-Base paradox.

Ms., University of Manchester. Available online at www.bermudez-otero.com/Catalan.pdf

Clements, G. N. 1985. The geometry of phonological features. *Phonology Yearbook* 2: 225–252.

Hall, T. A. 2007. Segmental features. In Paul de Lacy (ed.), *The Cambridge Handbook of Phonology*. Cambridge University Press, 311–334.

Halle, Morris, and George N. Clements. 1983. *Problem Book in Phonology*. Cambridge, MA: MIT Press.

Hayes, Bruce. 2009. *Introductory Phonology*. Cambridge, MA: Blackwell.

Jakobson, Roman. 1942. The concept of phoneme. In Linda R. Waugh and Monique Moville-Burston (eds.), *On Language*. Cambridge, MA: Harvard University Press, 218–241.

Jakobson, Roman, C. Gunnar M. Fant, and Morris Halle. 1952. *Preliminaries to Speech Analysis: The Distinctive Features and Their Correlates*. Cambridge, MA: MIT Press.

Kenstowicz, Michael J. 1994. *Phonology in Generative Grammar*. Cambridge, MA: Blackwell.

Mascaró, Joan. 1976. Catalan phonology and the phonological cycle. Doctoral dissertation, Massachusetts Institute of Technology.

Mielke, Jeff. 2008. *The Emergence of Distinctive Features*. Oxford University Press.

Odden, David. 2005. *Introducing Phonology*. Cambridge University Press.

Sidharta (Sie Ing Djiang). 1976. *The Consonantal and Vowel Systems of Malay and Huayu: A Contrastive Analysis*. Singapore: Chinese Language Centre, Nanyang University.

van Driem, George. 1993. *A Grammar of Dumi*. Berlin: Mouton.

Youssef, Islam. 2013. Place assimilation in Arabic: contrasts, features, and constraints. Doctoral dissertation, University of Tromsø.

Zhang, Xi. 1996. The vowel systems of Manchu-Tungus languages of China. Doctoral dissertation, University of Toronto.

Zhang, Yanchang; Xi Zhang; and Dai Shuyan. 1989. *The Hezhen Language*. Changchun: Jilin University Press.

Review exercises

Yakut (Altaic, Siberia)

In Yakut, the initial consonants of suffixes can be observed to alternate as a function of the root-final segment. Consider the data below (from Kenstowicz (1994), v-final stems excluded):

Absolute	Plural	Dative	Gloss
at	at-tar	ak-ka	'horse'
kus	kus-tar	kus-ka	'duck'
oɣus	oɣus-tar	oɣus-ka	'bull'

kyøl	kyøl-ler	kyøl-ge	'lake'
sep	sep-ter	sep-ke	'tool'
et	et-ter	ek-ke	'meat'
ox	ox-tor	ox-xo	'arrow'
tobuk	tobuk-tar	tobuk-ka	'knee'
ubaj	ubaj-dar	ubaj-ga	'elder brother'
atɯɯr	atɯɯr-dar	atɯɯr-ga	'stallion'
tiiŋ	tiiŋ-ner	tiiŋŋe	'squirrel'
aan	aan-nar	aaŋŋa	'door'
olom	olom-nor	olomŋo	'ford'

a. List the alternants of the plural and dative suffixes.

b. List the environments in which each alternant of each suffix appears.

c. Is the form of either suffix predictable?

d. Write rules using binary features to derive the forms of the plural suffix. You may attempt to compose a single rule using alpha notation.

e. Write rules using binary features to derive the forms of the dative suffix.

Oroqen

Consider the following data from Oroqen (Zhang 1996):

açi	'now'
çii	'you (sg.)'
çɛɛn	'ear'
suxə	'axe'
suu	'you'
sʊnta	'deep'
sʊʊra	'flea'
sɔxɔ	'fill'
sɔɔti	'often'
sarbʊ	'chopsticks'
saa	'know'
sələ	'iron'
səəksə	'blood'
uskta	'fingernail'
asxa	'pinecone'[4]

a List all vowels that appear in the data.

b. Assuming the transcription is consistent with IPA notation, arrange these vowels in a table by their height and backness.

c. Describe using distinctive features the distribution of the sibilants [s] and [ç]. Are these allophones of a common phoneme? If so, what is the underlying phoneme?

d. Write a rule with distinctive features for the target and conditioning environment that accounts for the distribution of [s] and [ç].

Balinese

Recall the data from Balinese in §4.8, repeated here:

kədɪs	'bird'	kədise	'the bird'
sabʊʔ	'belt'	sabuke	'the belt'
bale	'hall'	balene	'the hall'
bwajɚ	'crocodile'	bwajane	'the crocodile'
təgal	'garden'	təgale	'the garden'
kambɪŋ	'goat'	kambiɲe	'the goat'
odalan	'temple festival'	odalane	'the temple festival'
məsolah	'dance'	məsolahe	'the dance'
əndəʔ	'Balinese ikat'	əndəke	'the Balinese ikat'
dʒaʊʔ	'type of demon'	dʒauke	'the type of demon'
pradɚ	'gold leaf'	pradane	'the gold leaf'
antʃʊr	'type of adhesive'	antʃure	'the type of adhesive'
dolɔg	'type of rice warehouse'	dologe	'the type of rice warehouse'
təbu	'sugarcane'	təbune	'the sugarcane'
tali	'rope, tie'	taline	'the rope, tie'
gɔŋ	'gong'	goŋe	'the gong'
gambəlan	'gamelan ensemble'	gambəlane	'the gamelan ensemble'
laŋɪt	'sky'	laŋite	'the sky'
borɛh	'skin lotion'	borehe	'the skin lotion'
idʊp	'life'	idupe	'the life'

a. List all the pairs of vowels that alternate based on their position within a word.

b. List all vowels that do not alternate in the data.

c. Differentiate using distinctive features the non-alternating vowels from the alternating vowels.

d. Using the feature [±tense], write a rule that accounts for the vowel alternations, and ensure that it does not apply to the non-alternating vowels.

Appendix: Feature charts for phonetic symbols

Note that these should be understood as general guidelines, and that the feature system used for a given language should adhere to the phonological system of that language. For example, palatals such as [c ɟ ɲ j] may function as [DOR, +high] in some languages, but [COR, −ant, −apical] in others. Similarly, [a] and [ə] could be considered [+ATR] or [−ATR] in different languages, depending on how they interact with other vowels in [ATR] harmony systems.

	p	b	m	ɸ	β	w	f	v
LAB	LAB	LAB	LAB	LAB	LAB	LAB	LAB	LAB
dental	−	−	−	−	−	−	+	+
cons	+	+	+	+	+	−	+	+
son	−	−	+	−	−	+	−	−
cont	−	−	−	+	+	+	+	+
nas	−	−	+	−	−	−	−	−
voi	−	+	+	−	+	+	−	+

	ṭ	d	θ	ð	s	z	n	l	ɹ	ʈ	ɖ	ɳ	ɭ	ʂ	ʐ	ʧ	ʤ	ʃ	ʒ
COR	COR	COR	COR	COR	COR	COR	COR	COR	COR	COR	COR	COR	COR	COR	COR	COR	COR	COR	COR
anterior	+	+	+	+	+	+	+	+	+	−	−	−	−	−	−	−	−	−	−
dist	+	+	−	−	+	+	+	+	+	−	−	−	−	−	−	+	+	+	+
cons	+	+	+	+	+	+	+	+	+	+	+	+	+	+	+	+	+	+	+
son	−	−	−	−	−	−	+	+	+	−	−	+	+	−	−	−	−	−	−
cont	−	−	+	+	+	+	−	+	+	−	−	−	+	+	+	−	−	+	+
nas	−	−	−	−	−	−	+	−	−	−	−	+	−	−	−	−	−	−	−
voi	−	+	−	+	−	+	+	+	+	−	+	+	+	−	+	−	+	−	+
lat	−	−	−	−	−	−	−	+	−	−	−	−	+	−	−	−	−	−	−
delayed release	−	−	−	−	−	−	−	−	−	−	−	−	−	−	−	+	+	−	−

	j	c	ɟ	ɲ	k	g	ŋ	x	ɣ	q	ɢ	χ	ʁ	R	N
	DOR	DOR	DOR	DOR	DOR	DOR	DOR	DOR	DOR	DOR	DOR	DOR	DOR	DOR	DOR
high	+	+	+	+	–	–	–	–	–	–	–	–	–	–	–
back	–	–	–	–	–	–	–	–	–	+	+	+	+	+	+
cons	–	+	+	+	+	+	+	+	+	+	+	+	+	+	+
son	+	–	–	+	–	–	+	–	–	–	–	–	–	+	+
cont	+	–	–	–	–	–	–	+	+	–	–	+	+	+	–
nas	–	–	–	+	–	–	+	–	–	–	–	–	–	–	+
voi	+	–	+	+	–	+	+	+	+	–	+	–	+	+	+

	i	ɪ	e	ɛ	æ	y	ø	ɨ	ə	ɵ	a	ɯ	ɤ	ɑ	u	ʊ	o	ɔ	ɒ
front	+	+	+	+	+	+	+	–	–	–	–	–	–	–	–	–	–	–	–
back	–	–	–	–	–	–	–	–	–	–	–	+	+	+	+	+	+	+	+
high	+	+	–	–	–	+	–	+	–	–	–	+	–	–	+	+	–	–	–
low	–	–	–	–	+	–	–	–	–	–	+	–	–	+	–	–	–	–	+
round	–	–	–	–	–	+	+	–	–	+	–	–	–	–	+	+	+	+	+
ATR	+	–	+	–	+									–	+	–	+	–	–

Endnotes

1 The implication here is one of sequential assimilation + deletion; one could analyze this subset as nasalization of the root followed by deletion of the prefix consonant, which places the boundary in a different locus, but which is consistent with the other rule that deletes nasals. A third option to explore is to call the pattern coalescence, in which the surface consonant is a blend of two underlying phonemes. Each approach has different implications, but each may fully account for these data

2 Some other alternations to note: /u/ → [ʊ] before n; /ɔ/ → [o] before [k, g, x] or]_WD; /a/ → [ɑ] after [k, x].

3 We can use binary features like [±low] and [±back] for vowels as well, as we will see later in this chapter.

4 These last forms have variants with medial [i], in which case the preceding consonant is palatal: [uçikta] and [açixa].

CHAPTER 7 RULE ORDERING, OPACITY, AND ABSTRACTNESS

Learning objectives

- Recognize interactions between different phonological processes
- Test competing hypotheses about ordering of rules
- Differentiate feeding and bleeding relationships
- Differentiate counterfeeding and counterbleeding relationships
- Motivate abstract underlying representations

Introduction

We have seen numerous phonological problems in which the ordering of two rules turns out to be critical to the account. For example, in §6.10, we examined the interaction of two deletion processes in Catalan: one process deletes word-final sonorants, as in /dur/ → [du], while another deletes word-final obstruents, but only after sonorants, as in /fɔrt/ → [fɔr]. We posited two separate rules to handle these processes, and determined that their ordering is crucial: if obstruent deletion applied first, then it would leave some sonorants in word-final position, subject to sonorant deletion, and this would yield inappropriate outcomes such as *[fɔ] from /fɔrt/. Since this does not match the appropriate output, we infer that the opposite ordering of these rules is necessary: obstruent deletion must follow sonorant deletion.

Relationships of rule-ordering are quite widely studied in phonology, and typically are seen in scenarios where multiple processes may apply to the same types of segments. We will explore some intricacies of rule ordering in more detail in this chapter.

Moreover, our ability to resort to ordered layers of rules means that sometimes the nature of an underlying form can be surprisingly different from its surface variants. At its most extreme, this phenomenon arises in the guise of abstractness, where a particular phoneme has an underlying representation which is never left untouched at the surface.

7.1 Serbo-Croatian: counterbleeding

To begin, let us return to the Serbo-Croatian data from §3.11, in which adjectives take different agreement suffixes according to gender and number.

Recall that we identified three suffixes: feminine [-a], neuter [-o], and plural [-i]. Masculine adjectives have no suffix. In Chapter 3, we concluded that the masculine forms in (8)–(13) contained an inserted vowel; for example, /sitn/ appears as [sitan] when unsuffixed, but when these roots receive suffixes, epenthesis is unnecessary, as in [sitna] and [sitno]. In contrast, the roots in (1)–(7) do not undergo insertion; their second vowels are underlying, which accounts for their appearance in suffixed forms as well. We used a rule of insertion to capture this generalization:

$$/ \emptyset \, / \rightarrow [a] \; / \; C \, \underline{\quad} \, C \,]_{\text{WD}}$$

Examine the data below, and note that we have added two more subgroups in (14)–(22).

	Masc	Fem	Neut	Pl	Gloss
(1)	mlád	mladá	mladó	mladí	'young'
(2)	púst	pustá	pustó	pustí	'empty'
(3)	zelén	zelená	zelenó	zelení	'green'
(4)	ʧést	ʧestá	ʧestó	ʧestí	'frequent'
(5)	bogat	bogata	bogato	bogati	'rich'
(6)	sunʧan	sunʧana	sunʧano	sunʧani	'sunny'
(7)	rapav	rapava	rapavo	rapavi	'rough'
(8)	ledan	ledna	ledno	ledni	'frozen'
(9)	dóbar	dobrá	dobró	dobrí	'good'
(10)	jásan	jasná	jasnó	jasní	'clear'
(11)	sítan	sitná	sitnó	sitní	'tiny'
(12)	óʃtar	oʃtrá	oʃtró	oʃtrí	'sharp'
(13)	mókar	mokrá	mokró	mokrí	'wet'
(14)	debéo	debelá	debeló	debelí	'fat'
(15)	posustao	posustala	posustalo	posustali	'tired'
(16)	béo	belá	beló	belí	'white'
(17)	mío	milá	miló	milí	'dear'
(18)	tséo	tselá	tseló	tselí	'whole'
(19)	okrúgao	okruglá	okrugló	okruglí	'round'
(20)	óbao	oblá	obló	oblí	'plump'
(21)	nágao	naglá	nagló	naglí	'abrupt'
(22)	pódao	podlá	podló	podlí	'base'

Exercise 7.1 The third group (14)–(18) illustrates a separate instance of alternation. Describe this pattern. Identify the underlying forms of each root, and propose a rule to account for the alternation seen here.

These roots illustrate an alternation between [l] and [o]. When there is no suffix, the root ends in [o], as in [beo]; before the vocalic suffixes, the roots instead have [l], as in [bela]. The /l/ is underlying in each root; for example, /bel/ 'white.' This motivates a rule that changes /l/ to [o] just in word-final position; when non-final (for example, before vowels, as in /bel + a/), the /l/ remains unchanged.

$$[l] \rightarrow [o] / \underline{\hspace{2em}}]_{\text{WD}}$$

An alternate hypothesis is available in which the masculine forms are identical to the underlying forms; this implies that /beo/ and so on are underlying. However, this forces an analysis in which underlying /o/ becomes [l] between vowels, and while this may work for the forms in (14)–(18), it falls apart when we turn next to the fourth group in (19)–(22).

Exercise 7.2 The fourth group in (19)–(22) illustrates both alternations: the [a ~ Ø] alternation and the [l ~ o] alternation. Describe this interaction. Identify the underlying forms of each root, and propose a rule to account for the alternation seen here.

Like the third group, these roots end in [o] in the masculine, as in [obao], but have [l] before the vocalic suffixes in the remaining forms, as in [obla]. Like the second group, these roots also have [a] in their unsuffixed masculine forms which is missing from the suffixed forms. In our analysis of the [a ~ Ø] alternation, we concluded that the [a] is inserted; it is absent from the suffixed forms but inserted in the masculine forms, where otherwise a word-final sequence of consonants would appear. We also concluded in Exercise 7.1 that the [l] is underlying, but is vocalized in word-final position.

Both of these patterns implicate the unsuffixed masculine forms: in other groups, unsuffixed /bel/ surfaces as [beo] and unsuffixed /ledn/ surfaces as [ledan]. In the fourth group, we are led to conclude that these roots have underlying final consonant sequences, the second of which is /l/. Thus, for example, /obl/ surfaces as [obao].

Exercise 7.3 Determine whether the l-vocalization rule and the a-insertion rule need to apply in a particular order.

The insertion rule must occur first. If l-vocalization applied first, then /obl/ would become [obo], in which case a-insertion need not apply. Thus, the ordering of l-vocalization followed by a-insertion predicts an inappropriate outcome. Conversely, however, if we order insertion first, /obl/ changes to an intermediate form of /obal/, which is then subject to [l]-vocalization, properly yielding [obao] at the surface.

In Serbo-croatian, then, these rules are said to be in a crucial order. This particular type of ordering is called **counterbleeding**, a label that draws its name from what would happen in the opposite ordering. That is, if l-vocalization were to apply first, its effect would *bleed* the later rule of a-insertion. Since this bleeding effect *does not* happen, the actual ordering of a-insertion first is called *counterbleeding*.

bleeding: a situation in which two rules are ordered such that the earlier rule removes the conditions for the later rule to apply in some forms.

counterbleeding: a situation in the ordering of two rules converse to a bleeding order. In counterbleeding order, the later rule removes the conditions that are implicated in the earlier rule.

We also refer to this as a scenario of **opacity**: a phonological phenomenon in which some surface form includes the output of a phonological process, despite lacking the motivation of that process. In these cases, the masculine roots contain an inserted [a], but the conditioning environment of two word-final consonants is absent at the surface, because of the effect of the counterbleeding order of rules.

opacity: a situation in which forms observe some phonological generalization despite the triggering environment not being present at the surface.

We suggested above that the [l ~o] alternation is best described as one of l-vocalization. The alternative analysis, that the /o/ is underlying, proves unwieldy in light of this fourth opaque group. Suppose that /o/ really were underlying here: then we are forced to make another choice about the representations for forms such as [obao]. Either we assume the /a/ is also underlying, and the UR is /obao/, or the /a/ is part of the [a~o] alternation, and the root is therefore /obo/.

If we follow the argument for /obao/, we then need a rule that changes intervocalic /o/ to [l] in suffixed forms, to predict /obao + a/ → [obla]. However, since the preceding /a/ is absent in the suffixed forms, we need a second rule that deletes it, to properly derive [obla]. Unfortunately, such a rule would overextend to [posustala], rendering it as *[posustla].

The last choice then is to explore /obo/ as a possible UR; one rule would be needed to change the root-final /o/ to [l] before a vowel, in order to effect /obo + a/ → [obla]. Another would be needed to insert [a] before word-final /o/, to yield /obo/ → [obao], but this rule risks overapplying to the many neuter forms which end in [o] without a preceding [a]. As a consequence, we can infer that the analysis which assumes /obl/, in tandem with rules of a-insertion and l-vocalization, fits the data much better.

7.2 Palauan

Another example of crucial rule ordering arises in Palauan. Take some time to peruse the data below (from Josephs 1975, 1990; Kie Zuraw p.c.), which are arranged into five groups. Each line contains a bare noun accompanied by a related form with a suffix indicating that the noun is possessed. Note that stress is included in these data as it is relevant to the analysis; also, you may consider all instances of word-final [ə] in the left column to be epenthetic.

(1)	ʔármə	ʔərm-έl	'animal'
(2)	málkə	məlk-έl	'chicken'
(3)	sέrsə	sərs-έl	'garden'
(4)	sέʔər	səʔər-έl	'sickness'
(5)	kέr	kər-έl	'question'
(6)	psípsə	psəps-έl	'drill'
(7)	kpókpə	kpəkp-έl	'wall'
(8)	səŋsóŋðə	səŋsəŋð-έl	'stick'
(9)	ʔúpsə	ʔəps-έl	'healing'
(10)	túrəʔə	tərəʔ-έl	'stamping'
(11)	ŋáklə	ŋkl-έl	'name'
(12)	ŋíkəl	ŋkəl-έl	'fish'
(13)	rásəʔə	rsəʔ-έl	'blood'
(14)	lúsəʔə	lsəʔ-έl	'luck'
(15)	láləʔə	lːəʔ-έl	'pus'
(16)	lík	lk-έl	'leaves'
(17)	bíːʔə	biʔ-έl	'sieve'
(18)	búːʔə	buʔ-έl	'betel nut'
(19)	ðέːl	ðεl-έl	'nail'
(20)	ðəkóːl	ðəkol-έl	'cigarette'
(21)	júŋsə	iŋs-έl	'island'
(22)	ʔajsə	ʔis-έl	'news'
(23)	bujlə	bil-έl	'moon'
(24)	wiŋəl	uŋəl-έl	'tooth'
(25)	swobəl	subəl-έl	'homework'
(26)	tawtə	tut-έl	'aim'

(27)	ðiálːə	ðilː-él	'ship'
(28)	tuáŋəl	tuŋəl-él	'door'
(29)	táɛm	tɛm-él	'time'
(30)	ɛáŋəð	ɛŋəð-él	'weather'
(31)	ɾoáklə	ɾokl-él	'rattling'
(32)	táoʔə	toʔ-él	'channel'

Exercise 7.4 Why would we conclude that word-final [ə] is epenthetic? Describe the alternations you see in the vowels of unsuffixed and suffixed roots.

We assume that word-final [ə] is always epenthetic for two reasons: first, this same vowel is absent from the suffixed forms, and second, it appears in a specific set of circumstances: only where the root ends in [ʔ] or a consonant sequence. All other roots end with some other single consonant.

The root vowel alternations differ across the arranged groups. In the first group, a stressed root vowel appears in the unsuffixed form, and alternates with unstressed [ə] in the suffixed form, as in [ʔármə, ʔərm-él]. In the second group, stressed root vowels in the unsuffixed form alternate with Ø in the suffixed forms, which also have syllabic consonants, as in [ŋáklə, ŋkl-él]. In the third group, a stressed long root vowel alternates with an unstressed short vowel, but with all the same vowel features, as in [bíːʔə, biʔ-él]. In the remaining groups, the stressed root vowel again alternates with Ø, and the suffixed forms contain high vowels instead, as in [bujlə, bil-él] and [ðiálːə, ðilː-él].

Since the specific vowels that alternate in each group vary across the unsuffixed forms, we can infer that the vowels in the unsuffixed forms are underlying, and that the schwa or zero alternant is a predictable variant that arises under suffixation. In the following exercises, we will develop analyses for each subgroup, and propose a unified approach to all the data.

Exercise 7.5 Describe the alternation in (1)–(10) in terms of distinctive features of both the alternating vowels and the conditioning environments. You may use [±stress] and [±long] as features for vowels. Account for this alternation with a formal rule.

The alternating vowels are [–long, +stress] in the unsuffixed forms, and they occur in roots in the environment [+cons]___[+cons]. When such roots are suffixed with [-ɛl], which receives stress, the vowels are reduced to unstressed [ə].

(1) ʔármə   ʔərm-él 'animal'

Reduction: [+syll, –long, +stress] → [ə] / [+cons]___[+cons] [+stress]

171

Exercise 7.6   Describe the alternation in (11)–(16) in terms of distinctive features of both the alternating vowels and the conditioning environments. Again, use [±stress] and [±long] as features for vowels. Account for these alternations with formal rules.

The alternating vowels are [–long, +stress] in the unsuffixed forms, and they occur in the environment [+son, +cons] ___ [–son]. When such roots are suffixed with [-εl], which receives stress, the vowels are deleted, and the preceding sonorants become syllabic.

(11)   ŋáklə   ŋkl-él   'name'
Post-sonorant deletion:
[+syll, –long, +stress] → Ø / [+son, +cons] ___ [–son] [+stress]
Sonorant consonant syllabification [+cons, +son] → [+syll] / $_{\text{WD}}$[___ [+cons, –son]

Exercise 7.7   Describe the alternation in (17)–(20) in terms of distinctive features of both the alternating vowels and the conditioning environments. Again, use [±stress] and [±long] as features for vowels. Account for this alternation with a formal rule.

The alternating vowels are [+long, +stress] in the unsuffixed forms, and they occur in the environment [+cons] ___ [+cons]. When such roots are suffixed with [-εl], the vowels are made [–long].

(17)   bíːʔə   biʔ-él   'sieve'
Shortening [+syll, +long, +stress] → [–long] ___ / [+cons] ___ [+cons] [+stress]

At this we can acknowledge a few interesting aspects of the analysis. First, the three subgroups we have handled so far each motivate different rules, but they share a common thread of weakening a vowel when stress shifts away from it. A short vowel that loses stress is either reduced or deleted, depending on its environment, while a long vowel is shortened. We may wonder on one hand whether reduction and deletion are really two manifestations of the same process, and on the other, whether the length of some vowels "protects" them from being reduced or deleted.

Certainly the fact that the shortening rule creates vowels which do not undergo further reduction is indicative of a crucial ordering of rules: the shortening rule applies to long vowels, but only after the reduction and deletion rules have applied to vowels which are themselves already short. This particular type of crucial ordering is called a **counterfeeding** relationship: the opposite ordering would be a **feeding** relationship (that is, shortening could feed reduction), but as this does not occur, the true ordering is counterfeeding.

feeding: a situation in which two rules are ordered such that the earlier rule generates the conditions for the later rule to apply.

counterfeeding: a situation in the ordering of two rules converse to a feeding order. In counterfeeding order, the later rule creates structure to which the earlier rule would have applied.

Counterfeeding is another example of a type of phonological opacity: in Palauan, there is a rule that reduces vowels to schwa, but the effect of this rule at the surface is partly obscured by the fact that some vowels are unreduced. Their immunity to reduction is a direct consequence of the counterfeeding relationship.

In addition, the rule of sonorant syllabification must follow the rule of deletion – it is the deletion rule that creates the conditions for sonorant syllabification, which provides an example of a feeding relationship.

As to the question of whether we can express deletion and reduction as the same process, the analytical choice we face is essentially as follows: in the circumstance of stress moving to the suffix, the root vowel either generally deletes (and surfaces as a schwa in a specific set of exceptions), or it generally reduces to schwa (and is further deleted in a specific set of circumstances). The remaining subgroups will inform this analytical choice, but we may already begin to favor the general-deletion approach, as it allows us to think of the overall pattern as one which deletes a single short vowel, or one half of a long vowel.

Exercise 7.8 Describe the alternation in (21)–(26) in terms of distinctive features of both the alternating vowels and the conditioning environments. Again, use [±stress] and [±long] as features for vowels. Account for this alternation with a formal rule.

The alternating vowels are [–long, +stress], and they occur in the environment [+cons] ___ [–cons, –syll] or [–cons, –syll] ___ [+cons]. When such roots are suffixed with [-ɛl], which receives stress, the vowels are deleted, and the adjacent sonorants become syllabic.

(21) júŋsə iŋs-ɛ́l 'island'

Pre- and post-vocoid deletion:

[+syll, –long, +stress] → Ø / [+son, –cons] ___ [–son] [+stress]
[+syll, –long, +stress] → Ø / [–son] ___ [+son, –cons] [+stress]
also: glide vocalization [–cons, –syll] → [+syll] / [+cons] ___ [+cons]

The rules we use here are very much like the deletion rule of Exercise 7.6, but also need to delete the vowel in the case of a following sonorant. The fact that

173

deletion again occurs provides further evidence that it is the default approach. Moreover, the process of glide vocalization is directly parallel to the rule of sonorant syllabification from the same exercise.

Exercise 7.9 Describe the alternation in (27)–(32) in terms of distinctive features of both the alternating vowels and the conditioning environments. Again, use [±stress] and [±long] as features for vowels. Account for this alternation with a formal rule.

The alternating vowels are [–long, +stress], and they occur in the environment [–cons, +syll] ___ [+cons] or [+cons] ___ [–cons, +syll]. When such roots are suffixed with [-ɛl], which receives stress, the vowels are deleted, leaving the adjacent vowels behind.

(27)   tuáŋəl   tuŋəl-ɛ́l   'door'

The same deletion rules from Exercise 7.8 work here.

Since we have several deletion rules throughout this analysis, we should consider revising the analysis by reducing them to a single general process, applying in a less specific environment.

General deletion: [+syll, –long, +stress] → Ø / ___ C [+stress]

This rule is so general that it will delete vowels from forms in which we expect schwa; however, such forms are readily described in terms of the natural classes of sounds that occur within them. In short, we can allow the general deletion rule to apply, and then rely on a rule that inserts schwa just in those forms that match the description of forms in (1)–(10).

Exercise 7.10 Describe the environment of the schwa in (1)–(10) using distinctive features for the adjacent sounds. Make sure your description exclusively describes these forms and none of the forms in (11)–(32). You do not need to worry about the third subgroup, since these have underlying long vowels and will not undergo deletion anyway. Propose a rule that inserts schwa in the environment you identify.

The schwa replaces the deleted vowel in the forms in (1)–(10) following an osbtruent and before any other [+cons] segment. The other subgroups do not fit this description: in (11)–(16), the initial segment before the deleted vowel is a sonorant. In (21)–(32), there is a [–cons] segment either before or after the vowel that is deleted.

The schwa insertion rule thus works as follows:

schwa insertion   Ø → [ə] / ᴡᴅ[[–son] ___ [+cons]

We have revised the analysis to comprise a rule of deletion, of schwa-insertion, and of shortening. We also still need an additional rule that makes leftover sonorants into syllabic consonants; we return to this issue in more detail in Chapter 8, but the following rule will suffice for the moment.

sonorant syllabification   [+son] → [+syll] / __ [+cons]

Both the schwa insertion rule and the sonorant syllabification rule are crucially ordered after the deletion rule. In fact, the deletion rule creates the circumstances under which the other rules apply, thus it feeds both of the later rules.

Furthermore, our earlier claim about the order of deletion and shortening is still necessary: deletion must occur first, and it applies only to short vowels; shortening applies later, and as a result, underlyingly long vowels are protected from deletion. The fact that shortening would feed deletion, but cannot because of its later application, makes this a counterfeeding relationship.

7.3 Extended case study: Isthmus Zapotec

In the following discussion we will take an extended look at alternations in the suffixes of Isthmus Zapotec. This problem brings together issues and skills from this chapter and the previous ones on morphophonemic analysis and alternation.

The table below contains three inflected forms for each of twenty-five roots (data from Merrifield *et al.* 1967, Jensen 1990). Note that the diacritic in symbols such as [å] indicates a glottalized voice quality; such vowels are always also stressed. Vowels which are stressed but not glottalized are transcribed with an acute accent. This notation is not standard IPA practice; when we return to stress in Chapter 9, we will learn more about stress notation.

In this discussion, we will be concerned primarily with the first-person singular forms, but the other forms are there in part to help us determine the form of each root independently of its affixes. Let us therefore first conduct some morphological analysis on the second singular and third singular forms.

Isthmus Zapotec verbs

	Gloss	2sg	3sg	1sg
(1)	'fall'	riábalu?	riábabe	riába?
(2)	'get up'	riásalu?	riásabe	riása?
(3)	'walk'	rizálu?	rizábe	rizája?
(4)	'save'	rulálu?	rulábe	rulája?
(5)	'scrape'	rurálu?	ruråbe	rurå?

(6)	'bathe'	rázeluʔ	rázebe	rázeʔ
(7)	'pinch'	rigiéluʔ	rigiébe	rigiéʔ
(8)	'err'	rutʃĕluʔ	rutʃĕbe	rutʃĕʔ
(9)	'take out'	ribĕluʔ	ribĕbe	ribĕʔ
(10)	'glean'	ribáguluʔ	ribágube	ribáguaʔ
(11)	'put on'	rákuluʔ	rákube	rákuaʔ
(12)	'faint'	riĕguluʔ	riĕgube	riĕguaʔ
(13)	'hunt'	rukuåguluʔ	rukuågube	rukuåguaʔ
(14)	'suppose'	ruzulúluʔ	ruzulúbe	ruzuluáʔ
(15)	'cough'	rurúluʔ	rurúbe	ruruáʔ
(16)	'put in'	rigůluʔ	rigůbe	riguåʔ
(17)	'enter'	riůluʔ	riůbe	riuåʔ
(18)	'get old'	riŏʃoloʔ	riŏʃobe	riŏʃuaʔ
(19)	'sell'	rutŏloʔ	rutŏbe	rutuåʔ
(20)	'get fat'	rirŏloʔ	rirŏbe	riruåʔ
(21)	'sleep'	rásiluʔ	rásibe	ráseʔ
(22)	'say'	rábiluʔ	rábibe	rábeʔ
(23)	'sit'	ribíluʔ	ribíbe	ribiéʔ
(24)	'cover'	rutʃíluʔ	rutʃíbe	rutʃiéʔ
(25)	'give'	rudíluʔ	rudíbe	rudiéʔ

Exercise 7.11   What are the forms for the second and third singular agreement suffixes in Isthmus Zapotec?

The third singular suffix is probably the easiest to approach. Each form in this column ends in the same segmental sequence, namely [-be]. We may therefore infer for the moment that in all such forms, [-be] is the suffix, and thus the root is always what remains when we remove [-be].

The same sequences – the segments we are presuming to be the roots – are present in the corresponding second singular forms. Indeed, shifting our attention to that column, whatever sequence follows these presumed roots is quite consistent. It is not identical in every case, but each presumed root is followed by some suffix beginning with [l], and in fact there are but two alternants of this suffix: [-loʔ] and [-luʔ]. The [-loʔ] form appears only after roots which end in [-o], and the [-luʔ] alternant appears in every other circumstance.

Based on second- and third-person suffixed forms, the analysis thus far is straightforward and simple. It gets more complicated when we turn to the first-person forms, because we will see that roots and affixes both alternate.

The next step is to locate boundaries within the first-person forms. We can use our conclusions from (1)–(25) above regarding the roots of each form to

make this determination. Examine the following data, which places the first-
person singular forms next to their presumed roots. As you look over the data,
consider the likely location of the boundary between the root and the first
singular suffix.

	Gloss	Root	1sg
(1)	'fall'	riába-	riábaʔ
(2)	'get up'	riása-	riásaʔ
(3)	'walk'	rizá-	rizájaʔ
(4)	'save'	rulá-	rulájaʔ
(5)	'scrape'	rurå-	ruråʔ
(6)	'bathe'	ráze-	rázeʔ
(7)	'pinch'	rigié-	rigiéʔ
(8)	'err'	ruʧĕ-	ruʧĕʔ
(9)	'take out'	ribĕ-	ribĕʔ
(10)	'glean'	ribágu-	ribáguaʔ
(11)	'put on'	ráku-	rákuaʔ
(12)	'faint'	riĕgu-	riĕguaʔ
(13)	'hunt'	rukuågu-	rukuåguaʔ
(14)	'suppose'	ruzulú-	ruzuluáʔ
(15)	'cough'	rurú-	ruruáʔ
(16)	'put in'	rigů-	riguåʔ
(17)	'enter'	riů-	riuåʔ
(18)	'get old'	riðʃo-	riðʃuaʔ
(19)	'sell'	rutð-	rutuåʔ
(20)	'get fat'	rirð-	riruåʔ
(21)	'sleep'	rási-	ráseʔ
(22)	'say'	rábi-	rábeʔ
(23)	'sit'	ribí-	ribiéʔ
(24)	'cover'	ruʧî-	ruʧiĕʔ
(25)	'give'	rudî-	rudiĕʔ

Exercise 7.12 Identify the alternants of the first-person suffix for the forms above.

Many of the first-person forms include a segment sequence which is identical
to what appears in the corresponding third- and second-person forms; for
example, the first singular form for (1) [riábaʔ] includes the sequence [riába-],
which also appears in the second singular form [riábaluʔ]. Thus we
conclude that the form of the first singular suffix in this word is [-ʔ].

The same analysis applies to everything in (1)–(13). By this logic, among
such roots, there are three suffix alternants. In (1), (2), and (5)–(9), the suffix is
[-ʔ]; in (3) and (4) the suffix is [-jaʔ], and in (10)–(13) the suffix is [-aʔ].

	Gloss	*Root*	*1sg*
(1)	'fall'	riába-	riába-ʔ
(2)	'get up'	riása-	riása-ʔ
(3)	'walk'	rizá-	rizá-jaʔ
(4)	'save'	rulá-	rulá-jaʔ
(5)	'scrape'	rurȁ-	rurȁ-ʔ
(6)	'bathe'	ráze-	ráze-ʔ
(7)	'pinch'	rigié-	rigié-ʔ
(8)	'err'	rutʃȅ-	rutʃȅ-ʔ
(9)	'take out'	ribě-	ribě-ʔ
(10)	'glean'	ribágu-	ribágu-aʔ
(11)	'put on'	ráku-	ráku-aʔ
(12)	'faint'	riȅgu-	riȅgu-aʔ
(13)	'hunt'	rukuȁgu-	rukuȁgu-aʔ

The remaining forms undergo a certain amount of root alternation, either in the position of stress, the nature of the root's final vowel, or both.

For example, consider (14) [ruzuluáʔ]. Like the forms in (10)–(13), its root ends in /u/ and its suffix includes a vowel. However, the stress placement differs across forms: its third-person form is [ruzulúbe], which leads us to infer /ruzulú/ as its underlying root. In the first-person form [ruzuluáʔ], stress has shifted from the final vowel of root to the vowel of the suffix. The same pattern applies in (14)–(17), with the additional complication that glottalization also shifts in (16) and (17).

	Gloss	*Root*	*1sg*
(14)	'suppose'	ruzulú-	ruzulu-áʔ
(15)	'cough'	rurú-	ruru-áʔ
(16)	'put in'	rigȕ-	rigu-áʔ
(17)	'enter'	riȕ-	riu-ȁʔ

In (18)–(20), the root-final vowel changes; for example, consider (18) [riȍʃuaʔ]. Its root ends in /o/ in the other inflected forms such as [riȍʃoloʔ, riȍʃobe], but appears as [riȍʃu-aʔ] here. Since there are other roots that end in [-u] in all three columns (for example, (11) [rákuluʔ, rákube, rákuaʔ]), we must conclude that the /o/ of [riȍʃobe] is underlying and becomes [u] before the [aʔ] suffix in [riȍʃuaʔ].

In addition to a change in vowel quality, the two forms (19) and (20) also move their stress and glottalization from their final root vowel to their suffix vowel, analogous to the forms in (14)–(17).

	Gloss	*Root*	*1sg*
(18)	'get old'	riȍʃo-	riȍʃu-aʔ
(19)	'sell'	rutȍ-	rutu-aʔ
(20)	'get fat'	rirȍ-	riru-ȁʔ

The forms with root-final /i/ present some additional complications. For example, consider (21) [ráseʔ]. Its corresponding third-person form is [rásibe], which, by the logic we have used, has a root /rási-/. Yet the final /i/ of the root is absent from the first-person form [ráseʔ]. The same issue arises in (22) [rábeʔ], whose corresponding third singular form is [rábibe].

As a result, more than one possible morphological analysis may be posited for each such first singular form: we may analyze [ráseʔ] as [ráse-ʔ], with a suffix [-ʔ], or as [rás-eʔ], with a suffix [-eʔ]. While the former is a simpler choice, in that all other root alternants also end in vowels, we can note that the latter is also consistent with several facts. In particular, the analysis that considers the breakdown as [rás-eʔ] posits [eʔ] as a suffix alternant with a root which underlyingly ends in /i/, a pattern seen elsewhere, particularly the forms in (23)–(25). Moreover, the roots in (21) and (22) are the only ones ending in unstressed /i/; the analysis can capitalize on this fact and limit a process of i-deletion only to roots of such type.

(21) 'sleep' rási- rás-eʔ
(22) 'say'   rábi- ráb-eʔ

That there is root alternation is unavoidable; if we instead assumed [-ʔ] to be the suffix alternant in [raseʔ], we would be left with a different alternation in which the root /rasi-/ lowers its final vowel in the first-person form, but remains [rasi-] elsewhere. We will see below that this alternative analysis is less wieldy, and therefore will follow the assumption that [-eʔ] is the suffix here.

The last set of forms also has roots with final /i/, which also happens to bear stress (and glottalization in one case). As with other root-final stressed forms, stress shifts in these cases, but here, the vowel of the suffix is [e].

(23) 'sit'   ribí-   ribi-éʔ
(24) 'cover' ruʧí-   ruʧi-èʔ
(25) 'give'   rudî-   rudi-èʔ

To summarize so far, we have a host of different alternants in the first-person forms; in some cases, the suffix has no vowel, in others it includes either [a] or [e]. Moreover, some root-final vowels alternate. Last, the vowel of the suffix is sometimes stressed, sometimes glottalized, and sometimes neither.

Let us attempt to account for these changes as a function of the form of the root. Re-examine the first-person data, repeated below but with boundaries included, with an eye for the conditions that predict each alternant. Try to sort your ideas in terms of processes: which roots have suffixes with vowels, and which have just [ʔ]? What distinguishes the stress-shifting forms from those with static stress position? What distinguishes the roots which alternate in their final vowels from those that do not?

	Gloss	Root	1sg
(1)	'fall'	riába-	riába-ʔ
(2)	'get up'	riása-	riása-ʔ
(3)	'walk'	rizá-	rizá-jaʔ
(4)	'save'	rulá-	rulá-jaʔ
(5)	'scrape'	rurå-	rurå-ʔ
(6)	'bathe'	ráze-	ráze-ʔ
(7)	'pinch'	rigié-	rigié-ʔ
(8)	'err'	ruʧě-	ruʧě-ʔ
(9)	'take out'	ribě-	ribě-ʔ
(10)	'glean'	ribágu-	ribágu-aʔ
(11)	'put on'	ráku-	ráku-aʔ
(12)	'faint'	riěgu-	riěgu-aʔ
(13)	'hunt'	rukuågu-	rukuågu-aʔ
(14)	'suppose'	ruzulú-	ruzulu-áʔ
(15)	'cough'	rurú-	ruru-áʔ
(16)	'put in'	rigů-	rigu-åʔ
(17)	'enter'	riů-	riu-åʔ
(18)	'get old'	riðʃo-	riðʃu-aʔ
(19)	'sell'	rutð-	rutu-åʔ
(20)	'get fat'	rirð-	riru-åʔ
(21)	'sleep'	rási-	rás-eʔ
(22)	'say'	rábi-	ráb-eʔ
(23)	'sit'	riɓí-	riɓi-éʔ
(24)	'cover'	ruʧǐ-	ruʧi-ěʔ
(25)	'give'	rudǐ-	rudi-ěʔ

Exercise 7.13 Identify the conditions under which each alternant of the first-person suffix appears. You may find it helpful to code the data by repeating the root-final vowel.

The predictability of the first-person forms begins to emerge when we see how they correlate with the form of the root.

First, the suffix is [jaʔ] when the root ends in non-glottalized stressed /á/, as in (3) and (4).

Otherwise, it is [ʔ] after other types of /a/, as in (1), (2), and (5), and after any type of /e/, as in (6)–(9).

The suffix is [aʔ] after roots ending in [u], as in (10)–(17), as well as those that underlyingly end in /o/), as in (18)–(20).

The suffix is [eʔ] after roots ending underlyingly in /i/, as in (21)–(25). In Exercise 7.12 we had a choice about how to analyze the forms in (21) and (22), specifically whether to consider the [e] as part of the suffix or part of the root. As we explore this in more detail below, it will emerge that assigning the [e] to the suffix in (21) and (22) is a more plausible route.

Stress shifts to the suffix vowel only if it is associated with the root's final vowel, as in (14–17), (19), (20), and (23)–(25).

Two alternations in root form are also observable. Root-final /o/ raises to [u] before the suffix, as in (18)–(20), and root-final /i/ lowers to [e], only if unstressed, as in (23)–(25).

The next step in the analysis is to decide upon the nature of the suffix's underlying representation, and in particular, whether the vowel of the suffix is present underlyingly. If it is not, our analysis must account for when that vowel is inserted; if it is, our analysis must account for when it is deleted.

We can rule out the insertion approach fairly easily; this would have us assume that /ʔ/ is the underlying form of the first-person singular suffix. If this were the case, then we would have to propose a rule that inserts vowels between root-final vowels and the /ʔ/ suffix. For example, this rule would need to insert /a/ in /raku + ʔ/ to derive the first singular form (11) [rakuaʔ]. The problem here is that other forms allow [uʔ] as a sequence, for example in second-person forms such as (23) [ribíluʔ].

Let instead propose that /-aʔ/ is the form of the suffix. Thus, the vowel needs to be deleted in some circumstances; changed to [e] in others, and separated from the root with a glide in still others. In addition, the analysis must account for the movement of stress or glottalization, as well as for changes in some root-final vowels.

Exercise 7.14   Construct rules that handle the number of segments in the suffix. You'll need a rule to insert a glide, and a separate rule to delete the /a/ of the suffix under a particular circumstance. Specify whether they need to be ordered.

$$\emptyset \rightarrow j \: / \: \text{á} \: \underline{\quad} \: a$$
$$a \rightarrow \emptyset \: / \: [\text{--back}] \: \underline{\quad}$$

The glide-insertion rule is quite straightforward.

The vowel-deletion rule deletes /a/ only after [–back] vowels, under the assumption that [a] is [–back]. If we do not want to commit to this claim, we could instead specify the environment as [–round], or as {–back, +low}. For their ordering, the deletion rule should come second, to ensure that the suffix vowel is not deleted after stressed [á].

However, the vowel-deletion rule is still somewhat problematic. In its current form, it deletes the suffix /a/ after [a, e, i], but not after [o, u].

Overall this is a decent fit, but the forms in (23)–(25) maintain a suffix vowel despite having roots ending in [i], as in (23) [riɓi-éʔ]. Without addressing this issue, the rules as they are stated risk deleting the suffix vowel in these forms.

We can address this by taking advantage of the fact that the suffix vowel is [e] in the (23)–(25) forms – as such, we can claim that the a-deletion rule does not apply. To hold this analysis, we need to propose a rule which raises /a/ and orders it before the deletion rule.

Exercise 7.15   Amend the analysis with an additional rule that prevents a-deletion from applying to the forms in (23)–(25). Does this rule need to be ordered crucially, and if so, what kind of ordering relationship can be observed?

a → e / [i] ____

This rule needs to occur before a-deletion, so that any raised vowel is not deleted. The ordering of the two rules is a bleeding order: the earlier a-raising rule results in a structure to which the later a-deletion rule can no longer apply.

glide insertion	Ø → j / á ____ a
a-raising	a → e / [i] ____
a-deletion	a → Ø / [–back] ____

Recall that we faced an analytical choice regarding the forms in (21) and (22), such as (21) [ráseʔ]. While our analysis assumes the breakdown to be [rás-eʔ], the alternative [ráse-ʔ] is also possible. Either approach requires some work on the nature of the root alternation.

Indeed, there are still several types of root alternation to account for. We have acknowledged the following patterns of root alternation in the first-person forms: the roots in (21) and (22) have a final /i/ which disappears; the roots in (18)–(20) have a final /o/ which raises to [u], and all roots with final stress see their stress shift to the suffix vowel.

Exercise 7.16   Write rules to account for the alternations in root-final vowels, and state whether their order relative to other rules is crucial.

| o-raising | o → u / ____ a |
| i-deletion | i → Ø / [+stress vowel] C ____ e |

The o-raising rule is simple and has no apparent ordering restrictions relative to other rules.

The i-deletion phenomenon is more complicated because of its interaction with our morphological analysis. Following our assumption of final-vowel deletion in (21) and (22), as in [rás-eʔ], we need a rule specified only to delete /i/ in some circumstances.

This rule must be ordered after the a-raising rule, to ensure that the suffix vowel can be raised. If i-deletion were ordered earlier, a-raising could not apply in (21) or (22), as the preceding /i/ would be missing. As such, the two rules stand in a counterbleeding order.

If we had followed the alternative analysis whereby these roots have a lowered final vowel, parsed as [ráse-ʔ], the rule instead would need to change /i/ to [e]. The conditioning environment for this i-lowering rule is problematic: if the rule occurs later than a-raising, then i-lowering must occur before [e] (as above); this would create a sequence of two [e]s in an intermediate form /rase-eʔ/, motivating an additional rule to remove one of them. If the rule occurs prior to a-raising, then the environment needs to be __ [a]; however, i-lowering would then also incorrectly apply in forms (23)–(25), since the root-final /i/ in such forms precedes [a]. Consequently, we can determine that an analysis which assumes [ráse-ʔ] and [rábe-ʔ] for (21)–(22) either requires an additional rule or produces a paradox in its ordering of rules.

The remaining alternation involves the position of stress, a phonological phenomenon that we have not technically addressed yet. Since we do not yet have the notational tools to characterize stress, we can for this analysis acknowledge in an informal sense a rule which moves the position of stress from a root-final vowel to a suffix vowel. The rule must be specific enough to keep stress static when it occurs on non-root-final vowels.

Stress shift: v́]$_{\mathrm{ROOT}}$v → / vv́

We can summarize the analysis as follows

j-insertion	Ø → j / á __ a
a-raising	a → e / i __
a-deletion	a → Ø / [-rd] __
i-deletion	i → Ø / __ e
o-raising	o → u / __ a
move stress	v́]$_{\mathrm{ROOT}}$v → / vv́

Now with all the rules revised, and their ordering determined, we may test the analysis against all forms. The table below summarizes this test; moving from left to right it takes the underlying representation of each first singular form and sends it through the sequence of rules. Where forms are unaffected because a rule cannot apply, the cell is left blank.

Gloss	UR	j-insertion o-raising	a-raising	a-deletion	i-deletion	move stress	SR
(1) 'fall'	riába-aʔ		riába-ʔ				riába-ʔ
(2) 'get up'	riása-aʔ		riása-ʔ				riása-ʔ
(3) 'walk'	rizá-aʔ	rizá-jaʔ					rizá-jaʔ
(4) 'save'	rulá-aʔ	rulá-jaʔ					rulá-jaʔ
(5) 'scrape'	rurå-aʔ		rurå-ʔ				rurå-ʔ
(6) 'bathe'	ráze-aʔ		ráze-ʔ				ráze-ʔ
(7) 'pinch'	rigié-aʔ		rigié-ʔ				rigié-ʔ
(8) 'err'	rutʃě-aʔ		rutʃě-ʔ				rutʃě-ʔ
(9) 'take out'	ribě-aʔ		ribě-ʔ				ribě-ʔ
(10) 'sleep'	ribágu-aʔ						ribágu-aʔ
(11) 'say'	ráku-aʔ						ráku-aʔ
(12) 'sit'	riěgu-aʔ						riěgu-aʔ
(13) 'cover'	rukuågu-aʔ						rukuågu-aʔ
(14) 'give'	ruzulú-aʔ					ruzulu-áʔ	ruzulu-áʔ
(15) 'get old'	rurú-aʔ					ruru-áʔ	ruru-áʔ
(16) 'sell'	rigǔ-aʔ					rigu-åʔ	rigu-åʔ
(17) 'get fat'	riǔ-aʔ					riu-åʔ	riu-åʔ
(18) 'glean'	riǒʃo-aʔ	riǒʃu-aʔ					riǒʃu-aʔ
(19) 'put on'	rutǒ-aʔ	rutǔ-aʔ				rutu-åʔ	rutu-åʔ
(20) 'faint'	rirǒ-aʔ	rirǔ-aʔ				riru-åʔ	riru-åʔ
(21) 'hunt'	rási-aʔ		rási-eʔ	rás-eʔ			rás-eʔ
(22) 'suppose'	rábi-aʔ		rábi-eʔ	ráb-eʔ			ráb-eʔ
(23) 'cough'	ribí-aʔ		ribí-eʔ			ribi-éʔ	ribi-éʔ
(24) 'put in'	rutʃî-aʔ		rutʃî-eʔ			rutʃi-ěʔ	rutʃi-ěʔ
(25) 'enter'	rudî-aʔ		rudî-eʔ			rudi-ěʔ	rudi-ěʔ

Now that we have situated all these processes together in a single analysis, we can see how the data exemplify a range of types of phonological alternations. The first singular suffix invokes epenthesis and deletion – alternations with zero – as well as several vowel-to-vowel effects. The process of o-raising can be seen as dissimilatory, in that the vowel becomes less like the adjacent [a]; meanwhile, the process of a-raising can be seen as assimilatory, because by raising a low vowel, it makes the target more like the adjacent [i]. Many of these processes are obscured by the variety of crucial rule-orderings we have needed for the analysis, but viewed individually, each seems to be a sensible rule.

7.4 Hungarian

A distinct type of hidden process in phonological systems involves a phenomenon we call abstractness, for reasons that emerge in the following discussion. Take some time to revisit the following data from Hungarian (Kornai 1987), which we saw in §4.4.

	Stem	Dative	Ablative	As an X	Gloss
(1)	had	hadnak	hadtoːl	hadul	'army'
(2)	haːz	haːznak	haːztoːl	haːzul	'house'
(3)	juk	juknak	juktoːl	jukul	'hole'
(4)	kuːt	kuːtnak	kuːttoːl	kuːtul	'well'
(5)	hold	holdnak	holdtoːl	holdul	'moose'
(6)	loː	loːnak	loːtoːl	loːul	'horse'
(7)	in	innak	intoːl	inul	'tendon'
(8)	hid	hidnak	hidtoːl	hidul	'bridge'
(9)	heːj	heːjnak	heːjtoːl	heːjul	'crust'
(10)	bab	babnak	babtoːl	babul	'bean'
(11)	baːb	baːbnak	baːbtoːl	baːbul	'puppet'
(12)	rum	rumnak	rumtoːl	rumul	'id.'
(13)	huːr	huːrnak	huːrtoːl	huːrul	'chord'
(14)	bot	botnak	bottoːl	botul	'stick'
(15)	droːt	droːtnak	droːttoːl	droːtul	'wire'
(16)	ʒir	ʒirnak	ʒirtoːl	ʒirul	'fat'
(17)	ceːl	ceːlnak	ceːltoːl	ceːlul	'goal'
(18)	hit	hitnek	hittøːl	hityl	'belief'
(19)	viːz	viːznek	viːztøːl	viːzyl	'water'
(20)	fej	fejnek	fejtøːl	fejyl	'head'
(21)	eːrv	eːrvnek	eːrvtøːl	eːrvyl	'argument'
(22)	hølɟ	hølɟnek	hølɟtøːl	hølɟyl	'lady'
(23)	tøːɟ	tøːɟnek	tøːɟtøːl	tøːɟyl	'udder'
(24)	sylt	syltnek	sylttøːl	syltyl	'roast'
(25)	tyːz	tyːznek	tyːztøːl	tyːzyl	'fire'
(26)	tøk	tøknek	tøktøːl	tøkyl	'pumpkin'
(27)	bøːr	bøːrnek	bøːrtøːl	bøːryl	'skin'
(28)	fyst	fystnek	fysttøːl	fystyl	'smoke'
(29)	byːn	byːnnek	byːntøːl	byːnyl	'sin'

Exercise 7.17 What are the alternants of each suffix? Under what conditions does each alternant appear?

The forms of the dative suffix are [nak] and [nek]. The alternant [nak] appears after roots with [u, o, a, i, e], while the alternant [nek] appears after roots with [i, e, y, ø]. Note that the choice is predictable for most root vowels, but where the root is [i] or [e], either alternant could appear.

Some parallel generalizations are evident for the other suffixes: for the ablative suffix, the alternant [toːl] appears with [u, o, a, i, e], and the alternant [tøːl] appears with [i, e, y, ø]. As before, roots with [i] or [e] could receive either suffix. A parallel alternation affects the "as an X" suffix, whose alternants are [ul] and [yl]. Crucially, those roots that receive [nak] also receive [tol] and [ul], while those that receive [nek] also receive [tøːl] and [yl].

Exercise 7.18 a. Using distinctive features, describe the vowels that co-occur with [nak], [toːl], and [ul], but do not include [i] and [e].
b. Using distinctive features, describe the vowels that co-occur with [nek], [tøːl], and [yl], but again do not include [i] and [e].

The vowels that co-occur with [nak], [tol], and [ul] are all [+back] vowels. The vowels that co-occur with [nek], [tøːl], and [yl] are all [−back] vowels.

These data show that many Hungarian suffixes alternate in their backness: roots with back vowels take back suffixes, and roots with front vowels take front suffixes.

Exercise 7.19 Describe the generalization that applies to the Hungarian suffixes and propose a rule or rules to account for their alternation.

Each suffix has one alternant with a front vowel and another with a back vowel. Where the root vowel is not [i] or [e], the alternant is determined by the vowel of the root. Back-vowel alternants appear with back-vowel roots, and front-vowel alternants appear with front-vowel roots. This is a simple example of a backness vowel harmony process, and we can capture this generalization with the following rule:

[+vowel, +back] → [−back] / [vowel, −back] C ____

This rule assumes that the [+back] alternants are underlying, and will change /u/ to [y], /o/ to [ø], and /a/ to [e].

Some Hungarian words seem to resist the harmonic pattern; in fact, only those with /i/ or /e/ may do so, but not every such root does. That is, some roots with /i/ or /e/ take front suffixes, but others take back suffixes. We may divide the roots into two groups: those that show front-vowel harmony, as in [hitnek], and those that show back-vowel harmony, as in [hidnak].

As with the roots with unexceptional vowels, any root with [i] takes consistently back or consistently front suffix alternants.

Exercise 7.20 Recall in our discussion of natural classes in Chapter 6 that segments with similar phonological properties can be inferred to share some feature specification. Conversely, segments that behave differently must differ from each other in some respect. Apply this reasoning to the different behavior of surface [i] in [hidnak] versus the surface [i] of [hitnek]. Propose the underlying representations of the vowels of each root.

Since /hid-/ takes back suffixes, we may presume it has an underlying back unround vowel, represented as /ɯ/. This is an **abstract** analysis because we are proposing a phoneme which never appears at the surface.

abstractness: a scenario in which there is evidence of some element (e.g., a phoneme) in the underlying inventory of a language, but that element is never realized in the surface forms of the language.

Abstractness usually coincides with rules of **neutralization**, in which the underlying abstract phoneme surfaces as identical in form with some other phoneme.

neutralization: a scenario in which two or more contrastive phonemes are identical at the surface.

Exercise 7.21 The vowel of [hidnak] is obviously [–back] at the surface. Propose a rule that accounts for this.

[–rd, –low, +back] → [–back]

This rule has no context in which it operates; it changes all instances of /ɯ/ to [i]. It also must follow the backness harmony rule, to ensure that the underlying vowel has a chance to affect the alternation of the suffixes.
The rule of neutralization in Hungarian is in both a counterbleeding and counterfeeding order with respect to vowel harmony. It changes an underlying [+back] vowel to a front vowel, but is ordered later than harmony. With the opposite ordering (neutralization first), the sytem would prevent [+back] from spreading, but would create conditions for [–back] to spread.
The exceptional back-harmony vowels of words like [hid] are not just opaque; they also act as if they are back vowels despite not appearing as such at the surface. This is inferred simply from the fact that, like other roots with obviously back vowels, they take suffixes with back vowels. This makes it an abstract analysis: it relies on the possibility that despite being identical in form at the surface, the [i] of [hid] and the [i] of [hit] are different vowels at an abstract level of representation.

7.5 Okpe verbal conjugation

Now let us turn to another complex pattern, from the verbal system of Okpe. Take some time to peruse the following data (Halle and Clements 1983).

		Imp.	*3sg pst*	*2sg pst*	*Inf.*
(1)	'pull'	ti	o tiri	wi tiri	etjo
(2)	'do'	ru	o ruru	wi ruru	erwo
(3)	'bury'	si	o siri	wi siri	esjo
(4)	'fan'	zu	o zuru	wi zuru	ezwo
(5)	'buy'	dɛ	ɔ dɛre	we dɛre	ɛdɛ
(6)	'drink'	da	ɔ dare	we dare	ɛda
(7)	'dig'	tɔ	ɔ tɔre	we tɔre	ɛtɔ
(8)	'run'	zɛ	ɔ zɛre	we zɛre	ɛzɛ
(9)	'fill'	se	o seri	wi seri	ese
(10)	'steal'	so	o sori	wi sori	eso
(11)	'defecate'	ne	o neri	wi neri	ene
(12)	'rot'	gbo	o gbori	wi gbori	egbo
(13)	'eat'	re	ɔ rere	we rere	ɛrjɔ
(14)	'sing'	so	ɔ soro	we soro	ɛswɔ
(15)	'refuse'	te	ɔ tere	we tere	ɛtjɔ
(16)	'come'	rhe	ɔ rhe	we rhere	ɛrhjɔ

Exercise 7.22   There is a range of different processes occuring in these data. Let us begin by identifying the alternants of the pronouns and past-tense suffix. List each alternant, and describe the environment in which it occurs.

The pronouns precede the verb and each has two alternants. The third singular is either [o] or [ɔ]. It is [o] before roots with [+high] vowels, as in (1) [o tiri], [ɔ] before roots with [–high] lax vowels, as in (5) [ɔ dɛre], and can be either [o] or [ɔ] if the root contains a [–high] tense vowel, as in (9) [o seri] and (13) [ɔ rere].

Some parallel is observable in the second singular: it is either [wi] or [we]; [wi] before roots with [+high] vowels, as in (1) [wi tiri], [we] before roots with [–high] lax vowels, as in (5) [we dɛre], and either [wi] or [we] before roots with [–high] tense vowels, as in (9) [wi seri] and (13) [we rere]. The parallel is quite consistent: any root that has [o] in the third person has [wi] in the second person, and likewise any root that has [ɔ] in the third person has [we] in the second person.

The past-tense suffix seems to be more complicated because of alternations in roundness, but another parallel pattern emerges here. Its forms include [ri],

[ru], [re], and [ro]. It is [ri] or [ru] after roots that co-occur with the pronoun forms [o] and [wi], and it is [re] or [ro] after roots that co-occur with the pronoun forms [ɔ] and [we]. The vowel of the suffix is round only if the root also has a round vowel, as in (2) [o ruru] and (14) [ɔ soro] 'sing,' but there are some cases in which a round root vowel co-occurs with a non-round suffix vowel, as in (10) [o sori] 'steal' and (7) [ɔ tɔre].

In summary, we note the following overall generalization: [o], [wi], and [-ri/-ru] all occur within the same subsets, while [ɔ], [we], and [-re/-ro] all occur within the converse subsets. There is an alternation in tenseness and vowel height observable across groups, plus an additional alternation in roundness.

Let us begin by treating the tenseness and height alternations, and we will return to the roundness issue later. For the most part, we could conclude that the forms of the pronouns and suffixes are predictable from the vowels of the root, except if the root contains a [–high] tense vowel. Some roots with [–high] tense vowels call for the same forms as [+high] vowels, as in (9) [o seri]; others call for the same forms as [–high] lax vowels, as in (13) [ɔ rere].

The rest of the analysis hinges on the freedom we have to make the following claim: that if two apparently identical segments behave differently in their phonology, then underlyingly they must be distinct along some dimension, or in some feature.

Let us summarize the issue so far by choosing one form to represent each group for comparison's sake.

(1)   'pull'   o tiri
(5)   'buy'   ɔ dɛre
(9)   'fill'   o seri
(13)   'eat'   ɔ rere

Differentiating (9) and (13), the two groups of roots that have [–high] tense vowels, is a lot like looking for natural classes: sounds that act similarly can be inferred to share some feature. By this argument, the [–high] tense vowel in (9) [o seri] has something in common with the [+high] tense vowel in (1) [o tiri], since they both take [o] as a pronoun. Likewise, the [–high] tense vowel in (13) [ɔ rere] has something in common with the [–high] lax vowel in (5) of [ɔ dɛre], since they both take [ɔ] as pronoun.

Exercise 7.23 Propose a feature that distinguishes the two subsets of surface [–high] tense roots represented by (9) and (13). Ideally this should be a feature that is already present in the data.

The fact that the pronoun and suffix vowels respond to the root vowels suggests that vowel harmony is at work here. We could say that the [o/ɔ] pronoun is tense before tense roots, and lax before lax roots. Thus, the root vowel of (13) [ɔ rere], which is [–high, +tense] at the surface and takes [ɔ] as its pronoun, is actually underlyingly [–tense]. Conversely, the root vowel of (9) [o seri], with [o] as its pronoun, is underlyingly [+tense].

For the time being, this analysis shifts the problem elsewhere: if (13) [ɔ rere] is derived from a root with a lax vowel, the simplest preliminary assumption is that underlyingly it is /rɛ/. If so, why would this vowel become [e], especially when there are surface [–high] lax vowels in other roots, as in (5) [ɔ dɛre]?

We address this by following similar reasoning: if two forms behave differently at the surface, we infer that they have some underlying difference as well. Thus, since the underlying vowel of (13) [ɔ rere] surfaces as [e], while the underlying vowel of (5) [ɔ dɛre] surfaces as [ɛ], they are not the same underlying vowel, and are thus distinct in at least one other feature, despite both being underlyingly lax.

Exercise 7.24 Propose another feature from the language that you could use to differentiate the underlying lax vowel of the root in (13) [ɔ rere] from the underlying lax vowel of the root in (5) [ɔ dɛre].

We can choose from among several other vowel features that are relevant in the Okpe vowel system, namely [±round], [±back], or [±high]. Since vowels of both values of [±round] and [±back] are found in both groups, we cannot say that (5) [ɔ dɛre] has a different underlying value of [±round] or [±back] from (13) [ɔ rere].

However, (5) [ɔ dɛre] and (13) [ɔ rere] are both [–high] at the surface, as are all the roots in each of their groups. Meanwhile, there are no [+high, –tense] roots at the surface. We may therefore appeal to [±high] to differentiate (5) [ɔ dɛre] and (13) [ɔ rere]: one is [+high] underlyingly, the other is [–high].

Exercise 7.25 Construct an argument that determines which of the two underlyingly lax subgroups is also underlyingly [+high]. That is, which of (5) [ɔ dɛre] and (13) [ɔ rere] has an underlying [+high] vowel?

The simplest proposal is that the (13) [ɔ rere] type roots are underlying [+high, +lax]. There are two general arguments to be made in favor of this: one looks to the simplicity of the rule system that results from your proposal, while the other looks to other aspects of the data to test the fit.

To pursue an argument based on rule simplicity, suppose tentatively instead that the roots of forms like (5) [ɔ dɛre] were underlyingly [+high], as in /dɪ/; we would then need a rule to lower it to [ɛ]. Moreover, we would be forced to assume that [ɔ rere] has an underlying [–high] lax vowel, as in /rɛ/, which needs a separate rule to make it tense. On the other hand, if instead forms like (13) [ɔ rere] had the underlying [+high] vowel, we only need a rule that changes them to [–high] lax vowels. The [ɔ dɛre] group would be unchanged.

A more convincing argument follows from an inspection of the rest of the data. Note first that the past suffix [ri/ru/re/ro] changes according to the root's vowel. If we again think tentatively that (5) [ɔ dɛre] is underlyingly [+high], then there is a difficult consequence for our analysis when we turn to roundness harmony. We would have to propose that the past suffix receives a round vowel after [+high +tense] round vowels, as in (2) [o ruru], and after [–high –lax] round vowels, as in (14) [ɔ soro] (which, according to this tentative analysis, has [–high] /sɔ/ as its root). When we get to the point of proposing a rule to predict proper suffix rounding, this would be problematic.

Conversely, if we hold to the idea of (13) [ɔ rere] roots being [+high], then the generalization is that the past suffix is round only after underlyingly [+high, +round] roots, as in (2) [o ruru] and (14) [ɔ soro] (which, in this view, has /sʊ/ as its root).

We will thus maintain the assumption that the vowels of the roots in (13)–(16) are [+high, –tense]. Essentially, this group of roots behaves as if its vowels are high, and also behaves as if its vowels are lax, despite them being neither at the surface.

Exercise 7.26   Construct a rule that accounts for the changes in the vowels of the roots in (13)–(16).

[+high, –tense] → [–high, +tense]

This rule categorically lowers all high lax vowels; since it occurs in any context, it requires no statement of a conditioning environment. This proposal, and the claim that some vowels are underlyingly [+high, –tense], is at the heart of the abstract nature of these data: Okpe vowels differ in height and tenseness, and some roots clearly behave as if they have [+high, –tense] vowels. Yet such vowels never themselves appear as such at the surface, and instead the contrast between [+high, –tense] vowels and [–high, +tense] vowels is subject to neutralization. Our only way of detecting the abstract vowels is through the behavior of nearby vowels that respond to their underlying features.

We will see that any processes that are sensitive to the underlying nature of these abstract vowels will need to be encoded as rules which are crucially ordered ahead of this lowering rule. Indeed, several other aspects of the analysis come together very neatly with this in mind.

Exercise 7.27   Describe the distribution of the pronoun and suffix alternants in terms of the underlying features of the root vowels.

The pronouns vary quite simply in the tenseness of the root vowels. Lax roots receive [ɔ] and [we], even if the root vowel is rendered tense at the surface, as in (13) [ɔ rere] and [we rere], and tense roots receive [o] and [wi], as in (9) [o seri] and [wi seri].

One could argue that the second-person pronoun [wi ~ we] also varies in its tenseness; it has tense [i] before tense roots, but this vowel is made lax before lax roots, and drops to [e] by the same process that lowers the underlying /ɪ/ in roots such as /rɪ/. The same claim can apply to the past suffix; it is [ri] after tense vowels and [re] after lax vowels. We may then infer that it is uderlyingly [+high] and assumes the [±tense] value of the root. When it is rendered [–tense], it is lowered by the general lowering rule above. In other words, the underlying form for (13) is /wi + rɪ + ri/; harmony renders it /wɪ rɪ-rɪ/, and the high-lax lowering yields [we rere].

Exercise 7.28 Construct rules to spread [±tense] from the root to the pronouns and suffixes.

Tensing harmony   V → [α tense] / __ C [α tense] *or* [α tense] C __

The suffix also assumes roundness if the root has an underlying [+high, +round] vowel. This roundness harmony accounts for (2) [ruru] and (14) [soro] (from /sʊ + rɪ /). Since the vowels in the other groups are underlyingly [–high], roundness does not spread: (7) [ɔ tɛri], (10) [o sori].

Exercise 7.29 Construct a rule that spreads [+round] to the suffix.

Roundness harmony   V[+high] → [+round] / [+high, +round] C ___

As we suspected in Exercise 7.26 above, these rules must precede the lowering rule. If the lowering rule were to apply first, then the tensing harmony rule would apply to the wrong roots, and the roundness harmony rule would fail to apply to forms such as [ɔ soro]. Since the lowering rule would make the other rules inapplicable, but is actually ordered later, this serves as another example of counterbleeding opacity.

Exercise 7.30 Create some sample derivations for the second-person past Okpe forms of (1), (2), (5), (7), (9), (10), (13), and (14). Remember that the underlying roots are identical to the roots in the surface forms in (1)–(2), but that the roots have underlying [+high, –tense] vowels in (13)–(16).

	(1)	(2)	(5)	(7)
UR	wɪ ti rɪ	wɪ ru rɪ	wɪ dɛ rɪ	wɪ to rɪ
tensing harmony	wi tiri	wi ruri	wɪ dɪ rɪ	wɪ tɔ rɪ
round harmony	–	wi ruru	–	–
lowering	–	–	we dere	we tɔre

	(9)	(10)	(13)	(14)
UR	wI se rI	wI so rI	wI rɪ rI	wI sʊ rI
tensing harmony	wi seri	wi sori	wɪ rɪrɪ	wɪ sʊrɪ
round harmony	–	–	–	wɪ sʊrʊ
lowering	–	–	we rere	we soro

We conclude our analysis of Okpe with a discussion of the ordering interactions. First, it should be clear that the order of roundness harmony before high lax lowering is a counterbleeding interaction; the opposite order would have the lowering rule bleed the roundness harmony rule, as the lowering rule would remove the structural conditions for the harmony rule. Second, the order of the tenseness harmony rule ahead of the lowering rule is also a counterbleeding interaction, as the lowering rule would again remove the conditions for the harmony rule if their order were reversed.

Nevertheless, it is also a counterfeeding interaction, since the opposite ordering – lowering first – would create a tense root vowel that would then generate tense vowels in the pronouns and suffixes. As such, lowering would actually feed harmony; for example, if the form /O dɪ rI/ underwent lowering first, we might see something like *[o deri].

The fact that the order of two rules can be qualifed as more than one type of ordering interaction suggests that these phenomena – bleeding and feeding and so forth – are not actual objects of the phonology of languages. Instead, they are merely convenient labels we use to describe different types of rule interactions, and indeed emerge as descriptions only in a theory of phonology that models complex alternations with sequences of rules.

Last, recall from Chapter 4 that a common harmonic feature is [±ATR], where roots and affixes share the same specification for this feature. Vowels specified as [+ATR] are often transcribed with the same symbols we use to represent tense vowels, such as [i, u, e, o], while [–ATR] vowels are transcribed with symbols also used for lax vowels, such as [ɪ, ʊ, ɛ, ɔ]. Okpe is most likely an [ATR] harmonic system; sensibly the analysis here could be recast such that all references to [±tense] are relabeled as [±ATR], but the details of rule ordering, underlying representations, and other features remain the same.

Summary

In this chapter we have seen numerous examples of languages in which multiple phonological processes are in effect. In such cases, each process can be modeled with one or more specific phonological rule; some patterns are challenging to analyze, but nonetheless can be modeled fittingly by supposing that multiple rules stand in a crucial order with respect to each other. We saw in Zapotec and Palauan examples of how analyses can be tightened up when we create rules that feed each other. In some interactions, the later rule hides the activity of the earlier rule. We saw this in Serbo-Croatian as well as Okpe.

Other challenging cases arise when it becomes clear that a language appears to have underlying phonemes that are lost at the surface, often by changing in form to become identical to some other phoneme in the same language. This was certainly the case in both Hungarian and Okpe, which both provide evidence of certain phonemes which never appear unaltered in surface forms. We are only able to detect such abstract phonemes by the effects they have on surrounding sounds – abstractness thus always entails some degree of opacity, where a later rule of neutralization obscures the abstract phoneme, but only after (in counterbleeding fashion) it has been able to affect nearby segments.

At this point we have neared the limit of segmental phonology: we have handled alternations and phonemic analysis, and we have seen how distinctive features can simplify the analyses of such patterns. We have also seen that the decisions we make about underlying forms can lead to abstract claims, and that the processes we propose as rules sometimes need to be applied in a specific order.

In this and other earlier chapters, we have occasionally made reference to phonological elements beyond the segment: syllables, and even in some cases, stress. We return to these phenomena in detail in the following chapters, where we see that the syllable can be a helpful element in the representation of word forms and in the expression of phonological rules: quite simply, we will encounter phenomena which cannot readily be modeled without appealing to the syllable as a higher-order unit that organizes segments into combined units.

Key terms

crucial ordering
feeding
counterfeeding
bleeding
counterbleeding
opacity
abstractness
neutralization

References and further reading

Bakovic, Eric. 2007. A revised typology of opaque generalisations. *Phonology* 24.2: 217–259.

Bakovic, Eric. 2011. Opacity and ordering. In John Goldsmith, Jason Riggle, and Alan C. L. Yu (eds.), *The Handbook of Phonological Theory*. Hoboken, NJ: Wiley-Blackwell.

Halle, Morris, and George N. Clements. 1983. *Problem Book in Phonology*. Cambridge, MA: MIT Press.

Idsardi, William J. 2000. Clarifying opacity. *The Linguistic Review* 17: 377–350.

Jensen, John T. 1990. *Morphology: Word Structure in Generative Grammar*. Amsterdam: Benjamins.

Josephs, Lewis. 1975. *Palauan Reference Grammar*. Honolulu: University of Hawaii Press.

Josephs, Lewis. 1990. *New Palauan–English Dictionary*. Honolulu: University of Hawaii Press.

Kiparsky, Paul. 1973. Abstractness, opacity and global rules (part 2 of "Phonological representations"). In Osamu Fujimura, *Three Dimensions of Linguistic Theory*. Tokyo Institute for Advanced Studies of Language, 57–86.

Kornai, András. 1987. Hungarian vowel harmony. In Megan Crowhurst (ed.), *Proceedings of the 6th West Coast Conference on Formal Linguistics*. Stanford Linguistics Association, 147–161.

McCarthy, John. 2007. *Hidden Generalizations: Phonological Opacity in Optimality Theory*. London: Equinox.

Merrifield, William R, and Benjamin F. Elson. 1967. *Laboratory Manual for Morphology and Syntax*. Santa Ana: Summer Institute of Linguistics.

Vago, R. M. 1976. Theoretical implications of Hungarian vowel harmony. *Linguistic Inquiry* 7: 243–263.

Vago, R. M. 1976. 1980. *The Sound Pattern of Hungarian*. Georgetown University Press.

Vaux, Bert, and Andrew Nevins (eds.) 2008. *Rules, Constraints, and Phonological Phenomena*. Oxford University Press.

Review exercises

Okpe revisited

Look again at the Okpe data from Exercise 7.22. Use the infinitive column to find additional evidence that the forms in (13)–(16) are underlyingly [+high,–tense].

a. How is the infinitive indicated?

b. What are the alternants of the infinitive morpheme?

c. Describe how the choice of alternant for the infinitive depends on the features of the root vowel.

d. Write any additional rules you need to account for alternation in the infinitive.

Tagalog

	Isolation	Suffix1	Suffix2
'open'	bukas	buksin	buksan
'fill'	laman	lamnin	lamnan
'redeem'	tubos	tubsin	tubsan
'cut'	putol	putlin	putlan
'embrace'	kapit	kaptin	kaptan
'clothe'	damit	damtin	damtan
'stop'	opos	upsin	upsan
'tuft'	posod	pusdin	pusdan
'suffer'	bata	bathin	bathan
'buy'	bili	bilhin	bilhan
'open'	dipa	diphin	diphan
'saddle bag'	pujo	pujhin	pujhan
'ask for trifles'	polo	pulhin	pulhan
'mat'	banig	baŋgin	baŋgin
'fulfill'	ganap	gampin	gampin
'thatching'	atip	aptin	aptan
'plant'	tanim	tamnin	tamnan
'penetrate'	talab	–––	tablan

a. Describe any alternation you find in the roots.
b. Describe the alternants you find in the two suffixes in Tagalog.
   What conditions their appearance?
c. Develop rules to handle these alternations, and make sure to order
   them appropriately.

Polish

vjadeɾ	'pail gen.pl.'	vjadɾ-o	'pail nom.sg'
sveteɾ	'sweater'	svetɾ-ɨ	'sweater nom.pl'
meandeɾ	'meander'	meandɾ-a	'meander gen.sg.'
bimbeɾ	'moonshine'	bimbɾ-u	'moonshine gen.sg.'
sen	'dream'	sn-u	'dream gen.sg.'
mex	'moss'	mx-u	'moss gen.sg.'
krateɾ	'crater'	krateɾ-ɨ	'crater nom.pl.'
lideɾ	'leader'	lideɾ-a	'leader gen.sg.'
teɾen	'terrain'	teɾen-u	'terrain gen.sg.'
ʃmeɾ	'rustle'	ʃmeɾ-u	'rustle gen.sg'

bjes	'devil'	bjes-a	'devil gen.sg.'
kɾet	'mole'	kɾet-a	'mole gen.sg.'
teatɾ	'theater'		
metɾ	'meter'		
vjatɾ	'wind, gale'		
litɾ	'liter'		
ʃɨfɾ	'cipher, code'		

a. Describe any alternation you find in the roots in Polish. Try grouping them together based on how they behave phonologically. How many groups of roots are there?

b. Propose an underlying form for each root, based on how you answered the above question.

c. Develop rules to handle the root alternations, and make sure to order them appropriately.

Yokuts

We encountered these data in Chapter 3 as an exercise in analyzing segment/zero alternations. We return to them here to examine alternations in vowel quality.

	Aorist passive	Aorist	Future	
(1)	xatit	xathin	xatnit	'eat'
(2)	gopit	gophin	gopnit	'take care of infant'
(3)	gijit	gijhin	gijnit	'touch'
(4)	mutut	muthun	mutnut	'swear'
(5)	saːpit	saphin	sapnit	'burn'
(6)	goːbit	gobhin	gobnit	'take in'
(7)	meːkit	mekhin	meknit	'swallow'
(8)	ʔoːtut	ʔothun	ʔotnut	'steal'
(9)	panat	panaːhin	panaːnit	'arrive'
(10)	hojot	hojoːhin	hojoːnit	'name'
(11)	ʔilet	ʔileːhin	ʔileːnit	'fan'
(12)	cujot	cujoːhun	cujoːnut	'urinate'
(13)	paxaːtit	paxathin	paxatnit	'mourn'
(14)	ʔopoːtit	ʔopothin	ʔopotnit	'arise from bed'
(15)	hibeːjit	hibejhin	hibejnit	'bring water'
(16)	sudoːkut	sudokhun	sudoknut	'remove'

197

a. Propose a tentative underlying form for each root.
b. Identify the alternants of the aorist and future suffixes. Can their form be predicted from the underlying form of the root?
c. Identify any roots which are problematic for the suffix alternations. Can these roots be distinguished from other roots in any way? To answer this question, think of all the possible ways in which vowels are distinct from each other at the surface in Yokuts, and check which combinations of features are actually observed in the data.
d. If necessary, revise your proposed underlying roots from (a).
e. Construct a rule to generate the appropriate suffix alternants, and an additional rule to make any other necessary changes.

CHAPTER 8 SYLLABLES

Learning objectives

- Recognize and differentiate components of syllables such as onset, nucleus, coda, and rhyme
- Infer maximal syllables and syllable constraints from segmental representations
- Be able to determine whether an alternation is sensitive to syllable structure
- Create rules that refer to syllables as phonological objects
- Frame alternations with zero as syllable-driven patterns

Introduction

In previous chapters, we have encountered numerous segmental alternations. Many of the patterns we have seen have been expressible using targets (i.e., segments) that change their features under certain circumstances, usually the adjacency of other segments. Segmental phonology, then, has appeared here as a linear phenomenon – we make sense of patterns in one-dimensional sequences of segments.

For some of these patterns, however, we have drawn upon the notion of the syllable, yet we have not pursued the concept of the syllable in detail as a component of phonological rules or representations. In this chapter, we will explore the role of syllable structure in phonological processes more deeply, examining patterns that can be modeled by grouping segments into larger components. We will examine the internal structure of the syllable and observe its interaction with alternations and allophonic effects. We will also see that we may make sense of a number of facts about word form in various languages by appealing to the syllable.

8.1 Syllable-based alternations

In §2.15 we encountered a pattern in German whereby underlying voiced obstruents in forms such as /tag/ 'day' alternate between voiced and voiceless forms at the surface. We concluded that underlying root-final voiced consonants retain their voicing only when followed by vowel-initial suffixes, as in [taːgə]. The alternating consonant is voiceless when word-final, as in [taːk], or when preceding another consonant, as in [zaːktə] (from /zaːg/) and [bʁaːfhaɪt] (from /bʁaːv/). The full data set is repeated below.

(1) [taːgə]   'days'   [taːk]   'day'
(2) [fɔl.kəʁ]   'peoples'   [fɔlk]   'people'
(3) [ʁɛːdəʁ]   'wheels'   [ʁaɪt]   'wheel'
(4) [laɪdən]   'to suffer'   [laɪt]   'sorry'
(5) [ʁaːtən]   'to advise'   [ʁaːt]   'advice'
(6) [bʁaːvəʁ]   'obedient'   [bʁaf]   'good'
(7) [høfə]   'courtyards'   [hɔf]   'courtyard'
(8) [ʁegʊŋ]   'movement'   [ʁɛksam]   'active'
(9) [zaːgən]   'to say'   [zaːktə]   'said'
(10) [ʁaːdɛln]   'to pedal'   [ʁaːtfaʁən]   'to cycle'
(11) [bʁaːvəʁ]   'obedient'   [bʁaːfhaɪt]   'good behavior'
(12) [ʃtɔɥ.bən]   'to dust'   [ʃtɔɥpçən]   'dust particle'
(13) [bøzə]   'wicked'   [boshaft]   'malicious'

In Exercise 2.20, we created two rules to account for such behavior: one devoices word-final voiced obstruents, while the other devoices them before other consonants.

[voiced consonants] → [voiceless] / ___]$_{WD}$
[voiced consonants] → [voiceless] / ___ [consonant]

Given that there is a single process of devoicing observed in these data, but two rules are needed to account for the pattern, we may wonder if there is a different way to express this alternation. In Chapter 6, in the face of multiple or disjunctive rules for particular processes, we turned to the notion of natural classes to express a uniform process with a single formal rule. If we were to do so with the two German devoicing rules, we would need a way to combine the two environments into a single expression. In other words, we need a way to rephrase the set of environments to conflate following consonants and word boundaries. However, it is difficult to conceive of these two types of environments as a natural class.

Thus, we turn to positional ways of expressing the environment. Invoking the syllable as a way of organizing sounds can help us do this. In the German voicing alternation, the alternating consonants are not simply devoiced in some disjunctive set of scenarios; rather, their devoiced alternants are never followed by vowels – by extension, they do not have any kind of release, and in more abstract terms, they are never syllable-initial.

If we appeal to the syllable, we can combine the two rules into a single expression: whether word-final or before a consonant, voiced obstruents are rendered voiceless just where they occur in syllable-final position. The following rule expresses this:

[voiced consonants] → [voiceless] / ___]$_{\text{SYLL}}$

We need to be careful with such claims, however, because we cannot take the location of syllable boundaries for granted. Even so, we can make some very reasonable guesses as to where syllable breaks occur within words. We will explore this further as we encounter some basic principles of syllabification.

8.2 Principles of syllabification

It is tempting to think of the syllable as an easily identifiable phonetic entity. We can count syllables in words, and we can "feel" them in lyrics and poetry. Even without a precise and unambiguous working definition of "syllable," we can ask English speakers to identify the number of syllables in words such as *soft, blanket,* or *pelican,* and expect consistent answers of one, two, and three respectively. In phonetic terms, we can associate syllables with relative peaks and valleys of loudness or power – there is one pulse or peak in energy over time for each syllable, so that a two-syllable word has two peaks and a three-syllable word has three peaks.

The role of the syllable in phonology goes far beyond counting peaks in physical energy. By turning to syllable structure, we now have a way of grouping segments together, in effect adding another dimension to our conception of phonological forms. A multi-syllabic word can be represented as a string of segments along one linear dimension, but each component segment is a member of some syllable along a different dimension of representation. These dimensions are hierarchical: a phonological form may consist of one or more syllables, and each syllable contains one or more segments.

Our representations can be illustrated to reflect this organization. For example, the word *soft* [sɑft] contains one syllable: the segments in it belong to the higher-order component. Visually, we represent syllable constituents with the symbol σ on one level, placing member segments on a lower level, linked by lines that indicate membership in their syllable.

σ

s ɑ f t

As we further explore such details of syllabification, let us acknowledge some terminology: all syllables by definition contain a **nucleus**, usually a vowel, which provides its peak or maximum energy. Consonants which precede the nucleus occur in the **onset**, while those that follow the nucleus are in the **coda**.

nucleus: the peak or loudest part of a syllable.

onset: the segments that occur before a nucleus, within a syllable.

coda: the segments that occur after a nucleus, within a syllable.

We should note that the rules may differ across languages about what can serve as a syllable nucleus. In some languages, syllabic consonants can function as the nucleus of a syllable: in English, nasals and liquids may act as syllable nuclei, as in [bɒtm̩/bɑɾm̩] *bottom*, [kɪtn̩] *kitten*, [bɹ̩d] *bird* (in rhotic accents), and [tɪkl̩] *tickle*. Likewise, sequences of vowels may be treated as diphthongs in some languages, and as such comprise a single nucleus, while the same two physical vowels might behave as the nuclei of two separate syllables in a different language.

If we have sufficient data about segment sequences within a language, we can engage in syllabification. This is a type of analysis in which we use linear segmental representations to infer the syllable structure of phonological forms, determining which syllabic position each segment occupies.

syllabification: the manner by which segments are associated to positions within syllables.

Syllabification of monosyllabic forms is straightforward. The nucleus contains the vowel, while the onset includes any segments beforehand and the coda includes any segments afterwards. For example, in the word *train* [treɪn], the nucleus is occupied by the diphthong vowel [eɪ]; the preceding [tr] is in the onset, and the final [n] is in the coda. We represent this by using a line of association to link the segment to its position.

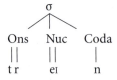

The decisions we make about syllabification may differ across languages, with respect to how to handle vowel sequences, potentially nuclear consonants, and consonant sequences. The choices we make about sequences of vowels or about potentially nuclear segments often depend on data we draw from other aspects of a language, usually ones that involve counting syllables. For example, if we are studying a language with adjacent vowels, and the stress system of that language is simpler to describe by assuming them to be tautosyllabic (belonging to the same syllable), then we infer that they comprise a diphthong. Likewise, if we ask native speakers to count syllables in words and they consistently lump the adjacent vowels together, then we again have evidence to treat them as tautosyllabic.

The approach is similar for potentially nuclear consonants like /ɹ/, /l/, or /n/. We consider them nuclear if the stress system of the language seems to count them as syllabic, or if speakers have intuitions about them counting in rhythmic tasks. When we are doing an explicit syllabification task, we assign them to nuclei only if they are not adjacent to vowels. Thus, for something like [ɹoʊ] *row* or [kaɹ] *car*, we would not project a separate nucleus for the consonant [ɹ], because it is adjacent to a nuclear vowel in both cases, allowing [ɹ] to occupy a syllable margin. However, in [bɹ̩d], we would indeed assume that the [ɹ] is the nucleus of a syllable.

We will see below that syllabification of consonant sequences is often critical to a phonological analysis, and needs to be sensitive to other facts about the positional distribution of consonants in a language. The next several exercises develop this point more deeply.

Exercise 8.1 Perform syllabification for each of the segments in the following words: *soft, plate, fee, sick, oak*.

One thing to note about these representations is that while every syllable has a nucleus, not every syllable has a coda or onset. Consequently, the initial segment in some syllables (such as in [fiː] *fee*) is in the onset, but in others (such as in [oʊk] *oak*), it is in the nucleus. Likewise, the final segment in some syllables (such as in [sɪk] *sick*) is in the coda, but in others (such as in [fiː]) it is in the nucleus.

The introduction of syllable structure and its use of elements on different tiers associating with each other creates an opportunity to reframe how some phonological rules work, and we have not yet exploited this in detail. Now we can add syllable structure to our set of analytical tools. In the rules we compose hereafter, we may use the notation $_{\text{SYLL}}[\_\_$ as shorthand for onset position, and $\_\_]_{\text{SYLL}}$ as shorthand for coda position. In later chapters, we will encounter some phonological processes which we'll need to represent using fully indicated syllable structure.

Syllabification is more complicated when we move to polysyllabic forms. Consider now words such as *blanket* [blæŋkət] and *locate* [loʊkeɪt], which each contain two syllables. The segments in each group belong to different higher-order components, and we represent this with segments on one level linked with association lines to their respective syllables on a higher level.

While we may be able to count syllables easily, syllabification of segments that exist at the margins of syllables can be a complex task. Nevertheless, by adhering to the following steps, it is often possible to achieve complete analyses of syllable structure.

As we did with monosyllabic forms, we assume each nuclear segment serves as the head of its own syllable. Thus, in a polysyllabic word, the first step is to identify the nuclear segments and associate them with syllables. Once again, this step is complicated wherever we encounter diphthongs or segments which may occur as nuclei or as margins.

Exercise 8.2 Identify the nuclei and link them to syllable nodes in the following words: *mistake, surface, pelican, restriction.*

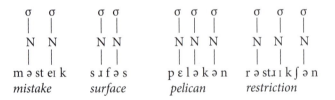

Having established the nuclear consonants within a word, our next task is to determine whether the non-nuclear segments occur in onset or coda position. Trivially, word-initial consonants are necessarily in onset position, while those that are word-final are in coda position. Intervocalic consonants present an analytical choice, however, as to whether they are onsets or codas. When a consonant occurs between two nuclei, overwhelmingly across languages it tends to syllabify as an onset to the second syllable rather than a coda to the first. We may refer to this phenomenon as the principle of onset preference; exceptions to this are rare and have some other explanation for their occurrence.

onset preference: languages favor onset consonants over coda consonants.

Given this preference, the next step in an analysis of syllabification is to syllabify consonants which precede nuclei as onsets. We associate the consonant to the left of each nucleus to the onset position of its syllable.

Exercise 8.3   Identify the preliminary onsets and link them to syllable nodes for the following words: *mistake, surface, pelican, restriction.*

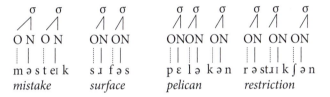

The remaining task is to figure out what to do with leftover segments. Again, word-final consonants can be assumed to be codas, but consonants in medial position which precede onsets are less straightforward. That is, in a medial sequence of [...VC1C2V...], we can infer that the second consonant is an onset without controversy, but the first consonant could be analyzed as a coda of the preceding syllable or as part of the onset of the second.

When faced with such a choice, we often must consider multiple analyses and look for evidence that favors one over the other. As we will see throughout this chapter, whether to assign a pre-consonantal consonant to a coda or to a complex onset is an analytical choice that may differ across languages, and which may even vary within a language, depending on the features of the consonants involved.

One question to ask is whether the same two consonants ever occur as a complex onset in absolute word-initial position elsewhere in the language. For example, in [blæŋ.kət], the medial sequence [ŋk] never occurs as a complex onset at the beginnings of other words in English, so we infer that it cannot be a complex onset in medial position in *blanket,* thus favoring [blæŋ.kət] with [ŋ] in a coda position over *[blæ.ŋkət]. Conversely, in *oblique,* the medial sequence [bl] is one that occurs initially in other words like [blæk], so we allow [oʊ.bliːk] as a syllabification, with [b] in an onset.

Another question is whether the consonants behave phonologically like syllable-initial or final allophones in other contexts. For example, in *mistake*, the medial *t* is not aspirated, so we infer that it cannot be syllable-initial.

Exercise 8.4 Syllabify the remaining consonants in the following words: *mistake, surface, pelican, restriction.*

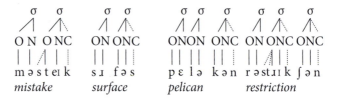

Thus, while the choice of how to syllabify medial segments is guided by principles such as the onset preference, your analysis needs to be consistent with other aspects of a language's phonology. Indeed, the best evidence for syllable boundaries is often phonological rather than phonetic: for example, we can take the activity of German syllable-final devoicing itself as evidence for the syllable as an organizing principle: since the appeal to the syllable allows us to express the alternation of voiced obstruents in simpler terms (i.e., with one rule), we have a better account of the alternation than we would if we relied on rules that make no reference to the syllable.

For the German data in §8.1, we assumed that single intervocalic consonants were necessarily onsets, while sequences of consonants were necessarily broken up into a sequence of a coda followed by an onset. The following exercise will test this assumption.

Exercise 8.5 Syllabify the German data. Assume that diphthongs comprise single nuclei, and assume that each vowel is a nucleus. You may use periods to indicate syllable boundaries.

(1)	[taː.gə]	'days'	[taːk]	'day'
(2)	[fɔl.kɐʁ]	'peoples'	[fɔlk]	'people'
(3)	[ʁɛː.dɐʁ]	'wheels'	[ʁaːt]	'wheel'
(4)	[laɪ.dən]	'to suffer'	[laɪt]	'sorry'
(5)	[ʁaː.tən]	'to advise'	[ʁaːt]	'advice'
(6)	[bʁaː.vɐʁ]	'obedient'	[bʁaf]	'good'
(7)	[hø.fə]	'courtyards'	[hɔf]	'courtyard'

(8) [ʁe.gʊŋ] 'movement' [ʁɛk.sam] 'active'
(9) [zaː.gən] 'to say' [zaːk.tə] 'said'
(10) [ʁaː.dɛln] 'to pedal' [ʁaːt.fa.ʁən] 'to cycle'
(11) [bʁaː.vəʁ] 'obedient' [bʁaːf.haɪt] 'good behavior'
(12) [ʃtɔʏ.bən] 'to dust' [ʃtɔʏp.çən] 'dust particle'
(13) [bø.zə] 'wicked' [bos.haft] 'malicious'

These representations clarify that the voicing alternation is sensitive to syllable position: underlying voiced obstruents remain voiced in onset position (to the right of a syllable boundary), but become voiceless in coda position (to the left of a syllable boundary, or in final position).

So far we have assumed that word-medial sequences of consonants are broken up so that they belong to different syllables, and the data we have seen have supported this. However, there are other scenarios in which a language may instead choose to syllabify both consonants into the onset of the second syllable. We may call this the principle of onset maximization.

onset maximization: given any intervocalic sequence of consonants, languages favor as many consonants in onset position as the language will allow.

We have seen that onsets are not necessarily maximized in every case of an intervocalic consonant sequence; for example, in the above German data, syllabification favors a single coda followed by a single onset over a complex onset. In those data, such syllabification emerges because the potential onset sequences are not possible. German syllabification is more nuanced than this, however, as there are other polysyllabic word forms which do syllabify a medial sequence as a complex onset, and in fact this is true of many languages that allow complex onsets. Typically the choice of how to syllabify medial sequences involves more than a language's tolerance of onset sequences; it depends also on the features of the specific consonants involved.

8.3 Barbareño Chumash

Examine the following data from Barbareño Chumash (Applegate 1972), paying attention to what consonants may occur together in word-initial, word-medial, and word-final position.

(1) ku 'person, Indian'
(2) woqo 'hard tar, asphalt'
(3) nukumi 'to bring (home)'
(4) kuwajapi 'to turn back'

(5)	sloq	'hole'
(6)	spɨl	'pitch, wax type'
(7)	sjep	'cactus leaf'
(8)	tsweq	'grass'
(9)	klawaʃ	'piece, broken'
(10)	qlowowon	'to be short'
(11)	xwapʃ	'nettle plant'
(12)	noqʃ	'head'
(13)	tupmektʃ	'child'
(14)	ʃmuwitʃ	'Coast Indians'
(15)	ʃlaqpe	'mushroom species'
(16)	nɨ	'flame, fire'
(17)	muhu	'owl species'
(18)	potʃoji	'lizard species'
(19)	skam	'wing, fin'
(20)	stapan	'round tool'
(21)	swelen	'earthquake'
(22)	ʃtajit	'willow'
(23)	tʃtaniw	'to be small'
(24)	kwelu	'tanned hide'
(25)	pleʔ	'to perish'
(26)	kikiʃ	'to be alone'
(27)	ʔasejt	'oil' (Spanish loan)
(28)	ʃkaʃ	'thread'
(29)	xlɨwɨxʃ	'devil fish'
(30)	ʃjaxawutʃ	'limpit species'

Exercise 8.6 Syllabify the above words using principles of onset maximization and onset preference.

All the monosyllabic words have no controversy in their syllabification, but many such forms do tell us whether certain consonant sequences are possible in onsets or codas. Word-initial sequences may consist of obstruents followed by sonorants, or sibilants followed by apparently any consonant. Word-final sequences consist of osbtruents followed by sibilants.

As for intervocalic consonants, wherever there is a single segment between vowels, we may assume them to be syllabified as onsets for the second syllable, in accordance with the principle of onset preference. There are only two medial sequences observed, [pm] in (13) and [qp] in (15). Since these both involve consonant sequences not observed as word-initial complex onsets, we can assume they belong to different syllables.

Exercise 8.7   Based on what you determined above, syllabify the following words:

(31)	saqpjun	'breeze'
(32)	zalqlaw	'to fly down'
(33)	ʔoqspololon	'to slap, yell'
(34)	polopswojon	'to be corded or twisted'
(35)	ʔaqʃmul	'to make a sound'
(36)	ʔaqʃwalaw	'to like, love, want'

(31)	saq.pjun	'breeze'
(32)	zal.qlaw	'to fly down'
(33)	ʔoq.spo.lo.lon	'to slap, yell'
(34)	po.lop.swo.jon	'to be corded or twisted'
(35)	ʔaq.ʃmul	'to make a sound'
(36)	ʔaq.ʃwa.law	'to like, love, want'

Each of these items has a problematic sequence consisting of three consonants. In (31), we can infer that the second and third consonant form a complex onset, as the sequence [pj] is a stop followed by a sonorant, matching the possible onset sequences we observed in Exercise 8.6. Moreover, were we to propose the alternative syllabification of [saqp.jun] or [sa.qpjun], we would be claiming either that [qp] is a possible coda or that [qpj] is a possible onset, yet neither sequence matches the observed types of syllable margins from Exercise 8.6.

The remaining forms could actually syllabify in two ways; for example, in (32) [zal.qlaw], the middle consonant is [q], which could occur in a coda following [l] (if we adhere to a generalization that codas may comprise sonorants followed by obstruents), or in an onset before the second [l], if we adhere to the generalization that onsets may comprise obstruents followed by sonorants. In other words, [zalq.law] and [zal.qlaw] are both possible, but the principle of onset maximization favors the latter. The same is true of the remaining forms, all of which have medial sibilants.

In general, we may assume that a language will syllabify medial consonants together in an onset only if the same two consonants are observed as possible word-initial onsets. In English words like *aspire, mistake,* or *askance,* we assume that the medial consonant sequences comprise complex onsets, which is supported by the allowability of such onsets in monosyllabic words like *spire, stake,* and *scant.* This assumption accounts for the lack of aspiration in the plosives of the bisyllabic forms.

Conversely, we syllabify *compile, intake,* and *encode* differently, with the nasal consonants in codas and the plosives in onsets, because word-initial sequences like [mp-], [nt-], or [ŋk-] are not found in English. Likewise, the syllable-initial position of the plosives renders them aspirated, hence [kəmpʰaɪl, ɪntʰeɪk, əŋkʰoʊd].

What this means is that syllabification is sensitive to the nature of adjacent consonants. Some languages syllabify all CC sequences as C.C, while others may vary. The choice is often a function of sonority: if the two sequences rise in sonority, CC is often treated as a complex onset. If the sequences are of equal or falling sonority, CC is broken into two separate syllables. There is often more nuance than this, however: stops followed by nasals are often syllabified separately despite their rise in sonority, while stops preceded by [s] are often syllabified together, despite their fall in sonority. Because of these facts, it is important for us to remember that the syllabification of an internal CC sequence can only be assumed as tautosyllabic if the same sequence is observed word-initially.

8.4 Minhe Monguor

Put in different terms, we can say that determining word-internal syllable boundaries is easiest if we can establish knowledge of possible syllables within a language. The following data from Minhe Monguor (Slater 2003) help illustrate this.

(1)	pulajsi	'boys, children'
(2)	çan	'first'
(3)	paŋ	'to be (2/3)'
(4)	ala	'to kill'
(5)	pawpa	'I went down'
(6)	asis	'herd animals'
(7)	panfa	'method, means'
(8)	tini	'I will eat'
(9)	akwer	'daughter'
(10)	wakʰe	'to dig'
(11)	çweʂeŋ	'student'
(12)	tʰjemer	'iron'
(13)	qʰoni	'sheep'
(14)	pejla	'to carry'
(15)	jaw	'to go, to walk'
(16)	jawpa	'I went'
(17)	injantu	'in one year'
(18)	jow	'oil'
(19)	swar	'to pour, to learn'
(20)	kʰwarpa	'I arrived'

(21)   ljaŋ   'two'
(22)   njaŋ   'mother'
(23)   mjawtur   'today'
(24)   pʰusa   'another'
(25)   ʂini   'to smile'
(26)   niŋke   'to do this'
(27)   tʰike   'that one'
(28)   ʂarsi   'urine'
(29)   ʂwer   'chopsticks'
(30)   çija   'I'll go'
(31)   ẓa   'I'll come'
(32)   ẓwaŋdu   'in a hole'

Exercise 8.8   Syllabify the Minhe Monguor data. Wherever you see internal sequences of consonants, you should assign at least one consonant to the onset of the second syllable. You may assign two consonants to a medial onset if a similar sequence is also found word-initially.
After you have syllabified each word, produce a short list of possible syllable types, using C and V for short.

The observed syllable types are summarized below.

CV
CVC
CCV
CCVC

In short, the Minhe Monguor syllable allows up to two consonants in the onset, and no more than one consonant in the coda.

Exercise 8.9   Take another look at the Minhe Monguor syllabification and answer the following questions:

a.   Can any consonant occur in coda position? If not, what consonants do you see in coda position?
b.   Where two consonants occur within an onset, is there any apparent restriction on what can appear, or are any two consonants allowed?

a.   Only sonorants can occur as codas.
b.   For complex onsets, the second consonant must be a glide, either [j] or [w].

We can summarize our findings for Minhe Monguor so far with a statement about the maximal syllable in the language. The maximal syllable is a generalization that summarizes possible syllables in a language, expressed as a sequence of C and V. Any C that precedes the V is understood as an onset consonant, and any C that follows it is understood as a coda.

In addition, some elements seem to be required, while others are optional. Optional elements are expressed in parantheses, while required ones are not. In this language, every syllable has a vowel, and at least one consonant beforehand. The second onset consonant is only sometimes present, so we conclude that it is an option or a possibility, and we place it in parentheses; the same is true of the coda consonant. With this in mind, the syllable template in Minhe Munguor is as follows:

C(C)V(C)

We can enrich this statement with some description of the types of consonants that appear: notably, the second onset consonant can only be a glide, while the coda consonant can only be a sonorant.

C(G)V([+son])

Placing the second onset consonant in parentheses rather than the first allows us to enrich this statement with generalizations about the types of consonants that can appear in each position, without creating too complicated a statement.

Now examine the following additional data from Minhe Monguor:

(33)	ʂatzi	'sand'
(34)	atsʰaja	EXCL
(35)	nutɕʰi	'pass by'
(36)	jawtɕan	's/he went'
(37)	tʰjantʐwaŋ	'skylight'
(38)	aŋtʂʰiqwo	'feeding through'
(39)	tzaj	'again'
(40)	tsʰaj	'food, dish'
(41)	tɕʰimaj	'2sg.dative'
(42)	tɕu	'therefore'
(43)	tʐwa	'catch, chase'
(44)	tʂʰenli	'to hear'

Exercise 8.10 Do these data conform to your syllable template from above? If not, what needs to be added to that statement?

These data illustrate two new facts. First, complex onsets may also include [t] followed by coronal fricatives. Second, onsets with three consonants are possible, so long as the sequence is consistent with the previously established sequences. In particular, the first two consonants may be [t] followed by a coronal fricative, while the third must be a glide.

8.5 Quechua

Using this level of detail about syllable types helps corroborate our analysis of Quechua in §6.18, where we saw that dorsal consonants have stop and fricative allophones. Dorsals in Quechua appear as stops before vowels, but as fricatives in syllable-final position. The data are repeated below.

(1)	qori	'gold'
(2)	q'omir	'green'
(3)	moqo	'runt'
(4)	phulju	'blanket'
(5)	tulju	'bone'
(6)	suti	'name'
(7)	tʃilwi	'baby chick'
(8)	tʃhaɴqaj	'granulate'
(9)	qetʃuŋ	'he disputes'
(10)	musoχ	'new'
(11)	jaɴqaŋ	'for free'
(12)	qhelja	'lazy'
(13)	tʃeqaŋ	'straight'
(14)	noqa	'I'
(15)	tʃeχniŋ	'he hates'
(16)	aχna	'thus'
(17)	qosa	'husband'
(18)	alqo	'dog'
(19)	karu	'far'
(20)	qaŋkuna	'you pl.'
(21)	t'eχwaj	'pluck'
(22)	wateχ	'again'
(23)	waχtaj	'hit!'
(24)	waqaj	'tears'
(25)	waxtʃa	'poor'
(26)	thakaj	'drop'
(27)	tʃoχlu	'corn on the cob'
(28)	niŋri	'ear'
(29)	hoq'ara	'deaf'
(30)	jujaŋ	'he recalls'
(31)	api	'take'

(32) oɴqoj   'be sick!'
(33) ʧhiʧiŋ   'he whispers'
(34) aɴqosaj   'toast'
(35) p'isqo   'bird'
(36) ʧuŋka   'ten'
(37) ʧulju   'ice'
(38) q'eɴqo   'zigzagged'
(39) qaŋ   'you'
(40) ʧaxra   'field'
(41) soχta   'six'
(42) ljixlja   'small shawl'
(43) qara   'skin'
(44) seɴqa   'nose'
(45) atoχ   'fox'
(46) pusaχ   'eight'
(47) ʧ'aki   'dry'
(48) aŋka   'eagle'
(49) haku   'let's go'
(50) kaŋka   'roasted'
(51) waleχ   'poor'
(52) reχsisqa   'known'

Exercise 8.11 Syllabify the Quechua data. Wherever you see internal sequences of consonants, you should assign at least one consonant to the onset of the second syllable. You may assign two consonants to a medial onset if a similar sequence is also found word-initially.

Your syllabification should illustrate that dorsal fricatives are always in coda position, while dorsal stops are always in onsets. There are a few important test cases that bear on the analysis; for example, (27) [ʧoχlu] contains a medial uvular fricative followed by [l]. We syllabify this as [ʧoχ.lu] with confidence, since no forms in the data contain word-initial onset CC sequences containing [l] as the second consonant. In fact, among the complex onsets of Quechua, the only consonants ever seen in second position are [h] and [j].

Exercise 8.12 Write a rule that expresses the allophonic distribution of dorsal stops and fricatives in Quechua.

Either of the following rule formulations would handle the allophony; the first works for underlying representations in which the dorsal is a stop (and thus spirantizes in coda position). The second works for underlying representations in which the dorsal is a fricative, and thus becomes a stop in onset position.

214

$$[\text{DOR}] \rightarrow [+\text{cont}] / \_\_\_]_{\text{SYLL}}$$
$$[\text{DOR}] \rightarrow [-\text{cont}] / \_\_\_ [+\text{syll}]$$

Whichever formulation we adopt, a fortuitous consequence is that we can express the allophony with a unitary conditioning environment: dorsals have different allophones depending on syllable position. Without the notion of the syllable as a concept that we can incorporate into rules, we would need to employ special notations for environments such as ___ {C, #}, which indicates that an allophone appears before consonants *or* word boundaries. Since consonants and word boundaries are not a natural class (as the reliance on a disjunctive notation suggests), this expression fails to capture the Quechua pattern as a coherent phenomenon.

So far, our appeal to syllable structure has helped us reframe some alternations in more coherent terms, and has also helped us express apparent limits on the number of consonants that may occur before or after vowels, and thus at the margins of words.

The fact that some segments can be seen to have a syllabically restricted distribution leads us in some cases to revisit what counts as a phoneme or as a sequence. Before we embark on this next step, consider the case of English affricates, which we consider to be single segments despite combining a sequence of a stop gesture and a fricative gesture. While English syllable structure can be relatively lax, allowing sequences of two or three syllable-initial segments, the nature of those segments is quite restricted: generally a two-syllable sequence may only combine [s] plus another consonant, or an obstruent followed by a liquid or glide.

Sequences of stops followed by fricatives are not otherwise found in English: since there are no tautosyllabic sequences of [p] or [k] followed by any fricatives, nor of [t] or [d] followed by any other fricatives besides [ʃ] and [ʒ], we infer that [tʃ] and [dʒ] are single segments.

8.6 Yagua

A similar argument can be made, albeit with different kinds of sounds, in the syllable structure of Yagua. Examine the following data (from Payne and Pullum 1990), focusing on where you think you should place medial syllable boundaries:

(1)	suwõ	'woven bag'
(2)	samũũsi	'his tail'
(3)	sapuunjĩ	'is hari guard'
(4)	pupa	'white color'

(5)   satanū   'he pounds'
(6)   jɨtu   'vocative for woman without children'
(7)   kɨɨwã   'fish'
(8)   mũkandɨɨ   'mud'
(9)   mããnjū   'sleepy-head/sleeping person'
(10)   samũū   'its feather'
(11)   sũūmbaaj   'he's stingy'
(12)   sũūmbuuj   'he barks'
(13)   mbaanjū   'one who chases or is being chased'
(14)   rɨ̃ɨ̃njãã   'my great feast'
(15)   nɨ̃ɨ̃tju   'pineapple'
(16)   sanduu   'he blows'
(17)   hɨɨndaj   'fire, campfire, cooking fire'
(18)   sandɨɨ   'his fat'
(19)   ruundihjũū   'rope for tying up a hammock'
(20)   ruwoo   'type of vine'
(21)   ratandaj   'to go down (as of a river)'
(22)   rawinjẽ   'type of monkey'
(23)   nũūwɨ   'is this the road'
(24)   wawjetju   'sparrowhawk'
(25)   nɨ̃ɨ̃hãã   'oil'
(26)   hawanu   'grub worm'
(27)   nĩjãã   'type of wild edible fruit'
(28)   rapjuka   'my big river tortoise'
(29)   rɨ̃ɨ̃tjãã   'my breasts'
(30)   risjuu   'kapok'
(31)   randjindɨ   'my meat sauce'
(32)   randjeetu   'my daughter'
(33)   rambjeerja   'I guard it'
(34)   ramĩsjãã   'my lupuna tree'
(35)   nĩkjẽrja   'angry person'
(36)   ramjẽẽj   'I am sleeping'
(37)   kõõtu   'rabbit'

Exercise 8.13 a. Should the sequences [mb] and [nd] be considered sequences of
                   phonemes or as single segments?
               b. Should the sequence of a consonant followed by [j] be considered a
                   sequence of two segments or as a single segment?

               a. Any sequence of homorganic nasal-stop consonants should be syllabified
                   tautosyllabically. Such sequences are found word-initially and between
                   vowels, as in (13) [mbaanjū] and (18) [sandɨɨ].

b.   Any sequence of a consonant followed by [j] should be syllabified as [.Cj] and not [C.j]. In fact, we could consider these to be complex phonemes, since no other consonant sequences are observed.

None of the forms in Yagua end in consonants, suggesting that coda consonants are not permitted. There is a limited set of possible sequences of sounds: consonants followed by [j], and homorganic nasal-stop sequences. The fact that no other sequences of sounds are permitted initially or medially suggests that such sequences should be considered complex onsets, if not complex segments.

In these data we may be tempted to assign [Cj] to separate syllables, for the basic reason that no words begin with this sequence. Nevertheless, while many consonants may precede [j] word-medially, none may precede any other consonant, and none may occur word-finally. The fact that only [j] may occur as the second of two consonants (aside from [mb] and [nd], which we also analyze as onset sequences) suggests that Yagua adheres to a very stringent limit on which two consonants may occur in onsets, not unlike the pattern we saw in §8.11 where only [h] or [j] occurs in the second position of an onset sequence.

Exercise 8.14   a.   Are nasal and oral vowels in complementary distribution in Yagua?
b.   Compare the distribution of oral and nasal vowels with the distribution of nasal consonants and nasal-stop sequences. Does any pattern emerge here?

While there are no minimal pairs, oral and nasal vowels have an overlapping distribution. Either may occur word-finally after [w], as in (1) [suwõ] and (20) [ruwoo]; either may occur after [r] and before a voiceless obstruent, as in (29) [rĩĩtjãã] and (30) [risjuu], and either may precede nasal consonants (14) [rĩĩnjãã] and (17) [hĩĩndaj]. These facts suggest that nasal and oral vowels are contrastive phonemically, and thus do not have a complementary distribution.

Nevertheless, nasal consonants are followed by nasal vowels, as in (9) [mããnjũ] and (25) [nĩĩhãã], but nasal–stop sequences are followed by oral vowels, as in (13) [mbaanjũ] and (16) [sanduu]. There clearly is a relationship between the nasality of vowels and the sounds that precede them, but it is not simply that a nasal consonant makes a following vowel nasal. Indeed, nasal vowels may follow voiceless stops, as in (37) [kõõtu], or non-nasal sonorants, as in (14) [rĩĩnjãã].

We thus maintain the claim that the nasality of a vowel itself is not predictable, and consequently that the appearance of the voiced stop is driven by the presence of an oral vowel, and not the other way around. Therefore, plain nasals and nasal–stop sequences are in complementary distribution.

In Yagua, we have relied on principles of syllabification to such an extent that our analysis has ultimately settled upon treating certain apparent sequences as unitary complex segments. Without the benefit of syllable structure, our analysis would lack a coherent account of the distribution of [Cj] sequences and nasal-stop sequences.

8.7 Syllable typology

The principles of onset preference and onset maximization tell us, in brief, that languages favor placing consonants into onsets over codas. These principles are useful for us as we explore syllable-based alternations, and they help us determine syllable boundaries within polysyllabic words, but these claims are also related to a general understanding of constraints on syllable structure. Indeed, they are grounded in robust typological trends that emerge from the analysis of a large number of the world's languages.

Among the languages of the world, onsets are either required or allowed – but no language forbids onsets. Conversely, codas are either allowed or forbidden – but no language requires codas. Considering all possible combinations of onset patterns and coda patterns gives us four basic syllable systems. The following table summarizes the syllable shapes that are available in each of these four types of systems.

	Onsets required	Onsets allowed
Codas forbidden	CV	CV, V
Codas allowed	CV, CVC	CV, V, CVC, VC

Syllable typology becomes more complicated when we acknowledge that some languages allow no more than one consonant in their margins, while others allow complex margins. Still, just as no language requires a coda, no language requires complex margins, so despite the larger number of syllable-system types that we encounter, we would not encounter any language that allows onsetless syllables or complex onsets, but no simple onsets.

In fact, overall what we see for possible onset systems are languages that (i) require onsets but limit them to single consonants, (ii) allow onsetless syllables, and limit onsets to single consonants, (iii) require onsets and allow complex ones, and (iv) allow onsetless syllables, and onsets otherwise may be simple or complex. In the dimension of coda systems, languages may forbid codas, allow only simple codas, or also allow complex codas. Each combination of onset type and coda type is found among the world's languages, as summarized in the following table.

Allowable syllable types in languages (adapted from Blevins 1995)

		Onsets			
Codas		C	C, –	C, CC	C, CC, –
	–	Hua*	Cayuvava	Arabela	Mazateco
		PNG	*Bolivia*	*Peru*	*Oaxaca*
	–, C	Thargari	Mokilese	Sedang	Spanish
		W. Australia	*Micronesia*	*Vietnam*	*Spain etc.*
	–, C, CC	Klamath	Finnish	Totonac	English
		Oregon	*Finland*	*Veracruz*	*England etc.*

Exercise 8.15   For each made-up syllable below, identify which languages from the table above it would be allowed in. Assume for this exercise that the segments are part of each language's phonemic inventory.

1. fru
2. pleŋ
3. arp
4. krent
5. jif
6. uk
7. tamp

1. fru   Arabela, Mazateco, Sedang, Spanish, Totonac, English
2. pleŋ   Sedang, Spanish, Totonac, English
3. arp   Finnish, English
4. krent   Totonac, English
5. jif   Thargari, Mokilese, Spanish, Finnish, Klamath, Sedang, Totonac, English
6. uk   Mokilese, Spanish, Finnish, English
7. tamp   Klamath, Totonac, English, Finnish

Our exploration of syllabification shows that languages may differ in the types of syllables they have: some languages have a wider range of possible syllables than others, largely as a function of how many consonants they tolerate within syllable margins. With this in mind, let us turn to some examples of segment-zero alternations, which we can now frame as effects of syllabification that emerge when borrowing or morphological concatenation introduces problematic consonant sequences.

219

8.8 Turkish

Re-examine the following data from Turkish, repeated from §3.10. Let us assume that the underlying forms of the roots are identical to the unsuffixed forms, and that the suffix is underlyingly /-msɪ/.

(1) kara   'black'   karamsɪ   'blackish'
(2) maɟara   'cave'   maɟaramsɪ   'cavernous'
(3) rapor   'report'   raporumsu   'report-like'
(4) duvar   'wall'   duvarɪmsɪ   'wall-like'

Exercise 8.16 Syllabify these data. What is the maximal syllable observed in the data? Are there any complex onsets or codas?

The maximal syllable is CVC; there are no complex onsets or margins here.

Exercise 8.17 Now let us work with the underlying forms of the morphemes here, prior to the application of any epenthetic process. Consider the sequences of underlying morphemes, and syllabify them, but do not allow more than one consonant in any syllable margin. What do you find?

The concatenation of /rapor + msɪ/ contains a sequence of three consonants; if we apply the maximal Turkish syllable to this form, we are left with /ra.por.m.sɪ/, in which /m/ is stranded. In other words, the process of syllabifying the underlying forms leaves some consonants outside the syllable margins. Thus, we can conceive of the epenthesis rule as one that creates a syllable nucleus, so as to generate a syllable in which the stranded consonant may find a home within a margin.

8.9 Japanese

For another example of a language adhering to strict limitations on its syllable structure, we turn next to data from Japanese. Take some time to look over the following data, paying attention to anything that would indicate limits on what kinds of consonants may occur in certain positions (data adapted from Itô (1990), Grignon (1985), Mizuki Miyashita (p.c).

(1) su   'vinegar'
(2) ta   'rice field'
(3) no   'field'
(4) ne   'root'
(5) ja   'arrow'
(6) ko   'child'
(7) ka   'mosquito'

(8)	hi	'fire'
(9)	te	'hand'
(10)	ki	'tree'
(11)	to	'door'
(12)	hi	'blood'
(13)	e	'picture'
(14)	ha	'tooth'
(15)	taberu	'eat'
(16)	tabenai	'not eat'
(17)	kaku	'write'
(18)	kakanai	'not write'
(19)	haʃiɾu	'run'
(20)	haʃiɾanai	'not run'
(21)	keɾu	'kick'
(22)	keɾanai	'not kick'
(23)	nomu	'drink'
(24)	nomanai	'not drink'
(25)	aɾuku	'walk'
(26)	aɾukanai	'not walk'
(27)	neɾu	'sleep'
(28)	nenai	'not sleep'
(29)	saɴ	'three'
(30)	saŋka	'participate'
(31)	maŋga	'comic (book)'
(32)	sampo	'taking a walk, a stroll'
(33)	samba	'three (birds)'
(34)	kantoo	'the Kanto area'
(35)	bando	'a band'
(36)	akka	'a change for the worse'
(37)	kappa	'kappa, a water imp'
(38)	patto	'a putt'
(39)	tanniɴ	'a homeroom teacher'
(40)	samma	'sanma (fish)'
(41)	hossa	'a stroke, seizure'
(42)	zutto	'for a long time'
(43)	zu:tto	'for a long time (rhetorical lengthening)'
(44)	ki:ɴ	'high pitched sound (onomatopoetic)'
(45)	kiɴ	'gold'
(46)	o:	'king'
(47)	se:to	'student'
(48)	senjo:	'battle field'

(49)	kata	'shoulder'
(50)	katta	'bought'
(51)	kite	'Come (here)!'
(52)	ki:te	'Listen!'
(53)	kitte	'stamp'
(54)	kite:	'regulations'
(55)	kippo:	'good news'
(56)	suko:N	'scone'
(57)	kami	'god'
(58)	kao	'face'
(59)	kai	'shell'
(60)	hon	'book'
(61)	hakkiɾi	'certainly'
(62)	obaa	'grandmother'
(63)	hjaku	'one hundred'
(64)	sentoo	'public baths'
(65)	kendoo	'fencing'
(66)	sampoo	'stroll'
(67)	samba	'midwife'
(68)	seŋkoo	'stick of incense'
(69)	maŋga	'comic book'
(70)	semmee	'clearness'
(71)	tenno	'emperor'
(72)	tʃansu	'chance'
(73)	tʃuumoN	'order'
(74)	tʃoottʃo	'butterfly'
(75)	ʃabondama	'bubble'
(76)	ʃuukaN	'custom'
(77)	ʃooguN	'military leader'
(78)	dʒaɾimiti	'gravel road'
(79)	dʒuutaN	'rug'
(80)	dʒoodaN	'joke'

Exercise 8.18 Examine these data and produce a preliminary analysis of syllable structure. Assume single intervocalic consonants belong to the following syllable. If you see any intervocalic sequences of two consonants, you will need to decide how best to syllabify them. What kinds of syllables do you find?

There are V syllables, CV syllables, CVC syllables, and CVV syllables. The intervocalic sequences of consonants include [-mp-], [-mb-], [-nd-], [-nt-], [ŋg], [ŋk], [ss], [tt], [kk], [mm], and [nn]. None of these appears in any word-initial position, so we can infer that each such sequence is split into separate syllables, where the first is the coda of one syllable and the second is the onset of the next syllable.

Exercise 8.19   Now look at all of your CVC syllables. What can you say about the nature of the coda consonant in each?

The coda consonant is either the first half of a voiceless obstruent geminate (long consonant) or a nasal consonant. Medial nasals have the same place of articulation as the following consonant, while word-final nasals are always [N].

geminate: a long consonant, contrastive with a short consonant with otherwise identical features.

Now examine the following additional data:

(81)	happjaku	'eight hundred'
(82)	pjuuto	'whizzing'
(83)	pjoNpjoN	'hop'
(84)	bjakureN	'white lotus'
(85)	bjuukeN	'fallacy'
(86)	bjooki	'sickness'
(87)	mjakudoo	'pulsation'
(88)	mjuudikaru	'musical'
(89)	mjoobaN	'tomorrow'
(90)	rjakusetu	'brief explanation'
(91)	rjuukoo	'fashion'
(92)	rjokaN	'Japanese-style inn'
(93)	njannja	'kitty'
(94)	njuumoN	'introduction'
(95)	njoobo	'wife'
(96)	kjanpasu	'campus'
(97)	kjooiuku	'education'
(98)	gjaŋu	'gang'
(99)	gjuunjuu	'milk'
(100)	gjogjoo	'fishing industry'
(101)	hjaku	'one hundred'
(102)	hjuzu	'fuse'
(103)	hjobaN	'reputation'

Exercise 8.20   Do you need to amend your generalizations about Japanese syllables? If so, how? Is the place of articulation of any consonant relevant here?

223

Japanese allows complex onsets if the second sound is [j]. Moreover, this only happens where the first consonant is not a coronal obstruent.

Clearly there is a stringent set of demands in place on the shape of syllables in Japanese. Only a very small set of onset sequences is permitted, and coda consonants are tightly bound to the place of articulation of the following onset. Nevertheless, Japanese has borrowed a large amount of vocabulary from other languages with a wider array of syllable types, including English. The data below illustrate such borrowings; take some time to peruse these forms, paying attention to the way in which complex English syllables are rendered in Japanese. You should also take note of any changes in segmental form that occur.

8.10 Borrowings in Japanese

Consider the following data from Japanese (Itô 1990):

(1)	amatʃua	'amateur'
(2)	puɾofeʃʃonaɾu	'professional'
(3)	heɾikoputaa	'helicopter'
(4)	tʃokoɾeeto	'chocolate'
(5)	teɾoɾizumu	'terrorism'
(6)	biɾudiŋgu	'building'
(7)	opeɾeeʃoɴ	'operation'
(8)	haŋkatʃiifu	'handkerchief'
(9)	fuɾasutoɾeeʃoɴ	'frustration'
(10)	iɾasutoɾeeʃoɴ	'illustration'
(11)	sukatoɾodʒii	'scatology'
(12)	akuseɾuɾeetaa	'accelerator'
(13)	intoɾodakuʃoɴ	'introduction'
(14)	konsaabatibu	'conservative'
(15)	asupaɾagasu	'asparagus'
(16)	sutoɾaiki	'strike'
(17)	adoɾesu	'address'
(18)	itaɾukku	'italic'
(19)	negatʃibu	'negative'
(20)	redʒisutaa	'register'
(21)	piɾiodo	'period'
(22)	podʒitʃibu	'positive'
(23)	hazubandu	'husband'
(24)	ɾokeeʃoɴ	'location'
(25)	teɾoɾisuto	'terrorist'

(26)	ɾaboɾatoɾii	'laboratory'
(27)	dekoɾeeʃoɴ	'decoration'
(28)	konekuʃoɴ	'connection'
(29)	maikuɾohoɴ	'microphone'
(30)	saikedeɾikku	'psychedelic'
(31)	paamanento	'permanent'
(32)	sandoitʃi	'sandwich'
(33)	daijamondo	'diamond'
(34)	ʃimpasaizaa	'sympathizer'
(35)	ampuɾifaiaa	'amplifier'
(36)	impotentsu	'impotence'
(37)	kombineeʃoɴ	'combination'
(38)	paŋkutʃaa	'puncture'
(39)	waado puɾosessa	'word processor'
(40)	hebii metaɾu	'heavy metal'
(41)	sukeeto boodo	'skate board'
(42)	pantii sutokkiŋgu	'panty stocking'
(43)	demonsutoɾeeʃoɴ	'demonstration'
(44)	anaunsaa	'announcer'
(45)	anaakisuto	'anarchist'
(46)	gjaɾantee	'guarantee'
(47)	saɾada doɾeʃʃiŋgu	'salad dressing'
(48)	haŋgaa sutoɾaiki	'hunger strike'
(49)	ɾimooto kontoɾooɾu	'remote control'
(50)	dʒiinzu pantsu	'jean pants'
(51)	paasonaɾu kompjuutaa	'personal computer'

Exercise 8.21   Describe any changes you can identify in the segments of the borrowings: which English segments are rendered differently in the loanwords? Do not yet be concerned with inserted or deleted segments.

- The English phonemes [ɹ] and [l] are both realized as [ɾ], as in (4) [biɾudiŋgu], (5) [teɾoɾizumu], (6) [tʃokoɾeeto], and (7) [opeɾeeʃoɴ].
- English [v] is changed to [b], as in (14) [konsaabatibu], (22) [negatʃibu], and (40) [hebii metaɾu].
- Some instances of [s] appear instead as [ʃ], as in (34) [ʃimpasaizaa] and (47) [saɾada doɾeʃʃiŋgu].
- Some instances of [t] appear as [tʃ], as in (22) [podʒitʃibu].
- Some instances of [n] appear as [ɴ], as in (7) [maikuɾohoɴ], (27) [dekoɾeeʃoɴ], and (29) [opeɾeeʃoɴ].
- Some sequences of vowel + [ɹ] appear as long vowels.

225

- The large number of English vowels is mapped to a much smaller Japanese vowel inventory. In particular, [i] and [ɪ] merge to [i]; [e] and [ɛ] merge to [e], [æ] and [ʌ] merge to [a], [ɑ] and [o] merge to [o], and reduced vowels in English are rendered with any of [o], [a], or [e] in Japanese.

Exercise 8.22   Describe what happens to English words that end in consonants.

- Word-final /ɹ/ is lost in the borrowed forms, as in (1) [amatʃua] and (3) [heɹikoputaa].
- Word-final /n/ is rendered as [N], as in (7) [opereeʃoN], (27) [dekoreeʃoN], and (29) [maikurohoN].
- All other words with final consonants receive an additional vowel in their borrowed form, as in (2) [puɹofeʃʃonaɹu], (5) [teɹoɹizumu], and (18) [itaɹukku].

Exercise 8.23   Describe what happens to word-initial and word-medial English consonant sequences. If any remain unchanged, describe the conditions under which a change should and should not occur.

- Word-initial sequences are always broken up with inserted vowels, as in (2) [puɹofeʃʃonaɹu], (11) [sukatoroʤii], and (16) [sutoɹaiki].
- Some word-internal consonant sequences remain adjacent, but only if they adhere to the conditions we identified in Exercise 8.19, as in (8) [haŋkatʃiifu], (14) [konsaabatibu], (35) [ampuɹifaiaa], and (49) [kontorooɹu]. That is, homorganic nasal-obstruent sequences remain unchanged.
- Sequences that do not meet these conditions are broken up in a similar way to word-initial sequences, as in (3) [heɹikoputaa], (6) [biɹudiŋgu], (12) [akuseɹureetaa], and (15) [asupaɹagasu].

Curiously, voiceless obstruent geminates are allowed in these borrowings, despite the fact that English does not have contrastive consonant length, and it is not obvious what conditions their appearance. One possibility is that gemination applies to /k/, /s/, or /ʃ/, and only if the preceding vowel is short in English, as in (39) [puɹosessa], (42) [sutokkiŋgu], and (47) [doɹeʃʃiŋgu].

    The Japanese data illustrate several concepts: the fact that vowels are inserted into onset sequences in borrowed words shows how the language adjusts such forms to fit its stringent constraints against complex syllable margins. Furthermore, these data serve as a clear example of what linguists call a Coda Condition: a limitation on what kinds of consonants can occur in coda position. Different languages show evidence of this phenomenon to varying extents.

Coda Condition: a coda consonant must share features with a following onset.

Languages with coda conditions typically may allow a subset of their consonant inventory to occur in coda position, or they may require that coda consonants somehow be similar or identical to a following onset consonant. This second type of conditioning is often called licensing: an onset consonant licenses a preceding coda consonant, as long as they share place features.

licensing: a consonant's features are licit only if the consonant is linked to a particular position.

8.11 Yokuts

As another example of an alternation with zero driven by syllabification, let us re-examine Yokuts, presented as an exercise in Chapter 3 and again in Chapter 7. Let us refamiliarize ourselves with the data below, which requires some steps of morphological analysis. In the following data, note that there are four groups of four forms each; we will use the first form in each group to represent that group.

	Aorist passive	*Aorist*	*Future*	
(1)	xatit	xathin	xatnit	'eat'
(2)	gopit	gophin	gopnit	'take care of infant'
(3)	gijit	gijhin	gijnit	'touch'
(4)	mutut	muthun	mutnut	'swear'
(5)	saːpit	saphin	sapnit	'burn'
(6)	goːbit	gobhin	gobnit	'take in'
(7)	meːkit	mekhin	meknit	'swallow'
(8)	ʔoːtut	ʔothun	ʔotnut	'steal'
(9)	panat	panaːhin	panaːnit	'arrive'
(10)	hojot	hojoːhin	hojoːnit	'name'
(11)	ʔilet	ʔileːhin	ʔileːnit	'fan'
(12)	cujot	cujoːhun	cujoːnut	'urinate'
(13)	paxaːtit	paxathin	paxatnit	'mourn'
(14)	ʔopoːtit	ʔopothin	ʔopotnit	'arise from bed'
(15)	hibeːjit	hibejhin	hibejnit	'bring water'
(16)	sudoːkut	sudokhun	sudoknut	'remove'

Exercise 8.24
a. Identify the three suffixes represented in these data.
b. Some roots have an alternation in the length of their vowels: explain how this alternation works, focusing on the forms in (1), (5), (9), and (13).

a. The aorist and future suffixes both have two alternants: [hin, hun] for the aorist passive, and [nit, nut] for the aorist. The aorist passive has three alternants: [t, it, ut].

b. The roots in (1)–(4) have no length alternation; for example, in (1), the vowel of the root is short in the aorist passive [xatit] and the future [xatnit], so we can tentatively infer that they have underlyingly short vowels.

The remaining roots have vowels which are long in some contexts but short in others:

- In (5), there is a long vowel in the aorist passive [saːpit], but a short vowel in the future [sapnit].
- In (9), there is a short vowel in the aorist passive [panat], but a long vowel in the future [panaːnit].
- In (13), there is a long vowel in the aorist passive [paxaːtit], but a short vowel in the future [paxatnit].

Exercise 8.25 a. Determine the underlying forms for the aorist passive suffix. What conditions its alternants?

b. Determine underlying forms for the alternating roots. What conditions the length of alternating vowels?

a. The aorist suffix is underlyingly /t/, and a vowel appears between it and root-final consonants. For example, in (1) the root is /xat/, and /xat + t/ receives an inserted vowel. In (5) the root is /saːp/, and /saːp + t/ also receives an inserted vowel. In (9), no vowel is inserted in [panat], since the root ends in a vowel.

If we were to assume the suffix has an underlying vowel, we would have to propose that it is deleted after vowel-final roots.

b. As for the root representations, since underlying short vowels always stay short, we can propose that the alternating vowels in (5)–(16) are underlyingly long, and shorten in some circumstances. For example, some roots include (5) /saːp/, (9) /panaː/, and (13) /paxaːt/.

The long vowels of (5)–(8) and (13)–(16) are shortened before consonant sequences in the aorist and future forms, as in (5) /saːp + nit / → [sapnit] and (13) /paxaːt + nit/ → [paxatnit].

The long vowels in (9)–(12) are shortened before word-final consonants, as in the aorist passive of (9), /panaː + t/ → [panat].

Exercise 8.26 a. Syllabify these data.
b. What types of syllables do you find?
c. Are there any complex onsets or codas?
d. What is the maximal syllable observed in the data?

	Aorist passive	*Aorist*	*Future*	
(1)	xa.tit	xat.hin	xat.nit	'eat'
(5)	saː.pit	sap.hin	sap.nit	'burn'
(9)	pa.nat	pa.naː.hin	pa.naː.nit	'arrive'
(13)	pa.xaː.tit	pa.xat.hin	pa.xat.nit	'mourn'

There are CV, CVC, and CVː syllables. None of the syllables has a complex coda or onset. The largest syllable is either CVː or CVC; a syllable may have a long vowel or a coda, but not both.

Exercise 8.27 Now instead of syllabifying the data, assemble each word as a sequence of its underlying morphemes.

  a. Syllabify these sequences.
  b. Are there any potential syllable types that you did not observe in Exercise 8.26?

	Aorist passive	*Aorist*	*Future*	
(1)	xatt	xat.hin	xat.nit	'eat'
(5)	saːpt	saːp.hin	saːp.nit	'burn'
(9)	pa.naːt	pa.naː.hin	pa.naː.nit	'arrive'
(13)	pa.xaːtt	pa.xaːt.hin	pa.xaːt.nit	'mourn'

There are several syllable types here that are not seen in the surface data. The aorist passive of (1), (5), and (13) has a complex coda, as in /xatt, saːpt, paxaːtt/. The aorist and future forms of (5) and (13) have CVːC syllables, as in /saːphin/ and /paxaːthin/.

Exercise 8.28 a. Write a rule to handle the inserted vowels in the aorist passive forms.
  b. Write a rule to handle the shortened vowels in (5)–(16).
  c. Do these rules need to be ordered? Explain your answer.

  a. Epenthesis: $\emptyset \rightarrow$ [i] / C __ C]$_{\text{SYLL}}$
  b. Shortening: Vowel $\rightarrow$ [-long] / __ C]$_{\text{SYLL}}$
  c. The insertion rule must occur first. This will add a vowel to the aorist passive forms in (5) /saːpt/ and (13) /paxaːtt/, yielding [saːpit] and [paxaːtit]. If Shortening were instead to apply first, these roots would have shortened vowels in their aorist passives.

We infer that several phenomena are occurring in Yokuts. First, there is an avoidance of complex syllable margins – the epenthesis that occurs in the aorist passive can be seen as a response to this. Second, there appears to be an upper limit on the size of syllables: they may contain a long vowel, or a coda consonant, but not both. The shortening pattern that occurs in various roots appears to be a response to this limit.

The notion of a limit on syllable size suggests that Yokuts is aware of the weight of syllables: the occurrence of a segment after the nucleus adds a unit of weight to the syllable, regardless of whether this additional segment is a consonant or a vowel. This calls for a way of representing the idea of syllable weight in formal terms, and phonologists use the mora to do so. The mora distinguishes heavy from light syllables: light syllables have one mora, while heavy syllables have two. A heavy syllable may be bimoraic by having a long vowel, but languages vary as to whether coda consonants carry a mora; in Yokuts, they clearly do. We will explore the notion of syllable weight in greater detail in the following two chapters, where other phonological phenomena can be shown to respond to the number of moras within a syllable.

Summary

In this chapter we have introduced and explored the notion of the syllable. It has given us a concept to describe certain allophonic and alternation patterns more succinctly than we could do otherwise. We have seen that some alternations are sensitive to the syllabic position of segments, or can be framed as patterns that make the choice of allophone or alternant sensitive to the syllabic position of the phoneme. We have also been able to incorporate syllabic components into the formal mechanism of phonological rules.

By appealing to a nuanced conception of internal syllable structure, we have seen that languages range in terms of the types of syllables they allow. Some allow complex margins and some do not; some allow codas while others do not, and some have more stringent limits on syllable size and weight than others.

In the next two chapters, we will encounter phenomena that interact quite clearly with syllable structure: in particular, in Chapter 9, stress and tone are best treated as properties of syllables, sensitive to things like the number and weight of syllables within words. In Chapter 10, we will explore prosodic morphology, a branch of phonology that uncovers how syllable structure can serve contrasts and morphological functions in surprising ways.

Key terms

syllable

onset

nucleus

coda

rhyme

geminate

mora

Coda Condition

complex margins

syllabification

References and further reading

Applegate, Richard. 1972. Ineseño Chumash grammar. Doctoral dissertation, University of California, Berkeley.

Blevins, J. 1995. The syllable in phonological theory. In John Goldsmith *(ed.),* Handbook of Phonological Theory. Oxford: Blackwell, 206–244.

Elbert, Samuel H., and Mary Kawena Pukui. 1979. *Hawaiian Grammar.* Honolulu: University Press of Hawaii.

Gordon, Matthew K. 2002. A factorial typology of quantity insensitive stress. *Natural Language and Linguistic Theory* 20: 491–552.

Gordon, Matthew K. 2004. Syllable weight. In Bruce Hayes, Robert Kirchner, and Donca Steriade (eds.), *Phonetic Bases for Phonological Markedness.* Cambridge University Press, 277–312.

Grignon, Anne-Marie. 1985. On the structure of the Japanese rime. *McGill Working Papers in Linguistics* 2.2: 97–114.

Itô, Junko. 1986. Syllable theory in prosodic phonology. Doctoral dissertation, University of Massachusetts.

Itô, Junko. 1989. A prosodic theory of epenthesis. *Natural Language and Linguistic Theory* 7: 217–259.

Itô, Junko. 1990. Prosodic minimality in Japanese. *Chicago Linguistics Society 26: Papers from the Parasession on the Syllable in Phonetics and Phonology,* 213–239.

Levin, Juliette. 1985. A metrical theory of syllabicity. Doctoral dissertation, Massachusetts Institute of Technology.

Payne, Doris, and Thomas Payne. 1990. Yagua. In Desmond Derbyshire and Geoffrey Pullum (eds.), *Handbook of Amazonian Languages*, vol 2. Berlin: Mouton de Gruyter, 249–474.

Slater, Keith W. 2003. *A Grammar of Mangghuer: A Mongolic Language of China's Qinghai-Gansu Sprachbund.* London and New York: RoutledgeCurzon.

Review exercises

Meithei

Determine the maximal syllable template of Meithei based on the following forms. Give the syllabification of each item.

dari	'verandah'
səkti	'power'
əpokpə	'swollen'
lajdəŋ	'only God'
na	'ear'
kʰojtʰut	'enrage'
pʰəygan	'place on thigh'
məwpwa	'address term'
pʰreŋ	'a way birds flap their wings'
səmbre	'freckle'
piktru	'small child'
tiltʰrok	'earthworm'
mətʰwaj	'inheritance'
kaŋdrum	'hockey puck'
kruk	'resin'
kwak	'crow'
kjamləj	'a thorny tree'
pakʰra	'widower'
syam	'proper name for male'
swaj maŋ-	'vanish'

ʧel	'run'	ʧelli	'runs'
ʧəŋ	'enter'	ʧəŋŋi	'enters'
ləj	'be'	ləjji	'is'
thəm	'keep'	thəmmu	'keep!'
ɟeŋ	'look'	ɟeŋŋu	'look!'

Ashenica

maa.ro.ni	'all'
i.kjaa.piin.ti	'he always goes in'
no.ko.wa.we.ta.ka	'I wanted it in vain'
sji.ran.pa.ri	'man'
sjon.ki.ri	'type of partridge'

ha.ka	'here'
o.pi.na.ta	'it costs'
a.ti.ri.pa.jee.ni	'people'

Diola Fogny

Reconsider the following data from §3.4.

Underlying form	Surface form	Gloss
ni-maŋ-maŋ	nimammaŋ	'I want'
ni-ŋan-ŋan	niŋaŋŋan	'I cried'
na-ʤum-to	naʤunto	'he stopped'
ni-gam-gam	nigaŋgam	'I judge'
pan-ʤi-maɲʤ	panʤimaɲʤ	'you-pl will know'
na-tiŋ-tiŋ	natintiŋ	'he cut through'
ku-boɲ-boɲ	kubomboɲ	'they sent'
uʤuk-ʤa	uʤuʤa	'if you see'
let-ku-ʤaw	lekuʤaw	'they won't go'
kob-kob-en	kokoben	'yearn for'
a-ʤaw-bu-ŋar	aʤabuŋar	'voyager'
na-laɲ-laɲ	nalalaɲ	'he returned'
na-joken-joken	najokejoken	'he tires'
na-waɲ-am-waɲ	nawaɲawaɲ	'he plowed for me'
e-rent-rent	ererent	'it is light'
na-maɲʤ-maɲʤ	namamaɲʤ	'he knows'

a. Perform syllabification of these data.
b. Compose a deletion rule that refers to syllable structure.

CHAPTER 9 TONE

Learning objectives

- Understand tone as a contrastive property
- Differentiate tone from stress, pitch, and intonation
- Understand contours as sequences of simple tone units
- Detect patterns in distributions of tones
- Analyze tone patterns as separate levels of representation
- Interpret and construct representations with autosegmental melodies and association among tiers
- Compose and use rules that affect tone

Introduction

Now that we have established the notion of the syllable as an actual element of phonological representation, we can turn to other phenomena which are more easily analyzed with syllable structure than without. We often call such phenomena **suprasegmental**, meaning above the segment, with the idea that moras and syllables organize segments into larger units. In this chapter, we will focus on tone, a phenomenon that is best handled as a distinct layer of phonological units, separate from but linked to the layer of segments. In later chapters, we will address stress, which is intimately tied to syllable sequencing, and prosodic morphology, a domain of inquiry in which we investigate how syllable shape (among other things) can differentiate morphological functions.

suprasegmental: phenomena which affect units that are larger than individual segments.

As we investigate suprasegmental phonology, we will need to clarify certain terminology that has a very specific interpretation. In particular, stress, tone, and intonation are all terms you may have heard before, but each has a specific usage in this chapter and in the field of phonology.

9.1 Tone

Tone is a phonological property of some languages which allows for a separate dimension of contrast. Languages that use tone contrastively do so by altering **pitch** in the vowels of words. Pitch and tone both refer to frequency of the speaker's voice, but they are distinct concepts. Pitch refers to the absolute value of rate (i.e., frequency) of vocal cord vibration, while tone refers to a speaker's relatively higher and lower frequencies within their own register.

pitch: the frequency of vocal cord vibration.

In a tone language, a syllable with a relatively lower pitch represents one lexical item, but a change in the pitch corresponds to a different lexical item. In other words, in tone languages, minimal pairs can be identified which differ in form only by their tone.

tone: the use of pitch as a contrastive feature in the lexicon or morphology of a language.

Chinese languages are often cited as good examples to illustrate tonal contrasts, as the following forms illustrate.

Tones in Mandarin Chinese

Segmental form	Tone	Gloss
ma	high level	'mother'
ma	high rising	'hemp'
ma	low fall/rise	'horse'
ma	high falling	'scold'

The Mandarin tones are predominantly **contoured**, in that they often involve a rise or fall in pitch over the course of a syllable. Such contours can be decomposed into sequences of basic units of high and low tones, and in some systems, a mid tone between the two. By turning to the use of high and low as tonal units, we can simplify the nature of the tonal representation.

contour: a tone that includes more than one level of pitch.

It is very important to differentiate tone from both stress and pitch. Two different speakers may have vastly different pitch, as a function of their size, age, and culture-specific gendering practices, but use the same tones. Conversely, a word spoken by one speaker may have a different tone, but the same or similar pitch, to a different word spoken by another speaker of the same language.

Moreover, as we will see when we investigate stress in Chapter 10, languages tend to have one primary stress per word, but the distribution of tone is quite different. Stress is associated with exactly one syllable, and languages tend to interleave stressed and unstressed syllables in longer words. In contrast, all syllables of a given word may be high or low, which suggests that a tone element may be associated with more than one syllable. In addition, languages may allow more than one tone to associate to a single syllable, as contours. We must keep these notions in mind as we proceed through analysis of tonal phonology.

Tonal notation varies widely across transcriptional systems. Phonologists who study tone often use acute and grave accents to indicate high and low tones respectively. In turn, a circumflex can be viewed as a sequence of the two, thus indicating a fall in tone, while a caron is the reverse sequence, a rising tone. For systems with three level tones, a macron may be used for the middle (or mid) tone. The following table summarizes these symbols and terms.

Symbol	Name	Tone
á	acute	high
à	grave	low
â	circumflex	falling
ǎ	caron	rising
ā	macron	mid

We will adhere to such a system in this chapter in descriptions of data, except where noted. When we turn to analysis, we will follow the additional representational practice of representing tones on separate levels.

In the following examples, we can see sets of words which are contrasted only by their tonal characteristics.

9.2 Wapan

Examine the following data from Wapan (Welmers 1973). Unmarked vowels should be considered to have a mid tone.

(1) akwí 'knife'
(2) akwì 'chicken'
(3) akwĩ 'millstone'
(4) àkwì 'gourd'

Exercise 9.1 Identify pairs of words in Wapan that show contrast among high, mid, and low tones.

The pair (1) [akwí] and (2) [akwì] show that high and low tone are contrastive in Wapan, since they differ only in the tones on their second syllables. Similarly, the pair (2) [akwì] and (3) [akwɩ̀] show that low and mid tone are constrastive.

9.3 Igala

Now examine the following data from Igala (Welmers 1973). Again, unmarked vowels should be considered to have a mid tone.

(1) áwó 'guinea fowl'
(2) áwo 'an increase'
(3) áwò 'hole in a tree'
(4) àwó 'a slap'
(5) àwo 'a comb'
(6) àwò 'star'

Exercise 9.2 Identify pairs of words in Igala that show contrast among high, mid, and low tones.

The pair (1) [áwó] and (2) [áwo] show that high and mid tones are contrastive in Igala, since they differ only in the tones on their second syllables. Similarly, the pair (2) [áwo] and (3) [áwò] show that low and mid tone are constrastive.

9.4 Igbo

Often when we analyze sequences of tone, we resort to the abbreviations H, M, and L for High, Mid, and Low tones. Examine the following data from Igbo (Welmers 1973), in which each vowel has either H or L.

(1) ɔ́kà 'corn'
(2) úlɔ̀ 'house'
(3) ézì 'pig'
(4) éwú 'goat'
(5) ákpú 'cassava'
(6) ócé 'chair'
(7) égó 'money'
(8) ɔ́dʒí 'kola nut'

(9)   ágú   'leopard'

(10)   àkwá   'egg'

(11)   ìkó   'cup'

(12)   ɔ̀sá   'squirrel'

(13)   ìtè   'pot'

(14)   àkpà   'bag'

(15)   ùdɔ̀   'rope'

Exercise 9.3 Describe the sequences of tone that occur in two-syllable words in Igbo.

Any sequence of high and low tone is possible in Igbo.

- The forms in (1)–(3) have the sequence H–L, as in (1) [ɔ́kà].
- The forms in (4)–(9) have the sequence H–H, as in (4) [éwú].
- The forms in (10)–(12) have the sequence L–H, as in (10) [àkwá].
- The forms in (13)–(15) have the sequence L–L, as in (13) [ìtè].

Certainly tone acts as part of the phonemic system of some languages, in that we can see it functioning to provide conrast among lexical items. However, just as we see that phonemes have restrictive distributions and alternations, we can also see that tones and tone sequences have limited distributions and respond to morphological processes. The next several exercises illustrate these phenomena.

9.5 Efik

In the following data from Efik (Gleason 1955), we will examine the tonal patterns in a number of verb paradigms. Ultimately, we will detect the underlying tonal contours of each root and affix, and we will be able to describe the processes that affect these sequences. Note that vowels may carry high, low, or rising tone. Syllabic nasal consonants may also bear tone.

		a. 'buy'	b. 'live'	c. 'think'	d. 'put'	e. 'go'	f. 'run'
(1)	1sg.pres	ńdèp	ńdù	ŋ́kèrè	ńdòrì	ŋ́kà	m̀fèhè
(2)	2sg.pres	èdèp	òdù	èkèrè	òdòrì	àkà	èfèhè
(3)	3sg.pres	édèp	ódù	ékèrè	ódòrì	ákà	éfèhè
(4)	1sg.fut	ńjédép	ńjédù	ńjékéré	ńjédòrì	ńjékǎ	ńjéfèhé
(5)	2sg.fut	èjédép	èjédù	èjékéré	èjédòrì	èjékǎ	èjéfèhé
(6)	3sg.fut	éjédép	éjédù	éjékéré	éjédòrì	éjékǎ	éjéfèhé

(7)	1sg.pst	ŋ́kédép	ŋ́kódù	ŋ́kékéré	ŋ́kódòrì	ŋ́kákǎ	ŋ́kéfèhé
(8)	2sg.pst	èkédép	òkódù	èkékéré	òkódòrì	àkákǎ	èkéfèhé
(9)	3sg.pst	ékédép	ókódù	ékékéré	ókódòrì	ákákǎ	ékéfèhé

		'lay'	'dig'	'walk'	'come'	'pass'	'show'
(10)	1sg.fut	ńjésín	ńjédɔ̀k	ńjésàŋá	ńjétó	ńjébě	ńjéwút
(11)	3sg.fut	éjésín	éjédɔ̀k	éjésàŋá	éjétó	éjébě	éjéwút
(12)	1sg.pst	ŋ́késín	ŋ́kɔ́dɔ̀k	ŋ́kásàŋá	ŋ́kótó	ŋ́kébě	ŋ́kówút
(13)	3sg.pst	ékésín	ɔ́kɔ́dɔ̀k	ákásàŋá	ókótó	ékébě	ókówút

		'come'	'kill'	'pray'	'cover'	'fly'	'be called'
(14)	1sg.pst	ŋ́kédí	ŋ́kówòt	ŋ́kɔ̀bɔ́ŋ	ŋ́kékíbí	ŋ́kéfě	ŋ́kékèrè
(15)	3sg.pst	ékédí	ókówòt	ɔkɔ̀bɔ́ŋ	ékékíbí	ékéfě	ékékèrè

Exercise 9.4   Conduct a morphological analysis of these data, focusing first on the prefixes. Note any forms that alternate, including whether they have different tones in different morphological contexts.

The subject agreement morphemes are simple to extract. By comparing the three forms of 'buy' in the present tense, we can infer that /ń/ is first person, /è/ is second person, and /é/ is third person. Other allomorphs of the second- and third-person prefixes appear before other roots, as we will see below.

(1a)	ńdèp	'I buy'
(2a)	èdèp	'you buy'
(3a)	édèp	'he buys'

The tense morphemes can be identified in a similar manner: by comparing the three first-person forms of 'buy,' we can infer that /jé/ is future, while past is indicated by /ké/. Other allomorphs of the past prefix, as in /ká, kɔ, kó/, appear with other roots. There is no segmental form for the present tense, but we will return to this shortly.

(1a)	ńdèp	'I buy'
(4a)	ńjédép	'I will buy'
(7a)	ŋ́kédép	'I bought'

None of the affixes has any alternation in tone: the first- and third-person prefixes always have H, and the second person always has L. The future and past prefixes also always have H.

Some of the affixes do alternate in their segments:

- The first-person prefix is [ŋ́] when it occurs before [k], as in (1c) [ŋ́kèrè] and (7a) [ŋ́kédép].

- The past-tense morpheme changes its vowel; it is [kó] before roots with [o, u], [kɔ́] before roots with [ɔ], [ké] before roots with [e, i], and [ká] before roots with [a].
- The second- and third-person prefixes show a parallel alternation; independently of tone, they are [e] when the following vowel is [i, e]; [o] if the following vowel is [u, o], [ɔ] if the following vowel is [ɔ], and [a] if the following vowel is [a]. This alternation occurs when the agreement suffix precedes the root, as in (2a) [èdèp], (2b) [òdù], and (2e) [àkà], and also when it precedes the past-tense morpheme, as in (8a) [èkédép], (8b) [òkódù], and (8e) [àkákǎ].

The allomorphs of the prefixes are summarized as follows:

ń/ŋ́	1sg
é/ó/ɔ́/á	2sg
è/ò/ɔ̀/à	3sg
jé	past
ké/kó/kɔ́/ká	future

Exercise 9.5 Now turn the analysis to identify the roots.

a. Do any roots have different tones in different contexts?
b. What is the underlying tone of each root?

The roots constitute whatever remains after the tense prefix. For example, in (4c) [ŋ́jékéré], the root is [-kéré], and in (9e) [ákákǎ], the root is [-kǎ].

a. Many roots have different tone contours in different contexts. In the present, every root has only low tones, as in (1a) [ńdèp], (1b) [ńdù], and (1e) [ńkà], but in the other tenses, some roots have other tones. For example, the root /dù/ maintains a low tone in the other tenses, as in (4b) [ŋ́jédù], but the other roots have different tones, as in (4a) [ŋ́jédép] and (4e) [ŋ́jékǎ].
b. Since it is not predictable whether a root has high or low tone in future or past, we can infer that the root tones of these tensed forms are underlying. The present-tense forms, in contrast, always have low tone, so we infer that it is indicated by replacing the underlying tone with low tone.

The roots of Efik are summarized below:

dép	'buy'
dù	'live'
kéré	'think'
dòrì	'put'

kǎ	'go'
fèhè	'run'
sín	'lay'
dòk	'dig'
sàŋá	'walk'
tó	'come'
bě	'pass'
wút	'show'
dí	'come'
wòt	'kill'
bóŋ	'pray'
kíbí	'cover'
fě	'fly'
kèrè	'be called'

We have completed a morphological analysis of Efik in which the value of the tones is relevant, and we have discovered that in some cases, the tone of a morpheme changes because of its morphological context. There is more we can say about these data, however. One important observation is that only some combinations of tones are observed within roots. Every root has either only low tones, only high tones, a rising contour, or a sequence of a low tone vowel and a high tone vowel. Crucially, there are no falling tones, and no roots that contain a sequence of high tone followed by low tone. In addition, there are no bisyllabic roots that contain rises on either of their vowels.

There is thus an apparent restriction on the distribution of tones within roots; this lets us reduce the number of underlying tone sequences for the language. If we allow a particular tone unit to associate to more than one vowel, then roots with a single low tone or pair of low tones have an underlying L unit, and roots with a single high tone or pair of high tones have an underlying H unit. In so doing, we are in effect placing tone on a separate level or **tier** of representation, independent of vowels. In other words, segments and tones exist on separate tiers.

tier: an autonomous level of representation on which all phonological units of a particular type exist in sequence.

The elements on a tier that is distinct from the segmental tier are sometimes called **autosegments**: they resemble segments in that we can identify them in sequence, but they exist on an autonomous level. In the approach we are exploring here, tones are autosegments. We thus refer to this approach to phonology as **autosegmental**.

autosegment: a phonological unit found on some tier of representation distinct from the segment level.

The separation of tones and segments into different tiers can be illustrated literally with different levels of representation. The relationship between elements of different tiers (like tones and vowels) is called **association**, and the links joining them are **association lines**. The H and L roots in Efik are thus represented as follows; note how a single tone unit on the tone tier may associate to multiple vowels in the segment tier.

```
 H       H   L      L
 |      / \  |      / \
dep     kere du     dori
[dép    kéré dù     dòrì]
```

In turn, if we allow a single vowel to associate to more than one tone unit, then rising contours can be represented as single vowels linked to LH sequences. Contours and sequences of low tones and high tones thus share the same tone sequence.

```
LH      LH
 V      | |
ka      fehe
[kǎ     fèhé]
```

This approach identifies three basic tonal melodies for Efik: L, H, and LH, where a **melody** is a sequence of units (segments or autosegments) on some tier of representation.

melody: a sequence of phonological elements on some tier of representation.

If rising tone were some other basic tonal unit, distinct from L and H rather than composed of a sequence, we would have no explanation for why only monosyllabic roots have rising tone, and why rises never occur together with L or H in bisyllabic roots. Conversely, we have a simple explanation for the absence of both falling contours and sequences of high tones followed by low tones: HL is simply absent from the inventory of melodies.

A consequence of this representational approach is that the present tense can easily be modeled as the replacement of the root's lexical melody with L. The affixes all have tones associated with them as well, except the present-tense morpheme underlyingly is just a floating or unassociated L element.

The task of writing rules for tonal phonology is sometimes more complicated than what we typically see in segmental restructuring rules, because of the separation of tiers. In cases like the Efik present tense, a change

242

in tone can simply be expressed in terms of nearby tones. The manifestation of present tense suggests that there is a rule that operates just on the tone tier and deletes any tone element after an unassociated L, notated as *L.

Post-L deletion   Tone → Ø / *L ___

As the present tense underlyingly is simply a floating, unassociated L, its addition to a root will trigger Post-L deletion for any form in the present tense. A later rule of reassociation is needed to spread the floating L tone rightward to any vowels that have lost their tones. To exemplify this, the derivation of (1a) [ńdèp] from /ń + L + dép/ and (1c) [ŋ̀kèrè] from / ń + L + kéré/ is illustrated below. Note how newly added association lines are indicated with dashed lines.

UR	/1sg + pres + 'buy'/	/1sg + pres + 'think'/
	H L H | | n dep	H L H | ⋀ n kere
Post-L deletion	H L | n dep	H L | n kere
reassociation	H L | ⦙ n dep	H L | ⋀⦙ n kerè
Surface form	[ńdèp]	[ŋ̀kèrè]

Tonal phonology also involves tones changing in response to nearby tones, analogous to assimilation or dissimilation in segmental phonology. Sometimes the rules are more complex than the above example, as they involve changes in the relationships of association between segments and tones. In the exercises in the next section, we will see examples of underlying tones being affected by their proximity to tones of adjacent morphemes.

9.6 Ogbia (Nigeria)

Examine the following data from Ogbia (Williamson 1972), paying attention to how the suffix in the right hand column alters the segmental and tonal structure of each word.

	Unsuffixed	Definite	Gloss
(1)	ədírí	ədírə̂	'book'
(2)	ətúrú	ətúrə̂	'nail'
(3)	əwúdúm	əwúdúmə̂	'life'
(4)	ədè	ədə̀	'farm'
(5)	əbə̀dì	əbə̀də̀	'monitor lizard'
(6)	əgbùdùm	əgbùdùmə̀	'bush cow'
(7)	əpùsí	əpùsə̂	'cat'
(8)	ədùmó	ədùmə̂	'riddle'
(9)	əpíkò	əpíkə̀	'feather'
(10)	èmú	èmə̂	'head'
(11)	əgôl	əgólə̀	'gold'

Exercise 9.6 Rewrite the tone sequences using H and L. For convenience and clarity, separate tones of different syllables with periods, but place contour tones together. For example, you would notate [ədírə̂] as [L.H.HL].

(1)	ədírí	[L.H.H]	ədírə̂	[L.H.HL]	'book'
(2)	ətúrú	[L.H.H]	ətúrə̂	[L.H.HL]	'nail'
(3)	əwúdúm	[L.H.H]	əwúdúmə̂	[L.H.H.HL]	'life'
(4)	ədè	[L.L]	ədə̀	[L.L]	'farm'
(5)	əbə̀dì	[L.L.L]	əbə̀də̀	[L.L.L]	'monitor lizard'
(6)	əgbùdùm	[L.L.L]	əgbùdùmə̀	[L.L.L.L]	'bush cow'
(7)	əpùsí	[L.L.H]	əpùsə̂	[L.L.HL]	'cat'
(8)	ədùmó	[L.L.H]	ədùmə̂	[L.L.HL]	'riddle'
(9)	əpíkò	[L.H.L]	əpíkə̀	[L.H.L]	'feather'
(10)	èmú	[L.H]	èmə̂	[L.HL]	'head'
(11)	əgôl	[L.HL]	əgólə̀	[L.H.L]	'gold'

Exercise 9.7 a. Identify the segmental component of the definite suffix.

b. Describe whatever segmental alternation you find in the data.

c. Create a rule that handles this segmental alternation.

a. The suffix is underlyingly /ə/.

b. Root final vowels are deleted before this suffix, as in (1) /ədírí + ə/ → [ədírə̂] and (10) /èmú + ə/ → [èmə̂]

c. V-deletion:

$$V \rightarrow \emptyset \, / \, \_\_ \, V$$

Exercise 9.8   Describe the tonal alternation in the data.
  a.   What are the final tones of the definite forms?
  b.   Are these predictable alternants, and if so, what determines the tone contour?
  c.   What is the underlying form of the definite suffix?

  a.   The definite forms contain either a final L tone, as in (4) [ədə̀]
       and (5) [əbədə̀], or a final HL tone, as in (2) [ətúrə̂] and (3)
       [əwúdŭmə̂].
  b.   The definites end with HL tones where the unsuffixed forms end in
       H tones, as in (1)–(3), (7), (8), and (10); otherwise, the definite forms end
       with L, as in (4)–(6), (9), and (11).
  c.   The definite suffix consists of the vowel /ə/ marked with low tone.

Exercise 9.9   Describe in words what happens to roots with a final H tone when they receive
the definite suffix. Make sure to address both vowel-final and consonant-final roots.

  • H-final roots ending in vowels lose their vowel in the definite form.
    Their final H tone remains and associates to the vowel of the suffix,
    producing a HL contour, as in (2) /ətúrú/ → [ətúrə̂].
  • H-final roots ending in consonants do not lose any of their vowels, but
    their final tone nevertheless associates to the vowel of the suffix, again
    producing a HL contour, as in (3) /əwúdŭm/ → [əwúdŭmə̂]

Curiously, Ogbia differentiates lexical tones from affix tones, and
evidently requires that the final lexical tone associate to the final vowel of
the word, even if that vowel is a component of an affix. Where the affix
vowel has its own low tone, a root-final high tone combines with it to
form a falling contour. Thus, we do not need the rule to focus on
unassociated tones; instead, there is a process that spreads the final lexical
tone to the next syllable, even if the final vowel of the root is
not deleted.

  The rule that extends the root's final tone is presented as follows.

Tone spreading   Tone]ROOT   →   Tone
                                    \
                                 X]WORD

  The following derivations test this rule. Let us assume that within
representations, if two vowels have identical tone values, then they actually
share the same tone element. Likewise, if two identical tones are associated to
the same vowel, they coalesce into a single tone.

Exercise 9.10 Test these rules out on the definite forms in (1), (10), (9), and (3).

Here are some sample derivations:

The derivations show clearly that the tonal melodies themseves do not change in these forms. Only the segments change, through V-deletion, and the rule of Tone-spreading simply rearranges the alignment of tonal and segmental tiers.

Exercise 9.11 The definite form in (11) [əgólə] is problematic for the system we have developed so far. Identify its issue and propose an additional rule to account for its behavior.

The form [əgólə] is the only one whose unsuffixed root ends with a falling contour, as in /əgôl/. With our current set of rules, vowel deletion does not apply to its definite form, and tone spreading would spread the L tone rightward, yielding *[əgôlə]. We therefore need an additional rule that delinks the L from a non-final vowel, rendering [əgólə]. There are two ways of expressing this rule; one is to present a structure-changing rule in which the target includes a non-final HL contour, restructured to a form in which the L element is left unassociated.

H L   H L
 \/   → |
V C V   V C V

An alternative is to use a cross-hatch to mark whatever association line is to be removed. The result of this formalism is equivalent: after its application, there is a floating L unit that will subsequently look to associate to a different host.

H L
 \╳
V C V

246

The appeal to such a rule (regardless of how we formalize its expression) seems plausible given that there are no contour tones on non-final vowels anywhere else in the data.

The Ogbia data provide several pieces of evidence to support the idea of representing tones on a separate tier. First, sequences of H and L clearly converge to HL when associated to a single syllable; if tones were merely features of vowels, this process would not be adequately expressed.

Second, root-final tones are left behind even when the root-final vowel is deleted.

9.7 Margi

The notion that tones remain when their host vowels are lost is commonplace in the morphophonology of agglutinative tone languages. Now consider these data from Margi (Hoffmann 1963; Kenstowicz 1994), noting the definite suffix and the tones of both the roots and the suffixes.

(1)	sál	'man'	sálárì	'the man'
(2)	kùm	'meat'	kùmárì	'the meat'
(3)	ʔímí	'water'	ʔímjárì	'the water'
(4)	kú	'goat'	kwárì	'the goat'
(5)	tágú	'horse'	tágwárì	'the horse'
(6)	ʃèré	'court'	ʃèrérì	'the court'
(7)	tóró	'threepence'	tórórì	'the threepence'
(8)	ɔ́ncàlá	'calabash'	ɔ́ncàlárì	'the calabash'
(9)	tì	'morning'	tjǎrì	'the morning'
(10)	hù	'grave'	hwǎrì	'the grave'
(11)	úʔù	'fire'	úʔwǎrì	'the fire'
(12)	cédè	'money'	céděrì	'the money'
(13)	fà	'farm'	fǎrì	'the farm'

Exercise 9.12   Based on the forms in (1)–(2), what is the segmental and tonal structure of the suffix?

The suffix is /ari/, and its tones are HL. The suffix's first vowel is H, regardless of the preceding root tone.

Exercise 9.13   Now turn to the forms in (3)–(8). Describe the segmental and tonal alternations that are illustrated here.

The roots in (3)–(5) end in high vowels with H tone when unsuffixed, but the vowels become toneless glides before the vowel-initial suffix, as in (3) / ʔímí / → [ʔímjárì].

The roots in (6)–(8) end in non-high vowels with H tone when unsuffixed. The suffix loses its first vowel in the definite forms, as in (6) / ʃèré / → [ʃèrérì].

Exercise 9.14   Last, examine the forms in (9)–(13). Describe any segmental or tonal alternations.

The roots in (9)–(11) end in high vowels with L tone when unsuffixed. As in (3)–(5), these vowels become toneless glides before the vowel-initial suffix. The first vowel of the suffix gains a rising tone, presumably by absorbing the stranded L tone of the root and combining it with the initial H tone of the suffix, as in (9) /tì/ → [tjǎrì].

The roots in (12)–(13) end in non-high vowels with L tone. The suffix loses its first vowel in the definite forms, and the final root vowel has a rising tone in this context, as in (12) / cédè / → [céděrì]. Presumably this occurs as the final vowel of the root absorbs the stranded high tone of the suffix.

Exercise 9.15   Create phonological rules to handle the segmental alternations.

a.   Glide Creation   [+syllabic, +high] → [-syllabic] / ___ [+syllabic]
b.   Vowel Deletion   [+syllabic] → Ø / [+syllabic] ___

The rule of Glide Creation renders the root-final high vowels of (3)–(9) and (9)–(11) as glides before the initial vowel of the definite suffix. The rule of Vowel Deletion removes the vowel of the suffix if it follows a vowel, as in (6)–(8) and (12)–(13). Given that Vowel Deletion is ordered after Glide Creation, it only encounters vowels following non-high vowels, so it does not need precise specification of the environment. The ordering here is counterbleeding, in that the opposite ordering would have Vowel Deletion bleed the environment for Glide Creation. It is also partially a bleeding order, since the application of Glide Creation renders Vowel Deletion inapplicable for some forms.

Exercise 9.16   Create phonological rules to handle the tonal alternations.

We need two rules to handle the tonal patterns. A rule of Low Tone Anchoring is needed to associate any L that is left over after any root-final high vowel is changed to a glide. A separate rule of High Tone Anchoring is needed to associate any high tone left stranded by the Vowel Deletion rule.

Low tone anchoring: L* H → L H   *or*   L* H

High tone anchoring: L H* → L H   *or*   L H*

That there are two separate rules to handle stranded tones is a consequence of our approach here: we need one rule to target stranded high tones, and another to target stranded low tones, and whether the stranded tone combines to its left or right depends on the adjacent tones.

Note, however, that the two rules have the same outcome; thus, another way of approaching this phenomenon is to require that any unassociated tone simply and automatically associates to the nearest vowel after any operation that leaves it stranded, and place a condition on the outcome of this rule which stipulates that only rising contours are permitted.

reassociation: associate stranded tones to the nearest available vowel, but do not generate a HL contour.

Exercise 9.17   Test the rules that we have proposed for [tjǎrì], [cédĕrì], and [ʃèrérì].

	L H L	H L H L	L H H L
	| | |	| | | |	| | | |
UR	ti + a r i	c e d e + a r i	ʃ e r e + a r i

	L H L		
	| |		
Glide Creation	t j + a r i	--	--

		H L H L	L H H L
		| | |	| | |
Vowel Deletion	--	c e d e + r i	ʃ e r e + r i

	L H L	H L H L	L H L
Reassociation	t j + a r i	c e d e + r i	ʃ e r e + r i

| Surface | tjǎrì | cèdĕrì | ʃèrérì |

We can extract one additional implication from these derivations: that there is a need to address sequences of identical tones, as we see in [ʃèrérì], where at least in an intermediate stage, the middle vowel links to its own underlying H tone, as well as to the stranded H tone of the suffix. Let us propose that in such scenarios, sequences of identical tones may coalesce into a single tone of the same value.

The tonal phonology we have seen so far shows that tones operate on a separate level from segments. Often, a morphological operation might associate the tone of one morpheme to the vowels of another; in Efik, this occurred as the present tense L tone overwrote the lexical tone of the root. In Ogbia, lexical tone spread rightward, coalescing with the affix tone. In Margi, low and high tones combine if a vowel is deleted at a morpheme boundary.

Margi offers a few more patterns that show other ways in which tonal alternation can play out. For example, some affixes have no tone of their own, while others do. Examine the following data to look for examples of each.

(14) cʊ́   'speak'   cí-bá   'tell'
     ɣà   'reach'   ɣà-bá   'reach'
     fĭ   'swell'   fĭ-bá   'make swell'

(15) sá   'go astray'   sá-ná   'lead astray'
     dlà   'fall'   dlà-nà   'overthrow'
     bdlǔ   'forge'   bdlə̀-ná   'forge'

Exercise 9.18   a.   Which suffix has its tone underlyingly specified?
                 b.   Which has no tone, and how does it acquire tone at the surface?

a.   The suffix in (14) is consistently H, regardless of the tone of the root, so we can infer that it underlyingly is H.
b.   The suffix in (15) is H in some forms but L in others. In fact, it is H when the root has H and L when the root has L; it thus seems to adopt the tone of the root. We can therefore infer that it has no tone of its own. Indeed, when the root has a rising LH contour, as in [bdlǔ], the tones split in the suffixed form, such that the L tone remains on the root, but the H tone associates to the suffix, as in [bdlə̀-ná].

Just as stranded tones automatically seek out vowels, we can infer that toneless vowels seek out tones in Margi. Thus, a suffix not specified for tone would gain tone by associating to the final tone unit of the preceding root.

Now let us turn to another kind of affix whose tone also seems to reflect the tone of the root, but not in the same way as the suffix in (15) above. First, examine the following unaffixed verbs, taking note of the tone melodies that are exhibited.

(16) tsá   'beat'
     sá   'go astray'
     ndábjá   'touch'
     tə́dʊ́   'fall down'

(17) dlà   'fall'
      ghà   'reach'
      gə́rhú   'fear'

(18) hǔ   'grow up'
      və̌l   'fly'
      pə̀zú   'lay eggs'
      dzà?ú   'pound'
      ŋgùrsú   'bend'

Exercise 9.19 What tone melodies are seen in the data?

The roots in (16) have only H vowels; in (17) they have only L vowels. In both groups, if there are two vowels, they have the same tone. The roots in (18) have a LH contour, either combined in a single syllable, as in [hǔ], or with one tone on each of two syllables, as in [pə̀zú].

Now examine the following data, where each item includes a morpheme before the root and another afterwards.

(19) à sá gù   'you go astray'
      à tsú gù   'you beat'

(20) á wì gú   'you run'
      á dlà gú   'you fall'

(21) á və̌l gù   'you fly'

Exercise 9.20 Describe the alternation in tone for the pre- and post-verbal elements in (19) and (20).

In (19), the preverbal element /a/ has L when the root has H, as in [à sá gù]. In (20), it has H when the root has L, as in [á wì gú]. The alternation is similar for the post-verbal element /gʊ/: the same examples in (19) show that /gʊ/ is L when it follows a root with H, and in (20) /gʊ/ has H next to a root with L.

Such affixes can be called polarity affixes, because their tone is regularly opposite to the tone of the adjacent root vowel. Now turn your attention to the tone of these affixes in (21).

Exercise 9.21 Explain the tone of the preverbal and postverbal elements in (21).

The root's vowel has a rising tone, which we would analyze as L followed by H. Since the root's first tone is L, the preverbal polarity morpheme /a/ receives H tone. Likewise, since the root's second tone is H, the postverbal polarity morpheme /gʊ/ receives L tone.

Note that the pattern in (21) would seem like an arbitrary stipulation if we assumed that rising tones were not sequences of LH. As such, we would need separate rules to handle polarity morphemes in just such cases; but by adhering to the notion of LH contours, the polarity pattern for (21) is neatly accounted for.

The way in which polarity morphemes respond to contours in Margi provides yet more evidence for the idea of representing tones on a tier separate from the segment level – the morphemes respond to the rising tone as if it is a sequence of two tones, irrespective of the fact that these tones are sometimes associated to the same vowel.

Let us return briefly to a discussion of how to handle sequences of identical tones. Recall that in Exercise 9.17, some steps in the derivations associate two identical tone elements to the same vowel – we assumed that such representations result in the tones combining into a single unit. Later, in Exercise 9.19, we also assumed that some roots contain only a L tone, and others contain only a H tone, and that this tone is linked to both vowels of disyllabic roots. In other words, roots like [gɔ̀rhʋ̀] have a single L tone, not a sequence of two. Indeed, we made a similar assumption for Efik in Exercise 9.5, where we figured that the present tense L tone overwrote the tone of disyllabic roots, as in /kéré/ → [ŋ̀kèrè]. As a generality, these analyses work best when we assume that adjacent identical tones reduce to a single tone of that value, and that sequences of same-tone vowels within morphemes actually share a single tone unit.

9.8 Shona

We find additional evidence for this claim from Shona. Examine the following data (from Kenstowicz 1994), paying attention to the tones of the roots in the left column. The forms in the right column all contain some sort of preposed element; many of these are pro-clitics, which are morphemes that are appended to the beginning of the root but morphologically are not prefixes, and which are notated with a # boundary.

(1)	mbwá	'dog'	né # mbwà	'with a dog'
(2)	hóvé	'fish'	né # hòvè	'with a fish'
(3)	mbúndúdzí	'army worms'	sé # mbùndùdzì	'like army worms'
(4)	hákátà	'diviner's bones'	sé # hàkàtà	'like diviner's bones'
(5)	bàdzá	'hoe'	né # bàdzá	'with a hoe'

(6)	chàpúpù	'witness'	sé # chàpúpù	'like a witness'
(7)	bénzíbvùnzá	'inquisitive fool'	sé # bènzìbvùnzá	'like an inquisitive fool'

(8)	Fárái	'personal name'	nà # Fárái	'with Farai'
(9)	mbwá	'dog'	sá-mbwá	'owner of a dog'

Exercise 9.22 a. Rewrite the tone sequences of the roots and the preposed forms in (1)–(7) using H and L.

b. What happens to the tones of roots after H pro-clitics?

(1)	mbwá	H	né # mbwà	H # L
(2)	hóvé	H	né # hòvè	H # L
(3)	mbúndúdzí	H	sé # mbùndùdzì	H # L
(4)	hákátà	HL	sé # hàkàtà	H # L
(5)	bàdzá	LH	né # bàdzá	H # LH
(6)	chàpúpù	LHL	sé # chàpúpù	H # LHL
(7)	bénzíbvùnzá	HLH	sé # bènzìbvùnzá	H # LH

The tone melodies are represented here assuming that sequences of identically toned vowels share a single unit. For example, [hóvé] is represented with a single H associated to both vowels; likewise, [hákátà] is represented with H associating to the first two vowels and L to the third.

The pro-clitics have the effect of changing an initial H of the root to an L. For example, the H root [mbwá] is instead L after the H pro-clitic, as in [né # mbwà]. This lowering applies to every H vowel from the beginning of the root onward, as in [hákátà] → [sé # hàkàtà], but does not apply to a H that is separated from the proclitic by an intervening L. For example, in [bàdzá] → [né # bàdzá], the H of the final vowel stays unchanged.

Exercise 9.23 Construct a rule that changes the root's tone.

$$H \rightarrow L \; / \; H \; \# \; \underline{\hspace{1.5cm}}$$

This rule changes initial H to L, but only in the environment of a preceding H tone, as long as a clitic boundary intervenes. Thus, it will not apply to (8) [nà # Fárái], where the pro-clitic has a L tone, and it will not apply to (9) [sá-mbwá], where the pre-posed element is a prefix. It also will not apply to non-initial H tones.

The rule does apply to the H tones of (1–4), which are all made L, but the H tones of (5) [né # bàdzá] and (6) [sé # chàpúpù] are not affected, because these H units are not root-initial. Likewise, only the first H of the root in (7) [bénzíbvùnzá] is made L in [sé # bènzìbvùnzá]; the second H (on the final syllable) is not initial.

You may have elected to represent each vowel's tone separately in Exercise 9.22, and if so, you would have had representations like HH for (2) [hóvé] and HHH for (3) [mbúndúdzí]. Such representations match the data, but the tone-lowering process is very difficult to capture with them; the rule above would have been very challenging to express. As long as we adhere to the representations proposed in the feedback to Exercise 9.22, where several vowels share a single tone unit, we can capture this pattern with a simple phonological rule: it converts root-initial H, but actually converts the tone of all vowels linked to that H. This process, whereby all vowels linked to the initial H tone are changed, is called Meeusen's rule, named for the linguist who first identified and described it.

9.9 Lomongo

The following exercise combines a number of aspects of tonal phonology into a single problem. Examine the following data from Lomongo (Hulstaert 1961), which illustrate numerous prefixed verb forms. You will notice some opportunities for morphological analysis, which uncovers some patterns of phonological alternation, ordered processes, and several tone-based phenomena. Consider unmarked vowels to have low tone.

	Imperative	*1sg*	*2sg*	*3sg*	*Gloss*
(1)	saŋgá	ńsaŋga	ósaŋga	ásaŋga	'say'
(2)	kambá	ŋ́kamba	ókamba	ákamba	'work'
(3)	jilá	ńjila	ójila	ájila	'wait'
(4)	ɛ́na	ńjɛ́na	wɛ́na	ɛ́na	'see'
(5)	ísa	ńjísa	wísa	ísa	'hide'
(6)	iméjá	ńjimeja	wîmeja	îmeja	'consent'
(7)	iná	ńjina	wîna	îna	'hate'
(8)	bína	mbína	óína	áína	'dance'
(9)	báta	mbáta	óáta	ááta	'get'
(10)	bóta	mbóta	óóta	áóta	'beget'
(11)	mɛlá	mmɛla	ɔ́mɛla	ámɛla	'drink'
(12)	lɔ́ma	ńdɔ́ma	ɔ́lɔ́ma	álɔ́ma	'kiss'
(13)	lɔndá	ńdɔnda	ɔ́londa	álɔnda	'chase'
(14)	usá	ńjusa	wûsa	ûsa	'throw'
(15)	asá	ńjasa	wâsa	âsa	'search'

Exercise 9.24 Conduct a morphological analysis of these data, focusing on the segmental representations of the roots and prefixes.

a. What are the alternants of each prefix? Under what conditions do their alternants appear?
b. Do any root morphemes alternate?

There are four morphological functions represented in the data: an imperative form, and forms that agree with the subject for each of first-, second-, and third-person singular. There is no evidence of an actual imperative morpheme, and thus we can assume for the time being that the imperatives reflect the unaffixed form of each root.

a. The first-person form contains a tone-bearing nasal consonant prefix which alternates in its place of articulation as a function of the initial segment of the root, as in (1) [ńsaŋga], (2) [ŋkamba], and (8) [ḿbína]. It is palatal before vowels, as in (14) [ńjusa], suggesting underlyingly it is /ńj/, and assimilates to the place of any following consonant.

   The second-person prefix appears as [ó] or [ɔ́] before consonant-initial roots, as in (1) [ósaŋga] and (11) [ɔ́mɛla], where the vowel harmonizes, appearing as [ɔ] before roots with [ɔ] or [ɛ]. The prefix appears as [w] before vowel initial roots, as in (4) [wɛ́na] and (14) [wûsa]. Curiously, there are some roots that lose their initial consonant in these forms, but the prefix stays as a vowel, as in (8) /bína/ → [óína] and (9) /báta/ → [óáta]. This appears to occur only for roots with initial /b/. We can infer the prefix is underyingly /ó/, and that there are rules of Vowel Harmony and Glide Formation that account for its alternants.

   The third-person prefix appears as [á] before consonant-initial roots, as in (1) [ásaŋga] and (11) [ámɛla], but has no segmental form before vowel-initial roots, as in (4) [ɛ́na] and (14) [ûsa]. Roots with initial [b] again lose their initial consonant under prefixation, but the prefix stays as a vowel, as in (8) /bína/ → [áína] and (9) /báta/ → [ááta]. We can infer that the prefix is underlyingly /á/, and is deleted by rule before vowels, just not before roots that have lost initial /b/.
b. Several kinds of roots do alternate under prefixation. As noted in (a) above, roots with initial /b/ in their imperative lose this consonant after a vocalic prefix, as in (8) /bína/ → [óína] and (9) /báta/ → [óáta]. In additon, roots with initial /l/ see that consonant change to [d] following the first-person prefix, as in (12) /lɔ́ma/ → [ńdɔ́ma].

Exercise 9.25 a. Compose rules to account for each of the prefix alternation patterns.
b. Compose a rule to handle the deletion of root-initial /b/.

c. Describe whether any of these rules need to be crucially ordered, and describe such ordering using the terminology of ordering relationships from Chapter 7.

a. Nasal Assimilation   [+cons, +nas] → [α place] / ___ [+cons, α place]

    Vowel Harmony   [+syll, −high, −low] → [−ATR] / ___ [+syll, −high, −low, −ATR]

    Glide formation   [+syll, −low] → [−syll] / ___ [+syll]

    Vowel deletion   [+syll] → Ø / ___ [+syll]

b. /b/ → Ø / [+syll] ___ [+syll]

c. The rule of b-deletion must be ordered after the other rules, to ensure that the prefixes are not affected. The b-deletion rule would feed the other rules if they were in the opposite order, since it would create the conditions for vowel deletion to occur. That is, if b-deletion happened first to (8) /ó + bína/, the result would be /ó ína/, with adjacent vowels, a structure which would be subject to glide formation. This indicates that their actual order is counterfeeding.

Exercise 9.26 Describe the tone patterns of the prefixed forms and how they relate to the tone contours of the unprefixed roots.

a. What are the tone melodies in the roots?

b. How are the tones realized in the prefixed forms? Be sure to address the melodies in forms that lose their prefix vowel.

a. The unsuffixed roots all have one of two melodies: LH, as in (1) [saŋgá] (7) [iná] and (11) [mɛlá], and HL, as in (4) [ɛ́na], (8) [bína], and (12) [lɔ́ma].

b. The prefixes all have an H tone, which interacts with the tones of the roots in several ways. The tone on the first singular /nj/ prefix always stays associated to the prefix nasal.

For HL roots that keep their prefix vowel, the melody of the prefixed forms is HL, with H associating to both the prefix and the first syllable of the root, as in (8) /bína/ → [óína, áína] and (12) /lɔ́ma/ → [ólɔ́ma, álɔ́ma]. For HL roots that lose their prefix vowel through deletion or glide formation, the melody of the prefixed forms is HL, with H tone staying on the first syllable of the root, as in (4) / ɛ́na / → [wɛ́na, ɛ́na] and (5) / ísa / → [wísa, ísa].

For LH roots that keep their prefix vowel, the melody of the prefixed forms is HL, where the prefix H stays but the root H is lost, as in (1) /saŋgá/ → [ósaŋga, ásaŋga] and (11) /mɛlá/ → [ɔ́mɛla, ámɛla]. For LH roots that lose their prefix vowel through deletion or glide formation, the prefixed forms have a falling tone on their first vowel and L on subsequent vowels, as in (6) /iméjá/ → [wîmeja, îmeja] and (14) /usá/ → [wûsa, ûsa].

Exercise 9.27   a.   Write a rule that accounts for the changes in tone in LH roots when they are prefixed.

b.   Test your analysis against the derivations of (8) [óína], (12) [álɔ́ma], (4) [wéna], (1) [ósaŋga], and (14) [ûsa], using the segmental rules from Exercise 9.25 and the tone rule from (a). Make sure to acknowledge any steps of reassociation that may occur for stranded tones or toneless vowels.

a.   H → Ø / H L __

b.   Derivations

UR	H H L	H H L	H H L	H L H	H L H
	| | |	| | |	| | |	| | |	| | |
	o + bi na	a + lɔma	o + ɛ na	o + saŋga	a + u sa
V-deletion			H H L		H L H
Glide-formation			| |		| |
			w ɛ na		u sa
B-deletion	H H L				
	| | |				
	o + i na				
reassociation			H H L		H L H
			⌐⌐⌐⌟ |		⌐⌐⌐⌟ |
			w ɛ na		u sa
H-deletion				H L	H L
				| |	⌐⌟
				o + saŋga	u sa
reassociation				H L	H L
				| ⌐⌐	⌐⌐⌐
				o + saŋga	u sa
Surface	óína	álɔma	wéna	ósaŋga	ûsa

One last thing to note about the above derivations is that many of them contain sequences of HH; such forms could undergo coalescence of tone such that a single H results, associated to whatever segments had been linked to the original HH sequence. This coalescence process could occur at any point in the derivation without changing the results.

257

Lomongo thus provides an example of a phonological system that combines numerous types of phonological processes, including tonal alternations. Its segmental alternations illustrate an example of counterfeeding opacity which interacts with the distribution of tones over the segments of complex words. Its tonal phonology provides more evidence of stranded tones associating to other vowels, of distinct tones combining to form contours over individual vowels, and of tones changing via phonological rule.

Summary

In this chapter, we have observed phonological patterns involving tone as a contrastive feature. We have seen that tones may be simple or complex, where complex tones comprise a series of two or more simple tones. In fact, complex tones illustrate that a single tone-bearing unit (such as a vowel) may associate to multiple tone elements; conversely, a series of vowels may all associate to the same tonal element. The independent sequencing of tones and segments suggests the two exist on separate but associated tiers of representation.

We have also seen that tones may act as contrastive features, may serve as morphological elements, may interact with segmental phonology, and may alternate as a function of nearby tones. Indeed, each of these types of tonal processes is found widespread throughout tone languages, and the common theme is that they are more easily represented, and their alternations more readily modeled, as long as we can represent the sequence of tone units on a tier that is separate but nonetheless linked to a segmental level.

Tones, like syllable structure, therefore provide an example of phonological elements operating independently from the string of segments that we more typically associated with word forms. Moreover, their patterning and distribution is phonological in nature, in that the restrictions languages place on tone formation are abstract and language specific. In the next chapter, we will rely briefly on tones as a way of deconstructing intonational melodies, which in turn will lead us into a deeper discussion of stress and rhythm.

Key terms

tone
pitch
intonation
level tone
rising and falling tone

contour

level of representation

tier

autosegment

melody

association

References and further reading

Clements, George N., and John Goldsmith (eds.). 1984. *Autosegmental Studies in Bantu Tone*. Berlin: Mouton de Gruyter.

Gleason, H. Allan. 1955. *An Introduction to Descriptive Linguistics*. New York: Henry Holt and Company.

Goldsmith, John Anton. 1976. Autosegmental phonology. Doctoral dissertation, Massachusetts Institute of Technology.

Goldsmith, John Anton. 1990. *Autosegmental and Metrical Phonology*. Oxford: Blackwell.

Halle, Morris, and George N. Clements. 1983. *Problem Book in Phonology*. Cambridge, MA: MIT Press.

Hoffmann, Carl. 1963. *A Grammar of the Margi Language*. London: Oxford University Press for International African Institute.

Hulstaert, G. 1961. Grammaire du Lomóngo. Musée royale de l'Afrique centrale. Terveuren.

Hyman, Larry. 2007. Universals of tone rules: 30 years later. In Tomas Riad and Carlos Gussenhoven (eds.), *Tones and Tunes: Studies in Word and Sentence Prosody*. Berlin: Mouton de Gruyter, 1–34.

Hyman, Larry. 2014. Tone: is it different? In John Goldsmith, Jason Riggle, and Alan Yu (eds.), *The Handbook of Phonological Theory*, 2nd edition. Oxford: Wiley-Blackwell.

Kenstowicz, Michael. 1994. *Phonology in Generative Grammar*. Oxford: Blackwell.

Marlo, Michael R. 2008. Tura verbal tonology. *Studies in African Linguistics* 37: 153–243.

Marlo, Michael R. 2009. Khayo verbal tonology. *Africana Linguistica* 15. 77–129.

Marlo, Michael R. 2013a. Tonal melodies and Meeussen's Rule in Khayo. In Karsten Legère (ed.), *Bantu Languages and Linguistics: Papers in Memory of Dr. Rugatiri D. K. Mekacha*. Bayreuth: BASS, 93–118.

Marlo, Michael R. 2013b. Verb tone in Bantu languages: micro-typological patterns and research methods. *Africana Linguistica* 19: 137–234.

Merrifield, William R., and Benjamin F. Elson. 1967. *Laboratory Manual for Morphology and Syntax*. Santa Ana: Summer Institute of Linguistics.

Nash, Carlos. 2011. Tone in Ekegusii: a description of nominal and verbal tonology. Doctoral dissertation, UCSB.

259

Odden, David. 1995. Tone: African languages. In J. Goldsmith (ed.), *Handbook of Phonological Theory*. Oxford: Blackwell.

Pulleyblank, Douglass. 1983. Tone in lexical phonology. Doctoral dissertation, Massachusetts Institute of Technology.

Welmers, William E. 1973. *African Language Structures*. Berkeley and Los Angeles: University of California Press.

Williamson, Kay. 1972. Assimilation in Ogbia. Research Notes from the Department of Linguistics and Nigerian Languages, University of Ibadan 5.2 1–5.

Yip, M. 2002. *Tone*. Cambridge University Press.

Yip, M. 2007. Tone. In P. De Lacy (ed.), *The Cambridge Handbook of Phonology*. Cambridge University Press, 229–252.

Zhang, Jie. 2007. A directional asymmetry in Chinese tone sandhi systems. *Journal of East Asian Linguistics* 16: 259–302.

Zhang, Jie. 2010. Issues in the analysis of Chinese tone. *Language and Linguistics Compass* 4.12: 1137–1153.

Zhang, Jie. 2014. Tones, tonal phonology, and tone sandhi. In C.-T. James Huang, Y.-H. Audrey Li, and Andrew Simpson (eds.), *The Handbook of Chinese Linguistics*. Oxford: Wiley-Blackwell.

Review exercises

Kikuyu

Examine the following data from Kikuyu (Halle and Clements 1983).

torɔraya	'we are looking'	totomáya	'we are sending'
tomorɔraya	'we are looking at him/her'	tomotomáya	'we are sending him/her'
tomarɔ́raya	'we are looking at them'	tomatómáya	'we are sending them'
márɔraya	'they are looking'	mátómáya	'they are sending'
mámórɔraya	'they are looking at him/her'	mámótomáya	'they are sending him/her'
mámárɔ́raya	'they are looking at them'	mámátómáya	'they are sending them'
torɔrirɛ́	'we looked'	totomírɛ́	'we sent'
tomorɔrirɛ́	'we looked at him/her'	tomotomírɛ́	'we sent him/her'
tomarɔ́rirɛ́	'we looked at them'	tomatómírɛ́	'we sent them'
márɔ́rirɛ́	'they looked'	mátómírɛ́	'they sent'

260

mámórɔriré	'they looked at him/ her'	mámótomíré	'they sent him/her'
mámárɔriré	'they looked at them'	mámátómíré	'they sent them'

a. Conduct a basic morphological analysis, paying attention to segments but ignoring tone for the moment.

b. What tone alternants appear with each affix? Compile a list of the contexts under which each alternant appears. Note: ´ = high tone. Unmarked vowels have low tone.

c. Describe how you would predict the placement of tone in Kikuyu.

Mono-Bili

Examine the following data from Mono-Bili (Merrifield *et al.* 1967).

àbá dá mì	'Father spanked me'
àbá dà mì	'Father will spank me'
gbòlò lú màngè	'The child planted corn'
gbòlò ú lù màngè	'The child will plant corn'
kòmbá zɨ gbàgà	'The bird ate the peanut'
kòmbá zɨ gbàgà	'The bird will eat the peanut'
kàpítà ʃó kɨndɨ	'The chief burned the field'
kàpítà ó ʃò kɨndɨ	'The chief will burn the field'
jàsè zɨ gbàgà	'The woman ate the penaut'
jàsè í zɨ gbàgà	'the woman will eat the peanut'
múrú wó ʃè	'The leopard killed him'
múrú wò ʃè	'The leopard will kill him'
àbá dá ʃè	'Father spanked him'
àbá dà ʃè	'Father will spank him'

a. Perform a morphosyntactic analysis of these data.

b. Describe any segment alternations you detect, and make predictive generalizations to account for them.

c. Describe the distribution of tone for each word class.

More Shona

Examine the enclitics /wo/, /sa/, and /po/ in Shona below. Describe how tone is realized on these morphemes. Hint: one of the morphemes alternates in a way that is unlike the other two.

bwe	'stone'	bwe # wó	'tone also'
shámwarí	'friend'	shámwarí # wo	'friend also'
pfúpi	'short'	pfúpi # sá	'too short'
ndefú	'long'	ndefú # sa	'too long'
ákáénda	'he went'	ákáénda # po	'he went there'
ákaóná	'he saw'	ákaóná # pó	'he saw there'

CHAPTER 10 STRESS

Learning objectives

- Understand how stress differs from other suprasegmental phenomena like intonation and tone
- Differentiate the phonetic and phonological properties of stress
- Observe patterns of primary and secondary stress assignment
- Compose rules that assign stress to syllables
- Understand and operationalize foot structure
- Describe patterns of stress-driven segment alternations

Introduction

With the concepts of the syllable and tone at our disposal in our analyses, we can turn to another suprasegmental phenomenon closely related to syllable structure. In this chapter, we will focus on stress, which like tone is best handled as a property of syllables rather than of segments.
Stress refers to the relative prominence of a syllable amongst other syllables, and is detectable through some combination of loudness, length, and intonation.

The study of stress systems is called metrical phonology (related to the notion of *meter*), and it draws upon familiar concepts of the syllable and the mora, as well as an additional object we call the foot. Later, in Chapter 11, we will address prosodic morphology, a domain of inquiry in which we investigate how syllable and foot shape can differentiate morphological functions.

As we investigate metrical phonology, we will again need to clarify certain terminology that has a very specific interpretation. In particular, stress, tone, and intonation are all terms you may have heard before, but each has a specific usage in the field of phonology. Crucially, while stress and tone are separate phenomena, they are linked through the concept of intonation.

10.1 Intonation

We have observed that some languages are tone languages while some are not. In non-tone languages, changing a tone does not affect a lexical item's meaning: there are no minimal pairs where a difference just in tone provides a contrast between two words. Nevertheless, we can still observe a function in the pitch contours, particularly in intonation. Intonation is the relative sequence of pitch changes over the course of an utterance – often, changing the intonation of an utterance can add a layer of meaning to the utterance, but without changing the meanings of its component words.

intonation: the sequence of relative pitch changes over the course of an utterance.

As a basic example, think of the difference between a statement and a question intonation in the following utterances:

Statement: You forgot your keys.
Question: You forgot your keys?

The two utterances have the same sequence of words, and likewise of phonemes, and each individual word has the same meaning in either context. In both utterances, *you* always refers to the addressee; *forgot* is the past tense of a verb meaning to leave something behind or to fail to remember, and so on. But spoken aloud, the two utterances would have different intonational sequences. Different of types intonational sequences are called **melodies** or contours, and they often can be unpacked into sequences of tones. We saw in Chapter 9 that the term *melody* can apply to a sequence of elements on any tier of representation; an **intonational melody** is a melody of tones which together carry some discourse function within a language. The statement melody in many varieties of English is spoken with a mid tone that rises slightly and then falls in the last word. In contrast, the last word of the question melody has a sequence of a low tone followed by a high tone.

	M	H L
Statement:	*You forgot*	*your keys.*
	M	L H
Question:	*You forgot*	*your keys?*

intonational melody: a sequence of tones that carries a consistent function within a language.

We can readily see the same intonational melodies projected over different sequences of words; regardless of the sentence, the question melody always involves, at the very least, a low tone followed by a high tone at the end of the utterance. Indeed, similar intonational patterns can be projected over single words; consider the following example in which the same melodies are associated with just the personal name *Peter*.

Statement   *Peter.*   high low
Question   *Peter?*   low high

The statement melody has a high tone on the first syllable that drops in the second syllable. In contrast, the question melody has a sequence of a low tone followed by a high tone, with (in this case) one tone per syllable. This helps us clearly illustrate the difference between tone and intonation: here, in this non-tone language, the meaning of the lexical item *Peter* is stable across examples.

The way in which intonational contours associate to words or phrases is a vast topic in itself, and requires a deeper understanding of stressed syllables. Nevertheless, we can actually use intonation as a way of detecting stressed syllables. The question melody is particularly useful for this task, because it contains two very distinct tones in quick sequence. Consider first the following two words: *confuse* and *pocket*. If we project the question melody over them, the result differs depending on the word.

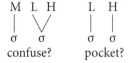

In *confuse?*, the LH sequence of the question melody is associated to the final syllable, giving it a rising tone, and there is a mid tone on the first syllable. In contrast, in *pocket*, the L tone associates to the first syllable, and the H tone to the second.

If we had the right means of measurement, we could also determine that the second syllable of *confuse* is longer and louder than the first; conversely, the first syllable of *pocket* is longer and louder than the second. The length and loudness of these syllables makes them more prominent, and we can infer that the more prominent syllables are stressed.

stress: the relative prominence of a syllable, detectable via loudness, length, and intonation.

Different languages rely on these cues to different extents; English uses all three. Thus, the two words have different stress patterns: *confuse* has final stress, and *pocket* has initial stress. Not coincidentally, the more prominent syllable of each word is also the one that happens to attract the L tone of the question melody. We can infer that the position of the L tone of the question melody can actually help us identify stressed syllables in longer words.

Let us perform the same test against three different trisyllabic words: *lullaby*, *agenda*, and *kangaroo*. Spoken with the intonation of the yes/no question melody, each word has a final H tone, but the location of the L tone differs across words. *lullaby* would have L tone on its first syllable; *agenda* would have it on its second, and *kangaroo* would have it on its third, combining with the final H to form a rising contour. The latter two words also contain a mid tone on the syllables that precede the one that bears the L tone.

We can again infer that the L tone is drawn to the stressed syllable; in these examples, an M tone appears on any syllable that precedes the stressed syllable.

It is important to note that it is not L tones in general that gravitate to the stressed syllable; instead, it is the L tone of the question intonational melody. This fact makes L the **nuclear tone** of that melody. Other intonational melodies have different nuclear tones that nevertheless also gravitate to the stressed syllable, as we will see shortly.

nuclear tone: the tone of a given melody that must associate to the primary stressed syllable.

Now we can apply the same methodology to the following longer list of polysyllabic English words (adapted from Hammond 1999).

(1)   table
(2)   data
(3)   bunny
(4)   flower
(5)   aspen
(6)   disturb
(7)   perverse
(8)   conceal
(9)   Canada
(10)   avenue

(11)   similar
(12)   metaphor
(13)   Portugal
(14)   contusion
(15)   computer
(16)   Nevada
(17)   Tennessee
(18)   macaroon
(19)   understand
(20)   America
(21)   community
(22)   Minnesota

Exercise 10.1   Describe the intonational melody of each word as if it were spoken aloud with a yes/no question melody. Where does the lowest tone occur? Where does the highest tone occur?

In the yes/no question melody, the highest tone is always on the final syllable, but the location of the lowest tone seems to vary across words. In some words, it occurs together with the high tone on the same syllable, as in *disturb* and *macaroon*; in others, it occurs on the penultimate sullable, as in *aspen* and *Nevada*, and on still others, it is in the antepenultimate syllable, as in *metaphor* and *America*. The full results are repeated below, with the symbol ' placed to the left of the syllable that contains the nuclear tone (and therefore the primary stress).

(1)   'table
(2)   'data
(3)   'bunny
(4)   'flower
(5)   'aspen
(6)   dis'turb
(7)   per'verse
(8)   con'ceal
(9)   'Canada
(10)   'avenue
(11)   'similar
(12)   'metaphor
(13)   'Portugal
(14)   con'tusion
(15)   com'puter

(16)   Ne'vada
(17)   Tennes'see
(18)   maca'roon
(19)   under'stand
(20)   A'merica
(21)   com'munity
(22)   Minne'sota

We have used the question melody to locate primary stress in all of these English words. Note that we did so without referring to length or loudness of the syllable, and indeed, the stressed syllable here is the one with lowest pitch, not highest pitch. This is a very clear example of using phonological rather than phonetic evidence for the location of stress.

Exercise 10.2 Repeat Exercise 10.1, but instead of using a question intonation, choose the "calling for dinner" melody and the "whiny" melodies, exemplified below with the word *Rebecca*. Assuming that you identified the primary stress syllable in Exercise 10.1, which tone is attracted to the stressed syllable in these melodies? How does the position of stress affect the melodies?

calling
L   H   M
| | |
σ   σ   σ
Rebecca

whining
M   LH L
| |/ |
σ   σ   σ
Rebecca

If you change the intonational sequence away from the question melody, you will still see some consistent results. Each melody has a particular component tone associated to the syllable that carries primary stress. The "calling" melody has an H tone that is attracted to the stressed syllable, while the "whiny" melody has an L tone that does so. Thus, each melody has its own specified nuclear tone, in addition to its sequence of tone elements.

Where stress is initial, the nuclear tone is also initial, and any preceding tones are dropped. We saw this already in the question melody; the same happens for calling and whining melodies. For example, the initial L of the calling melody is dropped when combined with forms such as *Thomas*, as is the initial M of the whining melody.

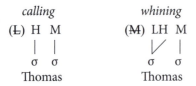

The behavior of post-nuclear tones differs across melodies in ways that are beyond the scope of this discussion; for example, the L and H in the whining melody link to the same syllable if stress is penultimate or later, but are on separate syllables otherwise. Likewise, the H of the calling tone distributes across all syllables from the stressed syllable to the penultimate syllable. What is critical for this discussion is that each melody has a nuclear tone, and that the nuclear tone is drawn to the syllable with primary stress.

When notating intonation, we mark the nuclear tone with an asterisk, and place optional pre-nuclear tones in parentheses. Thus the yes/no question melody is better transcribed as (M)L*H, while the calling melody is (L)H*M.

An important implication of the notion of the nuclear tone is that stress is not equivalent to highest or lowest tone; stressed syllables attract the central or nuclear tone of whatever melody is projected over them, which may be H, M, or L, depending on the melody.

Given that we now have some means of identifying stressed syllables, we can turn to a more thorough investigation of stress assignment. The position of stress within polysyllabic words varies within and across languages; as we saw above, a trisyllabic word in English may have initial, medial, or final stress. Metrical phonology is concerned with identifying and describing the patterns that underlie such systems.

10.2 Stress

The description of a language's stress pattern is part of the description of its phonological system in general – it is not up to us to infer stress for data in which stress is not notated. For our exercises above, our detection of stress relied on our own knowledge of English intonational melodies, which is a phonological task. We do not have the same luxury for languages that we do not speak; thus, in the data that we encounter, we are to treat syllables as stressed only if they are transcribed as such, just as we also only take segments to be voiced or nasal if we are told they are. Nervertheless, in any case where we do know the location of stress within given words, we can then ask whether its position is predictable in a given language.

Given knowledge of the number of syllables in a word, the weight of syllables within words, and the location of stress, metrical phonology is concerned with uncovering the regularities of stress assignment, ultimately with the goal of generalizing and predicting the position of primary and secondary stress. As we will see, in languages with predictable stress, the rules for assignment of stress are sensitive to the form and arrangement of other phonological elements.

10.3 English stress

We will start with stress in English, where you already have some familiarity with the phonological representations of words. Data in this secton are adapted from Hammond (1999). The following discussion is complicated, however, as the facts about the distribution of stress in English polysyllables are nuanced and complex. We will ultimately find that there is some degree of unpredictability in the assignment of English stress, but there are also stringent limits on its distribution; as a result, we will uncover a set of robust (but not absolute) generalizations.

Let us begin with the following data, comprising bisyllabic forms in English.

(1)	'aspen
(2)	'bottle
(3)	'convent
(4)	'council
(5)	'decent
(6)	'flavor
(7)	'flower
(8)	'happen
(9)	'open
(10)	'pocket
(11)	'revel
(12)	'robin
(13)	'tonsil
(14)	'wicker
(15)	'wriggle
(16)	ca'reer
(17)	com'pel
(18)	con'ceal
(19)	cor'rect
(20)	de'fer
(21)	des'cent
(22)	dis'turb
(23)	en'debt
(24)	per'verse
(25)	re'fer
(26)	re'veal
(27)	re'vert
(28)	re'vile
(29)	se'rene
(30)	ve'neer

Exercise 10.3 Is it possible to predict whether two-syllable words have primary stress on their initial or final syllable?

Roughly half of these words have initial stress and half have final stress. There are some forms with initial closed syllables and initial stress, such as (3) *convent*, or final stress, such as (18) *conceal*. There are other forms with heavy final syllables and final stress, such as (21) *descent*, or initial stress, such as (5) *decent*.

There does appear to be a relationship between vowel quality and stress; any phonemic vowel may occur in a stressed syllable, but the unstressed syllables here contain either [ə] or a nuclear sonorant, as in (14) ˈwicker, (2) ˈbottle, or (8) ˈhappen.

The set of vowels that can occur in English unstressed syllables is quite limited; the only others that may do so are [o] (as in *veto*) and [i] (as in *bunny* or medially in *polio*). That the stress pattern is initial in these can be confirmed with the yes/no melody test from Exercise 10.1.

The co-occurrence of [ə] or syllabic sonorants with unstressed syllables suggests a pattern. One possibility is that unstressed syllables have a limited range of possible vowels; as such, stress (or lack of it) predicts the distribution of [ə]. Another possibility is that syllables with [ə] cannot bear stress; that is, the quality of the vowel predicts the distribution of stress.

The following exercise should help tease apart these hypotheses. Consider the next group of bisyllabic forms: note that they have two stress options, and pay attention to their word class as well. Where UK and US pronunciations differ, both are provided.

		Verb/adjective	*Noun*
(1)	record	ɹəˈkɔːd/ɹəˈkɔɹd	ˈɹɛkəd/ˈɹɛkəd
(2)	reject	ɹəˈdʒɛkt	ˈɹidʒɛkt
(3)	convert	kənˈvɜːt/kənˈvət	ˈkɒnvɜt/ˈkɑnvət
(4)	protest	pɹəˈtɛst	ˈpɹoʊtɛst
(5)	pervert	pəˈvɜːt/pəˈvət	ˈpɜːvɜt/ˈpəvət
(6)	converse	kənˈvɜːs/kənˈvəs	ˈkɒnvɜs/ˈkɑnvəs
(7)	install	ənˈstɒl/ənˈstɑl	ˈɪnstɒl/ˈɪnstɑl
(8)	abstract	əbˈstɹækt	ˈæbstɹækt
(9)	content	kənˈtɛnt	ˈkɒntɛnt/ˈkɑntɛnt

Exercise 10.4 Describe the relationship between the stress pattern and the word class.

In these forms, there is a verb or adjective with final stress, but a noun with initial stress: the change of word class affects the position of stress. That the

271

pairs of words are related is not controversial; they overlap in meaning, but differ in syntactic interpretation.

We can thus conclude that the word class affects the position of stress. This is merely a trend, as there are some initial-stress nouns that do not have final stress in their related verb form (e.g., 'bottle can be made a verb, but retains initial stress). Likewise, there are some final-stress verbs that do not have initial stress in their related noun form (e.g., re'veal can be used as a noun, but retains final stress). Despite the gradient nature of this trend, it is relevant that no pair exists in which the noun has final stress and the verb has initial stress.

These data also speak to the relationship between [ə] and stress assignment; we have already observed that stressed syllables may contain any vowel, but unstressed syllables are limited to [ə, i, o], or syllabic sonorants. The initial vowel of the verb forms here is [ə] or [ɚ], but when there is initial stress, the quality of the initial vowel differs across forms: ['ɹɪʤɛkt, 'ɹɛkɔɹd, 'kɑntɛnt], which suggests that the alternating vowels are not underlyingly [ə]. We thus cannot presume that stress assignment is determined by whether a vowel is underlyingly [ə]; it is more appropriate to propose that vowels are reduced to [ə] when they are unstressed.

We should note here that the relationship between [ə] and stress is specific to English; there are other languages in which unstressed vowels need not be reduced to [ə], and others in which [ə] may bear stress.

Now consider the following forms, which all have primary stress on their initial syllable.

(1)   benzene
(2)   essay
(3)   mandrake
(4)   cuckoo
(5)   charcoal
(6)   argon
(7)   icon
(8)   centaur
(9)   decoy
(10)   Afghan
(11)   biceps
(12)   hygiene
(13)   decade
(14)   membrane
(15)   alcove
(16)   cosmos

(17)	crouton
(18)	hautboy
(19)	asset
(20)	apex
(21)	cognac
(22)	banshee
(23)	praline
(24)	encore
(25)	crayon
(26)	asphalt
(27)	bovine
(28)	magpie
(29)	accent
(30)	ambush
(31)	anthrax
(32)	rampage
(33)	parlay
(34)	mildew

Exercise 10.5 What can you say about the second syllable of such forms? Compare them to the forms with initial stress forms in Exercise 10.3.

These forms all have secondary stress on their final syllable, which also contains some vowel other than schwa. This supports our claim that unstressed syllables in English may only contain one of a limited set of vowels.

We know that stress may occur in the initial or final syllable of two syllable words; let us now turn to three-syllable words. Examine the following forms, paying attention to their location of primary stress, as well as secondary stress, which appears in some but not all of these forms. The words have been grouped together by similarity of stress pattern.

(1)	benefit	ˈbɛnəfət
(2)	Canada	ˈkænədə
(3)	carpenter	ˈkɑːpəntə/ˈkɑɹpəntɚ
(4)	Portugal	ˈpɔːtʃəgəl/ˈpɔɹtʃəgəl
(5)	sentiment	ˈsɛntəmənt
(6)	Switzerland	ˈswɪtsələnd/ˈswɪtsɚlənd

(7)	albacore	ˈælbəˌkɔː/ˈælbəˌkɔr
(8)	albatross	ˈælbəˌtɪɒs/ˈælbəˌtɪɑs
(9)	alcohol	ˈælkəˌhɒl/ˈælkəˌhɑl
(10)	anecdote	ˈænəkˌdoʊt

(11)	artefact	ˈɑːtəˌfækt/ˈɑɹəˌfækt
(12)	artichoke	ˈɑːtəˌtʃoʊk/ˈɑɹəˌtʃoʊk
(13)	aspartame	ˈaspəˌteɪm/ˈæspəˌteɪm
(14)	catacomb	ˈkætəˌkoʊm/ˈkæɾəˌkoʊm
(15)	creosote	ˈkriəˌsoʊt
(16)	detonate	ˈdɛtəˌneɪt
(17)	kerosene	ˈkɛrəˌsin
(18)	Lancelot	ˈlansəˌlɒt/ˈlænsəˌlat
(19)	Lebanon	ˈlɛbəˌnɒn/ˈlɛbəˌnan
(20)	limousine	ˈlɪməˌzin
(21)	lullaby	ˈlʌləˌbaɪ
(22)	marathon	ˈmæɹəˌθɒn/ˈmæɹəˌθɑn
(23)	nightingale	ˈnaɪtənˌgeɪl
(24)	ocelot	ˈɒsəˌlɒt/ˈɑsəˌlat
(25)	parakeet	ˈpæɹəˌkit
(26)	ricochet	ˈɹɪkəˌʃeɪ
(27)	tomahawk	ˈtɒməˌhɒk/ˈtɑməˌhɑk

(28)	agenda	əˈdʒɛndə
(29)	arachnid	əˈɹæknəd
(30)	condonement	kənˈdoʊnmənt
(31)	deferral	dəˈfɚəl
(32)	Kentucky	kənˈtʌki
(33)	Nevada	nəˈvædə

(34)	understand	ˌʌndəˈstænd/ˌʌndɚˈstænd
(35)	Tennessee	ˌtɛnəˈsi
(36)	decompose	ˌdikəmˈpoʊz
(37)	macaroon	ˌmækəˈɹun
(38)	kangaroo	ˌkæŋgəˈru

(39)	carbuncle	ˈkɑːˌbʌŋkəl/ˈkaɹˌbʌŋkəl
(40)	saltpetre	ˈsɒltˌpitə/ˈsaltˌpiɾɚ
(41)	boondoggle	ˈbunˌdɒgəl/ˈbunˌdɑgəl
(42)	cucumber	ˈkjuˌkʌmbɚ/ˈkjuˌkʌmbɚ
(43)	pinochle	ˈpiˌnʌkəl

Exercise 10.6   Can you predict the location of primary stress? Can you predict the presence and location of secondary stress?

Whether stress occurs on the first, second, or third syllable is not predictable in such forms, as each position is represented in these data, independently of syllable weight. For example, (2) ˈ*Canada* and (14) ˈ*catacomb* both have initial stress; (28) *a'genda* and (32) *Ken'tucky* both have stress on their middle syllables, and (34) *under'stand* and (38) *kanga'roo* both have final stress.

The appearance and position of secondary stress is partially unpredictable. Among initial-stress forms, some have no secondary stress, as in (1)–(6), some have a secondary stress on their third syllable, as in (7)–(27), and some on their second, as in (39)–(43). Among words with penultimate primary stress, secondary stress appears to be absent (28)–(33), while among final-stress words, the initial syllable always bears secondary stress (34)–(38).

What we are amassing here is a nuanced understanding of the distribution of primary and secondary stress in English. So far, we can assert that the position of primary stress is unpredictable, but that among polysyllables, there is some limit to the position of secondary stress – it can only be final in bisyllables, it can be final or penultimate in initial-stress trisyllables, and must be initial in final-stress bisyllables. Thus, while on the one hand we can say that stress position is unpredictable, there is still a limit to its distribution.

Exercise 10.7   Now let us turn to words with four or more syllables, again paying attention to the location of primary and secondary stress. The following forms again are grouped by similarity of stress pattern; UK and US pronunciations are both given. Describe the distribution of primary stress, in terms of its position within words, and with respect to the position of secondary stress, if any.

(1) convertible	kənˈvɜːtəbəl	kənˈvɚrəbəl
(2) impunity	əmˈpjunəti	əmˈpjunəri
(3) annuity	əˈnjuɪti	əˈnuɪri
(4) fanatical	fəˈnætəkəl	fəˈnærəkəl
(5) insanity	ənˈsænəti	ənˈsænəri
(6) America	əˈmɛɹəkə	əˈmɛɹəkə
(7) combustible	kəmˈbʌstəbəl	kəmˈbʌstəbəl
(8) geography	ʤiˈɒgɹəfi	ʤiˈɑgɹəfi
(9) orthography	ɔˈθɒgɹəfi	ɔɹˈθɑgɹəfi
(10) authority	əˈθɒɹəti	əˈθɔɹəri
(11) demonstrative	dəˈmɒnstɹətəv	dəˈmɑnstɹərəv
(12) certificate	sɜˈtɪfəkət	sɚˈtɪfəkət
(13) enthusiast	ənˈθjuziəst	ənˈθuziəst
(14) preoccupied	pɹiˈɒkjuˌpaɪd	pɹiˈɑkjuˌpaɪd
(15) appreciate	əˈpɹiˌʃieɪt	əˈpɹiˌʃieɪt
(16) apologize	əˈpɒləˌʤaɪz	əˈpɑləˌʤaɪz
(17) economize	əˈkɒnəˌmaɪz	əˈkɑnəˌmaɪz
(18) Piscataway	pəˈskætəˌweɪ	pəˈskærəˌweɪ
(19) Saskatchewan	səsˈkætʃəˌwɒn	səsˈkætʃəˌwɑn

(20) Kalashnikov	kəˈlæʃnəˌkɒf	kəˈlæʃnəˌkaf
(21) orangutan	əˈɹæŋəˌtæn	əˈɹæŋəˌtæn
(22) Baryshnikov	bəˈɹɪʃnəˌkɒf	bəˈɹɪʃnəˌkaf

(23) Ontario	ˌɒnˈtɛriˌoʊ	ˌanˈtɛriˌoʊ
(24) antipodes	ˌænˈtɪpəˌdiz	ˌænˈtɪpəˌdiz
(25) conquistador	ˌkɑnˈkistəˌdɔː	ˌkɑnˈkistəˌdɔr
(26) Afghanistan	ˌæfˈgænəˌstæn	ˌæfˈgænəˌstæn
(27) Uzbekistan	ˌuzˈbɛkəˌstæn	ˌuzˈbɛkəˌstæn

(28) Mississippi	ˌmɪsəˈsɪpi	ˌmɪsəˈsɪpi
(29) Minnesota	ˌmɪnəˈsoʊtə	ˌmɪnəˈsoʊɾə
(30) Tipperary	ˌtɪpəˈɹɛɹi	ˌtɪpəˈɹɛɹi
(31) variation	ˌværiˈeɪʃən	ˌværiˈeɪʃən
(32) independent	ˌɪndəˈpɛndənt	ˌɪndəˈpɛndənt
(33) circulation	ˌsɜːkjəˈleɪʃən	ˌsɚkjəˈleɪʃən
(34) explanation	ˌɛkspləˈneɪʃən	ˌɛkspləˈneɪʃən
(35) demonstration	ˌdɛmənˈstɹeɪʃən	ˌdɛmənˈstɹeɪʃən
(36) idiotic	ˌɪdiˈɒɾək	ˌɪɾiˈɑɾək
(37) adolescence	ˌæɹəˈlɛsəns	ˌæɹəˈlɛsəns

(38) Aristotle	ˈæɹəˌstɒtəl	ˈæɹəˌstɑɾəl
(39) centimeter	ˈsɛntəˌmitə	ˈsɛntəˌmiɾɚ
(40) commentator	ˈkɒmənˌteɪtə	ˈkamənˌteɪɾɚ
(41) calculator	ˈkælkjəˌleɪtə	ˈkælkjəˌleɪɾɚ
(42) demonstrator	ˈdɛmənˌstreɪtə	ˈdɛmənˌstreɪɾɚ
(43) architecture	ˈɑːkəˌtɛktʃə	ˈɑɹkəˌtɛktʃɚ
(44) caterpillar	ˈkætəˌpɪlə	ˈkæɾɚˌpɪlɚ
(45) dandelion	ˈdændəˌlaɪjən	ˈdændəˌlaɪjən
(46) lederhosen	ˈleɪdəˌhoʊzən	ˈleɪɾɚˌhoʊzən
(47) hootenanny	ˈhutəˌnæni	ˈhutəˌnæni
(48) ragamuffin	ˈrægəˌmʌfən	ˈrægəˌmʌfən
(49) cauliflower	ˈkɒliˌflaʊə	ˈkɑliˌflaʊɚ
(50) kindergarten	ˈkɪndəˌgɑːtən	ˈkɪndɚˌgɑɹtən
(51) periwinkle	ˈpɛɹiˌwɪŋkəl	ˈpɛɹiˌwɪŋkəl
(52) tabernacle	ˈtæbəˌnækəl	ˈtæbɚˌnækəl

(53) capitalize	ˈkæpətəˌlaɪz	ˈkæpəɾəˌlaɪz
(54) similitude	ˈsɪmələˌtud	ˈsɪmələˌtud
(55) gobbledegook	ˈgɒbəldəˌguk	ˈgabəldəˌguk
(56) toreador	ˈtɔɹiəˌdɔː	ˈtɔɹiəˌdɔr
(57) catamaran	ˈkætəməˌɹæn	ˈkæɹəməˌɹæn

(58) hullabaloo	ˌhʌləbəˈlu	ˌhʌləbəˈlu
(59) Kalamazoo	ˌkæləməˈzu	ˌkæləməˈzu
(60) Anapamu	ˌænəpəˈmu	ˌænəpəˈmu

Primary stress can appear on any syllable of four-syllable words: initial, as in (45) ˈdandelion, antepenultimate, as in (21) oˈrangutan, penultimate, as in (29) Minneˈsota, and final, as in (59) Kalamaˈzoo.

While primary stress seems possible in any syllable, the range of potential positions for secondary stress is limited.

- Where words have initial stress, secondary stress may be penultimate, as in (45) ˈdandeˌlion, or final, as in (54) ˈsimiliˌtude.
- For words with antepenultimate stress, secondary stress may be final, as in (21) oˈranguˌtan, or absent, as in (6) Aˈmerica. There are several examples in which two syllables bear secondary stress; initial and final, as in (26) ˌAfˈghaniˌstan.
- For words with penultimate stress, secondary stress must be initial, as in (29) ˌMinneˈsota.
- For words with final stress, secondary stress must be initial, as in as in (59) ˌKalamaˈzoo.

These results add some details to our growing body of observations about English stress. We could say that the stress system seems to spread the emphasis out over words: forms with adjacent stresses on the second and third syllables are not found. Sequences of two unstressed syllables are only tolerated after a stressed syllable. Words with initial primary stress and no other secondary stress are missing.

You may have been thinking of potential counterexamples to these claims, and in fact there are some to be acknowedged. Consider the following list in light of what we just saw.

(1)   accuracy
(2)   aerialist
(3)   alienable
(4)   amiable
(5)   associative
(6)   eligible
(7)   enviable
(8)   favorable
(9)   habitable
(10)   heritable
(11)   irritable
(12)   seasonable

(13)   spirituous
(14)   variable
(15)   violable
(16)   abominable
(17)   accompaniment
(18)   attributable
(19)   communicable
(20)   impenetrable
(21)   incalculable
(22)   indubitable
(23)   inestimable
(24)   inevitable
(25)   measurable
(26)   perishable

Exercise 10.8   Describe the stress pattern in these words. Is there anything else about them that they all have in common?

Primary stress in these words is pre-antepenultimate, with no secondary stress afterwards. As such, they are unlike the four-syllable words in Exercise 10.7, because they contain sequences of three unstressed syllables. These words are all morphologically complex, and their primary stress occurs on a syllable which is antepenultimate in the absence of the suffix. We can then infer that morphological structure is relevant in the assignment of stress in English.

Clearly a number of factors come into play for the determination of English stress: the class of the word, the weight of its syllables, and the quality of its vowels. Nevertheless, each of the tendencies we observe in English reflects certain cross-linguistic trends: that stress orients to the edges of words, and that stress gravitates toward heavy syllables.

While the position of stress in English may be quite variable, other languages can be characterized as having fixed stress. One could call it predictable: by knowing the number of syllables in a word, it is possible in such languages to predict where in a word the stress will occur.

10.4 Fixed stress

Languages with fixed stress systems have a stress assignment pattern in which the position of primary stress is regular and predictable. As such, given just a sequence of syllabifiable segments, one could compose formal rules to generate the appropriate location of the primary stressed syllable. To illustrate this, examine the following data from Maranungku (adapted from Kenstowicz 1994/Tryon 1970).

ˈtiralk	'saliva'
ˈmereˌpet	'beard'
ˈjaŋarˌmata	'the Pleiades'
ˈlaŋkaˌrateˌti	'prawn'
ˈweleˌpeneˌmanta	'kind of duck'

Inferring syllable structure for these forms is not problematic, and once we have done so, we see that primary stress is always on the initial syllable. We can account for this with the following rule:

$$\sigma \rightarrow \text{ˈ}\sigma \text{ / }_{\text{WD}}[\underline{}$$

The same data suggest that the position of secondary stress is also predictable: every odd-numbered syllable bears secondary stress, so that stressed and unstressed syllables are interleaved. This can also be captured with a rule; in this case we will use [+ stress] for stressed vowels in the environment of the rule.

$$\sigma \rightarrow \underset{}{\text{ˌ}\sigma} \text{ / } \overset{\displaystyle [+\text{stress}]}{\underset{\displaystyle |}{\sigma}} \quad \sigma \quad \underline{}$$

This rule will assign secondary stress to any syllable which is preceded by a sequence of a stressed and unstressed syllable. The stressed syllable in the structural environment is notated as [+stress] to indicate that it triggers the rule whether it carries primary or secondary stress. We also need to stipulate that the rule is *iterative*: it applies over the course of the word until it runs out of syllables to check. This is not unlike other segmental rules we have seen, which will (for example) check each plosive to see if it is subject to aspiration. Secondary stress rules may be iterative, but since there is only one primary stress per word, rules that assign primary stress cannot be iterative.

Now we can use the same devices to handle different manifestations of fixed stress systems. Examine the data from Weri below (adapted from Kenstowicz 1994/Boxwell and Boxwell 1966):

ŋinˈtip	'bee'
ˌkuliˈpu	'hair of arm'
uˌluaˈmit	'mist'
ˌakuˌneteˈpal	'times'

Exercise 10.9 Compose one rule to assign primary stress and another to assign secondary stress in Weri.

$$\sigma \rightarrow \text{'}\sigma \; / \quad \underline{\quad} \;]_{\text{WD}}$$

$$[\text{+stress}]$$
$$|$$
$$\sigma \rightarrow {}_{\backslash}\sigma \; / \quad \underline{\quad} \; \sigma \quad \sigma$$

The rules for Weri are a mirror-image of Maranungku: primary stress is assigned to the final syllable, and secondary stress to odd-numbered syllables counting from the end of the word.

While Maranungku and Weri both have clear examples of edgemost stressed syllables, fixed stress systems may orient to a word edge but leave an unstressed syllable at the very periphery. The result is penultimate or peninitial stress. Examine the data from Warao (Kenstowicz 1994/Osborn 1966) and Araucanian) Kenstowicz 1994/Echeverria and Contreras 1965) below for some examples:

Warao

(1) ji̖wara'nae   'he finished it'
(2) ̖japu̖ruki̖tane'hase   'verily to climb'
(3) e̖naho̖roa̖haku'tai   'the one who caused him to eat'

Araucanian

(1)   wu'le   'tomorrow'
(2)   ʈi'panto   'year'
(3)   e'lumu̖ju   'give us'
(4)   e'lua̖enew   'he will give me'
(5)   ki'muba̖luwu̖laj   'he pretended not to know'

Exercise 10.10 Compose one rule to assign primary stress and another to assign secondary stress in the Warao data above.

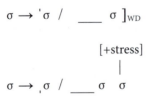

$$\sigma \rightarrow \text{'}\sigma \; / \quad \underline{\quad} \; \sigma \;]_{\text{WD}}$$

$$[\text{+stress}]$$
$$|$$
$$\sigma \rightarrow {}_{\backslash}\sigma \; / \quad \underline{\quad} \; \sigma \quad \sigma$$

Exercise 10.11 Compose one rule to assign primary stress and another to assign secondary stress in the Araucanian data above.

$$\sigma \rightarrow \text{'}\sigma \; / \quad _{\text{WD}}[\sigma \; \underline{\quad}$$

$$\begin{array}{c} [+\text{stress}] \\ | \\ \sigma \rightarrow \text{,}\sigma \; / \; \sigma \quad \sigma \; \underline{\quad} \end{array}$$

The penultimate and peninitial systems still share with the others the notion of a fixed position, oriented to one edge or the other of a word. Moreover, the rules of secondary stress assignment are quite similar, in that they separate stressed syllables with single unstressed syllables.

Several facets of stress assignment merit some additional attention: notably, in these fixed-stress systems, stressed syllables tend to be spaced apart from each other, separated by intervening unstressed syllables. This suggests the idea of adjacent stressed and unstressed syllables somehow pairing up with each other. Not coincidentally, the orientation of primary stress towards one edge, even in peninitial and penultimate systems, further suggests that stressed and unstressed syllables tend to occur adjacently.

To address these phenomena, phonologists invoke the notion of the metrical **foot**. A foot is a group of one or more syllables, exactly one of which is stressed. In representational terms, it is a higher-order phonological unit comprising one or more syllables.

foot: a group of one or more syllables, exactly one of which is stressed.

Across languages, numerous types of feet can be observed. In the study of poetic meter, there is a larger set of terminology used to refer to different types of two-syllable and three-syllable feet, but in phonological analysis, we tend to rely on representations that use two-syllable feet. Indeed, feet tend to be **binary**, comprising either two syllables or a syllable with two moras. In words containing three syllables but one stress, like those we saw in Exercise 10.6, one could analyze these as three-syllable feet, or as bisyllabic feet with an additional unfooted syllable.

Bisyllabic feet include **trochees**, with initial stress, and **iambs**, with final stress.

trochee: a bisyllabic foot with initial stress.
iamb: a bisyllabic foot with final stress.

There are several ways we can represent foot structure. An expanded view would place feet hierarchically above their constituent syllables.

A shorthand representation is also used where bracketing indicates foot boundaries. This notation is convenient in combination with the use of dots for syllable boundaries.

('ja.ŋar).(ˌma.ta)

With the notation of the foot, we can assign stress via rules that create feet. Such rules create foot structure over a sequence of syllables, in much the same way as our rules of syllabification in Chapter 8 create syllable structure over a sequence of segments. Here is an alternative way of constructing stress assignment for Maranungku:

$\sigma\,\sigma \rightarrow (\sigma\,\sigma)_{FT}$	This rule assigns feet to syllables; it must allow for a final monosyllabic foot. It must also apply iteratively left-to-right.
$(\sigma\,\sigma)_{FT} \rightarrow ('\sigma\,\sigma)_{FT} \,/\, _{WD}[\ \_\_\_$	This rule assigns primary stress to the initial foot.
$(\sigma\,\sigma)_{FT} \rightarrow (ˌ\sigma\,\sigma)_{FT}$	This rule assigns secondary stress to remaining feet.

The appeal to foot structure is a more restrictive approach to stress assignment than simple rules that count syllables. The foot-based approach precludes us from creating systems in which, arbitrarily, only the third or fourth syllable from a word edge receives primary stress. It also captures the tendency for stressed and unstressed syllables to be interspersed.

10.5 Predictable but unfixed stress

The fixed-stress systems we see above share the property of assigning stress merely by counting syllables (or more technically, by projecting binary foot structure), regardless of the segmental components of individual syllables. Other stress-assignment systems are more nuanced, and the position of primary stress may vary across words, but nevertheless in a predictable way.

Examine the following data from Hawaiian (Elbert and Pukui 1979, Pukui and Elbert 1971), paying attention to the position of stress and the shape of syllables.

(1)	a.ˈkaː.ka	'clear'
(2)	ˈha.le	'house'
(3)	ha.ˈnau.ma	'a place name'
(4)	ka.ˈna.ka	'person'
(5)	ma.ˈla.ma	'light'
(6)	ʔe.ˌka.le.ˈsi.a	'church'
(7)	ˌHa.na.ˈlei	'place name'
(8)	ˌhei.ˈau	'ancient temple'
(9)	ˌkaː.ˈna.ka	'people'
(10)	ˌmaː.ˈla.ma	'to care for'
(11)	ne.ˌne.le.ˈau	'sumac'
(12)	ˌho.ʔo.ˌlau.ˈle.ʔa	'celebration'
(13)	ˌkoː.ˌʔe.le.ˈʔe.le	'species of seaweed'
(14)	ˌkuː.ˌnaː.ˈnaː	'puzzled'
(15)	ˌmaː.ˌla.ma.ˈla.ma	'clear'
(16)	hu.ˌe.le.ˈe.lo	'having tails'
(17)	Ka.ˌme.ha.ˈme.ha	'personal name'
(18)	Ka.ˌpi.ʔo.ˈla.ni	'personal name'
(19)	Ka.ˌlaː.ˈkau.a	'personal name'
(20)	Ka.ˌi.mu.ˈkiː	'place name'

Exercise 10.12 On what syllables may primary stress occur? What is the relationship between the form of the final syllable and the position of primary stress?

Stress can occur on the final or penultimate syllable in Hawaiian. When the final syllable is monomoraic and light, primary stress is penultimate, as in (4) [ka.ˈna.ka] and (5) [ma.ˈla.ma]. When the final syllable is bimoraic and heavy, it bears primary stress, as in (7) [ˌha.na.ˈlei] and (14) [ˌkuː.ˌnaː.ˈnaː].

Exercise 10.13 Now describe the distribution of secondary stress.

If the syllable before the primary stress is heavy, it bears secondary stress, as in (10) [ˌmaː.ˈla.ma] and (12) [ˌho.ʔo.ˌlau.ˈle.ʔa]. Otherwise, the next precedent syllable bears secondary stress, as in (6) [ʔe.ˌka.le.ˈsi.a] and (11) [ne.ˌne.le.ˈau]. The same generalization applies to each subsequent iteration of secondary stress.

Hawaiian seems to generate feet from right to left, but with some notable limitations: feet are generally bisyllabic, but structures which place a heavy syllable as the rightmost of a pair of syllables are avoided. In other words, heavy syllables can only be in initial position within a foot. The system will place heavy syllables into feet by themselves in order to meet this requirement. The Hawaiian pattern illustrates the phenomenon of **quantity sensitivity**. In quantity-sensitive systems, the projection of foot structure and position of stress depends on the weight of syllables: heavy syllables attract stress, and stress otherwise occurs on light syllables if there are no heavy syllables to receive stress.

quantity sensitivity: a property of stress systems which favor heavy syllables over light syllables for stress assignment.

Exercise 10.14 Compose a rule or rules using foot structure to predict the position of primary stress in Hawaiian.

$$\sigma_{\mu\mu} \rightarrow (\text{'}\sigma_{\mu\mu})_{FT} \, / \, \underline{} \,]_{WD}$$
$$\sigma \, \sigma \rightarrow (\text{'}\sigma \, \sigma)_{FT} \, / \, \underline{}]_{WD}$$

These rules check for two possible word-final structures: first, a word-final heavy syllable is given its own foot; if there is no final syllable, then a bisyllabic foot is created by the second rule.

Exercise 10.15 Now consider the distribution of secondary stress in Hawaiian, and compose rules to predict its position, again using foot structure to do so.

Proceeding from right to left through the word, the location of each subsequent stressed syllable can be assigned by constructing quantity-sensitive feet to the left of each existing foot.

$$\sigma_{\mu\mu} \rightarrow (\text{,}\sigma_{\mu\mu})_{FT} \, / \, \underline{} \,_{FT}($$
$$\sigma \, \sigma \rightarrow (\text{,}\sigma \, \sigma)_{FT} \, / \, \underline{} \,_{FT}($$

The first rule checks if the immediately leftward syllable is heavy, and if so, places it in a foot by itself. The second rule then otherwise produces a bisyllabic foot.

The rules of secondary stress assignment are very similar to those for primary stress, but instead of orienting to the right edge of the word, they orient to the boundary of the following foot. These rules also need to operate iteratively: at the completion of a cycle of foot structure projection, the system repeats over the remaining unfooted syllables.

Some additional datapoints are worth noting. Consider the following two words, both of which have five syllables.

(21)   ˌʔe.le.ma.ˈku.le   'old man'
(22)   ˌlu.ma.luˈma.ʔi   'to upset'

Exercise 10.16   How do these forms differ from the generalizations in Exercise 10.13? Explain any problems that these present.

The secondary stress in these forms is word-initial, separated from the primary stress by two unstressed syllables instead of one. As such, these are problematic for our established generalizations, which suggest that secondary stress ought to occur on the second syllable rather than the first. In other words, the secondary foot inexplicably is one syllable farther to the left.

A deeper look at Hawaiian morphology indicates that these exceptions are principled; [ʔele-makule] is a compound, while [luma-lumaʔi] is a reduplicated form, and both words contain a morphological boundary between their second and third syllables. Thus, as we saw in Exercise 10.8, morphological structure can have an effect on stress assignment. In these examples, it seems as if the system is avoiding having a foot in which the two syllables belong to different morphemes. Such footing is not always avoidable, but given the choice between footing /ele-makule/ as [(ˌele)-ma(ˈkule)] or *[e(ˌle-ma)(ˈkule)], the language favors the form in which the morpheme and foot boundaries coincide.

Exercise 10.17   Examine the following forms to infer whether there are any internal morpheme boundaries that seem to affect the placement of secondary stress.

(23)	ʔau-i-ke-kai-loa	ˌʔau.i.ke.ˌkai.ˈlo.a	'swim in the distant seas'
(24)	ka-mehameha	ˌka.me.ha.ˈme.ha	'the lonely one'
(25)	ke-one-ʔoːʔio	ke.ˌo.ne.ʔoː.ˈʔi.o	'the sandy place with bonefish'
(26)	kaʔelele-o-ka-wanaʔao	ˌka.ʔe.ˌlele.ˌoka.ˌwa.na.ˈʔao	'the messenger of the dawn'
(27)	kau-i-ke-ao-uli	ˌkau.i.ke.ˌao.ˈuli	'place in the dark clouds'

In (23) [ˌʔau.i.ke.ˌkai.ˈlo.a], a secondary stress is placed on the initial syllable [ʔau], instead of the [i] that follows it. A similar result is seen in (24) [ˌka.me.ha.ˈme.ha] and (27) [ˌkau.i.ke.ˌao.ˈuli], where the second and third syllables are both unstressed. Thus, it seems that morphologically complex forms may receive initial secondary stress even if this results in a sequence of two unstressed syllables.

Exercise 10.18   Given what we have determined so far about Hawaiian metrical phonology, we can also use the position of stress to figure out whether two vowels are tautosyllabic or not. Examine the following data, using the location of stress to infer syllable boundaries. For each word, use the position of stress to indicate whether any sequence of vowels is a diphthong or two separate syllable nuclei.

(28)	ˌkaimuˈkiː	'oven for ti root'
(29)	ˌheiˈau	'shrine'
(30)	oˈnaona	'softly fragrant'
(31)	iˈlaila	'in that place'
(32)	ˌhoʔoˈuli	'dark'
(33)	ˌkanaˈiwa	'nine'
(34)	ˌkulaˈiwi	'native'
(35)	ˌkamaˈehu	'strength'
(36)	ˌpalaˈuli	'dark'
(37)	ˌkanaˈono	'sixty'
(38)	ʔeˈiwa	'nine times'
(39)	ˌhoʔoˈilo	'winter'

In (28)–(31), the position of stress indicates that the adjacent vowels comprise a diphthong.

In the remaining forms, the fact that stress occurs on the second of two adjacent vowels suggests that the stressed vowel is initial in its foot, and therefore serves as a syllable nucleus by itself. For example, in (33) [ˌkanaˈiwa], the stress on [i] suggests that the medial sequence [ai] must be tautosyllabic, with [a] serving as the unstressed syllable of the preceding foot, and [i] serving as the stressed syllable of the following foot, as in [(ˌka.na)(ˈi.wa)]. This analysis is supported by the observation that the initial vowel (the one that precedes unstressed [a]) also bears stress – thus [kana] clearly comprises a foot, further showing the vowels of the medial [ai] sequence not to be in the same syllable.

10.6 Mongolian

Now let us turn to Mongolian (Bosson 1964, Poppe 1970), which provides a more complicated example of a weight-sensitive stress-assignment system. The following data follow Walker (1995) in combining forms from Buriat and Khalkha Mongolian, two closely related languages that share the same stress pattern. Forms from Buriat are indicated with a B. Take some time to look over these data, paying attention to the length of vowels and the position of primary stress. It will help to consider that syllables in Mongolian are heavy only if they contain diphthongs or long vowels; coda consonants do not contribute weight.

(1)	ˈa.xa	'brother'	
(2)	ˈun.ʃi.san	'having read'	
(3)	ˈxa.da	'mountain'	B

(4)	da.ˈlae	'sea'	
(5)	ga.ˈluː	'goose'	
(6)	xa.ˈdaːr	'through the mountain'	B
(7)	ˈaː.ruːl	'dry cheese curds'	
(8)	ˈboː.soː	'bet, wager'	B
(9)	ˈuit.gar.tae	'sad'	
(10)	da.ˈlai.gaːr	'by sea'	B
(11)	uːr.ˈtae.gaːr	'angrily'	
(12)	øːg.ˈʃøː.xe	'to act encouragingly'	B
(13)	mo.ˈrjoː.roː	'by one's own horse'	B
(14)	mo.ri.ˈoː.roː	'by means of his own horse'	
(15)	na.maː.ˈtuːl.xa	'to cause to be covered with leaves'	B
(16)	xøn.diː.ˈryː.len	'to separate'	
(17)	da.lae.ˈgaː.raː	'by one's own sea'	
(18)	da.lai.ˈgaː.raː	'by one's one sea'	B
(19)	xyː.xen.ˈgeː.reː	'by one's own girl'	B
(20)	do.ˈloː.du.gaːr	'seventh'	
(21)	xu.ˈdaː.liŋ.daː	'to the parents of the husband in their mutual relation'	B
(22)	bae.ˈguː.lag.dax	'to be organized'	
(23)	bai.ˈguːl.la.gaːr	'by means of the organization'	
(24)	taː.ˈruː.lag.da.xa	'to be adapted to'	B
(25)	buː.za.nuː.ˈdiː.je	'steamed dumplings'	B
(26)	u.laːn.ˈbaː.ta.raːs	'Ulaanbaatar (ablat.)'	
(27)	u.laːn.baːt.ˈriːn.xan	'by the residents of Ulaanbaatar'	

Exercise 10.19 a. Under what conditions does stress occur on a light syllable?

b. Under what conditions does stress occur on a final syllable?

c. Where does stress otherwise occur?

a. Light syllables are stressed only if there are no heavy syllables in the word; stress is initial in such cases.

b. Stress is final if the final syllable is heavy, and there are no other heavy syllables.

c. Stress otherwise occurs on the last non-final heavy syllable.

While this system is succinctly describable, it pushes the bounds of capabilities of our rule notation system. We can, however, start by creating some rules of stress assignment without reference (yet) to foot structure.

Exercise 10.20 Make rules to assign stress for Mongolian. You may find it easier to do so without relying on foot structure.

The rules of stress assignment in Mongolian:

$\sigma_{\mu\mu} \rightarrow$ [+stress] / __ $(\sigma)_0$ $(\sigma_{\mu\mu})$]$_{WD}$
$\sigma_{\mu\mu} \rightarrow$ [+stress] / $_{WD}$ [$(\sigma)_0$ __]$_{WD}$
$\sigma \rightarrow$ [+stress] / $_{WD}$[__ σ_0]

The first rule assigns stress to the rightmost non-final heavy syllable, by targeting any syllable followed by any number of light syllables and a single final heavy syllable. The second rule assigns stress to a heavy syllable in final position, as long as all preceding syllables are light. The third rule assigns stress to initial position, and applies only if no heavy syllables are in the form.

While it is indeed possible to write rules that appropriately place stress in Mongolian, some additional commentary is warranted here. First, we have stipulated three separate rules, all of which assign stress; each rule only assigns stress in the absence of an already stressed syllable, and the three conditioning environments are more or less non-overlapping. As such, the rules are eerily coincidental in their current form. Moreover, if a theory of stress assignment allows us to specify arbitrary numbers of syllables between a stress target and a word edge, then certain typological trends regarding stress patterns remain accidental.

These problems stem from the fact that above the rules make no reference to foot structure; foot notation neatens the account somewhat. If you attempted to use foot structure in your rules, they would appear more as follows:

$\sigma_{\mu\mu}$ $(\sigma) \rightarrow$ (ˈ$\sigma_{\mu\mu}$ (σ))$_{FT}$ / __ $(\sigma)_0$ $(\sigma_{\mu\mu})$]$_{WD}$
$\sigma_{\mu\mu} \rightarrow$ (ˈ$\sigma_{\mu\mu}$)$_{FT}$ / $_{WD}$ [$(\sigma)_0$ __]$_{WD}$
σ $\sigma \rightarrow$ (ˈ$\sigma\sigma$)$_{FT}$ / $_{WD}$[__ σ_0]

Rather than assign stress to specific syllables, these rules assign foot structure in environments that are parallel to those formalized above. The first rule assigns a foot to the rightmost non-final heavy syllable, combining it with a light syllable to its right if one is available. The second rule assigns a monosyllabic foot to any final heavy syllable that is the only heavy syllable in its word. The third rule assigns a foot to initial position, in the absence of any heavy syllables.

As a quantity-sensitive system, Mongolian seeks out heavy syllables first, but ignores final ones. It creates a quantity-sensitive, left-headed foot as far as possible to the right, scanning from the penultimate forward. If it finds no non-final heavy syllable, it returns to the final syllable to see if is heavy, and failing that, it skips back to the initial syllables of the word. Using foot structure captures several things even about this system – for example, the idea that penultimate position takes primacy over final position, which foot structure succinctly models, and the idea that heavy syllables draw stress.

There are a few ideas we can summarize so far about stress systems. Across languages, stress is drawn to the edges of words, either edgemost or in the syllable next to the edgemost one. In some cases, antepenultimate stress is observed, which is nonetheless oriented to the end of a word. Stressed syllables tend to be spaced apart from each other, separated by unstressed syllables. Morphological structure sometimes interacts with stress assignment, as does syllable weight; in some languages, stress is drawn toward heavy syllables.

The converse effect may also be observed, in which stress syllables are made heavy; in the remainder of this chapter we can observe segmental phenomena that respond to the position of stress. Let us turn to Yup'ik to explore this further; examine the data below, paying attention to the position of stress. Note that while some vowels are long in these data, vowel length is not contrastive in Yup'ik.

10.7 Yup'ik

In quantity-sensitive systems, we see an interaction between syllable weight and stress assignment. Basically, stress is attracted to a particular position within a word, but can be pulled away from this position if the presence of a heavy syllable demands it. Conversely, in some languages, rather than syllable weight dictating the position of stress, stress dictates syllable weight. Consider the underlying and surface forms from Yup'ik below (Jacobson 1984, Reed *et al.* 1977).

	Underlying	*Surface*	*Gloss*
(1)	/qajaŋuq/	[qaˈjaːŋoq]	'he acquires a kayak'
(2)	/atata/	[aˈtaːta]	'later'
(3)	/aŋalkuq/	[aˈŋalkoq]	'shaman'
(4)	/juʁaŋuq/	[joˈʁaːŋoq]	'he is starting to dance'
(5)	/tumtaŋqəʁtuq/	[tum̩ˈtaŋqəχˌtoq]	'there are footprints'
(6)	/qajaɣtaŋqəʁtuq/	[qaˈjaxtaŋˌqəχtoq]	'there are kayaks'
(7)	/qajapiɣkani/	[qaˈjaːpixˌkaːni]	'his own future authentic kayak'
(8)	/qajaʁpaŋjuɣtuq/	[qaˈjaχpaŋˌjuxtoq]	'he wants to get a big kayak'
(9)	/iŋʁiq/	[iŋˈʁeq]	'mountain'

Exercise 10.21   Describe the position of primary and secondary stress in Yup'ik. You should attempt to syllabify the surface forms as you do this.

Primary stress occurs in the second syllable of each word. Secondary stress occurs in the fourth syllable, if there is one.

Exercise 10.22   Create rules that assign primary and secondary stress, using foot structure.

σ σ → (σ ˈσ) / $_{wd}$[___   Generate an initial iambic foot
σ σ → (σ ˌσ) /)$_{FT}$ ___   Iterate feet from left to right

Exercise 10.23   Describe the distribution of long vowels in Yup'ik.

Long vowels occur in stressed syllables, but only if the syllables have no coda consonants.

Exercise 10.24   Write a rule that predicts the length of vowels.

$$[+\text{stress}]$$
$$\sigma$$
$$|$$
$$V \rightarrow V\mu\mu \, / \, \underline{\quad} \,]$$

The rule detects vowels in open stressed syllables and renders them long. It is formulated so that vowel lengthening will not occur if the vowel occurs in a closed syllable.

The Yup'ik data suggest that vowels lengthen to provide sufficient weight for the syllable to be stressed. In other words, stressed syllables must be heavy in the language, and CVC syllables meet this demand, while CV syllables do not. The lengthening of the vowel in the latter case makes the syllable bimoraic.

We should also acknowledge that the evidence here is somewhat circumstantial: we have no direct evidence to support the claim that the alternating vowels are underlyingly short, only that long vowels are limited in their distribution (and thus somewhat predictable). If we could find independent evidence to show that vowel length is simply not contrastive in Yup'ik, or that the alternating vowels are short in other circumstances, we would have additional support for such a claim.

10.8 Rhythmic lengthening in Chicasaw

A very similar pattern is observed in Chicasaw, which also provides an example of the second sort of supporting evidence, in that vowels clearly alternate between short and long, depending on their position in the word. Examine the following data from Chicasaw (Munro and Ulrich 1984), paying attention to the position of stress and the length of vowels.

(1)	aˌbiːˈka	'S/he is sick'
(2)	aˌbiːkaˈtok	'S/he was sick'
(3)	aˌsaːbiˈka	'I am sick'
(4)	aˌsaːbiˌkaːˈtok	'I was sick'
(5)	aˌbiːkaˌʧiːˈtok	'S/he made it sick'
(6)	aˌʧiːbikaːˈtok	'You were sick'
(7)	ʧiˌhojjoˈtok	'S/he looked for you'
(8)	ʧiˌjimˈmi	'You believe it'
(9)	piˌsaːˈtok	'S/he saw it'
(10)	piˌsaːˈʧi	'S/he makes it see it'

Exercise 10.25 Describe the position of primary and secondary stress in Chicasaw.

Primary stress occurs in the final syllable of each word. Secondary stress occurs on the second syllable, as well as on the fourth, if there is one.

Exercise 10.26 Create rules that assign primary and secondary stress, using foot structure.

$\sigma\,\sigma \rightarrow (\sigma\,\text{'}\sigma) / \underline{\quad}]_{\text{WD}}$ Generate a final primary iambic foot
$\sigma\,\sigma \rightarrow (\sigma\,{}_{\backprime}\sigma) / {}_{\text{WD}}[\,\underline{\quad}$ Generate an initial iambic foot
$\sigma\,\sigma \rightarrow (\sigma\,{}_{\backprime}\sigma) /)_{\text{FT}}\,\underline{\quad}$ Iterate feet from left to right

Exercise 10.27 Describe the distribution of long vowels in Chicasaw.

Long vowels occur in stressed syllables, but only if the syllables have no coda consonants, and only if the syllables are not final.

Exercise 10.28 Write a rule that predicts the length of vowels.

The rule detects vowels in final position of feet, and lengthens them, so long as they are followed by another syllable (which prevents lengthening from applying to final vowels).

$V \rightarrow V_{\mu\mu} / \underline{\quad}]_{\text{FT}}\,\sigma$

The Chicasaw data illustrate for us another instantiation of stress patterns, one in which primary stress is oriented to one word edge while secondary stress orients to the other. In addition, we see (like in Yup'ik) that vowel length is predictable as a function of stress assignment – but unlike Yupik, the claim that these vowels are underlyingly short is unequivocal.

We infer this from a morphological analysis of these data. For example, there is a root /abika/ 'be sick' which uninflected carries present-tense and third-person subject agreement, as in [abiːka], where the vowel [iː] is lengthened in second position. When first-person agreement is added via the infix /-sa-/ and past tense indicated with the suffix /-tok/, we instead see [asaːbikaːtok], where now the root's [i] is short but its [a] is long. Hence we conclude that the vowels in the root /abika/ are underlyingly short and alternate in their length.

The Chicasaw stress pattern could conceivably be formalized without foot structure, but the appeal to feet readily captures the notion of stressed and unstressed syllables interspersed over a word. Moreover, the vowel length pattern could be modeled without reference to stress, but any account that does so would mischaracterize the co-occurrence of stress and length as a mere accident.

Summary

In this chapter, we have put the notation of syllable structure to work to allow us to examine and describe patterns of stress assignment. We have differentiated stress from other suprasegmental phenomena and acknowledged it as a phonological phenomenon with phonetic correlates. We have seen that stress can have a largely unpredictable distribution in English, but despite this, the assignment of stress in English is sensitive to a number of phonological conditions that are more categorically observed in other languages. Stress orients to edges of words, such that it is initial or final, or very nearly so; secondary stresses are distributed in such a way that unstressed syllables often occur between other stressed syllables; heavy syllables tend to attract stress, and morphological structure can have an influence on the location of stress.

We have been able to account for some of these tendencies using foot structure; for example, the interspersion of stressed and unstressed syllables. Yet we have also seen that there are certain phenomena that rules themselves do not capture, such as the association between syllable weight and stress; we have composed rules that draw this association, but we have not formalized a representational link between stress and weight (in the way that we have linked strong and weak syllables as daughters of the same foot). In Chapter 12, we will visit Optimality Theory, an approach which seeks to remedy this shortcoming of the rule-driven model.

Before doing so, in the following chapter we explore morphophonological phenomena in which suprasegmental structure quite clearly can be seen to carry contrastive or functional information. We refer to the study of such patterns as Prosodic Morphology, and we will see that while the structural notions of the syllable and foot help us discover the patterns that underpin prosodic morphology, the methods laid out in Optimality Theory often avoid some of the formal shortcomings of rule-driven approaches to metrical phonology and prosodic morphology.

Key terms

stress

intonation

intonational melody

meter

foot

foot structure

iamb

trochee

quantity sensitivity

References and further reading

Bosson, James E. 1964. *Modern Mongolian: A Primer and Reader*. Bloomington: University of Indiana.

Boxwell, H. and M. Boxwell. 1966. Weri phonemes. In S. A. Wurm (ed.), *Papers in New Guinea Linguistics* 5: 77–93. Canberra: Australian National University.

Echeverría, M. S. and H. Contreras. 1965. Araucanian phonemics. *International Journal of American Linguistics* 31: 132–135.

Elbert, Samuel H. and Mary Kawena Pukui . 1979. *Hawaiian Grammar*. Honolulu: University of Hawaii Press.

Halle, Morris, and George N. Clements. 1983. *Problem Book in Phonology*. Cambridge MA: MIT Press.

Hammond, Michael. 1999. *The Phonology of English*. Oxford University Press.

Hayes, Bruce. 1995. *Metrical Stress Theory: Principles and Case Studies*. University of Chicago Press.

Jacobson, Steven A. 1984. *Yup'ik Eskimo Dictionary*. Fairbanks, Alaska: Alaska Native Language Center.

Kenstowicz, Michael. 1994. *Phonology in Generative Grammar*. Oxford: Blackwell.

Kiparsky, Paul. 1979. Metrical structure assignment is cyclic. *Linguistic Inquiry* 10.4: 421–441.

Liberman, Mark, and Alan Prince. 1977. On stress and linguistic rhythm. *Linguistic Inquiry* 8.2: 249–336.

Munro, Pamela and Charles H. Ulrich. 1984. Structure-preservation and Western Muskogean rhythmic lengthening. In Mark Cobler *et al.* (eds.), *Proceedings of the Third Annual West Coast Conference on Formal Linguistics*. Stanford Linguistics Association, 191–202.

Osborn, Henry A. Jr. 1966. Warao I: phonology and morphophonemics. *International Journal of American Linguistics* 32: 108–123.

Poppe, Nicholas. 1970. *Mongolian Language* (Handbook Series 4). Washington: The Center for Applied Linguistics.

Pukui, Mary Kawena and Samuel H. Elbert. 1971. *Hawaiian Dictionary*. Honolulu: University Press of Hawaii.

Reed, Irene, Osahito Miyaoka, Steven Jacobson, Paschal Afcan, and Michael Krauss. 1977. *Yup'ik Eskimo Grammar*. Fairbanks: Alaska Native Language Center, University of Alaska.

Tryon, Darrell T. 1970. *An Introduction to Maranungku* (Pacific Linguistics, Series B, 15). Canberra: Australian National University.

Walker, Rachel. 1995. Mongolian stress: typological implications for nonfinality in unbounded systems. In Rachel Walker, Ove Lorentz, and Haruo Kubozono (eds.), *Phonology at Santa Cruz: Papers on Stress, Accent, and Alignment* 4: 85–102.

Review exercises

Stress and English vowels

Examine the following phonological representations, and answer the questions that follow. UK and US pronunciations are given where they differ.

table	ˈteɪbəl
veto	ˈvito
data	ˈdeɪtə/ˈdeɪɾə
bunny	ˈbʌni
sunny	ˈsʌni
flower	ˈflaʊə/ˈflaʊɚ
pocket	ˈpɒkət/ˈpɑkət
nightingale	ˈnaɪtənˌɡeɪl
robin	ˈɹɑbən/ˈɹɑbən
sparrow	ˈspæɹoʊ
flavor	ˈfleɪvə/ˈfleɪvɚ
conceal	kənˈsil

understand	ˌʌndəˈstænd/ˌʌndɚˈstænd
Canada	ˈkænədə
Nevada	nəˈvædə
Switzerland	ˈswɪtsələnd/ˈswɪtsɚlənd
Portugal	ˈpɔːtʃəgəl/ˈpɔɹtʃəgəl
Lebanon	ˈlɛbəˌnɒn/ˈlɛbəˌnɑn
armory	ˈaɹməri
vestibule	ˈvɛstəˌbjul
avenue	ˈævəˌnju
aspen	ˈæspən
sentiment	ˈsɛntəmənt
revision	ɹəˈvɪʒən
discontent	ˌdɪskənˈtɛnt
similar	ˈsɪmələ/ˈsɪmələ˞
metaphor	ˈmɛɹəˌfɔː/ˈmɛɹəˌfɔɹ
America	əˈmɛɹəkə
convertible	kənˈvɜːtəbəl/kənˈvɚ-ɾəbəl
Tennessee	ˌtɛnəˈsi
macaroon	ˌmækəˈɹun
disturb	dəstˈɜːb/dəsˈtɚ-b
perverse	pəˈvɜːs/pɚˈvɚ-s
contusion	kənˈtjuʒən/kənˈtuʒən
conference	ˈkɒnfəɹəns/ˈkɑnfəɹəns
computer	kəmˈpjutə/kəmˈpjuɾɚ
community	kəˈmjuəti/kəˈmjunɚi
impunity	əmˈpjunəti/əmˈpjunɚi
detonate	ˈdɛtəˌneɪt
deferral	dəˈfɚ-əl
annuity	əˈnjuəti/əˈnuɪɾi
relegation	ˌɹɛləˈgeɪʃən
fanatical	fəˈnætəkəl/fəˈnæɹəkəl
decompose	ˌdikəmˈpouz
insanity	ənˈsænəti/ənˈsænɚi
kangaroo	ˌkæŋgəˈɹu
carpenter	kaːpəntə/kaɹpəntɚ

a. Which vowels may occur in stressed syllables?

b. Which vowels may occur in unstressed syllables?

Mohawk

In the following data from Mohawk (Halle and Clements 1983), underlying forms and their morphological structure are provided for you. The morphemes are not glossed individually, but you can assume that recurrent forms have consistent function; e.g., the final /-s/ of (A1, B2, B4) is a recurrent morpheme, and the final /ʔ/ of (A3, A6, B1) is a recurrent morpheme.

A.	1. /hra+njahesʌ+s/	[ranaˈheːzʌs]	'he trusts her'
	2. /hra+ket+as/	[raˈgeːdas]	'he scrapes'
	3. /waʔ+hra+ket+ʔ/	[waˈhaːgedeʔ]	'he scraped'
	4. /o+wis+ʔ/	[ˈoːwizeʔ]	'ice, glass'
	5. /wake+nuhweʔ+u +neʔ/	[wagenuhwe ˈʔuːneʔ]	'I had liked it'
	6. /ʌ+k+ʌthe+ʔ/	[ʌkˈhʌːdeʔ]	'I shall go ahead'
B.	1. /ja+k+ni+rʌn+ot+ʔ/	[jageniˈrɔːnodeʔ]	'we two are singing'
	2. /ja+k+ni+ehjaraʔ+s/	[jagenehˈjaːraʔs]	'we two remember'
	3. /ja+k+wa+rʌn+ot+ʔ/	[jagwaˈrɔːnodeʔ]	'we (>2) are singing'
	4. /ja+k+wa+ehjaraʔ+s/	[jagwehˈjaːraʔs]	'we (>2) remember'
	5. /hra+jʌtho+s/	[raˈjʌthos]	'he plants'
	6. /hra+ehjaraʔ+s/	[rehˈjaːraʔs]	'he remembers'
	7. /je+k+hrek+s/	[ˈjekreks]	'I push it'
	8. /je+ʌk+hrek+ʔ/	[ˈjɔkregeʔ]	'I will push it'
C.	1. /hra+o+joʔtʌ+eʔ/	[rojˈoʔdeʔ]	'he works'
	2. /waʔ+hra+o+joʔtʌ+ʔ/	[wahoˈjoʔdʌʔ]	'he worked'
	3. /hra+kʌ+s/	[ˈraːgʌs]	'he sees her'
	4. /hra+o+kʌ/	[ˈroːgʌh]	'he has seen her'
	5. /k+esak+s/	[ˈgeːzaks]	'I look for it'
	6. /hra+esak+s/	[ˈreːzaks]	'he looks for it'

a. Describe the position of stress in Mohawk as a function of its position within words. You may find it helpful to approach these data by regrouping them based on their stress position.

b. If you were able to find two basic stress patterns, try to formulate a generalization about the choice between them, based on the phonological and morphological patterns seen in the data.

c. Compose a single rule of stress assignment in Mohawk. There may be at least one other phonological rule that is ordered crucially with respect to stress assignment; describe this rule and its order.

Selkup

In the following data from Selkup (Halle and Clements 1983), assume that adjacent consonants are syllabified into different syllables; apply this also to geminate consonants (e.g., /qummɨn/ → [qum.mɨn]).

ˈkə	'winter'
kɨˈpɔː	'tiny'
ˈamɨrna	'eats'
ˈqoʎcɨmpatɨ	'found'
pynakɨˈsəː	'giant!'
ˈyŋŋɨntɨ	'wolverine'
ˈqummɨn	'human being (genitive)'
ˈqumɨm	'human being (accusative)'
ˈqumɨnɨk	'human being (dative)'
quˈmoːqɪ	'two human beings'
ˈqumɨt	'human beings'
ˈqummɨ	'my friend'
qumˈmɪː	'our friend'
qumoːqlɪˈlɪː	'your two friends'
ˈsərɨ	'white'
ˈqoːkitiʎ	'deaf'
kanaŋˈmɪː	'our dog'
ilɨˈsɔːmɨt	'we lived'
ˈsæːqɨ	'black '
ˈkarman	'pocket'
ˈuːcɨqo	'to work'
ˈuːcak	'I work'
uːˈcɔːmɨt	'we work'
ˈuːcɨkkak	'I am working'
uːcɨkˈkoːqɪ	'they two are working'
ˈuːcitiʎ	'working (partitive)'
ˈuːcilæ	'working (gerund)'

a. Propose syllabifications for each word in the data. Do not attempt yet to determine the weight of every syllable – you may assume that CV syllables are light and that CVː syllables are heavy, but you should wait to decide whether CVC syllables are light or heavy.

b. Can stress ever occur on light syllables?
   - If so, where in the word can it occur?

- What else do you notice about words with stressed light syllables?
- What other syllables can carry stress, and where in the word can stress occur in such cases?

c. Summarize the Selkup stress system in general terms (i.e., not as a rule).

d. Would it make more sense to consider CVC syllables to be heavy or light? Why?

e. Propose a rule that properly assigns stress in all Selkup forms.

CHAPTER 11 PROSODIC MORPHOLOGY

> ## Learning objectives
>
> - Differentiate templatic and prosodic morphology from affixation
> - Discover the derivational steps in creating reduplicated forms
> - Address issues of base-reduplicant identity and their problems for derivational approaches
> - Understand the machinations of minimal word requirements
> - Observe and describe prosodic patterns in non-concatenative morphological systems

Introduction

In this chapter we delve into prosodic morphology, a set of phenomena that are quite closely linked to syllable and foot structure in language.

These include reduplication, word minimum effects, and non-concatenative morphology. Reduplication is a process in which some or all of a root is doubled, usually to indicate some morphological function, and often in a way that is best modeled by appending prosodic units such as syllables and feet. Word minimum effects are seen in languages where all words (or some category of words) are required to be at least of a certain prosodic size. Non-concatenative morphology is seen in languages where changing the prosodic organization of some segment melody helps indicate different morphological functions, in a way quite distinct from segmental affixation.

Prosodic morphology is also sometimes called templatic morphology, with the understanding that languages sometimes use templates to which segmental sequences are associated.

11.1 Reduplication

Reduplication is a process in which some or all segments of a root are repeated, and the appearance of the repeated sequence carries some morphological function. In reduplicated words, the source of copying is often called the **base**, which is sometimes but not always equivalent to the root. The reduplicated affix is called the **reduplicant**.

reduplication: a process in which some or all segments of a root are repeated to indicate some morphological function.

base: the stem to which a reduplicative affix is attached.

reduplicant: an affix which is created via reduplication.

For example, in Amele (Roberts 1987), one way for verbs to indicate simultaneous activity is to use initial reduplication. Examine the following data and note how each form has a CV prefix which is identical to the initial CV of the root.

11.2 Amele

ba-bacis-en	'as he came out'
be-be-n	'as he came up'
bi-bil-en	'as he sat'
bu-busal-en	'as he ran away'
ca-cad-en	'as he fought'
ca-cati-en	'as he cleaned'
ce-ced-en	'as he took'
ce-cegul-en	'as he met'
ci-cil-en	'as she boiled (it)'
co-cod-en	'as he beat'
fa-faj-en	'as he bought'
fe-fe-n	'as he saw'
fo-foj-on	'as he vomited'
ga-gaw-en	'as he desired'
ge-gel-en	'as he scraped'
gi-gis-en	'as she sewed'
ha-hagal-en	'as he tangled'
ho-hon-en	'as he came'
hu-hulu-en	'as he rotted'
ja-jab-en	'as he chased'
ja-jahin-en	'as he hated'
ja-jaq-en	'as he wrote'
le-le-n	'as he went'
le-let-en	'as he crossed over'
li-lib-en	'as he tied'

ma-masu-en	'as it proliferated'
me-men-en	'as he closed'
mu-mud-en	'as he made'
ne-nen	'as he came down'
ne-nesel-en	'as he chose'
no-non	'as he went down'
nu-nu-en	'as he went'
qa-qag-en	'as he tied'
qa-qasal-en	'as he confessed'
qo-qon	'as he hit'
sa-sabi-en	'as he increased'
sa-sal-en	'as he removed skin'
sa-sanij-en	'as he read'
ta-tanaw-en	'as he made peace'
ta-taq-en	'as he dressed'
te-te-n	'as he went up'
to-ton-en	'as he fell down'
wa-wagal-en	'as he demolished'
wa-walu-en	'as he swelled'
we-wet-en	'as he scooped'
o-on	'as he got'
o-od-on	'as he did'

The segments of the reduplicative prefix are predictable from the segments of the root; this is a definitive property of reduplicative morphemes. In this case, the first consonant of the prefix is identical to the first consonant of the root, and the subsequent vowel in the prefix is likewise identical to the earliest vowel of the root. We call this a pattern of partial reduplication, because only this much of the root is reduplicated.

From a formal point of view, reduplication patterns offer an immediate challenge to our technical means of notating phonological operations. On the one hand, reduplication is a morphological process, so the addition of a reduplicative prefix may seem to be outside the domain of phonological rules. On the other hand, we cannot posit any underlying segments for the prefix, because its segments are fully predictable and wholly differ from root to root. Consequently, we need to include in our phonological model a means of assigning the appropriate segments to the reduplicative prefix.

Let us briefly consider two plausible linear approaches, neither of which we will ultimately accept. First, it is plausible that the reduplicative morpheme really does have some underlying segments, but that there are rules which change each of them in the reduplicative circumstance to make them identical to other segments in the same form.

Thus, we could assume an underlying form such as /ba/ for the simultaneous prefix, which in turn motivates a rule to change /b/ to a consonant identical to the initial consonant of the root, and another to change /a/ in a similar fashion.

/b/ → [α everything] / __ V [Cα everything]
/a/ → [α everything] / __ C [Vα everything]

A second approach would be to imagine the segments of the root are indexed in order, and that a rule of reduplication forces a repeat of segments up to a certain number.

$C_1V_1\ldots \rightarrow C_1V_1C_1V_1\ldots$

Of course, this rule needs to be marked in such a way that it only applies in reduplicated forms.

While these approaches may capture the data in Amele quite easily, they open a number of potential problems. First, the default UR approach would need an additional rule for every segment of the reduplicant, and as we will see, sometimes the reduplicant is much longer than two segments. Second, the notion of complete identity is accidental in this account; a system of rules and features like this could generate an inordinate number of absurd systems that diverge in various ways from complete identity.

Both approaches invoke environments where the target segment is sensitive to another segment several positions away, in an unconstrained manner, leaving the relative linear order of reduplicative segments unexplained.

Most pressing, however, is the fact that many reduplicative patterns, including ones that we will see below, are more complicated than the repetition of a single consonant and vowel. They may alternate in form across roots, beyond simple reflection of the segments. The alternative we seek will couch reduplication as a process that creates a copy of the segmental level of the base to fill up some target syllabic or prosodic structure – and subsequent phonological rules then operate over the resulting form. To illustrate this, consider the following data from Ilocano (Gleason 1955).

11.3 Ilocano

| (1) | piŋan | 'dish' | piŋpiŋan | 'dishes' |
| (2) | talon | 'field' | taltalon | 'fields' |

(3)	dalan	'road'	daldalan	'roads'
(4)	biag	'life'	bibiag	'lives'
(5)	nua	'carabao'	nunua	'carabaos'
(6)	ulo	'head'	ululo	'heads'

Exercise 11.1 Describe the forms of the reduplicants in terms of C and V.

There are three types of reduplicants: CVC, as in (1) [pinpingan], CV, as in (4) [nunua], VC, as in (6) [ululo].

The fact that three types of reduplicants appear in these data is problematic for the linear approaches we suggested in the previous section. A default segment approach would have to choose one of the forms, say /tal-/, as the underlying form, and use rules to change each segment before other roots, as follows (note that ~ here indicates the morphological boundary between reduplicant and base):

/tal/
t → [C α everything] / __ VC~[C α everything]
a → [V α everything] / __ C ~ C [V α everything]
l → [C α everything] / __ ~ CV[C α everything]

This approach has a number of conceptual problems. First, characterizing reduplication like this really stretches the power of rules – for example, by assimilating one consonant to a non-proximate one, despite a vowel and another consonant intervening. Second, the appeal to three separate rules here loses the character of the process as one that copies part of the base. It is an accident that the rules happen to target the three earliest segments in the base, and that the rules instead don't randomly target some other subset of the base. Typologically, prefixing reduplication tends strongly to begin its copying with the initial segment of the base. Third, we actually need several additional rules to handle the allomorphs in which the reduplicant is VC or CV.

A linear indexing approach would instead double up the first several segments of the base, as follows:

$C_1V_1C_2 \ldots \rightarrow C_1V_1C_2\ C_1V_1C_2 \ldots$

As with the assimilation approach, several conceptual issues arise. First, the indexing system is confounded by forms such as [biag] and [ulo]. Since the rule calls for the second consonant to appear in the reduplicant, it predicts *[big-biag]. Similarly, since the first vowel occurs ahead of the first consonant in the base for [ulo], the rule inadvertently predicts *[lu-ulo]. Second, the linear approach again actually characterizes reduplication as an

303

accident: a system that allows indexing of rules does not preclude bizarre systems in which, for example, the indexes of the affix are in reverse order, or are odd-numbered only, yet the approach freely allows such rules to be written.

For these reasons, we will approach reduplication from a different angle: one that portrays it as the affixation of some prosodic unit, which is filled in with copies of segments from the root. In this approach, the copying process of reduplication occurs with exactly one rule, and other aspects of reduplicative patterns come about through rules that govern syllabification and other segmental patterns.

For example, in both Amele and Ilocano, we can posit an empty syllable as the reduplicative morpheme. We model the process of reduplication with the tandem acts of affixation of this empty syllable and the creation of a string of segments identical to those of the base. These segments associate to the empty syllable as much as they can, and extraneous unassociated material is left out of the form. The Ilocano derivations below illustrate this process for the forms /piŋgan/ → [piŋpiŋgan], /biag/ → [bibiag], and /ulo/ → [ululo].

UR:	/ σ_RED + piŋgan /	/ σ_RED + biag /	/ σ_RED + ulo /
syllabify	σ σ σ /|\ /|\ piŋ.gan	σ σ σ /| |\ bi.ag	σ σ σ 	/| u.lo
reduplicate	σ σ σ /|\ /|\ piŋgan piŋ.gan	σ σ σ /| |\ biag bi.ag	σ σ σ 	/| ulo u.lo
associate	σ σ σ /|\ /|\ /|\ piŋgan piŋ.gan	σ σ σ /| /| |\ biag bi.ag	σ σ σ |— /| ulo u.lo
stray erasure	σ σ σ /|\ /|\ /|\ piŋ piŋ.gan	σ σ σ /| /| |\ bi bi.ag	σ σ σ |— /| ul u.lo

An important aspect of this approach is that reduplication adds a prosodic unit and copies segmental material from the base as separate steps. Thus, despite its appeal to prosodic categories as crucial units, it does not simply copy a prosodic unit of the base. For example, the reduplicant syllable in [tal.ta.lon] includes segments whose base correspondents span more than a single syllable: the reduplicative [l] is in the coda position of the same syllable headed by [a], but the base [l] is in an onset of a syllable that follows [a]. Likewise, in [u.lu.lon], the reduplicated form is longer than the simple form by one syllable, but the reduplicative segments span two syllables, as the prefix [l] serves as the onset of the syllable that holds the base-initial vowel.

This analysis captures the divergent patterns with a simpler account than those of the linear approaches. That is, unlike an approach that uses a series of discrete segment-copying rules, this approach captures the smaller reduplicant of [bibiag] and the transsyllabic nature of the prefix in [ululo] with the same basic system of copy and associate. In particular, [bibiag] surfaces as it does, with just two segments, because the reduplicative /a/ cannot associate to either the prefix syllable or the initial root syllable. Likewise, [ululo] arises because the reduplicative /l/ can associate to the unfilled onset position of the base's first syllable.

Another notable facet of this approach is that the reduplicative rule temporarily creates a full copy of the base, only some of which persists to the surface. For example, in / σ + piŋgan /, the copying rule produces the intermediate form / piŋgan + piŋgan /. The association rule proceeds from left to right through the copied string of segments, using the first three segments rather than the last three or any other subset. In general, reduplicative prefixing works in this manner: the association moves from the left edge of the copy inward. However, suffixing reduplication, as we'll see, works in the mirror image: the copied portion follows the base, and association begins at the right edge of the copy, moving left and inward.

As we have seen, and as our perusal of other patterns will show, languages reduplicate in different ways. For example, while Ilocano copies up to a CVC syllable, as in [taltalon], Amele copies at most a CV, even if the root has another consonant available for copy, as in [bubusalen] (not *[busbusalen]). Likewise, Ilocano creates VC reduplicants in vowel-initial roots, as in [ul-ulo], while Amele creates only a V reduplicant, as in [o-odon]. Yet without amendment, the above system would reduplicate Amele as if it were Ilocano.

There are several ways we can address cross-linguistic differences in reduplication – we may posit different types of underlying templates for the reduplicant, and we may intersperse other phonological rules which interact with reduplicative processes.

The Amele pattern can be captured with a simple adjustment to the template. Rather than have the reduplicant absorb as much segmental material as can fit within a syllable, Amele avoids coda consonants in reduplicants, and also avoids having its reduplicative segments fill out any empty onsets held by the base. Thus, we can propose first that the template is a coda-less syllable, specified as σ_{CV}, and second, that the rule of association does not allow the reduplicative segments to associate across a morpheme boundary to the root's syllable structure.

UR: / σ_{RED} + busal + en /   / σ_{RED} + od + on /

UR: $/ \sigma_{RED} + \text{busal} + \text{en} /$ $/ \sigma_{RED} + \text{od} + \text{on} /$

syllabify   σ   σ σ   σ   σ σ
                   /| /|\ | /|\
                   bu.sal   o.don

reduplicate   σ   σ σ   σ   σ σ
                   /| /|\ | /|\
              busal bu.sal   od   o.don

associate   σ   σ σ   σ   σ σ
               /| /| /|\ | | /|\
              busal bu.sal   od   o.don

reduplicant segments cannot spread to right or occupy coda position

stray erasure σ   σ σ   σ   σ σ
               /| /| /|\ | | /|\
               bu   bu.sal   o   o.don

The restrictions on the applications of these rules are challenging to formalize in terms other than specific limits on how the association between segments and prosodic elements can proceed in any given language. We will explore this aspect of phonological derivation in more detail in Chapter 12.

In the next several cases, we will explore languages whose reduplicative systems call for either a different template or some other phonological rule, or both. Let us turn first to Hawaiian, which actually has several patterns of reduplication – we will restrict the discussion here to its suffixing pattern.

11.4 Hawaiian

Examine the following data from Hawaiian ((Pukui and Elbert 1973).

(1)	ʔaːkaʔa	ʔaːkaʔakaʔa	'peeling; ruffled'
(2)	ʔakiu	ʔakiukiu	Redup. of *ʻakiu*
(3)	aːloha	aːlohaloha	'friendly, loving, lovable'
(4)	haːʔupu	haːʔupuʔupu	'to recall again and again'
(5)	hoːkake	hoːkakekake	'to roil, as mud'
(6)	hulei	huːleilei	Redup. of *hulei*
(7)	kiːpoho	kiːpohopoho	Redup. of *kīpoho*
(8)	kiːpoʔi	kiːpoʔipoʔi	Redup. of *kīpoʻi*
(9)	maʔewa	maːʔewaʔewa	'to treat roughly'
(10)	ʔoːhea	ʔoːheahea	'drowsy, sleepy'
(11)	ʔoːheu	ʔoːheuheu	'fuzzy'
(12)	piolo	pioloolo	Redup. of *piolo*

(13) puːehu   puːehuehu   'tousled; flaky'
(14) puːhaka   puːhakahaka   Redup. of *pūhaka*

Exercise 11.2   Describe the prosodic shape of the reduplicants in Hawaiian. You may find it useful to conduct syllabification of the data, and as you do so, you may assume any sequence of vowels is a diphthong only if they rise in height (or fall in sonority). Under what conditions does each shape variant appear?

There are numerous reduplicative shapes in Hawaiian. Some reduplicants are a pair of light syllables, either CV.CV as in [ʔaːkaʔa-kaʔa] and [kiːpoho-poho], or V.CV, as in in [puːehu-ehu] and [piolo-olo]. Others include a sequence of vowels which either syllabify as CV.V, as in [ʔoːhea-hea], or as monosyllabic CVV, as in [huːlei-lei]. The monosyllabic CVV form appears where the root has a final heavy syllable, while the bisyllabic form appears otherwise; that is, where the root's final syllable is light.

Exercise 11.3   Propose a template for the Hawaiian reduplicant.

There are two possible approaches to consider: the reduplicative suffix could be a pair of syllables, or a single foot. Most of the variants have two syllables at the surface, but a subset of reduplicants comprise a single syllable, albeit with a sequence of vowels, as in [ʔa.nai.nai].

We will adopt the foot-based account, but the two-syllable approach is at least plausible: if the reduplicant were underlyingly /σσ/, the association process could yield [ʔa.nai-na.i], with a two-syllable suffix. Some additional rule would be needed to collapse the reduplicant's syllables together under specific conditions: only where they are not separated by an onset and where the vowel in the second is higher than that in the first. Note, however, that this approach requires us to assume that each of the last two vowels in the reduplicant gets its own syllable. Otherwise, the system could generate *[ʔa.nai.ʔa.nai], in which the reduplicant contains two syllables, the second of which has a diphthong. To handle this, a stipulation restricting the size of the reduplicant syllables to one mora each is not out of the question, as we had a similar limitation on the form of the prefix syllable in Amele.

The alternative of using a foot template is nevertheless a simpler account, as long as the template is satisfied by either a pair of syllables or by a single heavy syllable. Recall from §10.5 that Hawaiian feet can consist of (CVː), (CV.CV), or (CVː.CV) sequences, where CVː syllables include those with diphthongs, but not (CV.CVː) sequences. We can thus use the template to allow bisyllabic suffixes for most types of roots, as well as monosyllabic CVː in final-heavy stems. This way, the reduplicant is always larger than a single light CV, and may extend to two syllables, as long as they conform to the set of possible feet.

Exercise 11.4 Provide a derivation of [ki:poho-poho] and [ʔa:nai-nai]. Note that as you perform the step of association, you will need to proceed right to left, as this is a suffixing pattern.

UR: / ki:poho + FT_{RED}/   / ʔa:nai + FT_{RED}/

syllabify
```
σ   σ   σ      ()FT          σ   σ      ()FT
/||  /|  /|                  /||  /||
ki:.po.ho                   ʔa:.nai
```

reduplicate
```
σ   σ   σ      ()FT          σ   σ      ()FT
/||  /|  /|                  /||  /||
ki:.po.ho   kipoho          ʔa:.nai    ʔānai
```

associate
```
σ   σ   σ      (σ  σ)FT       σ   σ      (σμμ)FT
/||  /|  /|     /| /|          /||  /||     /||
ki:.po.ho   ki.po.ho         ʔa:.nai    ʔā.nai
```

stray erasure
```
σ   σ   σ      (σ  σ)FT       σ   σ      (σμμ)FT
/||  /|  /|     /| /|          /||  /||     /||
ki:.po.ho   po.ho            ʔa:.nai    nai
```

The Hawaiian reduplication pattern differs from Amele and Ilocano in two significant ways: it targets a foot rather than a syllable, and it is suffixing rather than prefixing. These two details are handled quite easily by appealing to a different template and positioning it differently with respect to the root. Other reduplicative patterns differ in ways that suggest other phonological rules are relevant.

11.5 Kamaiura

Consider the following data from Kamaiura (Everett and Seki 1985).

(1)	ohuka	ohukahuka	'he laughed'
(2)	ojenupa	ojenupanupa	'he hit himself'
(3)	ereo	ereoreo	'you go'
(4)	omotumuŋ	omotumutumuŋ	'he shook it'
(5)	omokon	omokomokon	'he swallowed it'
(6)	apot	apoapot	'I jumped'

Exercise 11.5 Conduct an analysis of the reduplicative suffix in Kamaiura. As part of your analysis, you should conduct syllabification of the data.
- Describe the prosodic shape of the reduplicants.
- Is there any alternation evident in either the root or the suffix? Under what conditions does each shape variant appear?

The Kamaiura reduplicant comprises two syllables, copied from the right side (i.e., end) of the base. For example, the root [ohuka] reduplicates as [ohuka~huka]. Both CV and V are possible syllables within the reduplicant. For example, in [ereo~reo], the second syllable of the suffix is V, while in [apoapot], the first syllable of the suffix is V.

If the root ends in a consonant in unreduplicated contexts, as in [omotumuŋ], the consonant is lost from the base in reduplication, but maintained in the suffix, as in [omotumu~tumuŋ].

Exercise 11.6 Propose a template for the Kamaiura reduplicant, and devise a a rule to account for the root-final consonant deletion. Illustrate their interaction ordering the deletion rule relative to other reduplicative processes. You may use the symbol ~ to refer to a reduplicative morpheme boundary.

The reduplicant is best captured with a foot template. The rule to delete the final root consonant is as follows:

$$C \rightarrow \emptyset / \_\!\_ \,]_{RT} \sim$$

This deletes root-final consonants only before reduplicative boundaries. As such, it will not delete the final consonant of unreduplicated forms, and it will not delete the final consonant of the reduplicative suffix. The rule must follow all steps of reduplication, and since it is restricted in its environment, it leaves absolute word-final consonants untouched.

UR: / omokon + FT$_{RED}$ /

syllabify   σ σ σ   ()$_{FT}$
              | /| /|\
              o.mo.kon

reduplicate   σ σ σ   ()$_{FT}$
              | /| /|\
              o.mo.kon omokon

associate   σ σ σ   (σ σ)$_{FT}$
              | /| /|\   /| /|\
              o.mo.kon o.mo.kon

stray erasure σ σ σ   (σ σ)$_{FT}$
              | /| /|\   /| /|\
              o.mo.kon mo.kon

C-deletion   σ σ σ   (σ σ)$_{FT}$
              | /| /| /| /|\
              o.mo.ko mo.kon

The Kamaiura data suggest something additionally notable about reduplication – that certain structures are not introduced that are not also seen in unreduplicated forms. For example, Hawaiian and Amele do not produce reduplicants with codas, and likewise neither language has coda consonants within words – Hawaiian even forbids them word-finally. Meanwhile, Ilocano tolerates reduplicative codas, and not coincidentally it tolerates codas within other words in non-final position. In Kamaiura, the roots clearly allow codas in word-final position, but when the root-final consonant is rendered a medial coda because of suffixation, it is deleted.

One last facet of these data is worth mentioning: the form [atoatop] is problematic. By the above analysis, the step of association would presumably generate the intermediate form of /a.to.p~a.top/, in which the final /p/ of the base serves as the onset for the penultimate syllable. There is nothing in our process of association which suggests onset positions are not to be filled with consonants. However, if the base-final /p/ is an onset, it does not meet the environment for C-deletion, so the analysis predicts that it will not be deleted. We therefore need to add some stipulation that blocks the step of association from allowing /p/ to syllabify as an onset. Essentially, the rule needs a condition requiring reduplicative segments and base segments not to occur in the same syllable – clearly languages like Ilocano do not obey any such generalization, but it is a necessary component for the analysis of Kamaiura to be complete.

11.6 Mangayari

Another example of an interaction between reduplication and other phonological processes of deletion can be seen in Mangayari. Examine the following data (from Merlan 1982), paying attention to which consonants of the base end up not being realized in the reduplicated forms.

(1) gabuɟi   gababuɟi   'old person'
(2) jirag   jirirag   'father'
(3) ɟimgan   ɟimgimgan   'knowledgeable one'
(4) waŋgiɟ   waŋgaŋgiɟ   'child'
(5) mujgɟi   mujgɟujgɟi 'having a dog'

Exercise 11.7 Describe the reduplicative system in more detail, and provide a specific description of any alternations that are evident in the data. As part of your analysis, you should conduct a tentative syllabification of the data.

• Describe the prosodic shape of the reduplicants.
• Is there any alternation evident in either the root or the prefix? Under what conditions does each shape variant appear?

The reduplicant is expressed with the addition of a syllable prefix. The prefix is more than simply a copy of the first base syllable: it includes a copy of any consonant that serves as onset of the base's second syllable; thus, for example, for /gabuɟi/, the /b/ of the root forms part of the reduplicative prefix in [gababuɟi]. Related to this, the reduplicant boundary does not coincide with a syllable boundary. In general, the reduplicant shapes include CVC and CVCC.

In all cases, the root-initial consonant is deleted from reduplicated forms, despite this consonant persisting in the prefix. In /gabuɟi/, the initial [g] remains in the prefix, but is deleted from the base in [gababuɟi].

Exercise 11.8 Propose a template for the Mangayari prefix and devise a a rule to account for the root-initial consonant deletion. Illustrate their interaction by ordering the deletion rule relative to other reduplicative processes. You may use the symbol ~ to refer to a reduplicative morpheme boundary.

The reduplicative template is a syllable, unspecified for weight. The rule to delete the root-initial consonant is as follows:

$$C \rightarrow \emptyset \, / \, {}_{RT}[\underline{\quad}$$

The Mangayari rule of consonant loss deletes base-initial consonants at reduplicative boundaries, and thus, like Kamaiura, it will not delete consonants in unreduplicated forms, nor will it delete consonants within the reduplicant itself. However, unlike Kamaiura, the deletion rule must precede the step of association, to ensure that a maximal number of consonants is retained in the reduplicant. The following derivation illustrates this.

UR: / σ_{RED} + ɾimgan /

syllabify
```
      σ          σ   σ
                /|\  /|\
                ɾim.gan
```

reduplicate
```
      σ          σ   σ
                /|\  /|\
    ɾimgan      ɾim.gan
```

C-deletion
```
      σ          σ   σ
                |\  /|\
    ɾimgan      im.gan
```

associate
```
      σ          σ   σ
     /|\        |\  /|\
    ɾimgan      im.gan
```

stray erasure
```
      σ          σ   σ
     /|\        |\  /|\
    ɾimg        im.gan
```

The position of C-deletion before association ensures that there is an empty onset position at the beginning of the base, to which a consonant from the reduplicant can associate. If C-deletion were to apply later, the [g] of the reduplicant would not have a syllabic position to associate to, and the result would otherwise be *[ɟimimgan]. The only other way to avoid such a result is to allow the reduplicative syllable to absorb a complex coda, intermediately allowing /ɟimg-ɟimgan/, and rely on reassociation to render the [g] as an onset following the deletion of the root's initial consonant. While this may work, it introduces the notion of allowing intermediate stages of syllabification to be tolerant of complex margins despite them being absent from surface forms.

The Mangayari data deserve some additional comment. First, like Kamaiura, there is a deletion process which affects the base in reduplicative contexts, and while the rule that does this seems to resolve consonant sequences, it may do more than necessary, since in this case, the language clearly does tolerate medial sequences in other contexts. Second, we have proceeded with this analysis assuming a very concrete sequence of steps in which reduplication of a prefix cleanly precedes a deletion process. Alternatively one could imagine an analysis in which reduplication is strictly infixing – thus, the initial segment *is* part of the base, rather than its stranded copy, and the VC or VCC sequence that follows is infixed between the base's initial consonant and the remainder of the root.

It is difficult to formalize infixation in the rule-based framework that we have adopted, but in the following chapter we will encounter a different approach to phonological derivation that allows such an analysis to hold sway.

11.7 Ponapean

Many of the reduplicative patterns we have seen thus far have involved what we elsewhere called alternations with zero – the size of the reduplicant adheres to a particular prosodic unit, and the number of segments that remain in partial reduplication may be more or less than the general target, as a function of processes of deletion.

Insertion processes are also possible, as are other types of alternations in which the segments of the reduplicant change form depending on their phonological context. Ponapean provides an illustrative example of each. Examine the following data (from Rehg and Sohl 1981), which represent a subset of the Ponapean reduplicative paradigm, and pay particular attention to the form of the reduplicative prefix.

(1)	cac	'to writhe'	cancac
(2)	cal	'to make a clicklike sound'	cancal
(3)	cir	'narrow'	cincir
(4)	kaŋ	'to eat'	kaŋkaŋ
(5)	kik	'to kick'	kiŋkik
(6)	lal	'to make a sound'	lallal
(7)	mem	'sweet'	memmem
(8)	nur	'contract'	nunnur
(9)	pap	'to swim'	pampap
(10)	pʷupʷ	'to fall'	pʷumpʷupʷ
(11)	rer	'to tremble'	rerrer
(12)	sar	'to fade'	sansar
(13)	sel	'to be tied'	sensel
(14)	sile	'to guard'	sinsile
(15)	sis	'to speak with an accent'	sinsis
(16)	tar	'to strike, of a fish'	tantar
(17)	til	'to penetrate'	tintil
(18)	tit	'build a wall'	tintit
(19)	tot	'frequent'	tontot
(20)	linenek	'oversexed'	lillinenek
(21)	lirooro	'protective'	lillirooro
(22)	pepe	'to swim to'	pempepe
(23)	rere	'to skin or peel'	rerrere
(24)	sarek	'to uproot'	sansarek
(25)	tilip	'to mend thatch'	tintilip
(26)	tune	'to attach in a sequence'	tuntune
(27)	cep	'to begin'	cepicep
(28)	cep	'to kick'	cepecep
(29)	lop	'to be cut'	lopilop
(30)	par	'to cut'	parapar
(31)	pet	'to be squeezed'	petipet
(32)	pʷil	'to flow'	pʷilipʷil
(33)	was	'obnoxious'	wasawas
(34)	caman	'to remember'	camacaman
(35)	cepek	'to kick'	cepecepek
(36)	kacoore	'to subtract'	kacikacoore
(37)	ker	'to flow'	kereker
(38)	lɔŋe	'to pass across'	lɔŋilɔŋe
(39)	sipet	'to shake out'	sipisipet
(40)	wasas	'to stagger'	wasawasas

Exercise 11.9   Identify the various shapes of the reduplicative prefix, and describe the condition under which each appears. Also make note of any segmental changes that occur. You may initially conduct this analysis in terms of C and V, but ultimately you should attempt to propose a template for the prefix using some prosodic unit.

Among these forms, there are two basic shapes that appear: some reduplicants are CVC, as in [memmem] and [sansarek], while others are CVCV, as in [kacikacoore] and [camacaman]. We can consider the CVC prefix to comprise one syllable, while the CVCV prefix is two.

In forms with monosyllabic prefixes, the final consonant of the reduplicant changes in some cases from its correspondent in the base, as in [kiŋkik] and [tintil]. Many of these examples involve nasalization of the reduplicative consonant, but some involve other kinds of sonorants, as in [lillirooro] and [lillinenek].

In forms with bisyllabic prefixes, the consonants of the reduplicant are always an exact copy of consonants in the base. The second vowel, however, can come from the base in some cases, as in [cepecepek], or be some other vowel, as in [kacikacoore] and [lɔŋilɔŋe]. For bisyllabic prefixes where the root is itself monosyllabic, the second vowel of the prefix varies between a copy of the root vowel, as in [cepecep] and [parapar], and some other vowel, usually [i], as in [cepicep] and [lopilop].

Note that in lots of forms, the root is so small that reduplication is complete – in such cases, it may seem debatable whether to maintain the assumption that prefixing is occuring. However, there are several reasons why this assumption should stay in place. First, since all longer forms reduplicate via prefixing, we can maintain consistency by assuming prefixing across the board – it would be a far more complex account to argue that longer forms are prefixed but shorter forms are suffixed. Second, even among some fully reduplicated forms, the first element sometimes undergoes some segmental change (often nasalization). Cross-linguistically, we tend to see phonological processes applying to reduplicative affixes and not bases, rather than to bases and not affixes. The converse is indeed possible, but the account again is simpler if we assume prefixing throughout.

The choice between the two reduplicative shapes is sensitive to the nature of the consonants of the root, as the second consonant of the prefix (which copies the second consonant of the root) is potentially adjacent to the initial consonant of the root. Where the consonants are of different places of articulation, the bisyllabic reduplicant form appears, as in [cepicep], [petipet], and [kereker].

If the consonants are of the same place of articulation, a monosyllabic reduplicant appears, but the pattern is more nuanced:

- Identical sonorants simply double up, rendering a CVC prefix, as in [memmem] and [rerrer].
- Sequences of non-identical sonorants assimilate, such that the final consonant of the reduplicant assimilates to the initial consonant of the base, as in [lillirooro] and [lillinenek].
- Other homorganic sonorants undergo nasalization in the prefix, where the second consonant of the prefix becomes a nasal consonant, as in [sensel] and [tantar].
- Identical consonants also undergo nasalization in the prefix, as in [kiŋkik], [pampap], and [tontot].

The descriptive facts about Ponapean reduplication are more complex than presented here, as several additional subsets occur, including a light-syllable form and vowel-initial forms, each of which only occur under very specific circumstances. There are also some homorganic coronal forms that nevertheless reduplicate with the bisyllabic shape. As these other subpatterns distract from the main point here, which is that segment alternations can be observed in reduplicated affixes, they are left out of the discussion. The reader should consult Rehg (1984), McCarthy and Prince (1986), and Kennedy (2003) for more thorough treatments of Ponapean reduplication.

Independently of the consonant alternations, the shape of the Ponapean reduplicant may be a single heavy syllable or a pair of light syllables. We thus have an analytical choice of whether to propose a syllable or foot as the template for the reduplicant. Other research on the language, and inclusion of other subsets of data not discussed here, would point us to the foot template, but we can entertain either approach here. In short, a syllable template approach would need the prefix to maximally fill to CVC, and other rules would be needed to bring out the second vowel to account for the bisyllabic forms. Conversely, the foot approach would always produce a CVCV prefix, and subsequent rules would remove the second vowel under several circumstances of homorganic consonants.

Exercise 11.10   Consider both the syllable-template and foot-template approaches to the Ponapean shape alternation. Propose a rule for each approach that generates the complementary shape form. That is, specify a rule that expands a monosyllabic prefix to two syllables under the appropriate circumstances, and another that reduces a bisyllabic prefix to a monosyllable, again under the appropriate circumstances. Use the roots /sel/ and /cep/, and develop systems that generate the intermediate forms /sel-sel/ and /cepi-cep/. We will worry about the nasalization in [sensel] in a later exercise.

The rule that accompanies a syllable template is as follows. It inserts a vowel between two consonants of non-identical place. The advantage of this rule is that it also produces the inserted vowel for monosyllabic roots. However, it relies on the odd convention of [−α] as a feature value for place features.

Insertion   Ø → V / [+cons, α place] __ [+cons, −α place]

The effect of the rule is shown below:

UR	σ + sel	σ + cep
Reduplicate	sel sel	cep + cep
Insertion	sel sel	cepi cep

The converse rule that accompanies a foot template is presented below. It deletes a vowel from between consonants that are homorganic. This rule more plausibly uses [α] as a feature value, but this approach needs to allow the foot template to generate an additional vowel for monosyllabic roots such as /cep/.

V → Ø / [+cons, α place] __ [+cons, α place]

The effect of this rule is shown below:

UR	Ft + sel	Ft + cep
Reduplicate	seli sel	cepi cep
Deletion	sel sel	cepi cep

Both approaches produce a set of intermediate forms in which homorganic consonants are adjacent and non-homorganic consonants are separated by a vowel. Thus, while the shape alternation is accounted for, the segment alternation is not yet.

Exercise 11.11 Propose a sufficient number of phonological rules to handle the segment alternations in the Ponapean prefix.

Sonorant assimilation   [+son, α place] → [β manner] / __ [+son, α place, β manner]

Nasal substitution   [+cons, α place] → [+nas] / __ [−son, α place]

The first rule assimilates a sonorant in manner to a following homorganic sonorant. The second rule nasalizes any consonant before a homorganic obstruent. These rules may co-occur with and follow either rule of shape alternation we used in Exercise 11.10, because the shape rules produce the same basic set of intermediate forms.

Like other patterns we saw earlier, this approach needs a rule of template satisfaction, plus other rules to handle alternations seen within subsets of data. In this case, one rule is needed to account for differences in syllabification

among the reduplications, while several other rules are necessary to account
for segmental alternations just among monosyllabic prefixes.

So far we have seen that reduplication challenges any attempt to describe
regularity in its form within a given language. A reduplicative morpheme may
alternate in size, copying more or less of the base, depending on other factors.
Meanwhile, if we see reduplicants as derived copies of their bases, they may be
seen to delete or insert segments in this copying process. Last, there are
examples where the copied segments may undergo some kind of feature-
changing alternation. Much of this is difficult if not impossible to capture
without an explicit model that duplicates the base's segmental string and
associates it to some sort of prosodic element.

The fact that prosodic elements are relevant units in morphophonological derivations is again why we include reduplication under the
aegis of prosodic morphology, but it is not the only manifestation of prosodic
morphology.

11.8 Word minimality

The morphological role of prosodic units in phonological representations is
seen in another domain, that of word minimality. Languages that show
minimality effects respect specific requirements about the size of at least some
of their word classes. In short, a minimality condition is a requirement that a
word be at least as large as some stipulated allowable mininum – often, such
minimum sizes are expressible in terms of prosodic units.

English provides a basic example. We may note that content morphemes
in English – nouns, verbs, adjectives, and adverbs, as well as quantifiers, are
always at least a certain size: they contain at least a long vowel (alternatively
called tense), or a short vowel (alternatively called lax) accompanied by a coda
consonant.

The traditional terminology of long and short to describe English vowels
distinguishes long vowels as the set of vowels which may occur in open final
syllables from short vowels, the set of vowels which cannot. In much modern
phonological work, this distinction is replaced by tense and lax; all short
vowels are lax, while long vowels are either tense or diphthongal. Irrespective
of the terminology, there are two sets of vowels in English, distinguished by
restrictions on their distribution.

We may establish a prosodic approach to this pattern, claiming that short
vowels are monomoraic but long vowels are bimoraic. The restricted
distribution of short monomoraic vowels – i.e., their absence from final open
syllables – is explained by a bimoraic minimal requirement, satisfied only if

317

the short vowel co-occurs with an additional moraic coda consonant. Since long vowels are themselves bimoraic, there is no need for an additional coda consonant to satisfy word minimality in English.

While this is an illustrative example, it is difficult to show concretely that long vowels are distinct from short ones in their moraic structure, because no two vowels are distinct just in their length. Indeed, the only evidence for moraic quantity of vowels in English is from this minimality requirement. Even so, the fact that the pattern relies on a bimoraic mininum in particular dovetails with numerous other cross-linguistic phenomena in which bimoraicity itself is implicated.

Another example of minimality can be seen in Minto (Hargus and Tuttle 1997: 190), where verbs alternate in size. In the data below, a verb that carries a prefix is itself monosyllabic, as in [dənæ-ʈəx], but if the verb is unprefixed, an epenthetic vowel is inserted beforehand, as in [ə-ʈəx]. This helps the form achieve a minimal size; from the given data the goal could be bimoraic or bisyllabic. Hypothetically a bisyllabic root would require no epenthesis, and if this were truly the case we would have direct evidence of a minimality effect, such that sufficiently sized forms would be unchanged while undersized ones undergo augmentation. Nevertheless, such forms are absent, but since all monosyllabic verb roots receive the same extra vowel, we infer that it is epenthetic, and we also infer that it is augmentative, since it only appears with words that would otherwise be monosyllabic.

11.9 Bisyllabic minimality in Minto verbs

Examine the following data from Minto (Hargus and Tuttle 1997: 190):

Unprefixed roots with epenthesis	Prefixed roots without epenthesis
ə-ʈəx 'he/she is crying'	cf. dənæ-ʈəx 'the man is crying'
ə-bæʈ 'it's cooking'	cf. łuk'æ-bæʈ 'fish is cooking'
ə-ʧaṣ 'it's melting'	cf. ṣəṣk'ʊx-ʧaṣ 'bear fat is melting'

11.10 Trukese

Now let us turn to a language that quite clearly illustrates a minimality effect in action. Examine the following data from Trukese (Goodenough and Sugita 1980), paying attention to the length of vowels.

	Unsuffixed	Gloss	Suffixed	Gloss
(1)	omos	'turban shell'	omosuj	'my turban shell'
	məkɨr	'head'	məkɨrej	'my head'
	pisek	'goods'	pisekij	'my goods'
	sæfej	'medicine'	sæfejej	'my medicine'
	səkɨr	'back'	səkɨrij	'my back'
(2)	tiip	'emotion'	tipen	'of emotions'
	tʃɨik	'basket'	tʃikɨn	'of baskets'
	pəək	'chip'	pəkən	'of chips'
	aatʃ	'handle'	atʃan	'of handles'
	wuut	'interior'	wutun	'of interiors'

Exercise 11.12 a. Identify the forms of the suffixes.

b. There are vowels that appear in the suffix column that are absent from the unsuffixed column. Where do these vowels come from? Compose a rule to account for their alternation.

The suffix meaning 'my' is /j/. The suffix meaning 'of' is /n/.

The vowels that directly precede these suffixes are actually associated with the roots. The consonant of the suffixes is invariant, but the vowel changes unpredictably across forms. Since the nature of the vowel is unpredictable, we presume it is part of the root. This effect is analogous to what we saw for Fijian in §3.2.

As a consequence, we conclude that the roots alternate between having a final vowel, retained in suffixed forms, which is deleted in unsuffixed contexts.

$$V \rightarrow \emptyset / \underline{\quad}]_{\text{WD}}$$

Exercise 11.13 Describe any other alternation you see in the forms of the roots in Trukese. Which roots alternate, and which don't? Describe the precise conditions under which this alternation occurs, and identify the underlying form of alternating roots.

The roots in (2) alternate in the length of their first vowel: there is a single long vowel in their unsuffixed forms and a pair of short vowels in their suffixed forms. The second vowel is missing when the root is unsuffixed, as seen by comparing [tiip] with [tipen] and [tʃɨik] with [tʃikɨn].

The non-alternating roots in (1) all contain two vowels in their unsuffixed forms, as in [məkɨr] and [pisek], but three in their suffixed forms, as in [məkɨrej] and [pisekij].

There are insufficient data here to choose a precise underlying form for the alternating roots. They could have either an underlying long vowel that is

shortened in one circumstance, or an underlying short vowel that is
lengthened in the opposite set of circumstances.

Exercise 11.14 Determine the conditions that would be necessary for a shortening rule and a
lengthening rule to work.

V → long / __ C]$_{WD}$
V → short / __ C V

Both rules achieve a similar result: the vowel is long if it is the only vowel, but
is short in the presence of another vowel. This suggests a basic fact of
minimality in Trukese nouns: each word must have at least two vowels, either
as a single long vowel, or as a pair of short vowels. Reframed in terms of
prosody, we can say that Trukese requires nouns to be at least bimoraic.

Exercise 11.15 Now examine the following subset. Describe the alternation you see here, and
propose a rule to account for it.

(1) petʃe   'foot'   petʃeej   'my foot'
     tikka   'coconut oil'   tikkaaj   'my coconut oil'
     etiru   'coconut matting'   etiruuj   'my coconut matting'
     tʃuutʃu   'urine'   tʃuutʃuuj   'my urine'

The second vowel of these roots alternates in length. Before the suffix [-j],
the root vowels are long; when word-final, they are short. We could propose a
rule that lengthens the root vowels before [j] or shortens them word-finally;
since vowels do not lengthen before suffix /-j/ in the forms in §11.10, we will
have a simpler account attributing this pattern to a rule of shortening:

V → short / __]$_{WD}$

This rule needs to follow the rule of final vowel deletion, to ensure that a word-
final long vowel is not first shortened and then deleted.

Exercise 11.16 Now examine this last set of data. What are the implications of these forms for
the final-vowel-shortening rule and the Trukese bimoraic minimum?

[təə]   'islet'
[maa]   'behavior'
[oo]   'omen'
[soo]   'precipitate'
[nɨɨ]   'unripe coconut'

These forms apparently have no suffix, and also do not undergo the rule of
final vowel shortening. Note that applying the rule would reduce these forms

to a single mora – thus, whatever motivates the rule in Exercise 11.14 (to account for the length alternation in CVC forms) also prevents the shortening rule from applying.

Trukese is an example of a system in which certain phonological rules apply – ones that delete word-final short vowels and shorten word-final long vowels. Yet the effects of these rules are mitigated by limits on how much structure they can remove from a form – evidently, the limit is that the rules can apply as long as they leave no less than a bimoraic minimum. This is similar to the Kamaiura condition on association from Exercise 11.6: a phonological rule generally applies, but not if it generates some kind of structure that the language apparently avoids.

11.11 Templatic morphology

Another way in which prosodic categories may play a role in phonology is in templatic morphology, a process in which the realization of some morphological function is via shape rather than by a string of segments.

Consider the following pairs of forms from Arabic:

darasa	'he studied'	darrasa	'he taught'
ħamala	'he carried'	ħammala	'he loaded'
rasama	'he drew'	rassama	'he made draw'
ʃariba	'he drank'	ʃarraba	'he made drink'

The first column contains forms in third-person past, while the second has derived forms with some element of causation. They differ in the length of their second consonant; we might assume that to derive a causative, one need only lengthen that consonant. However, the story is more complicated than this, as other derived forms have different shapes.

Before delving into the role of prosodic shapes, we should check for other dimensions of morphological complexity, because their third-person past interpretation suggests they include more than a root. Examine the following data, and determine whether any segmental afixes are present.

wadʒada	'he found'
wadʒadat	'she found'
wadʒadta	'you (m) found'
wadʒadti	'you (f) found'
wadʒadtu	'I found'
baʕaθa	'he sent'
baʕaθat	'she sent'
baʕaθta	'you (m) sent'

baʕaθti   'you (f) sent'
baʕaθtu   'I sent'

Exercise 11.17   Identify all affixes and their function in these data.

There are five agreement affixes that indicate person and gender agreement: /-a/ 'he,' /-at/ 'she,' /-ta/ 'you (m),' /-ti/ 'you (f),' and /-tu/ 'I.' This leaves [wadʒad-] as a stem meaning 'found' and [baʕaθ] meaning 'sent,' but these sequences are themselves still morphologically complex. Examine the next set of data and identify any new morphemes:

wudʒida   'he was found'
wudʒidat   'she was found'
wudʒidta   'you (m) were found'
wudʒidti   'you (f) were found'
wudʒidtu   'I was found'
buʕiθa   'he was sent'
buʕiθat   'she was sent'
buʕiθta   'you (m) were sent'
buʕiθti   'you (f) were sent'
buʕiθtu   'I was sent'

Exercise 11.18   Identify any morphemes that are not present in Exercise 11.17.

These forms differ in that the verbs are now passive. The vowels within the stems comprise [u] and [i], whereas in the previous exercise, the stems only contain [a]. This suggests that the vowels indicate voice: [u] and [i] interspersed among the consonants indicate passive, while [a] indicates active voice. As a consequence, it seems the consonants themselves indicate the verb roots.

The distinct function of the consonant and vowels leads us to refer to this phenomenon as non-linear or non-concatenative morphology. The segments of the voice morpheme are not placed as an affix before or after the segments of the root. Not all morphology in Arabic is non-linear, as the agreement morphemes are clearly suffixes, but the relationship between the root and other kinds of derivational morphology often is non-linear like this.

Exercise 11.19   Now examine the following set of data, with the non-linear nature of Arabic morphology in mind. Describe the relationship between prosodic shapes and morphology. You may refer to patterns with CV positions or with prosodic units.

darasa   'he studied'   ħamala   'he carried'
darrasa   'he taught'   ħammala   'he loaded'

darsun	'a lesson'	ħimlun	'cargo'
darraasun	'student'	ħammaalun	'porter'
diraasah	'studies'	ħimaal	'trade of porter'
madrasah	'Koranic school'		
daaris	'studying'	ħaamil	'carrying'
dasama	'he drew'	ʃariba	'he drank'
rassama	'he made draw'	ʃarraba	'he made drink'
dasmun	'a drawing'	ʃarbun	'a drink'
rassaamun	'draftsman'	ʃarraabun	'drunkard'
risaamah	'ordination'		
marsamun	'studio'	maʃrabun	'tavern'
raasim	'drawing'	ʃaarib	'drinking'

These data illustrate how specific prosodic shapes carry some derivational function; for example, the frame CVC:VC indicates some kind of causative, while CVCC-un indicates a nominalized form. We can observe the CVC:VC template by comparing [darasa] 'he studied' with [darrasa] 'he taught,' which is an idiosyncratic step beyond 'he made study.' A similar comparison is available for [ħamala] 'he carried' and [ħammala] 'he loaded,' for [rasama] 'he drew' and [rassama] 'he made draw,' and for [ʃaraba] 'he drank' and [ʃarraba] 'he made drink.' Likewise, the recurrent CVCC-un form is observable in [darsun] 'lesson,' [ħimlun] 'cargo,' [rasmun] 'drawing,' and [ʃarbun] 'drink (noun).'

Alternatively, we could use prosodic elements to indicate these derivational morphemes. For example, instead of expressing CAUSATIVE with CVC:VC, we could use /$\sigma_{\mu\mu}\sigma_{\mu\mu}$/ to show that the template includes two heavy syllables. However, this approach requires some way to ensure that the coda of the first syllable shares the same consonant as the onset of the second.

One way of doing this is to note that there are generalities over the set of different templates, which emerge as we inspect the full list of templates. Examine the following templatic forms, which are expressed in both CV terms and prosodic terms.

Example	*Gloss*	*CV template*	*Prosodic template*
darasa	'he studied'	CVCVC	$\sigma\sigma$ + a
darrasa	'he taught'	CVC:VC	$\sigma_{\mu\mu}\sigma$ + a
darsun	'a lesson'	CVCC-un	σ + un
darraasun	'student'	CVC:V:C-un	$\sigma_{\mu\mu}\sigma_{\mu\mu}$ + un
diraasah	'studies'	CVCV:C-ah	$\sigma\sigma_{\mu\mu}$ + ah
madrasah	'Koranic school'	ma-CCVC-ah	ma-σ + ah
daaris	'studying'	CV:CVC	$\sigma_{\mu\mu}\sigma$

Note that for any template, only penultimate syllables may contain long vowels. Other heavy syllables are always closed. A more detailed analysis of these forms would follow from this observation, but is beyond the scope of this chapter. In essence, the system must associate consonant melodies to prosodic templates in such a way to ensure that all root consonants appear, all affix segments appear, and non-penultimate syllables do not contain long vowels. We have not yet developed the notational tools to pursue this in this textbook, but the system would favor forms like [darsun] over alternatives like *[darasun] or *[drasun], and [darraasun] over *[daarassun] or [daaraasun]. In the following chapter, we will learn about an approach to phonology that centers on ensuring phonological forms meet output demands, rather than arise through an assembly line of phonological changes.

Summary

In this chapter we have seen how the prosodic categories of earlier chapters play a role in phonological systems beyond simply organizing segments into rhythmic units. The syllable and foot, which are relevant in other domains like tone and stress assignment, can act as units in underlying representations of morphemes. This is true of the reduplicative patterns we examined earlier in this chapter, as well as the derivational morphemes covered in Arabic at the conclusion. In the latter case, a prosodic element carries some morphological function, and rather than link to a reduplicated sequence, it merely provides the structure for the otherwise unassociated segmental melodies of roots and affixes.

With this chapter we have rounded out a broad representation of the phenomena to be observed in the phonology of the world's languages. Segmental phenomena such as alternations, insertion, and deletion provide insight into the nature of the phoneme, allophony, the role of features and natural classes, and representation of segments and rules that affect them. Not all phenomena are easily modeled with simple rules over linear sequences of sounds, however; we thus expanded the scope of phonological representation to include the syllable as an organizational unit, and in so doing we found that the same element plays a role in the distribution of tone and stress. Last, we arrived in this chapter at an understanding that the prosodic units may themselves be morphological objects, introduced in derivations and associated to the segmental components of other morphemes.

Along the way some recurrent questions have arisen – notably, whenever we have compared alternative analyses, we have chosen the one which requires fewer rules and fewer ad hoc notational devices. We have also noted that certain types of processes seem to recur across languages, and that certain rules have similar effects in languages that are unrelated and have no record of contact with each other. Last, we have begun to note phonological processes which seem to apply up to a point, but which are limited by some extra statement that blocks them.

Some of these questions have been so prominent in the field of phonology that our theories of representation and derivation have changed in ways intended to address them, and we turn to these advanced perspectives on phonology in the next and final chapter.

Key terms

reduplication
base
reduplicant
template
association
correspondent
stray erasure
minimality
non-concatenative
non-linear

References and further reading

Everett, Dan, and Lucy Seki. 1985. Reduplication and CV skeleta in Kamaiurá. *Linguistic Inquiry* 16: 326–330.

Gafos, Adamantios. 1998. A-templatic reduplication. *Linguistic Inquiry* 29: 515–527.

Gleason, H. Allan. 1955. *An Introduction to Descriptive Linguistics*. New York: Henry Holt and Company.

Goodenough, Ward H., and Hiroshi Sugita. 1990. *Trukese–English Dictionary*. Philadelphia: American Philosophical Society.

Hamp, Eric P. 1966. Studies in Sierra Miwok. *International Journal of American Linguistics* 32: 236–241.

Hargus, Sharon, and Siri Tuttle. 1997. Augmentation as affixation in Athabaskan languages. *Phonology* 14.2: 177–202.

Kaufman, Terrence. 1971. *Tzeltal Phonology and Morphology*. Berkeley: University of California Berkeley Press.

Kennedy, Robert. 2002. A stress-based approach to Ponapean reduplication. In *Proceedings of West Coast Conference on Formal Linguistics* 21. Somervill, MA: Cascadilla Press.

Kennedy, Robert. 2003. Confluence in phonology: evidence from Micronesian reduplication. Doctoral dissertation, University of Arizona.

Kim, Young-Seok. 1984. Aspects of Korean morphology. Doctoral dissertation, University of Texas, Austin.

McCarthy, John J. 1979. Formal problems in Semitic phonology and morphology. Doctoral dissertation, Massachusetts Institute of Technology.

McCarthy, John J., and Alan Prince. 1986. Prosodic morphology. Ms., University of Massachusetts and Brandeis University.

McCarthy, John J., and Alan Prince. 1990a. Foot and word in prosodic morphology: the Arabic broken plural. *Natural Language and Linguistic Theory* 8: 209–283.

McCarthy, John J., and Alan Prince. 1990b. Prosodic morphology and templatic morphology. In M. Eid and J. McCarthy (eds.), *Perspectives on Arabic Linguistics: Papers from the Second Symposium*. Amsterdam: Benjamins, 1–51.

Merlan, Francesca. 1982. *Mangarayi*. Lingua Descriptive Studies 4. Amsterdam: North-Holland.

Prentice, D. J. 1971. *The Murut Languages of Sabah*. Pacific Linguistics, Series C, no. 18. Canberra: Australian National University.

Pukui, Mary Kawena, and Samuel H. Elbert. 1986. *Hawaiian Dictionary*. Honolulu: University Press of Hawaii.

Rehg, Kenneth. 1984. Nasal Substitution rules in Ponapean. In B. W. Bender (ed.), *Studies in Micronesian Linguistics*. Canberra: Pacific Linguistics, 317–337.

Rehg, Kenneth, and Damian G. Sohl. 1981. *Ponapean Reference Grammar*. Honolulu: University Press of Hawaii.

Roberts, John R. 1987. *Amele*. Croom Helm Descriptive Grammar Series. London: Croom Helm.

Review exercises

Tzeltal

Examine the reduplicated forms in Tzeltal (Kaufman 1971). Conduct a morphological analysis of these data; you will note that reduplication co-occurs with another affix.

Root	Reduplicated	Gloss
nit	nititan	'push'
net'	net'et'an	'press'
haʃ	haʃaʃan	'feel with palm'
ʧol	ʧololan	'make rows'
p'uj	p'ujujan	'grind in fingers'

a. Describe the shape of the reduplicant and its position relative to the root.

b. Construct an analysis using sequential rules to model the pattern.

Korean

Examine the reduplicated forms in Korean (Kim 1984):

culuk	cululuk	'dribbling'
asak	asasak	'with a crutch'
t'aliŋ	t'aliliŋ	'ting-ting'
holok	hololok	'sipping'
allok	allolok	'mottled'

a. Describe the shape of the reduplicant and its position relative to the root.

b. Construct an analysis using sequential rules to model the pattern.

Timugon Murut

Examine the reduplicated forms in Timugon Murut (Prentice 1971):

bulud	bubulud	'hill'
tuluʔ	tutuluʔ	'point at'
dondoʔ	dondondoʔ	'one'
indimo	indidimo	'five times'
ompod	ompopod	'flatter'

a. Describe the shape of the reduplicant and its position relative to the root, with attention to any divergent subpatterns.

b. Construct an analysis using sequential rules that handles the range of reduplicative shapes and patterns.

Lardil

Take some time to examine the Lardil data (Halle 1973).

Uninflected	Acc. non-fut	Acc.fut.	Gloss
mela	melan	melaṛ	'sea'
wanka	wankan	wankaṛ	'arm'
kuŋka	kuŋkan	kuŋkaṛ	'groin'
tjempe	tjempen	tjempeṛ	'mother's father'

wiʈe	wiʈen	wiʈeɽ	'interior'
jalul	jalulun	jaluluɽ	'flame'
majar	majaran	majaraɽ	'rainbow'
wiwal	wiwalan	wiwalaɽ	'bush mango'
jilijil	jilijilin	jilijiliwuɽ	'species of oyster'

a. Conduct a morphological analysis in which you identify roots, affixes, and alternations that are relevant to each.

b. Compose rules to account for alternations you find in the suffixes and roots.

c. You will need one rule that affects word-final segments, but it does not apply in all circumstances. Describe the specific context in which this rule cannot apply.

Sierra Miwok

Examine the following data from Sierra Miwok (Hamp 1966). Each verb root has several shapes, and the shape is determined by the suffix that attaches to it. In other words, these are prosodic shape variants for the roots.

Stem 1	Stem 2	Stem 3	Stem 4	Gloss
loot	lot	lottuʔ	lotʔu	'catch'
ʔinn	ʔinih	ʔinniʔ	ʔinʔɨ	'come'
lakh	lakɨh	lakkɨh	lakhɨ	'appear'
mussa	musah	mussaʔ	musʔa	'be ashamed'
kowta	kowat	kowwat	kowta	'bump into'
hɨɨja	hɨjah	hɨjjaʔ	hɨjʔa	'arrive'
nocuu	nocuh	noccuʔ	nocʔu	'cry'
hasuul	hasul	hassul	haslu	'ask'

a. Determine the basic prosodic shape chosen by each group of stems. You may use CV templates or prosodic templates for this task. Note that the stem 2 form for 'catch' is exceptional; the data are otherwise regular.

b. Propose underlying representations for each root. Are any segments here inserted by default?

c. Comment on the relationship between the consonant melodies and vowel melodies.

CHAPTER 12 ADVANCED THEORIES

Learning objectives

- Recognize the shortcomings of linear phonology
- Interpret and manipulate feature-geometric representations
- Understand the mechanisms of Optimality Theory
- Propose plausible competing candidates
- Understand and propose formal constraints

Introduction

In this book we have encountered a number of different kinds of phonological phenomena, but at the same time we have had to touch upon a range of theoretical and analytical perspectives. The segmental phenomena in Chapters 1–7 were handled with linear approaches, but the later chapters introduced phonological phenomena that motivated multidimensional representations, with segments on one level linking to elements like tones, syllables, and feet on other levels.

The motivation for expanding the representations in this way came from a goal of fine-tuning analyses. Or, it came from addressing shortcomings of analyses. We have come across this type of argumentation already – if a representation allows a process to be modeled with a single rule instead of several coincidental ones, then it's a preferable analysis. Despite the complexity of representations, the analyses are simpler – the number of rules might be reduced, as is the number of technical tricks that a rule might need. Devices such as disjunctive notation or alpha notation are actually very powerful, more powerful than they need to be, and the suggestion that they form part of our actual phonological knowledge implies that there is a huge range of phonological computation that is hypothetically possible but never realized in human language. Thus, removing such devices from the repertoire of the phonologist brings us to a theory of phonological knowledge that more closely approximates phonological behavior.

329

As these advanced approaches developed through the later decades of the twentieth century, it became standard thinking to conceive of the formal representation of words as hierarchical, with larger-order elements containing smaller components, down to the segment. Indeed, this multidimensional conception extended into the segment itself. Meanwhile, as the types of rules phonologists proposed became more limited and restrictive in scope, it became clear that phonological processes are often driven by a shared (but sometimes conflicting) set of demands on form and representation.

12.1 Feature geometry

The hierarchical conceptualization of representation in phonology emerged first with analyses of tone. Recall from Chapter 9 that the analysis of tone patterns is quite complex if we assume that tone values are basic binary features of vowels. It works much more simply if we place tone units on a separate level of representation, with these elements linked to tone-bearing units on a segmental level of representation – as such, a single tone element may link to more than one vowel, and vice versa.

By analogy, the idea that other phonological features could link to multiple segments emerged as a way of modeling patterns like assimilation. When we have encountered assimilation in this textbook, we have relied on the device of alpha notation to model the change in one segment to adopt a feature value that matches the value of a nearby segment. Sometimes, however, assimilatory patterns affect more than single features; several features often assimilate together.

12.2 Nasal place assimilation

Let us return to the pattern of place assimilation we saw from Malay in §2.9 and §6.12, where the prefix /peŋ/ has a velar nasal consonant that adopts the place of articulation of following obstruents, but remains velar before vowels. A subset of data is repeated below to illustrate this phenomenon.

(1)	tulis	penulis	'writer'
(2)	sapu	peɲapu	'broom'
(3)	pukul	pemukul	'hammer'
(4)	pindah	pemindah-an	'a shift'

(5)	kenal	peɲenal-an	'introduction'
(6)	judi	peɲdʒudi	'gambler'
(7)	geli	peŋgeli	'ticklish one'
(8)	dapat	pendapat-an	'acquisition'
(9)	tʃari	peɲtʃari-an	'livelihood'
(10)	buka	pembuka	'opener'
(11)	atur	peŋatur	'arranger'

Once we had a grasp on the specifics of the pattern, we could easily describe it as follows: the nasal consonant of the prefix adopts the same place of articulation as the initial consonant of the stem; the stem-initial consonant then undergoes changes in some forms. Formalizing this process as a single rule was somewhat challenging, but we left it as a matter of the nasal consonant acquiring [α place] from the following segment.

$$\eta \rightarrow [\alpha\ place]\ /\ \underline{\quad}\ [+cons,\ \alpha\ place]$$

While this approach in Chapter 6 was preferable to our use in Chapter 2 of separate rules for each segment, it still has some shortcomings. Specifically, [α place] is not a sensible feature value when place features, as we saw, are not clearly binary. Bilabials and labiodentals are [labial], but not [+LAB, −COR, −DOR]. Moreover, even if they were truly binary, the rule needs to invoke more than [place] as an operative feature – that is, a different algebraic variable needs to stand in for each specific place feature that is involved in the rule. Thus, [α place] is really a shorthand for [α labial, β coronal, γ anterior, and δ dorsal]. Modeling complete assimilation with algebraic feature values like this requires us to draw on a long series of symbolic notation. However, the fact that all of these features assimilate at once is not coincidental, yet the algebraic approach portrays it as one.

A feature-geometric approach eschews the notion that each segment has a value for all features, and replaces it with representations in which features are elements that exist on separate levels, analogous to tone. Segments in Malay are represented as follows:

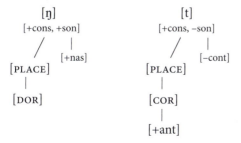

Consequently, instead of rules that change all place feature values for segments we can use rules that alter the association between segments and their features. The rule that assimilates place in Malay is represented as follows:

[+cons, +son]   [+cons, −son]

/ |

[+nas]

[PLACE]   [PLACE]

| |

[DOR]

Note that in a feature-geometric rule, the rule and representation can be collapsed together. The cross-hatched line is the association line that is removed, and the dotted line is the new association line. Elements left unassociated are deleted via stray erasure.

Exercise 12.1   Draw the representations before and after the rule, assuming the adjacent consonants are /ŋ+t/, as in /peŋ+tulis/. We are only concerned with deriving intermediate /pentulis/; a later rule would delete voiceless obstruents after nasals to derive [penulis]

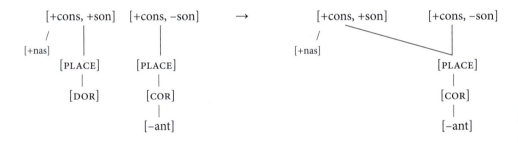

Note that these diagrams demonstrate the process quite precisely, but they do not clearly highlight the relevant changes: the old and new lines of association are harder for the reader to detect. This is one of the reasons that we instead use the reassociation notation of hatched and dotted lines.

It is also worth noting that these rules are no longer of the form A → B / C __ D, because the environment (which previously had always been C__D) is often geometric and not strictly linear.

A few additional ideas are important for this approach to the representation of the segment. First, the unit that stands in for the segment is called the **root** node, and typically comprises the features of [±son] and [±cons]. All other features are dependents of this node: [±nas], [±cont], [place] and so on, each with its own branch, and each on its own tier. The [place] node is useful in that it readily captures natural classes of phonological place. For example, in Malay, the nasal assimilation process adapts /ŋ/ to [n] or to [ɲ], because the association to a following [COR] place node also extends the [±ant] feature to the nasal consonant.

Indeed, intricacies of place specification and assimilation can be captured with an appeal to finer layers of representation, especially if we appeal to vowel specification. A re-examination of vowel-to-consonant effects will illucidate, so let us return to the phenomenon of palatalization, which we saw in Chapter 2 for Kongo and Japanese.

(1)   tobola   'to bore a hole'

(2)   ʧina   'to cut'

In a binary feature system, [+COR] consonants become [+palatal] before high front vowels. Using feature-geometric notation, we would represent alveolars and palatals both with a [COR] node, and distinguish them with different additional nodes, as follows:

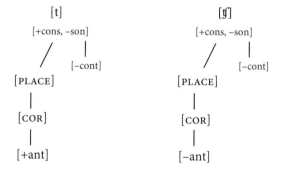

Here, we have presumed that the additional node for palatals is something like [–ant], as a dependent of [COR]. However, given that palatalization is triggered by the presence of a high front vowel, we may reconsider the process as one that spreads a place feature from [i] to the preceding consonant. Our options here [+high] and [–back]; [+high] is more plausible as the palatals do have a higher point of articulation, and we could not reasonably say that palatals are [–back] while coronals are not. Thus, alveolars in Kongo are [COR], while palatals are [COR, +high], and they acquire their [+high] feature via a rule of spreading, illustrated as follows:

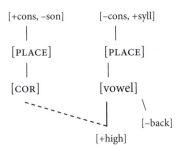

A similar approach can be applied to dorsal allophony in Hezhen, which we examined in §6.19. A subset of the data is repeated below.

(1)   qɔlu   'county'
(2)   qurpan   'boat'
(3)   kiaulu   'oar'
(4)   kɑskʰe   'bird'
(5)   ʒtatʰqʰuli   'cold'
(6)   qʰumakʰə   'deer'
(7)   kʰəku   'cuckoo'
(8)   soktu   'get drunk'
(9)   pitʰxə   'book'
(10) pʰitɕʰikə   'match'
(11) apʰkʰɑ   'universe'
(12) tʰuksu   'cloud'
(13) tʰikdə   'rain'
(14) tʰioqo   'chicken'
(15) tʰumakʰi   'tomorrow'
(16) pɔrqʰu   'color'
(17) iɬkɑ   'flower'
(18) luqʰu   'arrow'
(19) qʰuzʊŋkʰi   'energetic'

The uvulars occur before the vowels [o, ɔ, u, ʊ]. The velars occur elsewhere. Because of this complementary distribution, we can conclude that [k] and [q] are allophones of a common phoneme.

Exercise 12.2 Devise feature-geometric representations of dorsal consonants and of the triggering class of vowels in Hezhen. Allow your dorsal consonant representation to be general enough to include voiced and voiceless stops and fricatives, and allow your vowel representation to be general enough to include [o, ɔ, u, ʊ], but not [ɑ].

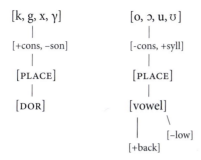

As [k] and [q] are both [DOR] in place, we can differentiate them by having an additional feature that is a dependent of the [DOR] node. Tentatively, we may call this [uvular]. But when we turn to the vowels, we see that the triggering vowels all have [+back] while additionally being [–low]. We can then theorize that [+back] is the feature that spreads: associating it to a [DOR] consonant such as [k] results instead in [q].

Exercise 12.3   Construct a feature-geometric rule that reassociates featural nodes to account for the dorsal allophony in Hezhen.

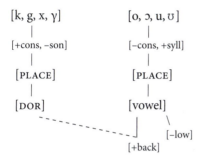

Other conceivable nodes in the feature-geometric hierarchy include the [laryngeal] node, which carries features of voicing and other aspects of the larynx, and the [ATR] node, which is useful for modeling vowel harmony as feature spreading. In fact, harmonic systems in which several features harmonize at once, such as height-dependent harmonic systems of Turkic languages, are neatly captured if we consider [±round] to be a dependent of [±high] in the vowel feature hierarchy.

The feature geometry approach to segmental representation is at once complex in its multidimensionality but elegant in its reduction of specification to a small set of branches from the root node. Feature-geometric research highlighted that some representations seemed impossible; others seemed recurrent across languages; meanwhile, some languages seemed to have stringent demands on how features could associate with each other, while others would provide conflicting evidence for different organizations of features. Phonologists thus found themselves debating whether the architecture of the geometric segment was universal. Nevertheless, the apparent dependent relationships among features and restrictions upon them within and across languages called for a further movement away from the conception of phonological derivation as a sequence of processual restructuring rules. Coupled with the recurrent emergence of analyses that required limits on rule application, these advancements led to an approach that entirely relinquishes the notion of sequential rules.

12.3 Optimality Theory

Phonological analysis has been a branch of linguistics throughout the modern era. Grammar sketches of newly described languages and other more well-known ones alike nearly always contain a description of the sound system – a phoneme inventory. Often such sketches include generalizations about allophony and alternation, even without using this terminology explicitly. It was the mid twentieth-century expansion of the field into developing a theory of internal knowledge of levels of grammar that brought theoretical adequacy into focus, beginning with the advent of distinctive binary features. The decomposition of segments into these operational components, and the expansion of representation into multiple dimensions with autosegmentalism and feature geometry in some ways simplifies, but in other ways challenges the notion of the phonological rule.

We have seen examples of such challenges – rules that need to be stipulated not to apply in some circumstances, as we saw for Amele, Trukese, and Lardil in Chapter 11. Other analyses often fall prey to an ordering paradox – contradictory evidence about rule order from within a single language. Moreover, multiple rules sometimes seem to have very similar outputs as their intention: for example, in Chapter 8 we saw recurrent rules that favor making consonants onsets, and in Chapter 10 we saw that there is some sort of link between syllable weight and stress.

This led a number of phonologists to reconsider the nature of phonological derivation and to reframe the patterns in linguistic data as a function of output-oriented constraints rather than on sequences of serially ordered restructuring rules. This forms the basis of Optimality Theory (OT; Prince and Smolensky 2004 [1993], McCarthy and Prince 1993a, b), which has become a widely used model of advanced phonological analysis.

Optimality Theory at once is a framework for analysis, a model of input–output relationships, and a theory of typology. In this chapter, we will primarily learn how an OT analysis works. One thing to remember is that the preliminary steps of describing generalizations and determining underlying forms is much the same as what you do for a rule-based analysis. The approach differs in the way we formalize the transition from underlying forms to surface representations.

Optimality Theory retains the notion of underlying representations and their derived surface representations, but the surface form is characterized as the optimal output, the one form that best satisfies an explicit set of requirements formalized as constraints. No form can satisfy all constraints; instead, constraints are ranked in their priority. The optimal form for a given lexical item is the one form (amongst *all conceivable competitors*) for which there is no other conceivable form that only violates lower-ranked constraints.

Let us explore with an example scenario. Consider the palatalization pattern we encountered in Kongo, in which underlying alveolar consonants become palatal only before high vowels, as exemplified in /tina/ → [tʃina]. In the following analysis, we will develop a system of constraints such that no other phonological form outperforms [tʃina] in satisfying these constraints.

We can observe that the underlying form /tina/ differs from the surface form [tʃina] in that underlying /t/ surfaces as [tʃ]. Both /tina/ and [tʃina], loosely speaking, are plausible forms, and we refer to them as **candidates**; other plausible forms can also be identified. An important step in the analysis is to assemble a larger list of candidates; to do so, we should consider what structure is avoided in the actual output. In this case, the underlying sequence /ti/ is avoided, so we will propose a constraint that /ti/ violates. As we do so, we realize there are other ways to avoid this sequence, such as changing the vowel or deleting the consonant. Thus, /tena/ and /ina/ are also plausible candidates. An optimality-theoretic analysis chooses the optimal output from this list of candidates by virtue of the constraints that each competitor violates.

Thus, our next step is to formalize the constraints and determine their relative priority. Central to this analysis is the need for a constraint that motivates palatalization. It is not to be framed as a rule that alters structure; instead, it is simply violated by the sequence of a non-palatal coronal followed by a high vowel. Below is formalization of the constraint that [ti] violates; note that when we operationalize constraints, we always refer to them with "small cap" typeface.

*[ɪɪ] The sequence of a [ɪ ant] coronal obstruent followed by [i] is forbidden.

Because /tina/ violates *[Tɪ] but [tʃina] does not, we infer that *[Tɪ] outranks any constraints that [tʃina] violates. Indeed, we can immediately identify a unique aspect of [tʃina], which is that it has a surface segment that does not match its underlying segment. These mismatches violate constraints of FAITHFULNESS, which are formal requirements that inputs and outputs match.

The fact that the output [tʃina] violates FAITHFULNESS but the fully faithful form /tina/ violates *[Tɪ] suggests that *[Tɪ] outranks FAITHFULNESS. In fact, no forms in the language appear to violate *[Tɪ], suggesting it is not itself outranked by anything. In such a scenario, we say the constraint is **undominated.**

Moreover, although FAITHFULNESS can be violated by the output, wildly unfaithful forms are not erroneously produced in the system. A second FAITHFULNESS violation is enough to sink a competitor such as *[tʃika]. Note as we develop this analysis, it is crucial that all forms in a language satisfy the same set of constraints, in the same ranking order.

We can illustrate the effects of constraint violations schematically with a **tableau**, a visual summary of an Optimality-Theoretic argument that lists plausible candidates and their performance on the relevant constraints. Each candidate is given a row, and each constraint has a column. Violations by candidates are noted by asterisks in the column of the constraints that they violate.

	/tina/	*[Tɪ]	FAITHFULNESS
a. ☞	tʃina		*
b.	tina	*!	
c.	tʃika		**!

A few more typographical details about tableaux require discussion. First, the violation that rules out a competitor is its **fatal** violation, and is noted with an exclamation point. The violation of *[Tɪ] incurred by /tina/ is that form's fatal violation, since it is the violation of a higher-ranked constraint. The lower-ranked FAITHFULNESS is still relevant in sorting out the remaining candidates; the one with two violations is ruled out, and thus the constraint acts as a tiebreaker. Second, any cells to the right of a failed candidate's fatal violation are shaded to show their irrelevance to the optimality algorithm. Third, the optimal candidate is the actual output, chosen as the one form with no fatal violations, and is marked with a pointing-finger icon.

In the grander scheme, the means of resolving the marked structure, and thereby satisfying *[TI], is a consequence of other constraints in the system, which we detect by considering other competitors. For example, forms with non-alveolar consonants and forms with alveolars followed by other kinds of vowels both satisfy *[TI]. These other competitors have more severe violations of FAITHFULNESS: the change from alveolar to palatal in [ʧina] is not as bad as the change in vowel in *[tena] or the deletion of the consonant in *[ina]. This suggests a more nuanced approach to FAITHFULNESS: a constraint requiring faithfulness to [+ant] is less important than a constraint requiring vowel faithfulness, or a constraint forbidding deletion (which in standard OT terms is usually called MAXIMIZE, or MAX for short). Meanwhile, the competitor *[ʧika] is ruled out by a different constraint over faithfulness to underlying [COR] features, which the output [ʧina] satisfies.

Each of these can be formalized as a unique constraint with its own rank; the FAITHFULNESS to [+ant] is violated by the output, which satisfies FAITHFULNESS for vowel features and for [COR]. In short, a larger set of competing candidates motivates a larger set of active constraints, which can be illustrated with a more enriched tableau, as below.

	/tina/	*[TI]	FAITHFULNESS-VOWELS	MAX	FAITHFULNESS-[COR]	FAITHFULNESS-[+ANT]
a. ☞	ʧina					*
b.	tina	*!				
c.	ʧika				*!	
d.	tena		*!			
e.	ina			*!		
f.	kina				*!	

Note that the set of FAITHFULNESS constraints formalizes the notion of structure preservation in this approach to phonology. They act to prevent outputs from being wildly different from lexical forms, and they also serve as a contrast-maintaining counterbalance to the opposing set of output-oriented constraints, many of which seem to favor easing the articulatory burden.

The present discussion illustrates the choice-making algorithm of Optimality Theory. In its foundational literature, a number of additional theoretical claims are bundled with the model: notably, that constraints are universal, that the candidate set is unbounded, and that the input itself is not constrained. The universality of constraints and the potentially infinite size of the candidate set are strong, controversial claims associated with Optimality Theory, but practitioners still rely on its mechanisms of attributing surface patterns to ranked, violable constraints.

That the input is not constrained is less of a controversial component of the theory; in fact, it is another important criterion (along with consistent ranking) by which we evaluate the fitness of an analysis. The unconstrained nature of the input is referred to as **Richness of the Base**: it is a general principle of OT that we do not place any explanatory burden on underlying representations themselves. While we still rely on underlying representations in our analysis, we cannot attribute a particular pattern to a stipulated claim about the nature of underlying forms in a language.

12.4 Richness of the Base

An analysis that conforms to the maxim of the Richness of the Base is one that attributes surface patterns to constraints that hold over the form of outputs and the faithfulness relationships between inputs and outputs. Diverging from this maxim would entail relying merely on patterns in the input to account for surface patterns; for example, if we were to attribute Kongo palatalization to the systematic absence of underlying /ti/, and instead claim that forms such as [tʃina] really are derived unaltered from underlying /tʃina/. The lack of underlying /ti/ in this alternate universe is unexplained.

To conform to Richness of the Base, we cannot bluntly claim that /ti/ is just missing from the lexicon of Kongo. Note, however, that by the same argument, /tʃ/ cannot be missing from the input either. Its absence from surface forms everywhere except before [i] must also be explained via constraint.

Exercise 12.4   Propose a constraint that rules out [tʃ]. Where is this constraint ranked in the Kongo system?

The constraint only needs to be *[tʃ]; further specification is unnecessary. Since it is violated in some forms, it is outranked by at least some constraints, and in fact we must rank it below FAITHFULNESS-[COR]. The following tableaux show how [tobola] is an optimal candidate regardless of whether the input contains /t/ or /tʃ/.

	/tobola/	*[Tɪ]	Faithfulness-Vowels	Max	Faithfulness-[cor]	*[tʃ]	Faithfulness-[+ant]
a. ☞	tobola						
b.	tʃobola					*!	*
c.	kobola				*!		

	/tʃobola/	*[Tɪ]	Faithfulness-Vowels	Max	Faithfulness-[cor]	*[tʃ]	Faithfulness-[+ant]
a. ☞	tobola						*
b.	tʃobola					*!	
c.	kobola				*!		

A last aspect of the analysis is to ensure that despite the position of *[tʃ] in the system, the palatal affricate may still occur before [i]. Thus, we repeat the evaluation of /tina/ → [tʃina], and include *[tʃ] as a constraint in the system. As the next tableau shows, we still predict [tʃina] as the output form, because all plausible competitors violate some higher-ranked constraint.

	/tina/	*[Tɪ]	Faithfulness-Vowels	Max	Faithfulness-[cor]	*[tʃ]	Faithfulness-[+ant]
a. ☞	tʃina					*	*
b.	tina	*!					
c.	tʃika				*!	*	
d.	tena		*!				
e.	ina			*!			
f.	kina				*!		

Exercise 12.5 Consider the form /knosi/ → [knoʃi]. Identify three plausible candidates in addition to the actual output.

*[knosi], *[knose], *[knosu], *[knos], *[knoi] are all plausible competitors; you may have found more, but they would be ruled out by whatever rules these out.

Exercise 12.6 Consider the remaining palatalized Kongo forms from §5.12. Do they motivate adding any additional constraints to the analysis?

All the other palatalized forms follow from the same system of constraints.

We have explored Optimality Theory here first with a pattern of segmental allophony, but some of the earliest work in the theory centered instead on syllable structure, stress patterns, and reduplication, domains in which it was particularly applicable. We will explore these in the following sections, where its fitness to these phenomena will be apparent.

12.5 Stress

In Chapter 10 we examined stress assignment for a number of languages. For example, in the Maranungku data repeated below, we saw that primary stress is assigned to the initial syllable, and secondary stress is assigned to each subsequent odd-numbered syllable.

ˈtiralk	'saliva'
ˈmere͵pet	'beard'
ˈjaŋar͵mata	'the Pleiades'
ˈlaŋka͵rate͵ti	'prawn'
ˈwele͵pene͵manta	'kind of duck'

To address the widely attested phenomenon of stressed and unstressed syllables occurring next to each other, we created rules that refer to foot structure:

$\sigma \ \sigma \rightarrow (\sigma \ \sigma)_{FT}$	This rule assigns feet to syllables; it must allow for a final monosyllabic foot. It must also apply iteratively left-to-right.
$(\sigma \ \sigma)_{FT} \rightarrow (\text{ˈ}\sigma \ \sigma)_{FT} \ / \ _{WD}[\ \_\_\_$	This rule assigns primary stress to the initial foot.
$(\sigma \ \sigma)_{FT} \rightarrow (͵\sigma \ \sigma)_{FT}$	This rule assigns secondary stress to remaining feet.

Even with the added formalism of foot structure, the rule system is quite unconstrained: by letting rules assign feet in arbitrarily defined environments, there is nothing in the theory that precludes a system that generates a foot every fourth syllable, or that produces alternate iambs and trochees. OT approaches to stress capture the distribution of stress over long words without creating the risk of such odd patterns.

One of the strongest aspects of OT approaches to stress is the ability to require all syllables to belong to feet. Combined with constraints requiring consistent foot structure, a stress constraint hierarchy can readily handle the rhythm of a language without introducing the risk of unattested patterns.

In Maranungku, the five-syllable word ['laŋka͵rate͵ti] is footed as follows: [('laŋka)(͵rate)(͵ti)]. While the feet are generally binary, in this case the final foot contains a single syllable, making it a degenerate foot. This violates a constraint of FOOT-BINARITY, but in an OT account, we look for other constraints that would force this as the optimal output. To ensure this result, we need to develop the account by considering competing stress patterns and finding constraints that would rule them out. For example, to ensure that the final syllable is placed in its own foot, the constraint PARSE-σ requires all syllables to belong to feet, ruling out [('σσ)('σσ)σ], [σ('σσ)('σσ)], and [('σσ)σ('σσ)].

FOOT-BINARITY   Feet are binary (bisyllabic or bimoraic)
PARSE-σ   Syllables belong to feet

Meanwhile, for a form in which the final three syllables combine into a single foot, we cannot simply use FOOT-BINARITY (since the optimal form also violates it); we thus appeal to LAPSE, a constraint against adjacent unstressed syllables. Another competitor would satisfy FOOT-BINARITY by deleting the final syllable, which we prevent by appealing to MAX.

LAPSE: Adjacent unstressed syllables are forbidden

A last form to consider is [(σ'σσ)(͵σσ)], which has no LAPSE violations and is fully parsed – and though its initial foot violates FOOT-BINARITY, this leaves it tied with the optimal candidate. Since all feet are left-headed in Maranungku, we can rule it out by appealing to a constraint requiring left-headed feet, formalized as TROCHEE.

TROCHEE: Feet have stress on their leftmost syllable.

The ranking system is thus formalized in the following tableau:

	σσσσσ	TROCHEE	MAX	PARSE-σ	LAPSE	FOOT-BINARITY
a. ☞	('σσ)(͵σσ)(͵σ)					*
b.	σ('σσ)(͵σσ)			*!		
c.	('σσ)(͵σσ)σ			*!	*	
d.	('σσ)σ(͵σσ)			*!	*	

343

e.	('σσ)(ˌσσσ)				*!	*
f.	('σσ)(ˌσσ)			*!		
g.	(σ'σσ)(ˌσσ)	*!				

Although the above analysis does not address the additional issue of directionality, other constraints can be invoked that orient stress toward the initial or final word edge. For example, we could require the primary foot to be binary, separately from FOOT-BINARITY, and also require it to be initial. This would guarantee [('σσ)(ˌσσ)(ˌσ)] over other competitors like *[('σ)(ˌσσ) (ˌσσ)] or *[(ˌσ)(ˌσσ)('σσ)]].

In the OT approach to stress, each of the individual constraints is a highly plausible claim about rhythm in languages, so their cross-linguistic recurrence is appealing. Differences in stress assignment patterns then follow from differences in constraint rankings, and phenomena like quantity-sensitive stress of the type we saw in §§10.6–7 can be handled with constraints requiring association between heavy syllables and stress. Moreover, stress systems that assign stress only to the middle syllable, or to every fourth syllable, or to every syllable, simply cannot be generated with these constraints in any configuration.

Exercise 12.7   Reconsider the following data from Araucanian:

(1)   wu'le   'tomorrow'
(2)   ṱi'panto   'year'
(3)   e'lumuˌju   'give us'
(4)   e'luaˌenew   'he will give me'
(5)   ki'mubaˌluwuˌlaj   'he pretended not to know'

Consider the fourth form, [e'luaˌenew]. Determine its likely foot structure, and comment upon its implications for constraint ranking. Using representations just with σ, provide a list of plausible competing candidates.

Since primary stress is always peninitial, with secondary stress on subsequent even-numbered syllables, we can infer iambic feet in this language. The form is thus footed as [(e'lu)(aˌe)new]. Since the final syllable follows the stressed syllable of an iamb, we can infer that it is not part of a foot. As a result, PARSE-σ is violable in this language, but since most syllables are nevertheless footed, we can also presume it has an emergent effect.

Some plausible competitors include *[(σ'σ)(σσˌσ)], *[(σ'σ)σ(σˌσ)], *[(σσ'σ)(σˌσ)], *[('σ)(σˌσ)(σˌσ)], *[('σσ)σ(ˌσσ)], and *[('σσ)(ˌσσ)(ˌσ)].

12.6 Reduplication

One of the most compelling domains for Optimality-Theoretic analysis is in reduplication, for several reasons. First, the templatic approach works neatly in OT, but without the rather awkward step of generating a complete copy of the base's segmental string. Templates are filled maximally via constraints that have an enriched notion of formalized FAITHFULNESS. A second aspect of this approach is an account of the observed tendency of the Emergence of the Unmarked. Moreover, reduplication is the site of curious Identity effects that are impossible to capture in rule-ordered approaches.

12.7 Ilocano

Let us first consider how a simple reduplicative pattern is handled in OT, starting with Ilocano, where reduplication is partial and without any complicating alternations. Recall the data below from §11.3, which illustrates how Ilocano reduplication creates a syllable prefix, filled maximally to CVC where possible, as in [tal~talon].

(1)	piŋgan	'dish'	piŋpiŋgan	'dishes'
(2)	talon	'field'	taltalon	'fields'
(3)	dalan	'road'	daldalan	'roads'
(4)	biag	'life'	bibiag	'lives'
(5)	nua	'carabao'	nunua	'carabaos'
(6)	ulo	'head'	ululo	'heads'

The reduplicative template can actually be modeled with a constraint, RED=σ, that is violated if reduplication creates more or less than a syllable. The prefix's segmental content is achieved with the correspondence constraint MAX-BR, which requires segments in the base to have correspondents in the reduplicant.

RED=σ   The reduplicant is a syllable
MAX-BR   Each segment in the base has a correspondent in the reduplicant

Systems with full reduplication are modeled with an undominated rank of MAX-BR, while partial systems have other constraints outranking MAX-BR. In Ilocano, the template constraint is ranked higher, thus preferring [tal-talon] over [talon-talon]. Even in its lower rank, however, MAX-BR has a role to play, choosing the more faithful [tal-talon] over the competitor [ta-talon]. These effects are summarized in the following tableau.

345

	RED + talon	RED=σ	MAX-BR
a. ☞	tal-talon		on
b.	ta-talon		lon!
c.	talo-talon	*!	

The smaller CV reduplicant in [bibiag] follows from the same system, whereby copying any more than [bi-] in the reduplicant would force an additional syllable, as in [bia-biag], which violates the template constraint.

12.8 The emergence of the unmarked: Sanskrit

One aspect of OT's approach to reduplication is its ability to capture effects in which the reduplicative string shows evidence of markedness effects – the avoidance of certain phonological structures – that are not otherwise seen in the language in question. This phenomenon is often referred to as the Emergence of the Unmarked (TETU). To illustrate, we can turn to classical Sanskrit (Whitney 1889, Steriade 1988, Kennedy 2011), in which there are several reduplicative morphemes, one of which generates a syllable prefix. Where the root begins with a consonant cluster, the prefix only copies one consonant, as the data below show. For example, the root /prat^h/ forms its perfect stem as [pa-prát^h-a], in which only one of two initial base consonants is reduplicated.

There are several other details to observe in the data; for example, many roots receive an additional [a] in the base component of their perfect stem, as in /b^{h}iː-/ → [biː-b^{h}aːj-]. We can put the base-internal issues aside for this discussion as we are more concerned with the nature of the prefix. Meanwhile, aspirated consonants have unaspirated correspondents, also exemplified in [biː-b^{h}aːj]. This is consistent with Grassman's Law, a general pattern in the language to avoid multiple aspirated consonants within words. In addition, velars are copied as palatals, as in [ɟa-gam-].

	Root	Perfect	Gloss
(1)	baud^h	bu-bód^{h}a-	'know, wake'
(2)	b^{h}id-	bi-b^{h}ed-	'split'
(3)	b^{h}iː-	biː-b^{h}aːj-	'fear'
(4)	ɕru-	ɕi-ɕraːv-	'hear'
(5)	d^{h}vans	da-d^{h}váns-a	'scatter'
(6)	gam-	ɟa-gam-	'go'

(7)	gʰas	ɟa-gʰása	'eat'
(8)	grabʰ	ɟa-grábʰ-a	'seize'
(9)	kʰjaː	ca-kʰjaú	'see'
(10)	kṣad	ca-kṣáda	'divide'
(11)	mjaks	mi-mjákṣ-a	'glitter'
(12)	mnaː	ma-mnúr	'note'
(13)	pat	pa-pát-a	'fly, fall'
(14)	pratʰ	pa-prátʰ-a	'spread'
(15)	spɽe-	pa-spɽe	'touch'
(16)	sarɟ	sa-sárɟ-a	'send forth'
(17)	smɽ	saː-smɽ-	'remember'
(18)	svaɟ	sa-sváɟ-a	'embrace'
(19)	svap	su-sváp-a	'sleep'
(20)	svar	sa-svár-a	'sound'
(21)	sjand	sa-sjadé	'move on'
(22)	tap	ta-tap-	'heat'
(23)	tvais	ti-tvéṣa	'be stirred up'
(24)	tjaɟ	ta-tjáɟ-a	'forsake'

The basic Sanskrit reduplicative system is not much different from that of Ilocano, in that the template constraint outranks MAX-BR. However, an additional constraint is relevant here, one that is violated by complex syllable margins, which we call *COMPLEX. It too needs to outrank Max-BR, to ensure that simplified reduplicants emerge instead of complex ones.

*COMPLEX Complex syllable margins are forbidden.

We call this an emergent effect because *COMPLEX is generally violable in Sanskrit, as the existence of roots like [grabʰ-] and [ɕru-] clearly shows. Thus, we infer that faithfulness to underlying roots (which we formalize as MAX-IO, short for Input–Output) outranks this markedness constraint, which in turn outranks MAX-BR. The reduplicant also lacks a coda consonant, unlike in Ilocano, suggesting that a constraint against coda consonants (NoCODA) is also emergent here.

MAX-IO   Every segment in the input has a correspondent in the output.
NoCODA   Syllables do not have codas.

Like complex margins, the language generally allows coda consonants, but avoids them only in the reduplicant. The activity of *COMPLEX and NoCODA in the Sanskrit reduplicant is illustrated below.

	RED + prat^h	RED=σ	*COMPLEX	NOCODA	MAX-BR
a. ☞	pa-pra.t^ha		*		rt^ha
b.	pra-pra.t^ha		**!		t^ha
c.	pat^h-pra.t^ha		*	*!	ra
d.	pra.t^ha-pra.t^ha	*!	*		

Exercise 12.8 Note that in the reduplicated forms that reduce consonant clusters, the current analysis has no mechanism for choosing one consonant over the other. Consider all such forms and provide a generalization about which consonant is chosen. Can you formalize this choice with constraints?

When the sequence consists of a stop followed by a fricative or sonorant, the stop is retained, as in [ca-kṣáda] and [pa-prát^h-a]. When the sequence consists of [s] followed by a stop, the stop is retained, as in [pa-spr̩e]. However, where [s] is followed by a sonorant, [s] is retained, as in [saː-smr̩-]. In general, the least sonorous consonant is always the one that is retained.

This effect can be captured by appealing to simple constraints such as *SONORANT and *FRICATIVE, ranking them below MAX-BR.

*Sonorant   Sonorants are forbidden.
*Fricative   Fricatives are forbidden.

With this ranking, the reduplicant is sure to include at least one consonant, and the choice among them is made with these lower-ranked constraints.

	RED + prat^h	MAX-IO	RED=σ	*COMPLEX	MAX-BR	*FRICATIVE	*SONORANT
a. ☞	pa-prat^ha			*	rt^ha		*
b.	pra-prat^ha			**!	t^ha		**
c.	ra-prat^ha			*	pt^ha		**!
d.	pa-pat^ha	*!			t^ha		
e.	a-prat^ha			*	prt^ha!		*

Exercise 12.9 The palatal pattern, where velar consonants are copied as palatals, could also be construed as a TETU effect. Propose a constraint that achieves this effect, rank it appropriately, and illustrate it with a tableau for [ɟa-gam-].

The constraint to avoid velars is simply *VELAR,

Unlike the additional consonant constraints like *SONORANT and *FRICATIVE from Exercise 12.8, we can rank *VELAR above FAITH-BR.

	RED + gam	FAITH-IO	RED=σ	*VELAR	FAITH-BR
a. ☞	ɟa-gam			*	*
b.	ga-gam			**!	
c.	ɟa-ɟam	*!			

TETU effects are challenging for rule-ordered approaches, but not insurmountable. They would require an additional rule that would alter certain segments or sequences only in the environment of the reduplicative boundary. Identity effects, however, are much more paradoxical for rule ordering, as we will see next.

12.9 Identity effects: Woleaian

Woleaian has a pattern of reduplication that produces a CVC prefix, where the second reduplicative consonant always combines with the base-initial consonant to form a geminate. As such, the second consonant in the base is never faithfully copied. For example, /metafe/ reduplicates as [mem-metafe]; the reduplicant is [mem-], with its second consonant adapting to the base-initial [m].

Several other aspects of Woleaian phonology are relevant to the pattern. First, as we saw in §4.9, the vowel /a/ raises to [e] in a dissimilatory way, so that the prefix contains [e] if the base's first vowel is [a], as in [ses-safe]. Second, and crucially to this discussion, consonants such as [x, ʃ, r, l] change their manner of articulation under gemination. For example, while [m] geminated is [mm], [x] is geminated to [kk], as in /xatapa/ → [kek-katepa].

(1)   xematefa   'explain it'   kek-kematefa   'be explaining it'
(2)   xettape   'touch'   kek-katepa   'to be touching it'
(3)   lʉwanee-j   'think (it)'   nʉn-nʉwane   'to think'
(4)   metafe   'to be clear'   mem-metafe   'to become clear'
(5)   mili   'stay'   mim-mili   'to be staying'

(6)	mmʷutu	'to vomit'	mʷum-mʷutu	'to be vomiting'
(7)	mʷoŋo	'eat'	mʷom-mʷoŋo	'to be eating'
(8)	pirafe	'steal'	pip-pirafe	'to be stealing'
(9)	raŋe	'yellow powder'	tʃetʃ-tʃaŋe	'apply powder'
(10)	ro-si	'decorate it'	tʃotʃ-tʃo	'to decorate'
(11)	saʃee-j	'scrutinize it'	ses-saʃe	'to scrutinize'
(12)	ʃalʉ-w	'water'	tʃetʃ-tʃalʉ	'to stick to'
(13)	taxee-j	'ride it'	tet-taxe	'to ride'
(14)	tela-ti	'discuss it'	tet-tale	'to discuss'
(15)	toro-fi	'catch it'	tot-toro	'to catch'

In a rule-ordered approach, we would use a template to produce a CVC prefix, and an additional rule that assimilates the final consonant of the reduplicant to the initial consonant of the base.

reduplicate   met-metafe   xet-xatepa
assimilate   mem-metage   xex-xatepa

Another rule would be needed to target [xx, ll, rr, ʃʃ] and render them as [–cont] sounds. After this, however, still another rule would be required to make the same change to the initial consonant. In essence, this is a second reduplicative process: the prefix copies the base twice.

make [-cont]   –   xek-katepa
fix initial C –   kek-katepa

A constraint-based approach does not rely on a second copying process. First, a template constraint is needed to derive a CVC reduplicant, and *GeminateX is responsible for the alternation in geminates.

*GeminateX: [+cont] geminates (aside from [ss]) are forbidden.

It is the BR-faithfulness constraint, the same one that derives any kind of copying at all, that drives the appearance of [k] in the initial position of the reduplicant.

	Red + xatepa	Red=σ	*GeminateX	Faith-BR
a. ☞	kek-katepa			epa
b.	xek-katepa			kepa!
c.	xex-xatepa		*!	epa
d.	xate-katepa	*!		pa

One last aspect of reduplicative phonology is worth mentioning. Recall in §11.3 how Amele reduplication avoids copying consonants for vowel-initial stems; for example, /odon/ reduplicates as [o-odon]. This is in contrast to the Ilocano pattern, which does allow a consonant in a vowel-initial reduplicant, as in [ul-ulo]. In Ilocano, the reduplicant [l] serves as the onset for the following base syllable, and this is readily modeled in both the rule-based approach of Chapter 11 and the constraint-based approach above in §12.7.

The Amele reduplicant, however, is blocked from associating a reduplicative [d] to the onset of the base's first syllable, as shown below. We acknowledged this in §11.3 but had no account.

associate   σ   σ   σ   σ   σ   σ
               /| /| /|\ | | /|\
           busal   bu.sal   od   o.don

In OT, we can attribute this block to a formalized limit on how far the reduplicant can extend. Here we are considering the output form [o.o.don] against the plausible competitor *[o.do.don]. Note that in this competing form, the reduplicant boundary and the syllable boundary do not coincide, whereas they do in the output [o.o.don]. As a consequence, we can attribute the choice of [o.o.don] to a requirement of such coincidence, formalized here as ALIGNMENT.

ALIGNMENT: morpheme boundaries and syllable boundaries coincide.

	Odon	RED=Syll	ALIGNMENT	FAITH-BR
a. ☞	o.o.don			***
b.	o.do.don		*!	**
c.	o.do.o.don	*!		*

12.10 Limits on rules

The Amele case sets up a discussion of other scenarios in which a phonological process seems to apply uniformly in a language except in certain circumstances that can't plausibly be reduced to a natural class in the structural environment of a phonological rule. For example, in the Lardil review exercise from Chapter 11, we saw a phonological process that deletes stem-final vowels. For example, /jalulu + n/ derives [jalulun], but in the absence of a suffix, the stem-final vowel is deleted, as in [jalul]. However, the deletion process is blocked in small stems, as in /mela/ → [mela]; basically, final-vowel deletion cannot apply if the remaining form is a single syllable. In a rule-based approach, the vowel-deletion rule is blocked from applying only if it creates a particular type of structure; it is as if it applies, realizes its effect is too drastic, and is undone.

Lardil

Uninflected	Acc. non-fut	Acc.fut.	Gloss
mela	melan	melaṛ	'sea'
wanka	wankan	wankaṛ	'arm'
kuŋka	kuŋkan	kuŋkaṛ	'groin'
tʲempe	tʲempen	tʲempeṛ	'mother's father'
wiṭe	wiṭen	wiṭeṛ	'interior'
jalul	jalulun	jaluluṛ	'flame'
majar	majaran	majaraṛ	'rainbow'
wiwal	wiwalan	wiwalaṛ	'bush mango'
jilijil	jilijilin	jilijiliwuṛ	'species of oyster'

The limit on the vowel-deletion rule's application is related to word minimality: words in Lardil must be at least a foot in size. We therefore can formalize this as an output-oriented constraint, at odds with whatever constraints are responsible for the vowel-deletion process. If we appeal to FINAL-C to motivate the deletion pattern, but also place WORD-MINIMALITY in the system, vowels will be deleted just so long as the result is not too small a word.

FINAL-C: Words end in consonants.

WORD-MINIMALITY   The word is no smaller than two syllables.

	mela	WORD MINIMALITY	FINAL-C
a. ☞	mela		*
b.	mel	*!	

12.11 Rule conspiracies

In this chapter, we have visited phonological patterns which are modeled more neatly with the mechanisms of Optimality Theory than with sequences of ordered structure-changing rules. Its elegant application to such patterns shows its usefulness for phonological analysis, but a different kind of support for the model comes from a theoretical perspective, identified as the Rule Conspiracy. As we have seen throughout this textbook, there are certain types of phonological patterns that are widely attested. Adjacent consonants assimilate; codas are avoided when possible; intervocalic position favors voicing; word margins favor voicelessness; stressed and stressless syllables are interspersed.

Across languages, sometimes a particular structure can be identified as an apparently dispreferred form, but the means of resolving it may differ. For example, numerous languages avoid sequences of nasal consonants and voiceless obstruents (Pater 1999). Some may delete the obstruent, some may delete the nasal, some may change the voicing of the obstruent. Thus, the process differs across languages, but the avoidance of a particular structure is recurrent, and we say the tendency for languages to do something, anything, is evidence of a conspiracy against that structure. In OT, the conspiracy is attributed to a constraint operative in multiple languages, with different means of satisfying that constraint.

Conspiracies within languages may also be found. Kisseberth (1970) demonstrates that a large number of distinct phonological rules need to be posited for Yawelmani Yokuts, but they all share an apparent common goal of avoiding complex syllable margins. The system is rendered much more simply if the rules are collapsed into a smaller set of statements, subject to a constraint that blocks their application should they derive illicit syllable margins. Optimality Theory takes such constraints as the only formal statements.

Summary

This chapter has introduced two advanced approaches to phonology that invoke complex formalisms intended to handle particular challenges in language data. It is difficult to present these models without framing the discussion as an advancement or progress in empirical thinking about phonological representation and derivation. Even so, it should not be taken as a recant of the previous eleven chapters in this book. All the preceding chapters have been devoted primarily to the investigation of specific phonological phenomena: alternation, allophony, syllables, meter, stress, tone, intonation, and prosodic morphology. The data should remain the focus of the discussion.

The choices we make about how to formalize processes – with rules or constraints, linear strings or geometric representations – these are analytical choices guided by the demands of the data. Indeed, much of segmental phonology can be modeled with linear representations and rules that operate over them. For more challenging types of patterns, other theories of phonology have been proposed, often to treat phenomena that we have not explored deeply here, such as Lexical Phonology, Underspecification, Exemplar Theory, and Evolutionary Phonology.

Lexical Phonology (Kiparsky 1982) divides the derivational process into blocks, where the earlier system treats morphophonological alternations that are triggered in scenarios of affixation, while the later system handles a different set of alternations and allophonic patterns. Lexical Phonology is useful in languages whose phonology seems sensitive to divisions or subsets within their lexicons, and also dovetails well with issues of opacity of the type we reviewed in Chapter 7.

Underspecification (Archangeli 1988) is an approach to segmental representations in which languages are theorized to encode lexical representations with minimal feature specification. Common combinations like voicing for sonorants or [+ATR] for high vowels are derived via rule. Especially in combination with geometric representations, this approach is tailored to the specifics of assimilatory patterns, particularly vowel harmony systems.

Exemplar Theory (Pierrehumbert 2001) is an extension of an approach in psychology, and adopts a completely different construal of the phoneme. Rather than frame segmental phonology as the association of a small number of allophones with an abstract (and prototypical) underlying form, Exemplar Theory posits that phonological knowledge of a category comprises the sum of encountered (perceived and spoken) tokens of it. For example, a category such as /a/ is really an amalgamation of all instances of a speaker having heard this sound, and speakers match new instances to that category if they are similar. The advantage of this theory is in how it captures the link between the widely variable physical instances of categories (within and across speakers) and a single, unitary category.

Evolutionary Phonology (Blevins 2004) is a theory that seeks to account for typological trends among phonological patterns, linking them to historically recurrent and phonetically likely types of language change. As such, it attributes the rarity of some patterns and prevalence of others not to what kinds of rules, constraints, or orderings are possible, but to what tends to happen as language varies and changes. As an explanation of typology and typicality, this is an alternative to models or theories that attribute markedness to formal statements that represent the capabilities of phonological acquisition and knowledge. It also allows room for the emergence of rare systems (e.g., onsetless languages) which explicit theories of markedness have trouble accounting for.

The range of theoretical approaches to phonological data underscores the sheer size of our collective body of empirical data from the world's languages. There are upwards of 7,000 languages in the world, each with a phonemic inventory and a set of generalizations as to how its phonemes may combine into prosodic and morphological units. Despite this huge degree of diversity, the pursuit of phonology continues to show that generalizations of patterns are emergent within and across languages, often expressible in elegant terms that belie the sophisticated knowledge of the speakers that acquire and develop these languages. There are more languages to be described and analyzed, and each approach to phonology allows room for amendment and improvement to its methods and notational tools wherever new data provide new challenges.

Key terms

feature geometry
feature hierarchy
place nodes
laryngeal node
Optimality Theory
constraint
ranking
undominated
violation
candidate
Richness of the Base
faithfulness
correspondence
The Emergence of the Unmarked
Rule Conspiracy
Lexical Phonology
Underspecification
Exemplar Theory
Evolutionary Phonology

References and further reading

Archangeli, Diana. 1988. Aspects of underspecification theory. *Phonology* 5: 183–207.

Archangeli, Diana, and D. Terence Langendoen. 1997. *Optimality Theory: An Overview*. Oxford: Wiley-Blackwell.

Bakovic, Eric. 2013. *Blocking and Complementarity in Phonological Theory*. Sheffield: Equinox.

Blevins, Juliette. 2004. *Evolutionary Phonology: The Emergence of Sound Patterns*. Cambridge University Press.

Clements, G. N. 1976. *Vowel Harmony in Nonlinear Generative Phonology: An Autosegmental Model*. Indiana University Linguistics Club.

Clements, G. N. 1985. The geometry of phonological features. *Phonology Yearbook* 2: 225–252.

Clements, G. N. and Elizabeth Hume, 1995. The internal organization of speech sounds. In John Goldsmith (ed.), *Handbook of Phonological Theory*. Oxford: Blackwell, 245–306.

Inkelas, Sharon, and Cheryl Zoll. 2005. *Reduplication: Doubling in Morphology*. Cambridge University Press.

Kager, René. 1999. *Optimality Theory*. Cambridge University Press.

Kennedy, Robert. 2002. Stress and allomorphy in Woleaian reduplication. In *Proceedings of the Texas Linguistics Society* 7, Austin.

Kennedy, Robert. 2008. Evidence for morpho-prosodic alignment in reduplication. *Linguistic Inquiry* 39: 589–614.

Kennedy, Robert. 2011. Reduplication in Sanskrit. In Marc van Oostendorp, Colin J. Ewen, Elizabeth Hume, and Keren Rice (eds.), *The Blackwell Companion to Phonology*. Oxford: Wiley-Blackwell, 2855–2878.

Kenstowicz, Michael, and Charles Kisseberth. 1977. *Topics in Phonological Theory*. New York: Academic Press.

Kiparsky, Paul. 1982. Lexical phonology and morphology. In Seok Yang (ed.), *Linguistics in the Morning Calm*. Seoul: Hanshin, 3–91.

Kisseberth, Charles. 1970. On the functional unity of phonological rules. *Linguistic Inquiry* 1: 291–306

McCarthy, John J., and Alan Prince. 1993a. Prosodic morphology I: constraint interaction and satisfaction. Ms., University of Massachusetts and Rutgers University.

McCarthy, John J., and Alan Prince. 1993b. Generalized alignment. In G. E. Booij and J. van Merle (eds.), *Yearbook of Morphology 1993*. Dordrecht: Kluwer, 79–153.

McCarthy, John J., and Alan Prince. 1994. The emergence of the unmarked. In M. González (ed.), *Proceedings of NELS 24*. Amherst, MA: Graduate Linguistic Student Association, University of Massachusetts, 333–379.

McCarthy, John J., and Alan Prince. 1999. Faithfulness and identity in prosodic morphology. In René Kager, Harry van der Hulst, and Wim Zonneweld, eds., *The Prosody–Morphology Interface*. Cambridge University Press.

McCarthy, John. 2002. *A Thematic Guide to Optimality Theory*. Cambridge University Press.

Pater, Joe. 1999. Austronesian nasal substitution and other NC effects. In René Kager, Harry van der Hulst, and Wim Zonneveld (eds.), *The Prosody–Morphology Interface*. Cambridge University Press, 310–343.

Pierrehumbert, Janet B. 2001. Exemplar dynamics: word frequency, lenition and contrast. In J. Bybee and P. Hopper (eds.), *Frequency and the Emergence of Linguistic Structure*. Amsterdam: Benjamins, 137–157.

Prince, Alan, and Paul Smolensky. 2004. *Optimality Theory: Constraint Interaction in Generative Grammar*. Oxford: Blackwell. [Originally distributed as a RUCCS technical report, Rutgers University, 1993; available as ROA-537.]

Sagey, Elizabeth Caroline, 1986. The representation of features and relations in non-linear phonology. Doctoral dissertation, Massachusetts Institute of Technology.

Sohn, Ho-Minh. 1975. *Woleaian Reference Grammar*. Honolulu: University Press of Hawaii.

Sohn, Ho-Minh, and Anthony F. Tawerilmang. 1976. *Woleaian–English Dictionary*. Honolulu: University Press of Hawaii.

Spaelti, Philip. 1997. Dimensions of variation in multi-pattern reduplication. Doctoral dissertation, University of California, Santa Cruz.

Steriade, Donca. 1988. Reduplication and syllable transfer in Sanskrit and elsewhere. *Phonology* 5: 73–155.

Stevens, Alan M. 1985. Reduplication in Madurese. In *Proceedings of the Second Eastern States Conference on Linguistics*. Columbus, OH: Linguistics Department, Ohio State University, 232–242.

Urbanczyk, Suzanne. 1999. Double reduplications in parallel. In Harry van der Hulst, René Kager, and Wim Zonneveld (eds.), *The Prosody–Morphology Interface*. Cambridge University Press, 390–428.

Whitney, W. D. 1889. *Sanskrit Grammar*. Cambridge, MA: Harvard University Press.

Review exercises

Arabic

Examine the pattern of complete assimilation in the Arabic definite article in §6.13. Develop an analysis that accounts for this pattern using feature-geometric representations. Make sure the account limits assimilation to coronal-initial stems.

Maasai

Re-examine the Maasai vowel harmony pattern from §4.7. Now focus on the data in Exercise 4.19, repeated below.

	1st sing.	*2nd pl.*	*Gloss*
(1)	a-rɪk-ɪta	ɪ-rɪk-ɪta-ta	'causing nausea'
(2)	a-ɪlɛp-ɪta	ɪlɛp-ɪta-ta	'ascending'
(3)	a-bɔl-ɪta	ɪ-bɔl-ɪta-ta	'holding its mouth'
(4)	a-bʊl-ɪta	ɪ-bʊl-ɪta-ta	'prospering'
(5)	a-raɲ-ɪta	ɪ-raɲ-ɪta-ta	'singing'
(6)	a-rik-ito	i-rik-ito-to	'leading it'
(7)	a-lep-ito	i-lep-ito-to	'milking it'
(8)	a-bol-ito	i-bol-ito-to	'opening it'
(9)	a-bul-ito	i-bul-ito-to	'piercing it'
(10)	a-iruk-ito	iruk-ito-to	'believing him'

Construct feature-geometric representations that illustrate the harmony process. Hint: it will help to consider the possibilty that surface forms of [o] and of [a] may each correspond to more than one type of phoneme.

German

Review the German final devoicing data from §2.15. Develop an Optimality-Theoretic constraint system that generates voiced and voiceless alternants in the appropriate contexts.

Hawaiian

Generate plausible competing candidates for the reduplicated forms [aːlohaloha], [ʔoːheahea], and [pioloolo] in Hawaiian.

Madurese

Examine the following data from Madurese (Stevens 1985):

neat	ĴãtnẽĴãt	'intentions'
moa	w̃ãmõw̃ã	'faces'
maen-an	ẽn-mãẽn-ãn	'toys'
ŋ-soon	ɔn-ɲɔʔɔn	'request (v)'
soon	ɔn-sɔʔɔn	'request (n)'

a. Describe the distribution of nasal vowels just within the bases of these forms.

b. Under what conditions do reduplicative segments become nasalized?

c. State why the distribution of nasal vowels in reduplicated forms is a problem for a rule-order approach. How would you instead account for these data using constraints?

Trukese

Recall the following data, which show a process of final-vowel shortening in Trukese:

(1) petʃe   'foot'   petʃeej   'my foot'
     tikka   'coconut oil'   tikkaaj   'my coconut oil'
     etiru   'coconut matting'   etiruuj   'my coconut matting'
     tʃuutʃu   'urine'   tʃuutʃuuj 'my urine'

(2) [tɐə]   'islet'
     [maa]   'behaviour'
     [oo]   'omen'
     [soo]   'precipitate'
     [nɨɨ]   'unripe coconut'

a. How are these data analyzed in a rule-ordering approach? How do you account for the lack of shortening in (2)?
b. Describe how these data would be handled in an OT approach.

INDEX